Cambridge Middle East Library

Merchants of Essaouira

Cambridge Middle East Library

Also in this series

Medicine and power in Tunisia 1780–1900
NANCY ELIZABETH GALLAGHER

Urban notables and Arab nationalism: the politics of Damascus, 1860–1920
PHILIP S. KHOURY

The Palestinian Liberation Organization: people, power and politics
HELENA COBBAN

Egypt in the reign of Muhammed Ali
AFAF LUTFI AL-SAYYID MARSOT

Women in nineteenth-century Egypt
JUDITH E. TUCKER

Egyptian politics under Sadat
RAYMOND A. HINNEBUSCH

Nomads and settlers in Syria and Jordan, 1800–1980
NORMAN N. LEWIS

Islam and resistance in Afghanistan
OLIVIER ROY

The Imamate tradition of Oman
JOHN C. WILKINSON

King Abdullah, Britain and the making of Jordan
MARY C. WILSON

The Ottoman Empire and European capitalism, 1820–1913
ŞEVKET PAMUK

The birth of the Palestinian refugee problem, 1947–1949
BENNY MORRIS

Jordan in the 1967 war
SAMIR A. MUTAWI

War's other voices: women writers in the Lebanese civil war
MIRIAM COOKE

Colonising Egypt
TIMOTHY MITCHELL

Womanpower: the Arab debate on women at work
NADIA HIJAB

Merchants of Essaouira

Urban society and imperialism in southwestern Morocco, 1844–1886

DANIEL J. SCHROETER

DEPARTMENT OF HISTORY
THE GEORGE WASHINGTON UNIVERSITY, WASHINGTON D.C.

CAMBRIDGE UNIVERSITY PRESS

CAMBRIDGE
NEW YORK NEW ROCHELLE
MELBOURNE SYDNEY

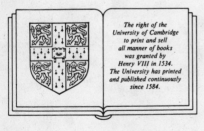

Published by the Press Syndicate of the University of Cambridge
The Pitt Building, Trumpington Street, Cambridge CB2 1RP
32 East 57th Street, New York, NY 10022, USA
10 Stamford Road, Oakleigh, Melbourne 3166, Australia

First published 1988

Printed in Great Britain at the University Press, Cambridge

British Library cataloguing in publication data

Schroeter, Daniel J.
Merchants of Essaouira : urban society and imperialism in Southwestern Morocco 1844–1886. – (Cambridge Middle East library).
1. Essaouira (Morocco) – Social life and customs
I. Title
964′.6 DT328.E8

Library of Congress cataloguing in publication data

Schroeter, Daniel J.
Merchants of Essaouira.
(Cambridge Middle East library)
Bibliography.
Includes index.
1. Essaouira (Morocco) – Economic conditions.
2. Merchants – Morocco – Essaouira – History – 19th century.
3. Merchants – Morocco – Essaouira – History – 19th century.
4. Capitalism – Morocco – Essaouira – History – 18th century.
5. Capitalism – Morocco – Essaouira – History – 19th century.
I. Title. II. Series.
HC810.Z7E857 1987 330.964′6 87-15163

ISBN 0 521 32455 6

VN

In memory of Paul Pascon and Ahmed Arrif
and my grandfather, Robert Strasser

Contents

Illustrations

Photographs

Figures

Maps

Tables

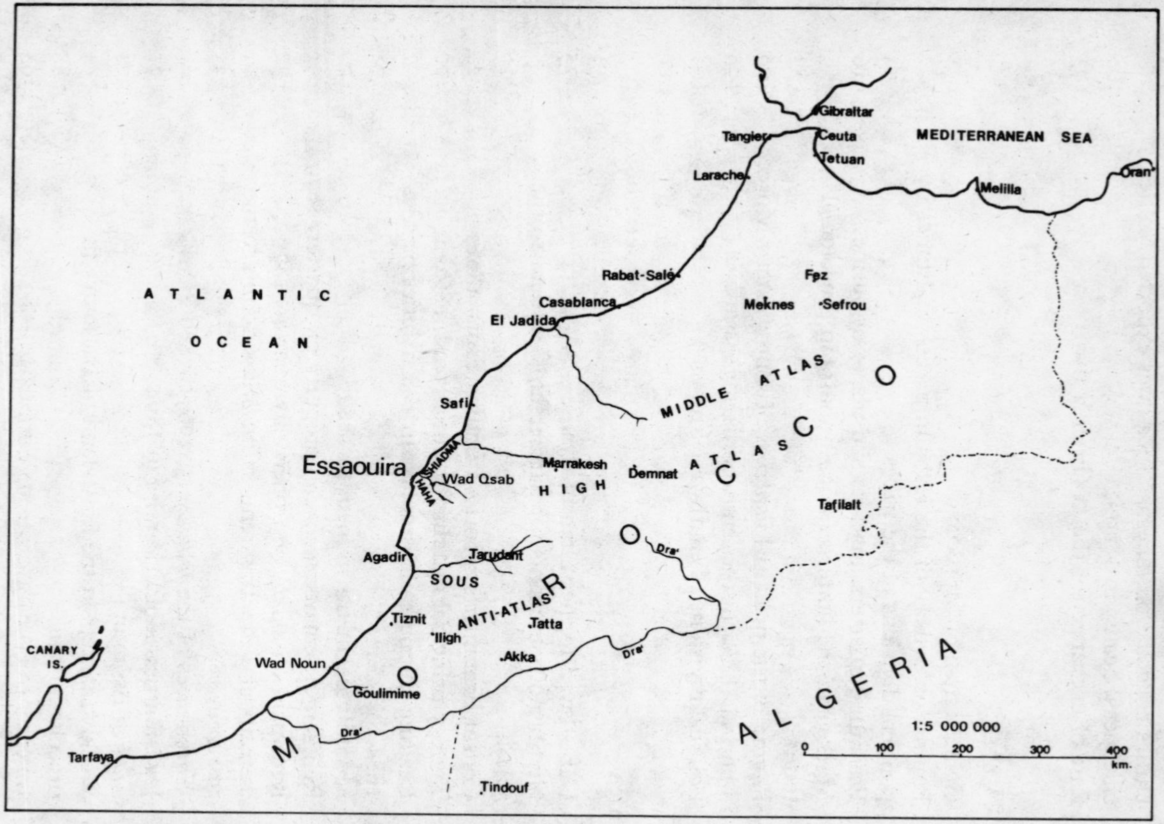

Map 1 General map of Morocco

Preface

The town of Essaouira, better known as Mogador to Europeans, is today a quiet, slow-paced, and relatively isolated fishing town. Most of the population of the town still resides within the *medina*, the area enclosed by ramparts which once constituted the city limits. The quaintness of the town today seems to contrast with its former position as a royal port. This is still marked by its formidable ramparts and rows of cannons which point outwards to the land and sea. In the eighteenth and nineteenth centuries, Mogador was among the few places along the North African littoral (called the 'Barbary Coast' by Europeans) known to foreign traders, sailors and adventurers. Its fame rivalled that of Algiers, Tunis and Tripoli.

From the 1770s through the 1870s, Essaouira was the most active seaport of Morocco. This present study is about the history of Essaouira from 1844 to 1886, the heyday of the town as an international port. These two dates mark crucial events in Moroccan history and in the life of Essaouira. In 1844, the town was bombarded by the French fleet, a punitive operation to deter Morocco from further involvement with the Algerian resistance movement along her eastern frontier. From that date on, Morocco had to recognize foreign intervention as a major factor in the life of the country. In 1886, Sultan Mawlāy al-Ḥasan embarked on an expedition to the Sous region of southwest Morocco in order to confirm Moroccan sovereignty over some of the more distant regions of the country. It was the last effort by the Moroccan government to demonstrate both to the Europeans and to the dissident tribes of the south that the royal port of Essaouira, a town closely controlled by government customs officials, was *the* port for the southern trade (see map 1).

This book is primarily concerned with the trading community of Essaouira in this period, and its relations with the Sultan, Europeans, and the regional powers of the southwest. By examining the history of a community on a local level, my aim is to discuss Moroccan society in precolonial times. What is being looked at in microcosm also reveals some of the dynamics of precolonial societies in the age of economic imperialism. The responses of the trading community of Essaouira to foreign penetration reflects more generally the way micro-populations reacted to European capitalist expansion.

Essaouira remained a relatively small town. Its population rose from about 10,000 in 1844, to about 18,000 in 1886. The relatively small size of Essaouira was one of the first things that attracted my attention. When I began research for my doctoral thesis at the University of Manchester, I had hoped to be able to exhaust virtually all the written documentation related to the town in the nineteenth century. This task seemed reasonable, in view of the presuppositions that historians have made about the absence of Moroccan archives. Nearly ten years later, it is now apparent that a lifetime of work would only reveal a small part of the existing material. And yet this mass of material, and the very density of its detail, makes one aware of the lacunae with which students of Moroccan history are faced. For every extant administrative letter, there are allusions to several others, for every tax register, there are lists of dozens of other account books formerly kept in the archives.

This study is based on four main types of primary sources: administrative documents and tax records of the Moroccan government, foreign consular records, descriptive accounts of foreign travellers and residents in Morocco, and the private papers of several Moroccan-Jewish merchants' firms. A recently discovered private archive, with papers from one of the principal Jewish merchant firms of Essaouira in the late eighteenth and early nineteenth century, has not been fully integrated into this present study. This material will be dealt with exhaustively in a separate monograph.

The kinds of documents available both circumscribe and guide this study. One of the principal sources used is the Corcos family papers. The Corcos was one of the most important merchant families in Essaouira, but no merchant house had such intimate ties with the Royal Palace in Marrakesh. More than two hundred Arabic letters sent by the Palace from 1843 to 1883 to members of the family in Essaouira have been preserved (see app. A). These letters, which span the period with which we are concerned, often provide a narrative of the events and processes discussed. The Corcos collection also includes legal documents in Hebrew and Arabic pertaining to property transfers and mortgages, notarized contracts in Hebrew, and several letters in Judeo-Arabic. I am indebted to Michel Abitbol, who first suggested I work on these documents. I was able to consult this material, thanks to the kind generosity of Georgette Corcos. Her assistance was extended in another way: through our lengthy conversations about the elite Jewish families, I have learned much about the social life of the Jews in the *casbah*.

The study of these documents was a first step in defining the subject of inquiry and research. Yet to build around these letters a more general history of the trading community of Essaouira required much more extensive research. Many of the letters are in fact only abbreviated responses to letters received, with summaries of the original letters sent. Painstaking research in the archives of the Royal Palace in Rabat revealed only a few letters actually sent by Corcos. Furthermore, Arabic letters of the period follow certain conventional styles. Descriptions are often ambiguous and relevant details are frequently absent. To impart meaning to these documents has demanded an understanding of the relationship between the correspondents and the events that they describe.

This task has been helped by the archives of the American consular agency of Mogador, recently transferred from Morocco to the diplomatic branch of the National Archives in Washington D.C. Abraham Corcos and his son Meyer served as U.S. consular agents in Essaouira for over thirty years. In addition to the correspondence between the Corcos and the consul-general in Tangier, numerous Arabic letters between the Mogador consulate and the local government of Essaouira have been preserved. Letters and documents in Spanish, French, and Judeo-Arabic concerning various local matters are also found in these consular archives. Most of the folios of letters in this collection were still sealed, and the volumes were not yet organized. I am most grateful to the helpful archivists of the National Archives for giving me the opportunity to work with this material.

I have also consulted the French and British archives of the Mogador consulates. Much work has already been accomplished in the Moroccan consular archives. Historians are particularly indebted to the voluminous study of Jean-Louis Miège (*Le Maroc et l'Europe: 1830–1894*, 4 vols., Paris, 1961–2). I have therefore concentrated more specifically on the Mogador consular archives rather than on the multi-volumed correspondence found in the general Morocco series of the Foreign Office and the Quai d'Orsay. The staffs of both the Public Record Office and the Ministère des Affaires Etrangères were most helpful in my research.

But to study Moroccan society purely from the standpoint of foreign consulates would obviously give us an unbalanced view of Moroccan history. I have therefore turned to the official correspondence of the central government, the *makhzan*. Apart from the numerous administrative documents pertaining to Essaouira, registers of customs duties, gate and market taxes, agrarian tithes, and *makhzan* property (the 'crown lands') have provided indispensable quantitative data for this study.

The systematic organization of the archives in the Royal Palace has only just begun, though the existence and value of these archives was noted long ago by the Moroccan historian, Germain Ayache. His insistence on the need to use the Moroccan archives has encouraged me in my task. A new generation of historians has begun to produce studies based on these archives, to which I will refer in the following pages. My debt to the historians of Mohamed V University of Rabat will become apparent in this book. Here I would like specially to mention Abderrahmane El Moudden, who was doing research in the archives at the time I was there. I am grateful for his help in guiding me through some of the material, and for later commenting on my thesis. My discussions with Tibari Bouasla, also doing research in the archives, were most helpful. Thomas Park, who was doing research on Essaouira, shared in the task of going through piles of as yet unorganized correspondence. The current work of Wilfrid Rollman in the archives of the Palace is of particular importance. As my first teacher of North African history, I owe him special thanks. I am immeasurably indebted to Monsieur Mohamed El Arbi El Khattabi, the Director of the Royal Palace Library (*al-Khizānat al-Ḥasaniyya*), who readily made available still unclassified archives. I should also like to thank the archivist, Hamid Moumou, who called to my attention many pertinent documents. I am grateful to Monsieur Abdel Wahab Benmansour, Royal Historiographer of the Direction des Archives Royales, who made numerous dossiers on Essaouira available for consultation. I should like to thank the Director of the Bibliothèque Générale, Monsieur Abdel Rahman El Fasi, for his assistance. To the numerous librarians and archivists I am especially indebted. In particular, I thank Abdelmajid Ben Youssef, who was extremely attentive to all my queries, and Mohamed El Aouene, who taught me much about the archives and libraries of Morocco.

Most of Morocco's archives still remain in private hands, located in often inaccessible places in the countryside. I am most grateful to Mustapha Naïmi of the Institut Universitaire de la Recherche Scientifique, who provided me with documents from the Bayrūk family of Goulimime, and discussed with me the history of southwestern Morocco at length. Much work has been done in the field by social scientists of the Institut Agronomique et Vétérinaire-Hassan II of Rabat. The Département des Sciences Humaines of the institute provided me with both facilities and an intellectual atmosphere which was most conducive to my research. My discussions with Mohamed Naciri and Abdallah Hammoudi have been invaluable. Most of all, I am indebted to the late Paul Pascon, who integrated me into a project in the Tazarwalt under the auspices of the Institut Agronomique and the University of Amsterdam. I was able to work extensively in the Sous and to examine the unpublished documents of the Bū Damī' a family of Iligh who controlled the caravan routes of the southwest. Paul Pascon's death in Mauritania, together with the sociologist, Ahmed Arrif, is a loss deeply felt by all concerned with Moroccan society. I learned a great deal from Paul Pascon about Morocco. His many new ideas, which challenged much of what has been written about Morocco – including his own publications – were just beginning to formulate at the time of his death. I hope that this book makes a contribution, in the direction that Paul Pascon was heading, by rethinking Moroccan society and history.

From a regional perspective, the people of Essaouira always took an active interest in my research. I would particularly like to thank the Abecassis family, whose door in their house of the *casbah* was always open. Both Boujemâa Lakhdar, the keeper of the Essaouira museum and *al-ustādh* al-Hadrī were always most informative about local culture. The authorities of Essaouira accommodated my research in many ways. The archives of the port and the *habous* were put at my disposal. I am particularly grateful to the *qā'id*, Aghigha Bassou, from the provincial government. Monsieur Belarbi of the Ministry of Culture was most helpful in my research. Many natives of the Essaouira 'diaspora' and their descendants, were anxious to share their knowledge and provide me with both personal documents and contacts. In particular members of the Afriat, Elmaleh, Abecassis, Corcos, and Knaffo families in Morocco, Israel, France, England, and the United States provided me with most useful information. I would here like specially to mention Messieurs Edmond Elmaleh, André Azoulay, Taïeb Amara, Samuel Levy, Shlomo Knaffo, and Haïm Zafrani. Special thanks go to Professor Haïm Zafrani, whose instruction on the complexities of Moroccan Hebrew and Judeo-Arabic has been of lasting value. Through his invitation to teach at the Université Paris VIII–Vincennes in 1984–5, I was able to continue my research on the Moroccan Jewish community.

Jews in Essaouira represented between 30 and 40 per cent of the population. But rabbinical sources for Essaouira, a city renowned for commerce rather than scholarship, are somewhat scanty. I have nonetheless found some relevant *responsa* in a few of the noted nineteenth-century works of Moroccan rabbis, and a few hagiographical texts on the Jewish saints (*ṣaddīq*s) of the town. I have also collected copies of a number of manuscripts from people with shared interests in the history of the Jews of Morocco. I thank Professor Miège, Arrik Delouya, Elias Harrus, and Victoria Ducheneaux for giving me copies of documents, photographs and other valuable information. I have learned much from Joseph Chetrit in our joint research on the Jewish community of Essaouira. Robert Attal, bibliographer and head librarian of the Ben Zvi

Institute, and Trude Levi of the Mocatta Library assisted my research in many ways. The most important source for the Jewish community of Essaouira is found in the archives of the Alliance Israélite Universelle in Paris. Monsieur Georges Weill, the director of the archives, and Madame Levyne, librarian of the Alliance Israélite Universelle, have been immeasurably helpful.

To all my teachers, colleagues, and friends who helped make the writing of this book possible, I am especially grateful. I have benefited enormously from the research done jointly with Thomas Park in Morocco. His meticulous reading of my thesis, and his many new ideas about Moroccan economic history have provided me with much insight. I am grateful to Paulo De Mas, colleague in the Tazarwalt project, for his useful criticisms. The valuable comments of Michael Brett, Lucette Valensi, Edmund Burke, and Raymond Jamous on my thesis have helped me rewrite this present work. I am particularly indebted to my teachers at Manchester. C.E. Bosworth gave me much encouragement throughout the writing of my thesis. Above all, Kenneth Brown has helped many of my ideas and writings about Morocco and social history take shape. Finally, I would like to thank my wife Hélène for her understanding and support in the difficult final stages of writing.

A large part of my research was made possible thanks to the support of the Faculty of Arts of the University of Manchester, the Memorial Foundation for Jewish Culture, and the Social Science Research Council/American Council of Learned Societies. I am most grateful for the financial assistance of these institutions. For the product of my research I am wholly responsible.

Notes on usage

For North Africa, purism seems inappropriate for spelling and transliteration. During the colonial period, Arabic and Berber were rendered from the colloquial pronunciation into French. Much literature on North Africa uses French spelling. For the English reader, French orthography can be problematic. But it would have been equally confusing to adopt a purely classical system of transliteration for all Arabic and Hebrew names. For most proper names and terms, I have used the system found in the *International Journal of Middle East Studies*, with the exception of eliding the definite article for sun letters. Hebrew transliteration has been adapted to the corresponding Arabic pronunciation.

For those words not transliterated from classical Arabic, a number of general guidelines have been followed. Words commonly known in English appear without diacritics. Terms which are specific to Morocco sometimes appear transliterated from the colloquial. The classical form is used for most names of persons, except when the name appears in its colloquial form in the text, or when the name is specific to Morocco. The European spelling is given for commonly known Jewish names. A number of words which are sufficiently well known from the French literature will appear in French. Values in pound sterling, Spanish piastres or hard dollars, and French francs are indicated, respectively, by £, $, and **f**. The five franc coin (the French riyāl) is represented by 5**f**. For the major cities, English spelling is used. For names of medium-sized places, I have sometimes used the French spelling. For most political divisions and tribes, a classical transliteration is used. However, for names of Berber tribes, French spelling is used for the prefix (Aït and Ida). Wad is used for wadi (lit., *wādī*, coll. *wād*, Fr. *oued*).

In chapter notes names which occur frequently are shortened or are referred to by their popular name (e.g., Bannīs for Muḥammad b. al-Madanī Bannīs, Bū ʿAshrīn for the *wazīr* aṭ-Ṭayyib b. al-Yamānī, Hay for Sir John Drummond Hay, etc.). It should be noted that for the K.H. archives, there are not yet reference codes available. Similarly, the folios in N.A., Record Group 84, for the Mogador Consulate have not yet been assigned reference codes.

Translations from Arabic and Hebrew attempt to be as literal as possible, but some formal terminology has been replaced. For example, the honorific title '*mawlānā*', literally 'our master', has been translated as 'the Sultan'. To help clarify meaning, words not found in the original text are added in square brackets.

Abbreviations

A.E.	Archives du Ministère des Affaires Etrangères, Paris (C.C.C. – Correspondance Consulaire et Commerciale; C.P. – Correspondance Politique; M.D. – Memoires et Documents)
A.I.U.	Archives de l'Alliance Israélite Universelle, Paris
A.J.	Anglo-Jewish Archives, London
A.N.	Archives Nationales, Paris and Aix-en-Provence
A.N., S.O.M.	Archives Nationales, Section Outre-Mer, Paris
B.A.	Bayrūk Archives, documents of the Bayrūk family, Goulimime
B.A.I.U.	*Bulletin de l'Alliance Israélite Universelle*
B.D.	Archives of the Bū Damīʿa family, Iligh, Tazarwalt
B.G.	Bibliothèque Générale (al-Khizānat al-ʿĀmma), Rabat
B.L.	British Library, London
B.N.	Bibliothèque Nationale, Paris
B.S.G.	*Bulletin de la Société de Géographie*, Paris
C.A.	Corcos Archives, documents of the Corcos archives, Jerusalem
C.A.H.J.P.	Central Archives for the History of the Jewish People, Jerusalem
C.H.E.A.M.	Centre des Hautes Etudes sur l'Afrique et l'Asie Moderne
D.A.R.	Direction des Archives Royales (Mudīriyya al-Wathā'iq al-Malikiyya), Rabat
E.I.[1]	*Encyclopedia of Islam*, 1st edn
F.O.	Records of the Foreign Office, Public Record Office, London
Halewī	Articles of Yaʿīsh b. Yiṣḥāq Halewī in *ha-Ṣefīra*
K.H.	al-Khizānat al-Ḥasaniyya, Rabat
M.C.C.	Manchester Chamber of Commerce, Manchester
M.G.	Archives du Ministère de la Guerre à Vincennes, Paris
Miège, I–IV	Jean-Louis Miège, *Le Maroc et l'Europe: 1830–1894*, 4 vols., Paris, 1961–2

Miège, *Doc.*	Jean-Louis Miège, *Documents d'histoire économique et sociale marocaine au XIXe siècle*, Paris, 1969
N.A.	National Archives, Diplomatic Branch, Washington, D.C. (R.G. – Record Group)
P.P.	Parliamentary Papers, *Accounts and Papers*
R.C.	*Renseignements Coloniaux* in *Revue de l'Afrique Française*
R.G.S.	Royal Geographical Society
S.L.	Archives of S. Levy, Paris

Chronology

ʿAlawid Sultans Of Morocco: 1757–1894

Muḥammad III	1757–1790
al-Yazīd	1790–1792
Sulaymān	1792–1822
ʿAbd ar-Raḥmān	1822–1859
Muḥammad IV	1859–1873
al-Ḥasan I	1873–1894

*Qāʾid*s Of Essaouira: 1830–1895*

ʿAbd al-Khāliq Ashʿāsh	1830–1833
ʿAllāl az-Zamrānī	1833–1842
al-ʿArabī aṭ-Ṭarrīs	1842–1854
Muḥammad Ibn Zākūr	1858–1859
ʿAbd al-Karīm ar-Razīnī	1859
al-ʿArabī al-ʿAṭṭār	1859–1860
ʿAbd al Qādir al-ʿAṭṭar†	1860–1861
al-Mahdī Ibn al-Mashāwrī	1861–1868
ʿAmāra Ibn ʿAbd aṣ-Ṣādiq	1868–1883
ar-Ragrāgī ad-Dawbilālī	1883–1895

*Also called governor (*ʿāmil*) and pasha (*bāshā*)
†Acting *qāʾid* and brother of above

Chapter 1

Introduction

Essaouira was the most important seaport in Morocco for a century, but compared with the growing port cities in the colonial area, this outlet to Europe was a backwater. Essaouira remained a small city, situated in a relatively barren region. The expansion of other Middle Eastern seaports, such as Beirut and Alexandria, was dramatic in the same period. Beirut's population grew from 6,000 to 120,000 in the nineteenth century.[1] At the beginning of the nineteenth century, Alexandria had a population of 10,000; already by the mid 1850s, the city had grown to about 150,000.[2] Wherever European commercial interests were strong, port cities began to grow into major emporiums of trade. In contrast, Essaouira's small scale growth from 10,000 to 18,000 seems insignificant (see app. B).

And yet, historians have often seen the development of Essaouira as highly significant in the modern history of Morocco. Abdallah Laroui argues that Sultan Muhammad III, the founder of Essaouira, can be regarded as the 'veritable architect of the "modern" Morocco described in numerous nineteenth- and twentieth-century accounts'. With the creation of Essaouira, in Laroui's view, the bulk of the state revenues were henceforth derived from customs duties on foreign trade. In this way the prosperity and the very existence of the state became dependent on an activity dominated by foreigners.[3]

The stress of almost all studies on Morocco, since the important book of Miège, has been on the social changes engendered by the integration of Morocco into the world capitalist system.[4] Miège postulates that Morocco's interaction with Europe, and in particular foreign trade, led to a structural transformation of society. Capitalism developed on the margins of the traditional economy, and the growing influence of the bourgeoisie – largely Jewish – effected the economic transformation of the country.[5] A capitalist class of farmers and landlords began to develop in both the towns and the countryside.[6] The inland cities declined as the coastal towns grew. As in other parts of the Middle East, traditional crafts were in crisis or disappeared altogether because of the influx of cheap European manufactured goods.[7] These assumptions have guided a number of in-depth studies on how Moroccan society was transformed in specific towns or regions during precolonial times.[8]

These studies are an important departure from the literature of the French colonial period, which depicts Moroccan traditional society before the French protectorate as unchanging. French writings on Moroccan cities tend to focus on the historic monuments of the town and the contributions of each successive Sultan to the urban topography, but are little concerned with social change.[9] Even the study of Fez by Roger Le Tourneau, one of the most important books on Moroccan urban life and the Islamic city generally, largely sees the precolonial city as timeless. Fez in 1900, in many respects, appears the same as in Marinid times.[10] Implicit in this interpretation is that change came about under the aegis of the French protectorate, but as the recent study of André Raymond has shown – in contradistinction to the notion of urban decadence in the Ottoman period – cities of the Middle East and North Africa were developing in significant ways in the centuries preceding the nineteenth century.[11]

In the precolonial period, social change in Moroccan cities was greatly accelerated because of the growing dependency of Morocco on Europe. European commercial expansion can be seen as the first phase in the process of foreign economic predominance, comparable to that which occurred in the countries of the Middle East.[12] Port cities in particular were susceptible to social change, because they were the principal points of contact between Europeans and the local population. Even more important, the ports served as agents of change, bridgeheads in subordinating the country as a whole to dominant western models.[13]

To what degree does Morocco's principal seaport in the nineteenth century fit this general model? How did the local merchants respond to the external forces of change, and how did they themselves act as agents of social and economic transformation? I hope to answer these questions throughout this book by examining local society and its relations with the interior of Morocco. But before I proceed, a few preliminary remarks about Essaouira are called for.

The town was founded by the Sultan to serve as a royal port, an entrepôt where all trade with Europe could be conducted. The aim of the Sultan was both to contain foreign influence and to limit the volume of trade. The town was situated in a relatively isolated location, and foreigners were not allowed to travel to the inland markets. In the town itself, foreigners and Moroccan-Jewish royal merchants were provided with special separate quarters in the *casbah*. Their premises belonged to the central government. Foreign trade, in theory, was to be closely administered by the *makhzan*. In many respects this calls to mind

Polanyi's 'ports of trade', in which the trading community was relatively isolated from the rest of society, playing the role of political intermediaries between political frontiers. In this paradigm, administered trade, which centres on long distance 'luxury' items, prevails over the economic process of competition.[14] In some respects, the Moroccan Sultan was able to contain foreign penetration and create an economic enclave in the same way, for example, that the Chinese were able to do in their treaty ports. In China, foreigners were confined to a specific quarter in Canton, and not allowed to travel elsewhere (except on special tributary missions to bring gifts to the Emperor) nor trade with other ports. Foreign trade became a state monopoly, and European merchants were compelled to trade with official Chinese intermediaries. Treaty ports grew rapidly in China in the nineteenth century, though their impact on the traditional Chinese economy remained limited.[15]

However, it would be misleading to carry this model too far. Essaouira's economic isolation and political neutrality were always relative, and certainly never complete. The urban patterns that evolved came to resemble those of other Muslim cities, and Moroccan cities in particular. Furthermore, the Sultan progressively lost his control of commerce. Essaouira's trade, even from the very beginning of the town's existence, operated according to the practices which were rooted in Moroccan society. Essaouira was therefore both unique, as an administered port of trade, yet similar to other cities.

In light of the size and economic position of the major inland cities of Morocco, the importance of the coastal ports in the socio-economic transformation of Morocco needs to be placed in perspective. The economic importance of the interior, and domestic trade generally, still greatly overshadowed that of the coast. Despite the assertions that the major inland cities of Fez and Marrakesh were in decline,[16] there is little solid evidence to suggest that the rather limited growth of coastal towns was necessarily at the expense, either demographic or economic, of the major inland cities of Morocco. Though there were probably dramatic fluctuations in Marrakesh's population in the nineteenth century, there are no obvious signs of an overall decline in this period.[17] Marrakesh still remained the capital and the most important commercial emporium for southern Morocco. Furthermore, the vast majority of Morocco's population of several million inhabitants resided in the countryside. It can be surmised that the urban population in Morocco ranged between five and ten per cent.[18] The rural population in the hinterland of Essaouira – in the Haha and Shiadma – numbered at least ten times as high as the inhabitants of the town (see map 2).[19] Morocco, therefore, remained essentially a rural society.[20] Bearing this in mind, the primary concern of

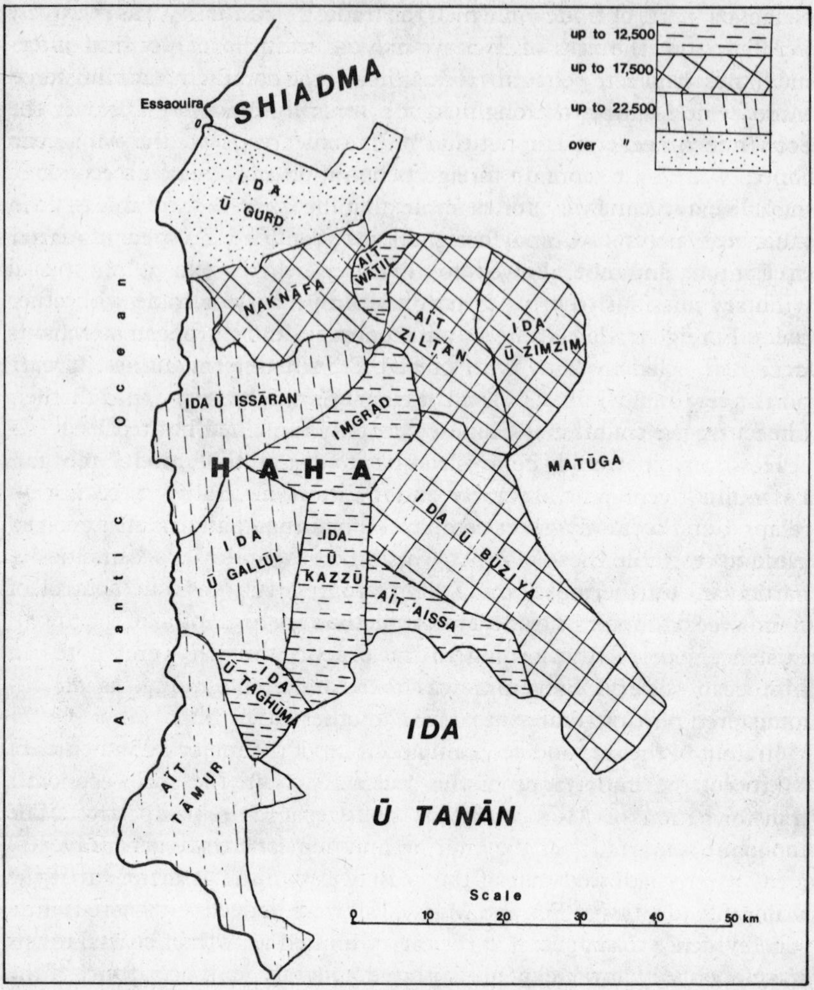

Map 2 Population density of the Haha in precolonial times by political divisions of the tribes (adapted from René de Segonzac, *Au Cœur de l'Atlas. Mission au Maroc, 1904–1905*, Paris, 1910, pp. 396–407)

the Moroccan Sultan was the control of the countryside. The largest potential source of revenue for the *makhzan* remained in the rural sector. Recent research in tax registers has revealed that the state derived much more income from the interior than from customs duties at the coast ports in the latter half of the nineteenth century.[21]

The significance of Essaouira, therefore, lay not only in the dependency of the *makhzan* on customs duties from foreign trade, which were important, but did not constitute the main fiscal resource of the state, but also in its geopolitical position in the control of southwestern Morocco. By linking the fortunes of potentially dissident chiefs of the Sous to the commercial activity of the royal port of Essaouira, the Sultan hoped to keep the more distant parts of the country within the fold. It should be borne in mind that at the beginning of the ʿAlawid dynasty the sultanate was threatened by a rival dynasty of *shurafāʾ* – men of sacred lineage – from Iligh in the Sous.[22]

This essentially domestic strategy had unforeseeable consequences. By opening up the Sous trade to Europeans, foreign penetration was facilitated, which was to undermine the Sultan's concomitant aim of containing foreign influence and keeping foreign trade at a minimal level. The native merchants of Essaouira themselves served as agents of foreign penetration. The closely controlled system of royal trade was challenged by the fact that the royal merchants (*tujjār as-Sulṭān*), like the Chinese compradors, became brokers for the foreign companies doing business in Morocco.[23]

Some of the *tujjār as-Sulṭān* became wealthy in their role as middlemen. Yet this wealth itself often implied dependency on Europe. The domestic possibilities for investment remained extremely limited, so the most successful Moroccan merchants invested in foreign banks and companies.[24] This underlines the limitations of their influence in Moroccan society as a whole. Though the *tujjār as-Sulṭān* may have tried to emulate western culture, they remained embedded in Moroccan society, and while they were responsible for distributing European imports domestically, they did not restructure the traditional Moroccan economy along western lines. European domination during colonial rule ultimately did transform the Moroccan economy, and integrated the country into a European-based capitalist market economy,[25] but the process of structural change took place much more gradually than historians have admitted. From hindsight one risks interpreting all events and activities relating to foreign trade as steps in the development of capitalism in Morocco. While the ports of trade served as bridgeheads for foreign penetration, in the nineteenth century, they did not subordinate Moroccan culture to a dominant western model. Despite the progress of foreign economic penetration, European interests were too limited, and the country remained too resilient for a significant restructuring to occur.

The approach of Miège, which focuses on Morocco's integration into a world economic system, needs to be reversed. In this book, I intend to place the trading community of Essaouira in a Moroccan context.

Immanuel Wallerstein's important theory on how the 'core' subjugated the 'periphery' provides an interesting conceptual framework for the development of a European world-economy,[26] but it does not take into consideration, as Eric Wolf points out, 'the reactions of the micro-populations habitually investigated by anthropologists'.[27] Morocco was in upheaval because of foreign political and economic penetration, but the continuities of 'traditional' Moroccan society were also propelled by their own dynamics. Through depicting the lives of the people of Essaouira, I hope to give a sense of what Moroccan culture and society was like in the age of European economic expansion.

Chapter 2

The royal port

He who comes [to Essaouira] poor, leaves rich.
A saying attributed to Sultan Sīdī Muḥammad b. ʿAbdallāh at the time of the foundation of Essaouira[1]

The situation of Mogadore [Essaouira] is the most desolate that can be imagined, and nothing but the advantages afforded to trade and the superiority of the harbour over the others of the Empire could ever reconcile merchants to an establishment here. An unbroken chain of high sandhills, totally bare of vegetation, meet the eye along the coast, and for miles inland the same aspect is presented, with the exception of here and there, a small cultivated spot, between the hills.
British vice-consul, Mr. Grace[2]

In 1764, the new town of Essaouira was founded by Sultan Sīdī Muḥammad b. ʿAbdallāh (1756–80) due west of Marrakesh on the Atlantic coast. It was to be Morocco's main seaport for trade with Europe. The Sultan, as legend suggests, intended to make the port a great and prosperous city where the principal Moroccan merchants could dwell and make fortunes.

Essaouira did indeed become the principal maritime port of Morocco within a decade after its creation, a status it maintained for over a century. But the legendary grandeur of the royal port of Sultan Muhammad III contrasts markedly with the stark reality portrayed by vice-consul Grace. Essaouira in its heyday in the mid-nineteenth century was an unexceptional and desolate place, certainly in comparison to other major ports of the Maghreb and the Middle East of the same era. It remained a small city, situated in a relatively barren region.

Mogador, the site

The creation from scratch of the new town of Essaouira was seen by the chroniclers of Moroccan dynastic history as one of the major achievements of the Sultan Muhammad III.[3] In many respects, it can be considered a bold decision. The immediate surroundings of the site were infertile; to the south, an almost constant wind caused the sands to shift and made cultivation extremely difficult. The small desolate village of Diabet (*Dhiyābāt*), situated immediately to the south of the site on the Wad Qsab (*qaṣab*), was the only settlement in the area.[4] The inland region of Haha (*Ḥaʾḥāʾ*) to the south of the site contained few villages, whose inhabitants usually resided in "homesteads" or small hamlets separated from their fellow tribesmen. This was quite uncharacteristic of most of Morocco, where the countryside was dotted with villages. Most of Haha is hilly or mountainous. Its inhabitants, then as today, were occupied with the cultivation of argan (a tree unique to southwestern Morocco, whose fruit is made into an oil and used as a staple in the diet) or olive trees, and raising goats.[5] In the Shiadma region to the east and the north of the town, the relief rises sharply. The first zone where grains and legumes were extensively cultivated was in the plains of Akarmūd some 30 kilometres to the north of Essaouira. Unlike most towns, Essaouira therefore lacked a fertile hinterland and food supplies had to be transported over considerable distances.

Despite the unfavourable terrain, the Essaouira's site did have a few assets which had attracted foreigners in the past. A natural harbour was partially sheltered by an island situated about 1,500 metres offshore, or about 900 metres from the port. In ancient times the island was settled by the Phoenicians and used as a trading station and a centre for the production of a purple dye. Archaeological discoveries show evidence of both a Roman and Byzantine presence on the island.[6] In 1506, the Portuguese constructed a small fortress on the mainland next to the sea, though their occupation was short-lived, in contrast to the long-lasting Portuguese settlement at Mazagan (later to become El Jadida when the Moroccans captured the town). In the sixteenth and seventeenth centuries, both the French and the British made periodic landings on the island. Only the Portuguese envisaged penetrating the hinterland from that part of the coast, but their plans were never realized and their occupation in the region was soon abandoned.[7]

The sparsity of population in the vicinity of Mogador may very well have been considered an advantage by the Sultan. Starting the town anew, the sovereign could establish a military and commercial colony which would be closely administered by the central government. The past had often proved that a rooted and disgruntled urban elite could challenge ʿAlawid authority. Furthermore, the central government had little control over the southern littoral, where the local chiefs were appropriating the customs' revenues from foreign trade for themselves.[8] The southern regions were the richest in the products of the Moroccan trade which were sought after by the Europeans: olive oil, ostrich feathers, goat skins, gum arabic, and almonds.

Royal plans

The notion of a royal port town, closely administered by the sovereign, has been considered as quite exceptional among North African cities. In both scholarly studies and travel books, the topography of the town together with its economy, are compared to foreign models. In one discussion, Essaouira is compared to the classical Chinese city, where the sovereign dominates commerce and urban activities, and allocates dwelling to an imported 'alien' population (here, the Jews are implied). In this paradigm, the town itself is built by the sovereign in a geometric chessboard pattern. Above all, it is a trading entrepôt and not a centre for the creation of wealth.[9]

To many French colonial writers, the architecture and layout of the city appeared different to that of other Moroccan towns. A legend, still popular in Essaouira today, attributes the design of the town to a Frenchman, Théodore Cournut, who had previously been employed by Louis XV for the fortifications of Roussillon. Cournut, however, is absent from contemporary Arabic sources, and a French account of the construction of Essaouira in 1765 makes no mention of a French engineer employed by the Moroccan Sultan. It is plausible that a plan for Essaouira was drawn up by Cournut, but according to tradition, Cournut was dismissed and the work was completed by Genoese renegades. An English renegade was also alleged to have played an important role in completing the construction. In the town itself, the few inscriptions on the old walls are ambiguous. Residents of Essaouira argue over the readings of the inscriptions at the gangway (*sqāla*, from the Italian *scala*) of the port: is it signed Aḥmad *al-ʿilj* (the renegade), the reputed English renegade? Or should the inscription read Aḥmad *Uharū* which linguistically would suggest Berber origin?[10]

To attribute the physical layout of the town to European influence is misleading. In the classic French colonial history of Morocco by Henri Terrasse, the construction of Mogador designed by the French engineer Cournut figures very prominently in the description of the period.[11] In the words of another French writer: 'Louis XV adds to this military work a charm which one would not expect to find there and which makes Mogador France's first town laid on the shore of Africa.'[12]

These assumptions, made on the physical layout of the town and its economic and administrative structure, are inaccurate and are based on faulty premises regarding the typologies of North African cities. The fact that Essaouira was planned from scratch in a way made it inevitable that some of the principal thoroughfares, markets, and royal and governmental domains would be constructed on a kind of geometric grid pattern, similar to planned cities found in western Europe since the

1 Inscription of the *sqāla* at the port of Essaouira

‘*1184. al-Ḥamdu lillāh hadhā al-bāb amara bi-binā’ihi fakhr al-mulūk Sayyid Muḥammad ‘alā yad mamlūkihi Aḥmad al-*[‘*Ilj*/*Ūharū*/*or possibly al-*‘*Ajj*]’

‘1770–1. Praise God, glory of the kings, Sayyid Muḥammad [the Sultan] ordered his slave Aḥmad al-[. . .] to construct this gate’

2 Engraving of Essaouira, early nineteenth century

From Jacopo Gråberg di Hemsö, *Specchio geografico e statistico dell’imperio di Marocco* (Genoa, 1834)

Renaissance. Yet this was not unusual either for Morocco or for other Middle Eastern or North African cities. One could equally compare the regularity of Essaouira to that of Meknes in the seventeenth and eighteenth centuries, which was also built to a royal design. One is struck by the formidable gateways and bastions, similar in some ways to European designs, but it is really no different from the other imperial cities of Morocco. Yet if one strays from the main thoroughfares of the commercial or governmental districts, intricately winding and narrow streets are immediately encountered.

This division between a well-ordered, open part of the city and a sector predominated by an intricate and irregular web of alleyways is distinctive of Arab cities generally. André Raymond has recently explained how this division is based on a notion of a fundamental differentiation between the 'public city', dominated by large-scale economic activity, and the 'private city', where family life is relatively segregated. This division was typical in the Mediterranean, and was clearly perceived and formulated by Muslim jurists.[13] It was the 'private city' that impressed the foreign observers as characteristic of the Arab city. In Essaouira the places of international commerce – the port, the customs house and other governmental buildings, and the main thoroughfare going through the central market – were what seemed to dominate the town. A foreign merchant would have had no need to venture into the poplular Muslim or Jewish residential quarters, which would have been harder to ignore in larger cities.

Foundation of the port

Essaouira is one of the most recent precolonial Moroccan cities, yet it is difficult to reconstruct with any precision the way in which the town actually came together. The naming of the town itself is subject to controversy. In documents of the eighteenth and the nineteenth centuries the Arabic letters *sīn* or *ṣād* are both used, sometimes indiscriminately in the same document. The official spelling which emerged, certainly by the mid-nineteenth century, was *aṣ-Ṣawīra* with a *ṣād*, which is a colloquial diminutive (lit. *aṣ-Ṣuwayra*) of the word *ṣūra*, meaning 'picture' or 'image'. However, most of the local ulama in the past, as well as the residents today, understood Essaouira to be the diminutive of *sūr* meaning wall. In the Berber dialect of Tashelḥit, the language of at least half the residents, the town was known as *Taṣṣūrt*, which despite the *ṣād*, connotes wall: thus the confusion between the official spelling and connotation, and local colloquial usage. Furthermore, *aṣ-Ṣawīra* or *aṣ-Ṣawīrat al-Qadīma* was a common name for a number of localities in the region before the foundation of the port of Essaouira. Foreigners called the town Mogador, a name found on European maps since the fourteenth century. The European name is probably a deformation of Sīdī Magdūl, the marabout buried near the beach facing the island.[14]

Both the naming of the town and the selection of the site, therefore, are subjects of speculation. Local traditions recount that Sīdī Muḥammad was attracted to Essaouira during an expedition down the coast from Safi.[15] The official inauguration of the new town was in 1764, though construction may have begun a few years earlier.[16]

In the construction of the new town, Sultan Sīdī Muḥammad clearly envisaged the consolidation of Moroccan power. One of the Sultan's contemporary courtiers, Aḥmad al-Ghazzāl, indicates that the estuary of Salé became blocked with sand for two months a year during the rainy season, impeding the movement of the Moroccan corsairs. The engineers were unable to resolve the problem and hence the new port of Essaouira was constructed, so that the 'corsairs could sail from it whenever they wished'.[17] The purpose of defending Islam against the infidel, the reason given by al-Ghazzāl for constructing Essaouira, legitimized the foundation of the new port. In fact, the activities of the Moroccan corsairs, seen as legitimate naval operations, were diminishing to the point of total disappearance.[18] Trade, through commercial treaties, was seen as another means of controlling foreign merchants to the benefit of the Moroccan state. Some foreign sources suggest that the Sultan wanted to put an end to the monopoly of trade at Safi, Agadir, Rabat-Salé, Mamoura, Larache and Tetuan accorded to the Royal Danish Merchants' Company (*Danske Afrikankse Kompagnies*) in 1751.[19] The Sultan clearly wished to concentrate all foreign trade into one port closely administered by the palace. This policy aimed at increasing state revenues through customs duties, curtailing the independence of foreign trade companies, and consolidating the power of the central government in the south by closing the port of Agadir to foreign commerce.

The settlers

The Sultan constructed a port for commercial trade, but to ensure that governmental authority would be secure, a sizeable military establishment was settled in the new town. In a sense, Sultan Muḥammad was creating a town in the tradition of the *ribāṭ*s, fortresses built along the coast in the fourteenth and fifteenth centuries to defend Islam against the enemy – the Portuguese during this period.[20] The new town was a mirror reflection of the Spanish and Portuguese garrisoned trading entrepôts, the *presidios*. The Portuguese and Spanish still tenaciously held on to their enclaves on the coast to the north – Mazagan by the former and Ceuta and Melilla by the latter. *Jihād* therefore remained a real issue, and it is in this context that al-Ghazzāl's point can be understood.

The descendants of the first soldier-settlers were an important element in the social composition of Essaouira. an-Nāṣirī states that there were about 2,500 men in all branches of the military settled in Essaouira in Sultan Muḥammad's time.[21] This figure seems fairly accurate, since a *makhzan* document of 1785 lists 2,214 soldiers receiving a salary of one mithqāl a month. There were more than twice as many soldiers on Essaouira's pay-roll as compared to any other garrison at an Atlantic port at that time.[22]

A large contingent of these soldiers was probably formed by the black soldiers known as *ʿabīd al-Bukhārī.*[23] According to an-Nāṣirī, *ʿabīd* from the Haha and Shabānāt were sent to Essaouira.[24] Their ranks were probably augmented in 1770 when, according to a contemporary source, some 7,700 *ʿabīd* were disbanded and dispersed to various ports.[25] A British source reveals that in 1793 there were about 1,800 *ʿabīd* in Essaouira.[26] Foreign observers in the nineteenth century often remarked that many of the inhabitants of the town were black, believing that this was due to the importation of slaves from the Western Sudan.[27] An American visitor to Essaouira in 1815 referred to 2,000 'free blacks' who had their own quarter.[28] In all probability, these foreigners were seeing the descendants of the *ʿabīd*, as they are referred to by the British representative Chaillet in 1829.[29] The actual number of slaves in town was probably small, particularly since the importation of slaves via the trans-Saharan route had diminished significantly in Mawlāy Sulaymān's reign (1792–1822). However, some of the black residents of the town may have been descendants of slaves employed by the *makhzan* in the former sugar plantations of Wad Qsab to the south of the town.[30]

There were two other major groups which formed part of the community of soldier-settlers: the Agadiris and the Banī ʿAntar. It is quite likely that a sizeable portion of the people of Agadir moved northwards to Essaouira. Contemporary sources recount that ten years after the foundation of Essaouira, Agadir was closed to commerce by the Sultan.[31] One tradition suggests that the people of Agadir initially refused to go to Essaouira, and as a consequence the town was attacked by a *makhzan* force marching from Marrakesh. The Sultan was said to have given the inhabitants little time to pack and move to Essaouira.[32] Another source gives the date when all the people of Agadir were forced to move to Essaouira as Thursday, 8 September 1774.[33] Thus an important, if not the largest, part of the first soldier-settlers must have come from Agadir. In 1847, a French consul in Essaouira refers to a pension from the customs duties, and among the recipients were descendants of the original 500 Agadiri families who settled the town.[34] If there were actually 500 original families, then it can be extrapolated that well over 2,000 settlers came from Agadir.

Less is known about the arrival of the Banī ʿAntar, or their exact identity. Local tradition recounts that they originated on the western flanks of the High Atlas Mountains.[35] Despite their ambiguous origins, they were regarded as one of the principal groups of soldier-settlers who populated the town in its nascent period, forming independent units in the militia of Essaouira, parallel to the Agadiri units throughout the nineteenth century. It is recorded in a military pay-roll register dated 1864 that the Banī ʿAntar formed a corps of 50 boatmen, an artillery (*tūbjiyya*) unit of 178, and an infantry (*jawāshīsh*) unit of 163. The Banī ʿAntar were the chief rivals of the Agadiris; the latter formed separate units for these three corps.[36]

A number of smaller groups were also among the first generation of soldier-settlers. A small contingent of renegades (*ʿulūj*) arrived with the first group of immigrants, and were employed in the construction of the town defenses and in manning the guns. In 1790, the Italian–Jewish poet and traveller, Rōmānellī, reported that some 200 renegades were guarding the city.[37] In the military register of 1864, independent contingents of *ʿulūj* still appear among the army ranks.[38]

Finally, an elite group of soldiers was sent from Fez to populate Essaouira. A tradition suggests that the Sultan had originally planned to send 300 men from Fez each year to construct the town, but after he saw the progress made in construction, only 50 militiamen (*rumāt*) were sent.[39] Several Arabic sources recount that the recruits destined for Essaouira at first refused to go and started a rebellion. Only when they realized that money could be made in trade during their service in the town did they go willingly, subsequently even offering bribes in order to be selected.[40]

The first generation of soldier-settlers left their mark on the social composition of Essaouira, and some of the quarters still bear their names (see map 3). In the first phases of the town's existence, these corporate groups appear to have resided in their own quarter. The shipwrecked American sea captain, Riley, remarks that the *ʿabīd*, though Muslims, 'are not allowed to live together promiscuously' with the other inhabitants.[41]

The specific corporate nature of the quarters established by the first generation of soldier-settlers broke down as immigrants from the surrounding regions settled in the thriving new town. The local historian, ar-Ragrāgī, enumerates the tribes from which recruits were drawn to populate Essaouira: Shabānāt, Masgīna, Aït Tamaʿīt, Adawār, *ahl* Agādīr, and Manābha from the Sous, and Banī ʿAntar and Raḥāla from the Anti-Atlas.[42] From another local historian, we can add the Fasis and the people from the surrounding countryside, the Haha and Shiadma.[43]

The eighteenth-century historian, al-Qādirī, refers vaguely to settlers from the Anti-Atlas (*Jabāl as-Sūsiyya*) and the region around Marrakesh.[44] For most of these groups, the circumstances of their arrival are unclear. Were some of them transferred *en masse* by the Sultan for political reasons? This may have been the case in some instances, but certainly the prosperity of the new port attracted immigrants. Rural pressures due to over-population or agrarian crisis were also important factors at times. Despite this mixture of diverse elements, eventually the largest proportion of the town was composed of people whose origins were connected to the hinterland: the Haha and Shiadma. Tribesmen from these regions formed a large contingent in the militia.[45] The bustling new port offered the possibility of finding work, and, above all, commission from traders at many levels. Petty artisans, hawkers, seasonal labourers, beggars and general riff-raff sought to scrape a living from the town's surplus. This influx from the Haha and Shiadma within several decades seems to have diluted any geo-ethnic specificity within the confines of the *medina*.

At a very early stage in Essaouira's development, natives of Haha and Shiadma were at the centre of the town's political and cultural life. In the eighteenth century, the control of the town and region was vested in two governors, one from the ranks of the ʿ*abīd* and the other from Haha.[46] Most of the ulama were also from Haha and Shiadma with their maraboutic traditions of the regional Ragrāga and Jazūliyya confraternities (*zāwiya*s). It became the custom in Essaouira for the *khaṭīb*s of the two largest mosques which date from the town's foundation – the Mosque of the Casbah and Sīdī Yūsuf – to be natives of Haha and Shiadma respectively.[47]

The legitimization of the new town required the formation of a religious establishment. The Sultan had to provide the town with its ulama to assure that his creation would be a city of 'civilization' (*al-ḥadāra*). The sovereign 'wished to make it civilized [*ḥadariyya*] like Fez in prosperity and wealth', writes Aḥmad Ibn al-Ḥajj, a nineteenth-century historian of Mawlāy al-Ḥasan's court.[48] A *muʾadhdhin*, *muwaqqit* and *mudarris* – muezzin, timekeeper and teacher – were sent so that the framework of the Islamic community could be established.[49] Ulama from Fez, according to a contemporary historian, ad-Duʿayyif, were granted huge sums of money to settle in Essaouira.[50]

The royal port of Essaouira was part of the sharifian ʿAlawid kingdom, and as such, it was established as an Islamic city. What really made the new town viable, however, was commerce, and most of the merchants were Jews. A powerful merchant sector has usually been an important component of Islamic urban society.[51] The decision to establish Jewish

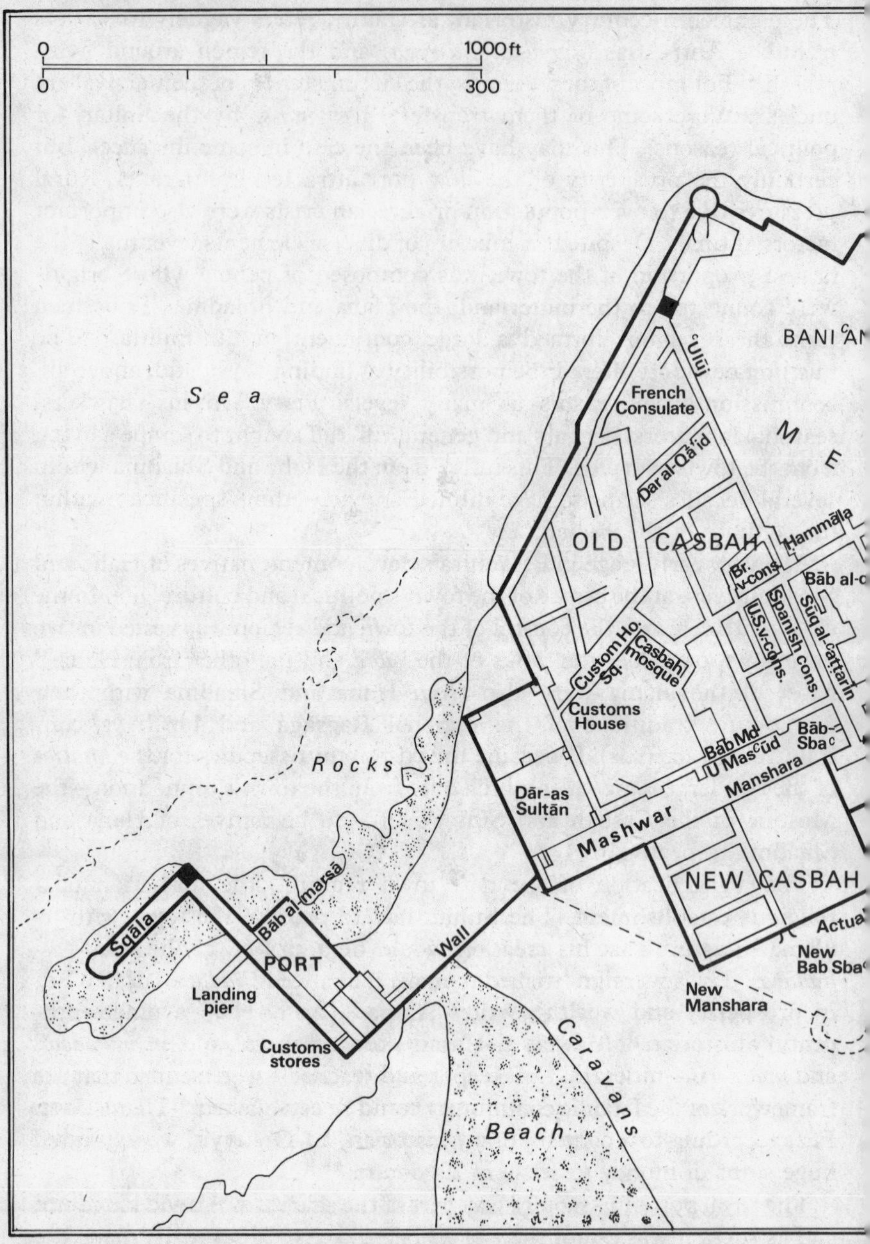

Map 3 Essaouira: quarters, markets and places of business (based on a map drawn by the British engineer James Craig, in the 1860s, in DAR/Ess. 9, in Arabic)

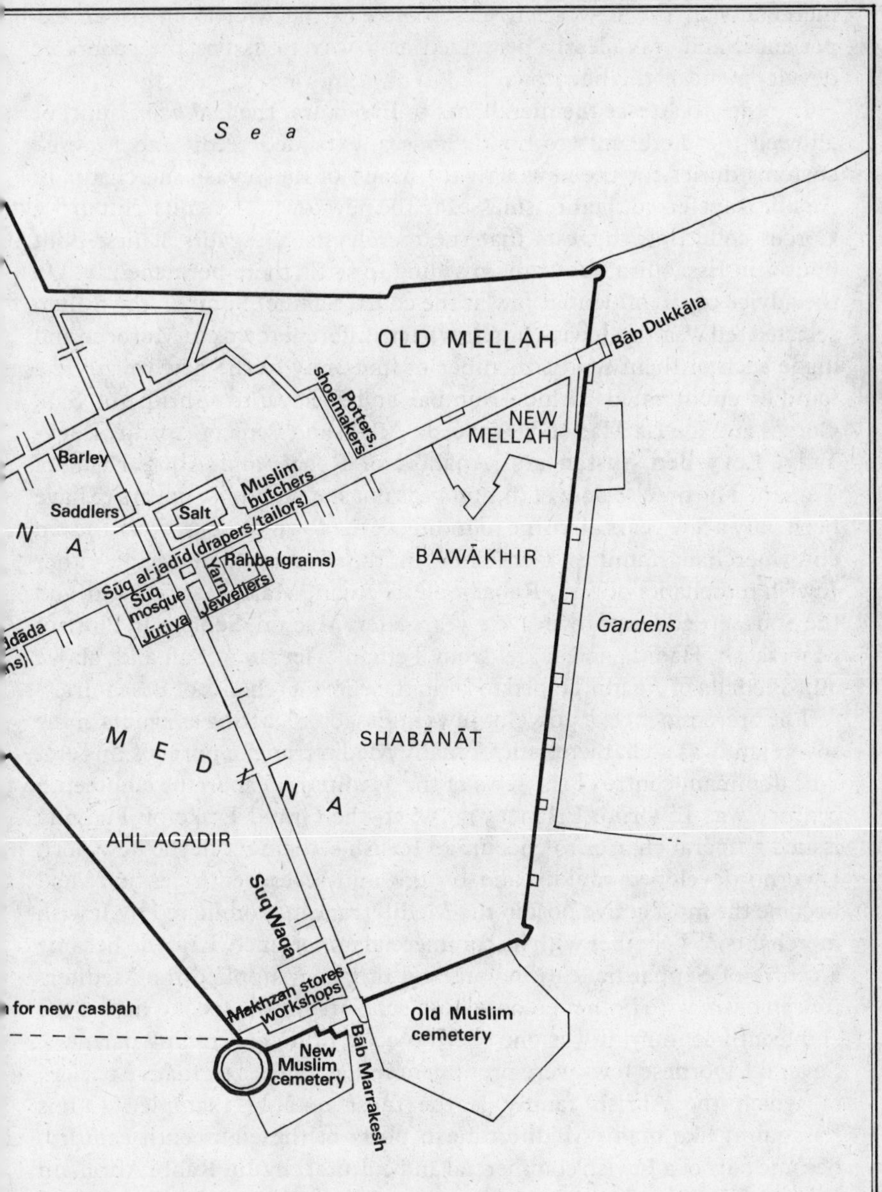
Sea
OLD MELLAH
Bāb Dukkāla
Potters, shoemakers
NEW MELLAH
Barley
Muslim butchers
Saddlers
Salt
Sūq al-jadīd (drapers/tailors)
Rahba (grains)
Yarn
Sūq mosque
Jewellers
Jūtiya
BAWĀKHIR
Gardens
SHABĀNĀT
MEDINA
AHL AGADIR
SuqWaqa
Makhzan stores workshops
for new casbah
New Muslim cemetery
Bāb Marrakesh
Old Muslim cemetery

merchants in the new town was rooted in the Moroccan urban experience, and was clearly perceived as a way to assure the economic development of the new town.

In order to attract the merchants to Essaouira, the *makhzan* built, or allowed the merchants to build, houses, extended credit and lowered customs duties for the new arrivals. Many of the Jewish merchants of Agadir transferred their businesses to the new town. A manuscript in the Corcos collection suggests that the merchants of Agadir at first built houses in Essaouira but were unwilling to settle there permanently. On the advice of an influential Jew at the court, Samuel Sumbal, the Sultan selected ten wealthy Jewish families from different towns in Morocco and made each of them send a member of its family to the new town. The families enumerated include Sumbal and Delevante (Shriqi) of Safi, Corcos and De La Mar of Marrakesh, Aflalo and Peña of Agadir, Levy-Yuly, Levy-Ben Sussan and Anahori of Rabat, and Abudurham of Tetuan. The precise date of this move is not stated, but it appears to have been only a few years after the founding of the town.[52] Apart from the ten elite merchant families mentioned in the Corcos manuscript, other Jewish merchants of Safi, Rabat-Salé, Tetuan, Marrakesh, Agadir and the Sous settled in the town a few years later. Macnin, Sebag and Pinto of Marrakesh, Hadida and Israel from Tetuan, Merran of Safi and, above all, Guedalla of Agadir helped to form the elite merchants of Essaouira.[53]

The pre-eminence of polyglot Jews in Essaouira, acting as agents of the sovereign, was a characteristic of many Mediterranean ports of this era. The dominant centre of the Jews of the Mediterranean in the eighteenth century was Livorno. From 1593, when the Grand Duke of Tuscany issued a liberal charter to encourage Jewish settlement in the new port, Livorno developed rapidly and by the mid-seventeenth century, had become the most active port in the Mediterranean, dominated by Jewish merchants.[54] Together with its commercial importance, Livorno became a centre of Sephardic learning and culture, and supplied the Mediterranean basin with both merchants and scholars. In the second half of the eighteenth century, it was one of Morocco's principal trading partners. Several Livornese Jews were prominent in Essaouira's formative period, of which the Akrish family is the most notable example.[55] Thus Essaouira, like many Mediterranean ports of the eighteenth century, became part of a Jewish commercial and cultural circuit. Rabbi Abraham Coriat of Tetuan, for example, moved to Essaouria after its foundation, but later left for Livorno to become the rabbinical judge (*dayyan*) at the request of Essaouira's Livornese Jews. Prominent Algerian Jews, such as Cohen-Solal and Boujnah,[56] settled in Essaouira soon after the foundation of the town. Amsterdam and London were also part of this commercial-cultural circuit of the eighteenth century – De Lara of Amsterdam came to Essaouira and married into the Guedalla family, and Guedalla himself had family and commercial ties with Amsterdam.[57]

This connection with the European network of Jewish traders was of crucial importance in conducting the import and export trade of Essaouira, but of equal importance was the Jewish network which stretched along the Moroccan inland trade routes. The bulk of the Moroccan foreign trade relied on the exchange of products imported and exported from the southwest. Some of the leading Jewish merchant families of Essaouira, such as Afriat and Ohayon, came from these regions. Their close ties with both Jewish and commercial agents and the tribal leaders of the southwest effectively facilitated the circulation of goods.

In the eighteenth century, representatives from foreign merchant firms of the major trading capitals of Europe established themselves in Essaouira. Initially French, Genoese and Portuguese were employed in the construction of the town. Later the Sultan exerted pressures to induce all European merchants to move from Rabat, Safi, Agadir and all other Moroccan ports to the new town.[58] Essaouira eventually became the only maritime port where foreign trade was allowed. Its foreign merchants (and this included Guedalla) formed a tribunal of commerce known as the *commercio*. In the first decade of the town's existence, Italians probably constituted the most privileged and largest foreign element in Essaouira.[59] The Spanish were also important, since we know that by 1769 a Franciscan church had been established.[60] With the resumption of the grain trade with Spain and Portugal in the 1780s,[61] the numbers of immigrants from the Iberian peninsula probably increased, and in addition, French, English, Dutch and Danish merchants settled in the new port.[62]

Most of the foreign merchants left Essaouira when trade with Morocco slackened at the end of the eighteenth century,[63] though new European merchants arrived around the mid-nineteenth century when foreign trade was liberalized through pressures from the European powers. But above all it was the Jewish merchants who left their imprint on the town. As the official merchants of the Sultan (*tujjār as-Sulṭān*), they were accorded houses in the lavish *casbah* quarter where the government administration and foreigners resided. Almost all the houses in the *casbah* belonged to the Moroccan central government which disposed of its properties as it wished. The *casbah* was surrounded by thick walls and was guarded at night much like the ramparts that encircled the city.

Most of the Jews who subsequently settled in Essaouira were not part of this privileged elite. Jewish commoners resided in the northwestern corner of the city in an exclusively Jewish quarter, which was known as the *mellah* (*millāḥ*) in Moroccan cities.[64] Initially, the common Jews of Essaouira lived in the *medina* with the Muslims, but in 1807 they were forced to move to a Jewish quarter by sharifian decree. It was part of a wider policy of Sultan Sulaymān who, for uncertain reasons, decided to confine the Jews in a number of coastal towns to *mellah*s. As the population of Jews increased in the coastal towns, there were probably pressures to confine Jews in *mellah*s, which was the arrangement in the major inland cities of Marrakesh, Fez and Meknes. The decree did not affect the Jews of the *casbah*, who continued to live in their *makhzan* residences.[65]

It was the coterie of Jewish merchants of the *casbah* that was the most influential of all groups in the town. Much of the economic activity of the town revolved around their commercial transactions, and the prosperity of the town depended on the successful operation of their trading firms. It was through these merchants that the traders of southern Morocco marketed their goods for the European trade. European firms were compelled to deal with these privileged royal merchants since most of Morocco's foreign trade was in their hands.

Chapter 3

Merchants of the Sultan

International trade was at the centre of Essaouira's economic life and the most influential men of the town were the merchants who were the Sultan's traders. Their special relationship to the Sultans gave them particular advantages over other traders, and at certain periods, they maintained a quasi-total monopoly of the import–export trade. The Sultan's merchants (*tujjār as-Sulṭān*) had the opportunity to make considerable profits, yet at the same time, they depended on the official recognition and patronage of the palace. The fact that the majority of them were Jews was also significant. As legally inferior members of the only religious minority in Morocco, they could almost never attain positions of political power or have a share in local government outside the confines of the Jewish community. For this reason, as a general rule, they were highly dependent on the Palace and, consequently, their loyalty was usually assured.

As merchants, however, they were able to exert considerable local influence since the prosperity of the town depended on their enterprises. In some ways, these royal merchants were similar to the 'court Jews' of central Europe in the seventeenth and eighteenth centuries. In both cases, elite Jews were economic instruments of the rulers. Equipped with foreign languages and international connections, the court Jews were used in diplomatic affairs as well. In both Morocco and Europe, the state treasuries relied on their financial activities for bringing in needed liquid cash, and Jewish merchants in both cases supplied the court with luxury goods and munitions. Finally, between Jew and ruler, there was a personal relationship which tied them together. Paradoxically, this tie was strengthened because both ruler and Jew, to some extent, separated from the rest of society on a social level, though for different reasons: the Jew as a member of a religious minority, and the ruler as a relatively inaccessible sovereign of holy lineage.[1]

Nonetheless, there were also fundamental differences between the court Jews of the German princes and the *tujjār as-Sulṭān*. The court Jews of Central Europe were essentially transitionary instruments of rulers in the first phase of the development of modern capitalism. In

Morocco in the eighteenth and nineteenth centuries, the royal merchants were vestiges of the old order, a historically embedded 'bourgeoisie' used as a final front against foreign capitalist penetration.

Historians who have written about the *tujjār as-Sulṭān* in the nineteenth century have focused on the Jewish merchants as agents of transition. Their contact with foreign commerce did indeed place them in an intermediary position, and enabled them to act as catalysts in the changing economic structures of Morocco. Miège sees the emergence of an inchoate capitalist class, which bears striking similarities to the rise of a Jewish bourgeoisie in Europe during the eighteenth century, characterized in both cases by long-term speculation on prices, exploitation of economic cycles, the formation of landed fortunes, rural expansion of capitalism from the cities and an ideological evolution.[2]

While there are some interesting points of comparison between the rise of the Jewish capitalist class in Europe and the *tujjār as-Sulṭān* in Morocco, the differences are just as important. In fact, the comparison itself is in some ways misguided because it transposes a European model of transition to a capitalist economy on a Moroccan context. A European capitalist economy did begin to impose itself on the peripheries of the Moroccan economy, and a number of Moroccan Jewish merchants became involved in foreign economic enterprises. Many took advantage of their intermediary positions by employing capital in novel ways. But except in very limited ways, they never became a clearly definable socio-economic group, nor constituted a cohesive class with any autonomous base of power. They became, in some respects, compradors in a new power-relationship with Europe.

But this is only part of the picture. The Jewish merchants remained embedded in a society which still operated by norms which had little to do with European capitalist economies, despite growing foreign economic penetration. The commercial world of the tenth- to twelfth-century Mediterranean, portrayed by S. D. Goitein, tells us as much about the ways in which nineteenth-century Moroccan merchants operated as do London, Amsterdam, Marseille, and Livorno of the eighteenth century. The *ancien régime* was under siege by foreign market forces, but it was not yet replaced by a new European economic order.[3] The Moroccan Jewish merchant operated on many different levels: comprador on the one hand, and royal merchant on the other, shipping agent of steam boats, and financier of caravans. The two seemingly irreconcilable worlds of European merchant capitalism and royal monopolistic trade, of camel and the steam boat, were intermeshed in a system which needs to be understood organically.

Tājir as royal merchant

In the cities of the Islamic world, the term *tājir* (pl. *tujjār*, from *t-j-r*, to trade), has always denoted more than someone who simply traded for his living.[4] The *tujjār* were first of all wholesalers, as distinct from those involved primarily in retail. The shopkeeper, therefore, would never be defined as *tājir*, and even a small-scale merchant who accumulated stocks might not be called a *tājir* if he was not actually a shipper of merchandise. In 1847, the French consul of Essaouira notes that only 17 or 18 Muslims and Jews 'bear the title of *tejer*'.[5] Furthermore, in Essaouira the title of *tājir* was limited to those privileged merchants who were associated with the Palace.[6] You could not become a shipper in the absence of sharifian authorization.

The Sultans' merchants, therefore, formed a corporate group into which admittance required royal favour and the formal sanction of the sovereign. The ties of interdependency between merchant and Sultan were reinforced by a particular kind of fiscal relationship. The *tājir* traded on interest-free loans from the Palace. Out of his profits, derived from commerce, the *tājir* repaid the Sultan in monthly instalments. The proscriptions regarding interest on loans in Islamic law prevented the Sultan from making direct profits from the royal advances. Indirectly, however, the *makhzan* was operating like a bank, investing in a *tājir* who was usually already a man of considerable means. By promoting the merchant's business enterprises, the *makhzan* could expect to gain substantial returns from custom duties paid by the *tājir* to government agents at the port.

In Essaouira, the relationship between the Palace and the *tujjār* was strengthened in another way: the royal merchants were granted *makhzan* houses in the *casbah* at low rents. This aspect of the relationship, together with the royal loan, was instrumental in the formation of the merchant elite of Essaouira, yet it was a relationship which prevented the merchants from becoming an independent social class. Once the relationship between *tājir* and Sultan was established, the former could move to another town or travel abroad only after receiving the personal authorization of the Sultan himself. This was only granted after the *tājir* left a guarantor (*ḍāmin*) and deposited money or property as collateral (*rahn*). The *tājir* Judah, for example, requests permission to travel to London where his brother had just died owing 788,116 ūqiya to the *makhzan*. Judah insists that if he is not allowed to travel, his inheritance would probably be lost. He claims to have property in the *mellah* and merchandise in the house where his children would remain in his absence. Ben Messas, the Marrakshi, would be delegated as guarantor of his monthly instalment to the *makhzan* in his absence.[7]

Finally, the relationship was symbolically maintained by an annual excursion of the merchants to Marrakesh to pay tribute to the Sultan. This included Jews and Muslims, and, in the first half of the nineteenth century, a few Christians. The merchants presented gifts to the Sultan on this occasion, and periodically the Sultan would give gifts of fine linen to the *tujjār* in return.[8] The reception of the merchants at the royal court was also a means of assuring royal control over the merchants' activities, yet, equally important, the merchants used the occasion to press demands concerning the administration of commerce in the town.[9]

In the first decades of the nineteenth century, the number of *tujjār* in Essaouira was limited. Few foreign merchants from the town's formative period in the eighteenth century remained. The plague of 1799–1800, the Napoleonic wars, and a change in Moroccan foreign policy, significantly reduced the number of *tujjār* required in the Moroccan–European trade. Sultan Sulaymān (1792–1822) made do with a handful of *tujjār* whose activities he could closely control. In 1805, there were six European and two Moroccan Jewish merchant firms in Essaouira. This ratio was reduced, and by 1828, only one European house (Renshaw and Willshire) remained, while the number of Jewish firms rose to nine.[10] One decade later the total number of merchant firms had only risen to sixteen.[11] By 1841, there had been a further slight increase in the number of firms in Essaouira: nineteen merchant houses are listed by the French consular agent as recipients of the royal loan (see tables 1 and 2). This privileged corps of merchants, though limited in number, was all that the Sultan required to handle Morocco's rather limited trade with Europe. Strict controls over foreign trade were enforced, and any exchange by merchants operating without the Sultan's authorization was considered contraband. Even the foreign Christian merchant houses of Willshire, Robertson and Bolelli, and the Algerian and Tunisian Jewish trading houses of Darmon, Boujnah, and Cohen-Solal, only operated by royal sanction and were tied to the Sultan in a contractual bond of royal debt.[12] Furthermore, it would be difficult for any kind of independent merchant to compete, since the *tujjār* received considerable advances in money, credit on customs duties, and monopolies of a number of commodities. In short, no merchant within the ports controlled by the *makhzan* could operate on a large scale without the official patronage of the Palace.[13]

By this contractual relationship of credit and debt, the Palace kept the merchants dependent and under its control. This system of closely administered trade began to change in the 1850s when foreign pressures induced Sultan ʿAbd ar-Raḥmān to abandon strict protectionist trade

Table 1 *Debts owed to the Sultan in riyāl*

Merchant	1841 debt	Merchant	1865 old debt	Merchant	1865 new loan
1 Willshire	138,900	A. al-Labār	2,900	A. al-Labār	
2 Robertson	90,000	A. Būhillāl	3,400	B. ʿAzūz	10,000
3 Bolleli	11,200	M. Ibn ʿAzūz	6,700	M^{jb} Tufal-ʿazz	
4 M^{hd} Tūfalʿazz	14,900	M^{jb} Tūfal-ʿazz (4)	9,900	A. Būhillāl	
5 M. az-Zarrār	50,000	aṭ-Ṭālib Būhillāl	2,000	al-Warzazi	5,000
6 J. Elmaleh	131,200	A. Afriat	7,200	U Tahālla	2,500
7 A. Elmaleh	163,300	Y. Acoca	2,500	S. Amar	7,000
8 A. Delevante	78,000	I. Coriat	8,400	J. Delevante (8)	7,000
9 Aflalo	96,600	Haim Toby	1,400	J. Levy-Yuly (18)	5,000
10 Boujnah	42,600	A. Corcos	22,600	Y. Acoca	7,000
11 Zagury	42,300	M^{jb} Ū Tahālla	3,500	S. as-Saqat	4,000
12 Cohen-Solal	37,200	J. de A. Delevante (8)	12,500	Bensemana	4,000
13 Benattar	38,800	S. Amar	3,500	J. Elmaleh (7) & son	15,000
14 Abitbol	19,000	S. Anahory (16)	9,000	aṭ-Ṭālib Būhillāl	4,000
15 Belisha	17,000	Jacob Pinto	200	Ibn ʿAzūz	5,000
16 Anahory	14,000	Cohen-Solal (12)	11,900	J. Levy-Yuly (18)	3,000
17 A. Corcos	19,000	Grace	8,200	(listed again)	
18 J. Levy-Yuly	1,600	*Musa Aflalo (9)*	34,300	J. Boujnah (10)	10,000
19 Darmon	4,300	M. al-Labār	6,300	J. Elmaleh (7)	5,000
		al-Ḥarīshī	500	(listed again)	
		al-Labādī	1,400	A. Afriat	6,000
		at-Tāʿī al-Qādirī	800	D. Ohana	7,000
		A.-Q. al-ʿAṭṭār	700		
		al-Makkī ash-Sharbī	100		
		Masʿūd	25		
		Curtis	200		
		J. de A. Elmaleh (7)	92,400		
		J. Levy-Yuly (18)	21,500		
		al-Ḥazān ʿAzir	200		
		D. de J. Levy Yuly (18)	600		
		Abraham Toby	1,800		
		Abraham Cohen	200		
		Aaron Corcos	100		

Note: The numbers are rounded up to the nearest 100. Jewish names are spelled according to a common European form of the time, except those which are unidentified. The numbers after the names in columns 2 and 3 correspond to the names in column 1, when the person is the same or a direct descendant. Column 2 is in mithqāl in the original source. I have converted it at the official exchange rate: 1 riyāl = 32.5 ūqiya.
Sources: A.E., C.C.C., Mogador 1, 2 January 1841, Delaporte. B.H., K^{295}. Between Dhū al-Qaʿda 1281 and the beginning of Dhū al-Qaʿda 1282, most of the merchants in the top half of column 2 are listed as having repaid the *makhzan* about 10% their debt.

Table 2 *Number of merchants (or partnerships) in debt to the Sultan*

Year	Jews	Muslims	Christians	Total
1841[a]	14	2	3	19
1865–6[b]	19	14	2	35
1881–4[c]	31	16	4	51

Sources: [a] Amounts of debts owed, listed by the French consul. A.E., C.C.C., Mogador 1, 2 January 1841, Delaporte.
[b] Amounts listed in *makhzan* register as 'old debt' and 'new loan'. K. H., K[295].
[c] From several lists in K.H., K[120].

policies. A commercial treaty with Great Britain in 1856, followed by similar treaties with other European countries, liberalized trade and encouraged increasing numbers of both foreign and Moroccan merchants to establish themselves in Essaouira. Although the total number of indebted merchants grew, many traders were able to operate without the direct control of the Palace. The French consulate counted 39 merchant firms in Essaouira in 1854, and 52 in 1866 (see table 3).[14]

Through either the system of consular protection or by obtaining foreign nationality, many Jewish merchants were able to attract foreign capital in place of royal contracts. The *makhzan*'s attempt to counteract this development by establishing new Muslim and Jewish merchants in Essaouira from Tetuan and Marrakesh met with failure. Despite royal favours, most of the Muslims were unable to survive the competition for more than a few years. Those who prospered, such as Mukhtār Ibn ʿAzūz, were largely successful because they built up the same kind of foreign connections as did the Jewish merchants. However, almost all the Muslim firms disappeared within two to three decades.

Growing numbers of minor wholesale merchants, some of whom originally were from Gibraltar, began to enter the arena of international commerce. Registers of customs duties show that there were about 65 to 70 individual merchants dealing in import or export, that is, more than those listed by Beaumier. However, since many of these merchants dealt only in small quantities of goods, the number of major trading firms was probably close to the figure given by the French consul: on the basis of duties paid, about 50 merchants appear to have been dealing in significant quantities of goods.[15]

Of the twenty shippers who paid the highest amount of duties from 1862–4, there were five Christians, two Muslims, and thirteen Jews. (See table 4.) Many of the leading shippers, such as Abraham Corcos and Joseph b. Amram Elmaleh, owed substantial amounts to the Sultan.

Table 3 *Consul Beaumier's report on trading firms, 1866*

Moroccan:	Jewish	30
	Muslim	7
English		11
Spanish		2
Italian		1
French		1
	Total	52

Source: A.E., C.C.C., Mogador 4, 15 April 1866.

Table 4 *Twenty principal merchants: duties paid, 1862–4*

Name in register	European form	Import	Export	Total ūqiya
1 Ka(r)tis	James Curtis	176,877	534,272	711,149
2 Barrī	David Perry	95,781	586,822	682,603
3 al-Ḥazān Bīhī	Abraham Afriat	366,484	314,115	680,599
4 Grīs(h)	Grace	183,197	250,871	434,068
5 Hannī az-Zagūrī	Abraham Zagury	119,597	248,701	368,298
6 Ya'qūb Naftālī	Jacob N. Afriat	85,893	247,915	333,808
7 Abrāham Qarqūz	Abraham Corcos	74,795	233,227	308,022
8 Ya'qūb Bintū	Jacob Pinto	120,591	94,668	215,259
9 Isḥāq Quriyāṭ	Isaac S. Coriat	3,752	197,075	200,827
10 Mukhtār b. 'Azūz	Mokhtar Benazuz	55,390	144,498	199,888
11 Yamīn Aqūqa	Yomin Acoca	104,020	63,205	167,225
12 Yūsuf b. 'Amrān al-Malīḥ	Joseph de A. Elmaleh	43,551	119,185	162,736
13 al-Ḥazān Isḥāq b. as-Saqand	(European spelling unknown)	85,730	72,919	158,649
14 al-Ḥazān Mas'ūd b. Naftālī	Messod Afriat	39,970	105,746	145,716
15 Ya'qūb Afriyāṭ	Jacob Afriat	67,078	73,352	140,430
16 Mas'ūd Turjumān	Messod Tugaman	56,737	73,400	130,137
17 'Akkān b. Ḥayyīm Qarqūz	Akkan Corcos	28,946	97,261	126,207
18 Raṭṭū	Manuel Ratto	5,394	114,004	119,398
19 Muḥammad Raghūn	Mohamed Aragon	29,517	82,752	112,269
20 Rāfa'il aṣ-Ṣbanyuli	Rafael Moll	6,220	102,295	108,515

Source: K.H., K[46]; K.H., *qawā'im ḥisābiyya*.

Other large-scale debtors were unsuccessful in commerce, and their property was eventually confiscated and sold off to pay their debts. While some merchant houses declined, others, such as Mukhtār Ibn 'Azūz and Dinar Ohana, were able to enter the scene because of royal favours. In the 1860s, two foreign merchant firms, Perry and Curtis, were able to trade in large quantities of goods virtually without credit from the *makhzan*.

Table 5 *Leading shippers of Essaouira in 1884: duties paid in 1884*

Name in register	European form	Import	Export	Total ūqiya
Yaʿqūb Naftālī	Jacob N. Afriat	34,918	67,020	101,938
Rabīl al-Malīḥ	Reuben Elmaleh	23,843	49,412	73,255
Dinār	Dinar Ohana	45,032	27,966	72,998
Abrāham b. Saʿūd	Abraham Bensaude	44,283	16,192	60,475
ʿAkkān b. Hammu	Akkan or Jacob Levy	28,412	27,589	56,001
Salām Naftālī	Solomon Afriat	34,203	8,215	42,418
Iṣḥāq Afriyāṭ	Isaac Afriat	23,381	16,071	39,452
Hannī az-Zagūrī	Abraham Zagury	6,547	30,288	36,835
Masʿūd ʿAṭṭiya	Messod Attia	33,529	2,720	36,249
Yaʿqub as-Saghir	Jacob M. Afriat[a]	27,098	5,883	32,981
ʿAkkān Qarquz	Akkan Corcos	14,876	14,743	29,619
Muḥammad al-Warzāzī	Mohamed Elwarzazi	21,087	3,183	24,270
Hananiya Kabisa	H. Cabessa	17,515	4,503	22,018
Dāʾūd Naftālī	David Afriat	15,994	1,050	17,044
Jakīṭī	Jacquetty	11,470	4,602	16,072
Iṣḥāq Alīwī	Isaac Halevy	15,010	972	15,982
Naftālī Afriyat	Naftali Afriat	13,183	2,363	15,546
Massān Biṭbūl	Messan Botbol	11,013	4,389	15,402
Iṣḥāq Quriyāṭ	Isaac S. Coriat	13,292	1,958	15,250
Abrāmī Biṭṭūn	Abraham Bitton	11,657	3,536	15,193

[a] Probable European equivalent.
Source: K.H., K[120] (approximately 112 persons were paying customs duties between 1882 and 1884, including 78 Jews, 18 Muslims and 16 Christians).

Other merchants successfully balanced their businesses through both foreign and royal credit. For this reason, the descendants of Naftali Afriat (*awlād* Naftālī) were probably the most successful merchants in Essaouira. While all the other major traders were still paying off the 'old debt' in 1884 (which is listed in the ledger of 1865–6), Abraham b. Naftali Afriat (known as al-Hazan Bihi) had met his obligations, despite the crisis of 1878–82.[16] It was through the combined credit of foreign firms and the *makhzan* that the town of Essaouira reached its apogee in the 1860s.

The total number of names listed in the ledgers of 1882–4 had increased, but this does not mean that there were a greater number of trading houses. Instead, it indicates the accumulated number of merchants over the past decades, of whom many were finding it difficult, if not impossible, to meet their obligations. The total number of persons paying import and export duties in 1884 was roughly the same as that of 1865, but the number dealing in any significant amount of goods appears to have been reduced to well under 50 and the quantity of trade was much lower than it had been 20 years earlier. Only one Muslim and one

Table 6 *Monthly payments in loans in 1884*

Name in register	European form	Monthly amount
al-Ḥājj Aḥmad Būhillāl	Hamed Bohlal	50 riyāl
al-Warzāzī	Elwarzazi	25
as-Saghīr	?	15
ʿUmar Bilhād	Omar Bilhod	5
Aḥmad Bilhād	Hamed Bilhod	5
al-Ḥājj Būshaʿīb	?	5
ʿAqūqa	Yamin Acoca	25
al-Ḥazān Bīhī	Abraham Afriat	20
Dinār	Dinar Ohana	25
Yūsuf al-Malīḥ	Joseph Elmaleh	20
ʿAkkān Qarqūz	Akkan Corcos	25
Yaʿqūb Naftālī	Jacob N. Afriat	20
Ibn Līshā'	Joshua Belisha	5
	Total:	245 riyāl
		× 32.5 (Official exchange rate)
	Fixed rate of exchange:	7,962.5 ūqiya

Source: K.H., K[120].

Christian appear among the top twenty persons in amounts of duties paid (see table 5).[17] As in the pre-1844 period, trade once again seems to have been almost entirely in Jewish hands. Some thirteen favoured merchants, six Muslims and seven Jews, were still receiving monthly advances from the customs officials (see table 6).

Property holders

The large and most valuable property in town was owned or leased to the wealthy merchants of the Sultan. The real estate which they controlled can be divided into three categories: private property (*mulk*), religious endowments (*ḥubus*, pl. *aḥbās*, Fr. *habous*; in the Muslim East, *waqf*, pl. *awqāf*), and *makhzan* property (*amlāk al-makhzan*). Less property was held as *mulk* than in older Moroccan cities.[18] The predominance of Jewish royal merchants, and the absence of a deeply-rooted Muslim elite may have been factors limiting the number of private holdings. Most of the merchants of Essaouira were leased both *ḥubus* and *makhzan* property at fixed rates of rent, which were only occasionally adjusted in the nineteenth century. Most of the large houses and stores in the two *casbahs* (the 'new *casbah*' was constructed in the 1860s) were *makhzan* properties held by the major merchants, who acquired what was known as 'key rights'. The right of possession was inherited by each new generation. Most of the houses of the new *casbah* were leased to foreign merchants and protégés at a monthly repayment rate of six per cent of the outlay for the construction. There were also numerous *makhzan* and *ḥubus* properties leased at low rent to the merchants in the two *mellah*s and *medina*. With increasing demands for both dwellings and warehouses, many of these properties were sublet at a profit. This was permitted by *manfaʿa*, the right to enjoy 'profit' from the property. Despite the low rents and the profits made by the tenants, the *makhzan* acquired more revenue from *makhzan* houses in Essaouira than for any other town in Morocco.[19]

Within this general structure of tenure, there existed an autonomous pre-emptive right among the Jews called *ḥazaqa*. The original tenant of a property received from successive tenants a quarter of the rent he paid to the landlord (the latter could be the *makhzan*, *ḥubus*, etc.), in theory to prevent property from falling out of Jewish hands. The *ḥazaqa* was juridically independent of Muslim law: the right of *ḥazaqa* could not be invoked in a Muslim court.[20]

The number of *ḥubus* and *makhzan* properties held by merchants reflects the position and status of Essaouira's elite. Equally it reflects the limitations encumbering the private accumulation of real estate. The ultimate possession of these properties was in the hands of the Sultan, who could legally sequester them from the lease-holder (the *ḥubus* was indirectly controlled by the Palace as a result of a series of reforms). While the *tujjār* were able to maintain lavish residences, they did so by the grace of the monarch.

Makhzan control of Essaouira's real estate may have inhibited the growth of the landed wealth of individuals, but it facilitated the functioning of the social and political system. Many holders of *makhzan* properties may have ceased to be active merchants in fact, but they continued to enjoy the favour of the Palace and still profited from subletting their holdings. Muslim notables also obtained *makhzan* properties owing to their position in the government administration or their function in the juridical establishment (i.e. qadis, *ʿudūl*, etc.). In addition, *qaʾids* and rural chiefs were granted rent-free houses as political concessions.

A roughly equal number of Muslims and Jews were paying rent to the *makhzan*, though the largest number of units are listed in the *medina* where the majority of holdings were in Muslim hands (see table 7). But the payment of rent on *makhzan* property had less to do with ethnic divisions than with the capacity of merchants to pay rent and the value

Table 7 *Religion of tenants:* makhzan *property by quarter, 1879*[a]

Quarter	Jews	Muslims	Christians	Unidentified	Total	Total units (houses, shops etc.)
medina	25[b]	102	7	11	145	170
Old *mellah*	38				38	44
New *mellah*	20	1			21	21
Old *casbah*	27	7		16	50	50
New *casbah*	19		12		31	33
All quarters	129	110	19	27	285	318

[a] Only a few slight changes had occurred since 1875 (in K.H., K[80]). It should be noted that many listed in the table as Jews were protégés of foreign powers or were foreign nationals, though often of Swiri origin. The names are not registered according to religion, so in a number of cases, the religion of the holder could not be identified.
[b] The numbers represent units, not aggregate total of persons. An additional three houses and one warehouse were under construction at the 6% agreement in the new *casbah* for three Jews and one Christian.
Source: K.H., K[93].

and location of the holdings. Since the majority of merchants were Jews, it was they who bore the greatest burden. It was from the two *casbah*s, the wealthy residential quarters of the merchants, that the majority of the rent was drawn (see table 8). The new *casbah* paid proportionally the highest rents because of the six per cent contracts. Though rents in the old *casbah* may originally have been assessed on a similar basis, constructions costs in the 1860s would have been much higher than in the time when the old *casbah* was built. It was therefore the foreigners and Jewish protégés who contributed proportionally the most to the *makhzan* coffers as rent-payers. In the *mellah* and *medina*, the popular quarters of town, *makhzan* property was rented at low rates. A large part of the dwellings and shops in these two quarters was held by the wealthy merchants of the old *casbah* in *manfaʿa*, sometimes sublet at exorbitant rates. This fact is not reflected in the *makhzan* registers.[21] Foreigners were banned from residing in the *mellah*, and neither foreigners nor Jews were allowed to live in the *medina* (though Jews rented shops in the *medina*). The consuls often contested these restrictions since rent was cheaper in the popular residential quarters, and in the case of the *medina*, there was more space available.

The old and well-established Swiri elite merchants were all to be found as tenants of *makhzan* property in the old *casbah* (see table 9). Not surprisingly, most of this coterie were the same as those listed as debtors to the Sultan (compare tables 9 and 1), and some were among those

Table 8 *Rent paid on* makhzan *property by quarter, 1879*[a]

Quarter	Amount (in ūqiya)	Units
medina	8,472 ūqiya	170
Old *mellah*	4,787	44
New *mellah*	2,518	21
Old *casbah*	24,113	50
New *casbah*	22,917	33
Total:	62,827	318

Note: For the *medina* and two *mellahs*, rent is listed in mithqāl, the money of account. For the *casbahs*, the rents have an initial listing in mithqāl, totalling 24,663.75 ūqiya. This is then divided by the official rate of exchange for riyāl (1 riyāl = 32.5 ūqiya). This is because the rents in the *casbahs* were counted in mithqāl, but collected in silver. The riyāl is then multiplied by the real market value exchange rate of 62 ūqiya the riyāl. The riyāl therefore revert back to the mithqāl system after compensation for the difference between the real and the official value of silver. In the register this calculation is done with the two *casbahs* combined. I have added up the rents and used this calculation for each town quarter separately.
Source: K.H., K[93].

paying the highest amounts of duties to the officials in charge of financial matters (*umanā'*). The merchant was therefore doubly tied to the Sultan as debtor and tenant. If the *tājir* was unable to meet his obligations, his private property was liable to be sequestered or sold, though he was generally allowed to keep his low-rent *makhzan* holdings. In 1868, for example, a *tājir* in Essaouira named Jacob. b. Adi [Delevante] requested from the Sultan (exalted by God), that his property be seized after its valuation, that the amount owed in the new debt be deducted from its sale and the remainder paid to him.[22]

This bond with the Palace, which involved extensive credit and leases of government property, effectively hindered capital accumulation and severely restricted the range of the merchants' investments.

Table 9 *Tenants and monthly rents of* makhzan *houses in the* casbah[a] in 1865

Tenant	Houses	Old rent (ūqiya)	Raise (ūqiya)	New rent (ūqiya)
ash-Sharīf Mawlāy aṭ-Ṭaʿi	1	32	8	40
Sīdī ʿAbd ar-Raḥmān al-Labār	3	100	30	130
Sīdī ʿAbd al-Majīd al-Ḥarīshī	1	30	15	45
Sīdī Muḥammad al-Warzāzī	1	50	15	65
al-Ḥājj Maḥjūb Tūfal-ʿazz	1	80	30	110
al-Ḥājj Maḥjūb Ū Tahālla	1	80	50	130
Sīdī aṭ-Ṭālib Būhillāl	1	130	30	160
Joseph b. Amram Elmaleh	3	276	84	360
Musa Aflalo	2	200	80	280
Isaac Bensaude	1	70	20	90
Jacob b. Adi Delevante	1	100	40	140
Haim b. Pinhas	1	120	40	160
Messan Knaffo	1	100	50	150
The Christian in Dār al-Aʿshār	1	80	40	120
John Grace	1	60	20	80
Ratto in Dār al-Sʿshār	1	80	40	120
Curtis	2	200	80	280
Saul Cohen-Solal	1	100	40	140
The French doctor	1	100	0	100
at-Tājir Abraham Corcos	3	290	90	380
Messod Turgaman	1	60	40	100
Yamin Acoca	1	110	40	150
Isaac Coriat	1	90	40	130
Consul Bolelli	1	100	0	100
Abraham Afriat	2	166	84	250
Akkan b. Miryam [Levy?]	1	50	30	80
Abraham Cohen	1	50	30	80
Judah Levy-Yuly	2	160	70	230
Abraham Bensaude	1	100	40	140
Pinhas Toby	1	124	66	190
Shemtob Abenhaim (son)	1	30	20	50
at-Tājir Perry	3	325	0	325
Thomas the Englishman	1	100	30	130
Sīdī Muḥammad Raghūn	1	30	10	40
Sidi al-Mukhtār b. ʿAzūz	1	120	40	160
Ratto [second listing]	1	50	20	70
al-Ḥājj Aḥmad Būhillāl	1	120	40	160
Bensemana	2	170	30	200
Total	51	4,233	1,432	5,665

[a] Former amount collected and new rent, raised in Rabīʿ I 1282/July–August 1865
Source: B.H., K[295].

The merchant elite

Essaouira's merchant elite numbered slightly more than those merchants appearing as residents of the *casbah*. Of these, less than ten stand out at the centre of Essaouira's commercial activities. Because foreign trade was so crucial for the town – indeed, Essaouira's *raison d'être* rested on its role as commercial entrepôt – the elite coterie of Jewish traders had a much more central role in the social and political life of the town than in any other major Moroccan city. In other cities as well, wealthy merchant families were high up on the social hierarchy. Wealthy families generally invested in real estate, such as urban and suburban houses and gardens. In Fez, for example, there was a deeply-rooted and wealthy Muslim elite or 'bourgeoisie' which maintained considerable real estate. Yet wealth was not the only criterion for elite status: learning, family ties, social and political functions were also crucial. Men of holy lineage (*shurafā'*), ulama, *makhzan* officials, and even artisans might have an important place in the social hierarchy. In addition to wealth, the elite maintained its position due to the respect that it was able to command from the population at large. One of its major functions was that of intermediary. Those men of venerated ancestry, such as the *shurafā'*, often arbitrated disputes in town and in the countryside.[23] In other towns in Morocco Jews might become wealthy merchants, but they could rarely attain a high position in the social hierarchy, except within their own society in the *mellah*. In Essaouira, through their close connections to the Sultan, the powerful chiefs of the southwest, and European countries, the Jewish merchants played a major role as mediators in urban life. Their high position in the social hierarchy, not just in the *mellah* but in the town and in the surrounding countryside, was perhaps unprecedented in Moroccan history.

Corcos and the Palace

The Corcos, like many families of the elite, trace their family back to an Andalusian past. Ancestors of the family came to Morocco from Spain and Portugal in the fifteenth century. A branch of the family appears to have established its position in Marrakesh in the eighteenth century. Maymon b. Isaac (see 'a' in fig. 1; subsequent lettering refers back to this genealogical tree) was probably among the first group of royal merchants to settle in Essaouira. He died of the plague in 1799.[24] His first cousin, Abraham (b), was another early settler.[25] A more distant cousin, also Abraham (c, who had lived in both Oran and London, was among the most important merchants of Essaouira in the 1830s and 1840s, and among the *tujjār* trading on the royal loan.

The most important Corcos for the period under study was Abraham (f), who moved from Marrakesh to Essaouira a few years before the French attack of August 1844. During the war, Abraham found refuge with a rural chief, Muḥammad Ū Mubārak, at Kūzimt in the Haha. It was there that his wife Miryam gave birth to their son Meyer, who was circumcised eight days later by Aaron Aflalo.[26] From Haha, the Corcos family continued their journey to Marrakesh where they remained until the summer of 1845. In 1846, Abraham's father Solomon (d) was ordered by royal edict (*dahir*) to move to Essaouira, 'to conduct his commercial affairs and to recover his debts and the rest of the debt of Willshire the Englishman'. Jacob (e) Corcos was left as Solomon's successor (*khalīfa*) or agent in Marrakesh. The debts referred to the royal loans of which all the *tujjār* were beneficiaries. This included Willshire, the British merchant and consular agent who absconded during the 1844 attack. Since Solomon Corcos was Willshire's agent in Marrakesh and held the latter's funds under his custody, Sultan ʿAbd ar-Raḥmān decided to keep Solomon in charge of this money to be used in foreign trade.[27]

Over the next decade, Essaouira's trade increased appreciably. In 1853, Solomon Corcos died in Essaouira, and in 1857, his son Jacob settled permanently in Essaouira leaving a cousin, Haim (h), in charge of the business in Marrakesh.[28]

With each successive Sultan or new *qāʾid* in Essaouira, the status of *tājir* was re-enacted by *dahir* for Abraham and Jacob. Shortly after Jacob's arrival in Essaouira in 1857, the two brothers were conferred with their investiture from the Sultan. The *dahir* proclaimed their eminence among the merchants of Essaouira, complimenting their contribution towards increasing the wealth of the treasury.[29] The Palace also made sure that the interests of the privileged merchants were looked after by local officials. In 1858, Khalīfa Muḥammad b. ʿAbd ar-Raḥmān wrote to Ibn Zākūr, the new *qāʾid* of Essaouira:

> The two merchants Abraham and Jacob, the sons of Solomon Corcos, are *our Jews*, and their father was *our Jew*. Among the Jews they are the cream of the crop [the fruit], and very few [Jews] are equal to them in yielding profits. So protect them and look after their well being.[30]

One year later, Sultan ʿAbd ar-Raḥmān died and Sīdī Muḥammad succeeded to the throne. In response to a worried letter from Abraham and Jacob, the *wazīr* Mūsā b. Aḥmad assured the two brother that their position would be maintained.[31] A few years later, the two brothers received a new *dahir* from Sultan Muḥammad IV.[32] The renewal of *tājir* status not only took place with the succession of a new monarch, but could also be inherited by the children of the royal merchants. In 1883,

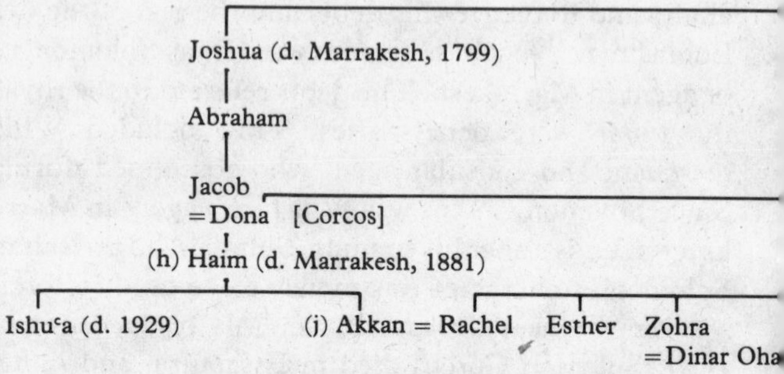

Fig. 1 Corcos genealogical tree (genealogical trees have been published by Michel Abitbol, *Témoins et acteurs: les Corcos et l'histoire du Maroc contemporain*, Jerusalem, 1977, and by Jean-Louis Miège, *Documents d'histoire économique et sociale marocaine au XIXe siècle*, Paris 1969, pp. 252–4). I am grateful to Sydney Corcos, who provided me with his own revised family tree. I have also drawn from dated tombstones in the Jewish cemetery of Essaouira. The above tree is an abbreviated version.

Meyer and Aharon were confirmed in the position of their father Abraham only six weks after his death.[33]

The eminent status that Abraham and Jacob Corcos enjoyed was largely due to their role as suppliers of luxury goods to the Palace. Many of the letters from Bū ʿAshrīṇ and Mūsā b. Aḥmad – the main ministers (*wazīr*s) to the Sultan's court in Marrakesh – to the two brothers pertain to requests for silk, fine linen, European tiles, English furniture, and chocolate. The port authorities were sometimes ordered by the Sultan to import these items duty-free. In addition to the luxury trade, the Corcos house also imported fabrics to be used for the uniforms of Essaouira's garrison and for soldiers in military expeditions (*ḥarka*s).[34]

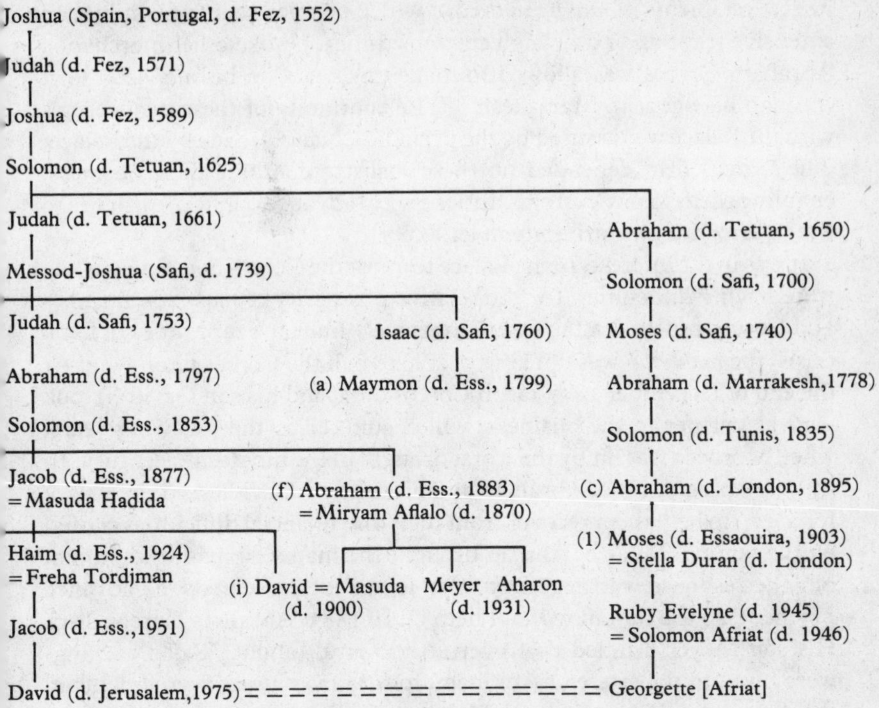

These close commercial ties with the Palace were also maintained by personal relations between the Corcos family and the entourage of the Sultan. When, for instance, Solomon Corcos died in Essaouira in 1853, Jacob Corcos, who was still in Marrakesh, received condolences from the *wazīr* Bū ʿAshrīn.[35] The Jewish merchant elite shared common interests with the ruling class that transcended religious boundaries. Members of the Sultan's entourage took into account Jewish holidays, marriages, and family quarrels.[36]

The Corcos family also served the Palace as informal political advisors, pertaining both to local administrative matters and to political developments in distant regions in the southwest.[37] Through their string of agents and connections with rural chiefs in southern markets, they were well informed on political developments all along the trade routes. Rural unrest was as damaging to the Corcos business as it was to successful government. The family often supplied the Palace with news of disturbances in the countryside.[38]

Such close connections to the Palace undoubtedly helped Jacob and Abraham Corcos to gain considerable wealth. They were among the largest recipients of *makhzan* credit, which enabled them to conduct an extensive trade and cover high customs duties. Unlike other merchants, Abraham Corcos was allowed to make payments on his *makhzan* loan through his agent in Marrakesh.[39] The continuity of these connections with the Palace was assured by the periodic advances made by the Palace. The Corcos firm depended on these loans to continue their business, enabling them to pay customs duties and to advance credit themselves to the interior for procuring items of export.

It was in the interests of the Palace to assist the Corcos house when they were having difficulties, for the relative prosperity of *makhzan* finances and Corcos business affairs were intricately linked. Yet at times of fiscal crisis, the *makhzan* was not always able to bail the Corcos family out. At the end of December 1877 Jacob Corcos died, and his son David (i) took over as partner in the business, which suffered in the following years, when Morocco was hit by the worst drought of the nineteenth century. In the beginning of 1880, Abraham and his nephew David asked the Palace for a loan to help them recover from their dire financial difficulties caused by the famine. Mūsā b. Aḥmad brought the matter up with the Sultan, but the response was negative: 'now is not the season for the advance payment, so the Sultan will not help'.[40] In 1883, Abraham Corcos died. His son Meyer claimed that over 40,000 riyāl (about £8,000 sterling) were owed to the estate of Abraham, mostly from unrecovered debts in the Sous, Aït Bāʿamrān and Haha, while some 19,000 riyāl (about £3,000) were still owed to the *makhzan*.[41]

Such considerable sums show that both the profits and the losses of the Corcos business could be high. Records of customs duties show that the Corcos firm dealt in all the main products of Essaouira's trade. Their principal imports were cotton fabrics (particularly bleached and unbleached calicoes), sugar, and tea. Exports, however, appear to have far outstripped imports, if we exclude goods imported expressly for the Sultan which may not have been marked in the customs' ledgers. The principal items exported included olive oil, goat skins, almonds, wax, and ostrich feathers. The Corcos business seems to have avoided specialization in a specific commodity. As general traders, the Corcos firm spread its risks.[42]

Members of the Corcos family were also important tax-farmers. After 1860, the gates and markets of Essaouira were farmed out to merchants, and Akkan Corcos (j) of Marrakesh became the leading tax-farmer in Essaouira. Akkan's brother Ishuʿa (k) was to become the head of the community of Marrakesh, and arguably the most influential Jew in Morocco at the turn of the century: 'the real court banker, when the court is in residence at Marrakesh', wrote a noted French observer of

Morocco.[43] In the 1860s, Akkan came to Essaouira with a considerable capital advance from the Sultan and was provided with a *makhzan* house.[44] For a decade he enjoyed many royal favours, and was alleged to have had a great influence over the *qā'id* of Essaouira because of his ties with the *wazīr* Mūsā b. Aḥmad. Akkan Corcos received credit on export duties, was allowed to purchase monopolies by royal decree and, for a period of time, was granted control of the octroi. He had a reputation for unscrupulous business practices, and consequently, Abraham Corcos sometimes felt compelled to disassociate himself from his relative. Jacob Corcos and his son-in-law, Dinar Ohana, co-purchasers of the octroi contract, apparently came to regret their association with the less diplomatic Akkan.[45]

These kinds of differences between *tujjār* were more the exception than the rule. Generally speaking, the interests of Abraham and Jacob Corcos were at one with other members of the merchant elite. The two brothers did not hesitate to use their connections to intercede on behalf of the other merchants. When the *makhzan* raised rents in 1864, the two brothers protested to the Palace about the harmful effects that the rise would have for the merchants of Essaouira. In the same letter of protest, they sought to secure more houses for their friends because of the housing shortage in town.[46] When other *tujjār* fell into difficulties, the Corcos brothers often intervened on their behalf. In 1875, when Musa Aflalo was unable to pay debts owed on his *makhzan* properties, Abraham Corcos was able to secure for him a delay on payment of rent, to enable him to recover from his financial problems.[47] Conversely, the Sultan's entourage on several occasions sent Muslim merchants to Essaouira, requesting help from Corcos in establishing their business in town.[48]

The Corcos family was therefore both an influential spokesman and a representative for the royal merchants of Essaouira. Its power and wealth owed much to royal favours, and it was able to use its privileged position to increase its profits in a number of ways, chiefly by property investments. Abraham Corcos was an important beneficiary of *makhzan* property in Essaouira. In the 1860s, he paid a higher rent on his *makhzan* house in the old *casbah* than any other tenant (see table 9). Rent on these houses was assessed proportionally to the value of the building at the time of construction. This suggests that among the *casbah* residents of his time Corcos held one of the most substantial houses. Besides his principal dwelling he rented six other houses in the *casbah*, and six shops, one mill, a bakery, and two apartments in town.[49] These properties had to be repaired periodically by the town authorities at considerable expense. Sometimes the *umanā'* objected to undertaking improvements because of high costs. In 1872, Abraham Corcos requested the construction of a new roof for his *makhzan* house because it had deteriorated. The costs of repairs appeared prohibitive to the local authorities. The principal *amīn* of Essaouira, Muḥammad al-Qabbāj, refused the request for a new roof, noting as well that Abraham Corcos was 'requesting repairs on many of his *makhzan* houses'.[50] Such refusals did not deter Abraham from circumventing local officials and bringing up his demands directly with his allies in the Palace. Mūsā b. Aḥmad interceded on his behalf a few years later. As a result, the Sultan ordered the *umanāʾ* to repair the house.[51] The acquisition of *makhzan* property by Corcos was clearly seen as a kind of investment: once the key-rights were purchased at some expense, rents paid to the *makhzan* were subsequently low and the properties could then be sublet at a profitable rate. As housing became scarce with the urban population growth, the holders of *makhzan* properties made increasing profits by subletting houses or rooms at high rates.[52]

Corcos also increased his wealth by accumulating free-hold property. It was reported that Abraham Corcos owned six houses in Essaouira in 1861, and he also owned numerous domains in the ʿAbda.[53] Between 1845 and 1861 Solomon, and after his death, his descendants, acquired some 13 houses in Essaouira, and mortgaged another four; further properties were owned by the family in Marrakesh.[54] More properties were purchased after 1861, though we do not have a complete record.[55] Corcos also profited from real estate not actually belonging to him through a type of proprietary agreement, made strictly between Jews, called *mashkanta* (in Hebrew). In this type of agreement a sum of money is given for a property to be held as a mortgage or in usufruct until the debt of the original holder is repaid, a parallel to the Muslim *rahn* agreement. This legally-binding act involved neither Muslim law nor the state. In 1848, for example, Abraham Corcos paid Ḥayyīm Ben Shemtōb Ben ʿAṭṭār 100 mithqāl as mortgage on a house in the *mellah*. Until the debt was repaid, and hence the property recovered, the former was not allowed to sublet, sell, or alter the premises in any way. In this way, rabbinical law aimed at protecting debtors from the excesses of speculators.[56]

The growing foreign presence in Essaouira gave Abraham Corcos another opportunity to enhance his position. In 1862, he was able to obtain the appointment of United States vice-consul in Essaouira. American interests in fact were quite limited in Morocco, and for this reason the United States government was satisfied to leave their affairs in the hands of a powerful intermediary, an advantage that Abraham Corcos emphasized to the American consul-general in Tangier: 'Our Establishment enjoys the advantage of the exclusive favor and protection of the Sultan of this Empire, and also of this local government.'[57] Corcos

3 Abraham Corcos, *circa* 1880
Courtesy of Madame Georgette Corcos

maximized his consular appointment to his own advantage by granting foreign protection to his agents in the interior.[58] The extraterritorial juridical rights enjoyed by Corcos as consular representative of the United States gave him considerable political influence, which he was able to use in mediating disputes not only in the Jewish community but also between Muslims and rural *qāʾid*s.

Abraham Corcos also exercised considerable influence over the Jewish community. He became indispensable to foreign Jewish organizations, a position which enhanced his prestige within Essaouira's Jewish community. He helped facilitate the Montefiore mission to Marrakesh in 1863–4,[59] and was subsequently at the forefront of the reforms of the Jewish community which were undertaken at the initiative of the foreign Jewish organizations. The Alliance Israélite Universelle and the Anglo-Jewish Association extended their influence through the wealthy oligarchs of the *casbah*. Abraham Corcos, 'the wealthiest and most influential man of the community', was viewed by the A.I.U. as having 'liberal' and 'advanced' ideas.[60] As foreign influence grew, such 'evolved' ideas became a requirement for those local Jewish leaders who wished to remain at the forefront of the community.

Abraham Corcos had manœuvred himself into an indispensable

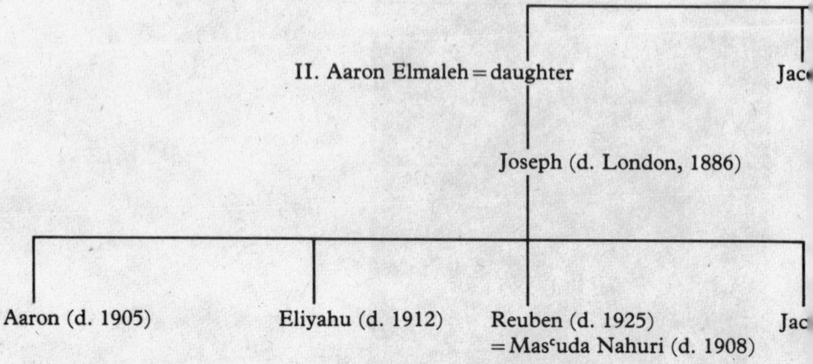

Fig. 2 Two branches of the Elmaleh family showing some marital links (based on research in the cemetery, two *ketūbas* of the family, and reported deaths in the archives).

position. He became the quintessential middleman: between the Palace and Europe, between foreign companies and southern chiefs, and between European Jewish organizations and the local Jewish community or the local authorities. His overall influence, as the A.I.U. director observed, was perhaps unparalleled. But within Jewish community life, Joseph Elmaleh had an overbearing position.

Elmaleh and the Jewish oligarchy

For over 80 years members of the Elmaleh family dominated Jewish community organization. Similar to the Corcos family, the multiplicity of their connections placed them in a particularly important position. Their role as rabbis and *dayyan*s of the Jewish community enhanced their position. Fulfilling rabbinical functions did not, however, prevent the Elmalehs from pursuing commercial activities. Jewish religious functions *per se* were never very remunerative in Morocco, and the specific

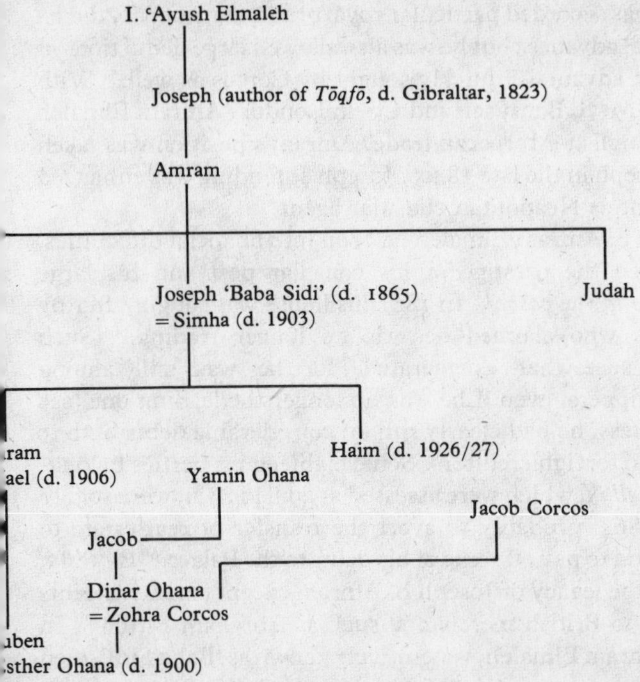

communal activities of the Elmalehs were rarely formally defined. Elmaleh's position as leader of the community, therefore, was rooted in his personal charisma. His religious functions and commercial activities legitimized his authority. For the Elmaleh family, piety and commerce went hand-in-glove. This position went unchallenged until the last decade of the nineteenth century.[61]

The two branches of the Elmaleh family most central to Essaouira's commercial and communal life were descended from Aaron and Ayush (see fig. 2).[62] One of the most distinguished rabbinical scholars of nineteenth-century Morocco was Joseph b. Ayush Elmaleh of Rabat, known as the author of a book of responsa (*she'eilōt ū-teshūbōt*), *Tōqfō shel Yōsef*, which was a compilation of legal opinions on sundry queries.[63] His son Amram, who was born in Rabat and lived in Gibraltar and Lisbon, settled in Essaouira in about 1820 and acquired a large *makhzan* house in the *casbah*.[64] He appears to have arrived with the new group of Jewish *tujjār* during the rejuvenation of trade in the 1820s.[65] For several decades Amram's position was unparalleled in Essaouira, except perhaps by his cousin Joseph b. Aaron who was the head of the corps of merchants from the 1830s, a position he maintained for many years.[66] After the 1844 war,

Amram Elmaleh was accorded particular royal privileges: not only did he receive large capital advances but he was also allowed large deductions in customs duties, an advantage quickly sought by Corcos as well.[67] With his correspondent M. S. Bensusan and Co. in London, Amram Elmaleh commanded the English–Moroccan trade. Amram's position was taken over by his son Joseph in the late 1840s. Joseph's standing was enhanced by his appointment as Neapolitan consular agent.

By 1860, Joseph b. Amram Elmaleh had run into financial difficulties. He still maintained the prestige of his consular post and his large *makhzan* residence in the *casbah*. In 1861 his house was sought after by British merchants who claimed he was no longer trading.[68] Such allegations were somewhat exaggerated, for he was still among Essaouira's top shippers, even if he was no longer the leading one (see table 3). Nevertheless, he had clearly run up considerable debts both to the *makhzan* and to foreign creditors. Some eighteen properties belonging to him in the *mellah*, which were assessed at 39,840 riyāl, were sold to the *makhzan* in 1864, probably to avert the transfer of real estate to foreign creditors and to pay off some of his debts to the Palace.[69] By 1865, little remained of the legacy of Joseph b. Amram except extensive debts to the Sultan and to British merchants, such as Abraham Bitton.[70] In 1865, Joseph b. Amram Elmaleh, veneratively known as 'Baba Sidi', died owing the Sultan some 20,000 riyāl from the 'new loan'. The *makhzan* transferred the responsibility of repayment to his brother Judah. In addition, the *umanā'* seized a part of his bail goods held by Moses Yuly, and all his property was sequestered. Abraham Corcos wrote to the Palace to point out his special friendship to Amram, and to ask that Joseph's younger brother Judah be helped back on his feet.[71] The British, who were interested in recovering their debts, had another idea: 'Should the Sultan decide on having nothing more to do with Elmaleks, and content himself with the scrapings he can get from the wreck of that once famous establishment, then it will be time to move on behalf of Bitton.'[72]

The disciple of Joseph b. Ayush Elmaleh was Joseph b. Aaron of the other Elmaleh branch. His combined honours as head of the corps of merchants, *dayyan*, consular agent for the Austro-Hungarian Empire, and Italian protégé enhanced his status as leader of the Jewish community.[73] His trade with Europe was substantial, and his *makhzan* holding was unparalleled. He was said to have occupied a house which was 'by far the largest and best house in the town'.[74] He seems to have been in possession of the houses of the Guedalla family, the most important Jewish merchant family of Essaouira in Sīdī Muḥammad b. 'Abdallah's time.[75] Moreover, Joseph b. Aaron was granted his cousin Joseph b. Amram's *casbah* house which contained a synagogue built by

Amram about 1830, after the latter's death.[76] In addition, he enjoyed *manfaʿa* rights to numerous houses in the *mellah*. He was to gain control of the largest *makhzan* house in the *mellah*, which had originally belonged to Joseph b. Amram.[77] It can be assumed that its 16 rooms were sublet as tenements, since we know that Joseph resided in the *casbah*. Undoubtedly Elmaleh, like Corcos, also held other properties in usufruct or mortgage. It is probably justifiable to say that Joseph b. Aaron Elmaleh derived much profit from property-holding in town, perhaps as much as any other merchant in the *casbah* in the nineteenth century.[78]

In the late 1870s and 1880s, Joseph's son Reuben increasingly assumed the responsibilities of his father's business, as Joseph was spending long stretches of time abroad. In 1876, for example, Joseph was authorized to travel abroad to settle accounts with his correspondent to enable him to pay back his *makhzan* debt. His son Reuben was left in charge in his absence.[79] In the 1880s Reuben was among the principal shippers of Essaouira. In 1886, Joseph Elmaleh died in London and Reuben, the eldest of four sons, was made responsible for his father's *makhzan* debt.[80] He succeeded his father as chief rabbi and vice-consul of the Austro-Hungarian Empire.

Although the commercial enterprises of the Elmalehs were at times unsteady, their position as heads of the Jewish community was assured for many years. The installation of foreign Jewish philanthropy gave the Moroccan Jewish leadership another card to play. Joseph, and later his son Reuben, dominated all benevolent charities and philanthropic societies established at the instigation of European Jews. The Alliance Israélite Universelle and the Anglo-Jewish Association depended on the moral and fiscal support of the Jewish oligarchy who controlled all communal activities. Joseph and Reuben Elmaleh were wary of European Jewish organizations such as the A.I.U., which posed a threat to their hitherto unchallenged leadership. At the same time, they could not disassociate themselves from what was perceived as a powerful new protector. Consul Beaumier, the Alliance's strongest proponent in town, reported to the organization in Paris in 1867 that since Elmaleh had travelled to Europe he recognized the benefit of the Alliance. In 1873, a more disillusioned Beaumier found that Joseph Elmaleh, in comparison to Abraham Afriat, had shown 'egoism, arrogance, and a lack of goodwill'.[81]

Despite the ambiguous support of Essaouira's Jewish leadership, foreign philanthropy was there to stay. The Jewish community was structurally unprepared to channel this philanthropy. As a result, important institutional developments took place: an Alliance committee was formed, various benevolent sodalities (*ḥebra*, pl. *ḥebrōt*) emerged, a

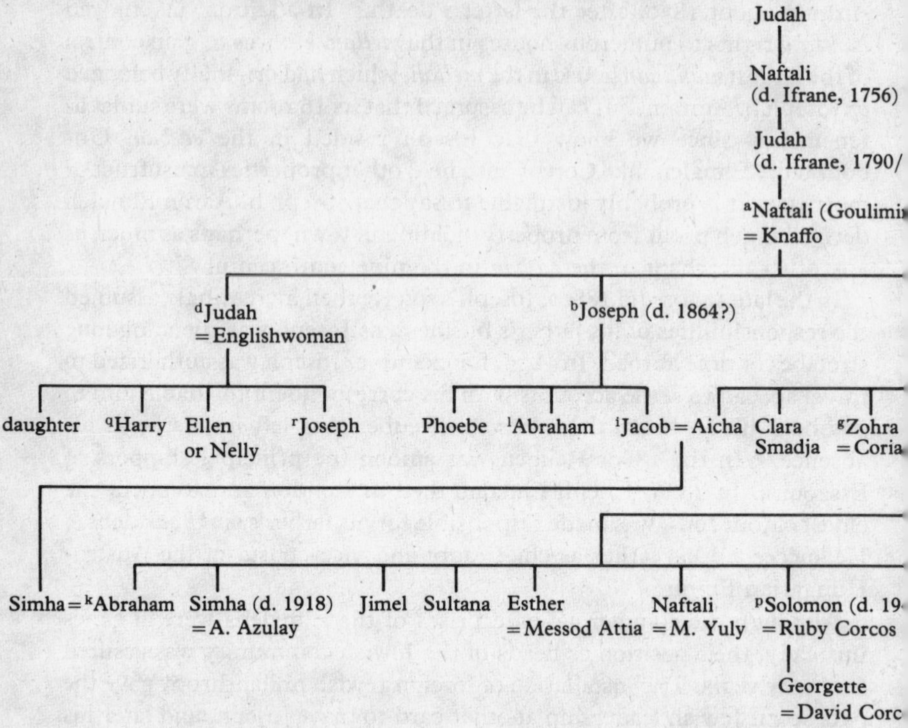

Fig. 3 Afriat genealogical tree (based on research of the National Geographical Society supplemented by cemetery data and miscellaneous archives).

moribund *ma*ʿ*amad* was constituted, and the community's fiscal organisms were reorganized.[82] Presiding over all these initiatives was Joseph Elmaleh, and later, his son Reuben.

Afriats – first capitalists

Of all the local entrepreneurs who were the most successful in adapting to western ways of commerce and breaking out of the traditional framework, the Afriats stand out. As *tujjār*, the Afriats had ties to the Palace, and as important Jews of the *casbah* they were part of the Jewish plutocracy that led Essaouira's communal life. But while the Corcos were tied down by their close dependence to the Sultan, the the Elmalehs by virtue of their position in the traditional Jewish leadership, and later, as protégés of foreign Jewish organizations, the Afriats enjoyed much greater mobility owing to their investments abroad. Intimately tied to

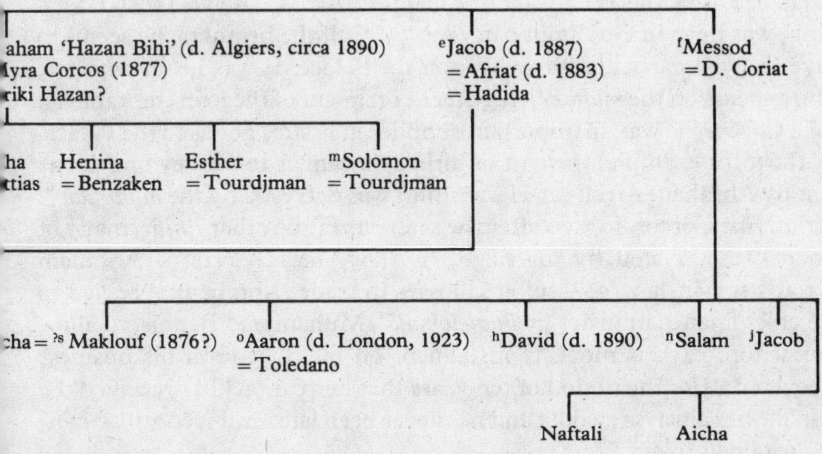

intermediaries in southwestern Morocco, the Afriats' ability to accommodate the trade of this region to the modern European sector ensured their continued solvency and mobility.

The transformation from traders of Sheikh Bayrūk in Goulimime to merchant-bankers of Essaouira, Marseille, and London took place in one generation. Although some Afriats may have claimed Andalusian descent, they appear to have had no connections with the Sephardic Mediterranean trading network which gave some Jewish families, such as Corcos, an advantage in extending business affairs in Europe. The basis of the Afriat business success was rooted in the close ties maintained by the family in the Sous.[83] The prestige of their family in Essaouira was enhanced by the legendary martyrdom of their ancestor Judah Afriat, the rabbi from Ifrane who was among the 50 Jews alleged to have been burned to death by the rebel Bū Iḥlās about 1790–2.[84]

The actual process of migration of the Afriat family from Ifrane to Essaouira is not entirely clear. Naftali (a) (see lettering in fig. 3), the son of Rabbi Judah, must have moved from Goulimime either during the Bū

Iḥlās revolt or in the years following. His move would have coincided with the growing prosperity of the Bayrūk dynasty of Wad Noun, which was tied to the development of commerce with Europe from the port of Essaouira.[85] Naftali Afriat's family became Sheikh Bayrūk's principal traders in Goulimime. In 1837, Naftali's son Joseph (b) came to Essaouira as Bayrūk's agent in order to negotiate a secret agreement with the French for opening up trade on the coast of Wad Noun.[86]

Some, if not all of the Afriat brothers, appear to have settled in Essaouira after the 1844 war. Abraham (c) Afriat, known as 'al-Hazan Bihi', was born in Goulimime in 1820.[87] Of all the brothers, he seems to have enjoyed particular favours from the Palace. It was he, at any rate, who appears on the *makhzan* register as recipient of the loan (see table 1). Like Corcos, he was an important supplier of luxury goods to the Palace. In 1863, for example, the cost of hiring six camels to convey fine linens sent by Abraham Afriat (al-Hazan Bihi) was defrayed by the *makhzan*.[88] Afriat, like Corcos, looked after the interests of the other *tujjār*, many of whom were related by marriage. In 1867, Isaac Coriat – Abraham Afriat's son-in-law (g) – suffered losses in trade. Abraham appealed to the chief finance minister *amīn al-umanā'*, Muḥammad Bannīs, to allow Coriat to delay his monthly instalment on the debt until his business recovered; 'For the period of ten years that he [Coriat] has received the loan, he has always repaid it and has never been late until [recently when] he sustained losses.'[89]

Members of the Afriat family soon acquired *makhzan* houses, like the other major merchant families. Jacob (e) Afriat resided in a house formerly held by one of the old established Muslim families, Tūfal-ʿazz. Apparently the house had been granted originally to Bayrūk, and consequently it served the sheikh's agents in Essaouira, of whom Tūfal-ʿazz and Afriat were the most prominent.[90] Jacob also held a large warehouse in the new *casbah*. In 1864, the *makhzan* granted Abraham Afriat a house in the old *casbah* after allegedly evicting a Muslim family, and a few years later he obtained a house in the newly-constructed *casbah*. His brother Messod (f) also acquired a *makhzan* house in the *casbah*.[91] One of the largest, if not the largest house in Essaouira, was constructed in the 1860s in the new *casbah* to be granted to Ḥusayn Ū Hāshim of Iligh. This grant was essentially symbolic, for in fact the house was built for French merchants who were increasing in number at that time. The Afriats, however, eventually took control of the house, and managed the property for the descendants of Ḥusayn. They later sublet it to the A.I.U. and the Paquet shipping company.[92]

The Afriats, unlike many *tujjār* families, continued to prosper through the last decades of the nineteenth century. All the members of the family either settled abroad or continued to enjoy foreign protection, usually

British or French. Members of the family invested their money in the Bank of England or in banks in Marseilles, and were behind all the capitalist ventures at Essaouira in the latter half of the nineteenth century: they became shareholders of Paquet, correspondents of various European firms, and agents or shareholders of newly-created banks.[93] Certainly the other *tujjār* families were involved in some of these ventures as well, but the Afriats prospered during times of crisis in Morocco because of their European establishments.

In the ledgers of customs duties, the scale of trade of all the Afriats combined was much greater than that of any other family of *tujjār*. For the months analysed between 1862 and 1864 (see table 3), the children and grandchildren of Naftali Afriat paid approximately 16.6 per cent of all the customs duties at the port of Essaouira. Abraham (c) had the most sizeable trade of all the family, followed by Jacob (e), Messod (f), another Jacob of the next generation (i or j), Aaron (o) son of Messod, and Abraham (k or l).

It was through foreign connections that the continued prosperity of the Afriats was assured. Abraham Afriat (Bihi) rapidly established these ties after settling in Essaouira. He married the daughter of Abraham Corcos (see fig. 1, c) of the Algerian branch, whose business Abraham was managing in Essaouira. As a result, he was accorded French protection. Abraham established important commercial relations with Marseille, while investing most of his capital in the Bank of England. In Essaouira he kept only enough capital required for commerce and a few small properties in the *mellah*. He served as interpreter (*censal-interprête honoraire*) for the French consulate, translating their correspondence with Jewish agents in the interior. In 1873 he began applying for French nationality and sought to move his business to France. According to Beaumier, Afriat well deserved French protection, owing to his constant devotion to French causes.[94] Despite the French consul's recommendation, it seems that Abraham's request was not accorded at this stage, but this did not stop Abraham from dividing his time between Essaouira and Europe. He left an agent, Ishuʿa [Afriat?], in his house in the old *casbah*.[95] About fifteen years after his initial appeal for French nationality, he died in Algiers (probably as a French citizen).[96]

Abraham's son Solomon (m) continued to enjoy French protection for many years, in his capacity as agent for a number of French companies and representative of Banque Transatlantique.[97] The new generation of Afriats were all strong advocates of French 'causes'. Solomon (p) Afriat, who had spent time in London, was a strong partisan of the A.I.U. He became one of Essaouira's leading merchants, described some years later as 'one of the rare capitalists of Mogador'.[98]

Commercial success of family firms required the establishment of a network both in Morocco and Europe. The Afriats not only sent capital abroad, but also members of their family. By 1870 several members of the family were permanently settled in London. Messod Afriat was an agent in Essaouira for his brother Judah (d) who resided in England.[99] Judah's two sons, Harry (q) and Joseph (r), already representing a new generation of Anglo-Moroccan Jewish merchants, were actively involved in the trade of southern Morocco from their establishment in London. Jacob (e) Afriat, one of Essaouira's most important merchants for many years, would spend extended periods of time in London. He invested money in the Bank of England and in other European countries, and held stocks in the British railways.[100]

Aaron (o), the son of Messod, who was born in 1847, was the most noted Afriat in England. He emigrated from Morocco as a young man, and already at the age of 15 or 16 he was importing large quantities of fabrics in Essaouira as an agent of a London firm, Alexander S. Pyke.[101] At the age of 20, he had already settled in England, became a member of the old established Sephardic Bevis Marks synagogue in London, and seven or eight years later, became a naturalized British subject.[102] Aaron Afriat and Co. became one of the most important British exporters to Essaouira, dealing in large quantities of tea and textiles. Aaron's brother, Maklouf (s), and Salam (n) (the latter divided his time between London and Essaouira) were the principal agents for the distribution of these goods in southern Morocco in exchange for Moroccan commodities. '*At-Tay Afriat*' was a well-known brand of tea in nineteenth-century Morocco.[103] The company's indigo linens, manufactured in Manchester, were famous throughout the south and the Sahara.[104] In London, the telegraphic address of Aaron Afriat and Co. was 'AWERWAL' (a kind of gum) symbolizing how their fortune was initially made in gum arabic.[105]

From gum traders of Sheikh Bayrūk to large-scale entrepreneurs of British manufactured goods, the Afriats, more than any other family in Essaouira, successfully made the transition from local traders to capitalists in the international arena.

Muslims of the *casbah*

The Jewish merchants of Essaouira were in the majority, but a certain number of Muslims from Tetuan, Fez, and Rabat-Salé were also among Essaouira's merchant elite and participated in such enterprises as the creation of a steamship line. They were linked to the Jewish elite merchants by common interests.[106] In the 1860s, Mukhtār Ibn ʿAzūz and Muḥammad Raghūn were both major exporters of olive oil, goat skins and almonds.[107] The *makhzan* spared no efforts in promoting the interests of the Muslim traders of Essaouira by advancing to them considerable sums of money. ʿAbd ar-Raḥmān al-Labār, Mukhtār Ibn ʿAzūz, the Būhillāls, Muḥammad al-Warzāzī, and Muḥammad Tūfal-ʿazz were among the recipients of the 'new loan' of 1865 (see table 1). Just like the Jewish merchants, some of the Muslims became protégés of European powers and invested money in foreign banks.

In many respects, therefore, the Muslim merchants of Essaouira did not differ from the Jewish merchants. However, the former were able to fulfil functions from which the Jews were excluded. While the Jewish *tujjār* could give informal political advice, they could not actually hold positions in government. A number of Muslim *tujjār* of Essaouira were also active in the local administration, of which Tūfal-ʿazz and Būhillāl were the most important.

The Tūfal-ʿazz family, originally of the Sous, played a central role in Essaouira's economic and political life from the town's first period until the end of the nineteenth century. Probably no other family of Muslim notables could claim such importance. Family tradition attributes the beginning of the family's wealth to the second visit of Sultan Sīdī Muḥammad b. ʿAbdallāh to Essaouira, which took place in 1198/1783–4. The tradition recounts that Aḥmad Tūfal-ʿazz, a simple miller and early Soussi settler to the new town, was blessed by the Sultan. He then began to trade in flour and 'God opened [the gates] for him and his wealth multiplied'.[108] His son Muhammad became well-educated and a friend of the future sultan, ʿAbd ar-Raḥmān, when the latter was *khalīfa* in Essaouira. When ʿAbd ar-Raḥmān became sultan, Muḥammad Tūfal-ʿazz was granted a *dahir* of *tawqīr* and *iḥtirām* (lit. 'respect' and 'veneration'), which usually implied exemption from paying taxes, or probably in this case, customs duties.[109] It granted the recipient the official protection (*ḥimāya*) of the sultan, and, in a sense, was tantamount to an act of ennoblement. In another *dahir* dated 1838, Muḥammad Tūfal-ʿazz was incorporated into the corps of *tujjār*, which allowed him to import and export. He was one of the only two Muslim merchants of the era to receive the royal loan (see table 1). Tūfal-ʿazz continued to accumulate privileges and responsibilities. In a *dahir* of 1842, he was designated to collect revenues from *makhzan* properties for the purpose of constructing fortifications near the harbour.[110]

Muḥammad Tūfal-ʿazz lost considerable merchandise and properties in the 1844 war. As a consequence, the Sultan granted him a reduction of one-fourth customs duties.[111] For five more years until his death in 1851, Muḥammad continued to ship goods to London.[112] His son Ḥadān, who was an *amīn* at the port, took over his late father's positon as *tājir*. He continued trading until his own death in 1862.[113]

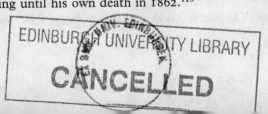

Although the heyday of the Tūfal-ʿazz business was over, Muḥammad's son al-Ḥājj Maḥjūb was still an important figure in Essaouira's economic and administrative life. In the 1860s his commerce was not negligible, mainly importing sugar and exporting olive oil and calf and goat skins.[114] His continued prosperity as a shipper depended on the fact that he received large sums of advanced credit from the *makhzan*, and at least in 1865, his debt of 321,352 ūqiya was higher than any other Muslim merchant (see table 1). Between 1865 and 1866 he was able both to pay back the required ten per cent on his loan and invest another 26,529 ūqiya in his house.[115]

For uncertain reasons, al-Ḥājj Maḥjūb ran into financial difficulties in the late 1860s (perhaps connected to the general Moroccan crisis of that period). He became insolvent and was unable to repay his debt to either the *makhzan* or to foreign merchants. In 1869, the *makhzan* seized his properties in order to recover money owed the treasury. The seizure was observed by the French and English consuls who demanded that debts owed by Tūfal-ʿazz to foreign merchants should also be recovered with the help of the authorities.[116] The *makhzan* property acquired by Maḥjūb's father Muhammad, and undoubtedly by his grandfather as well, was quite considerable. The rent on the various Tūfal-ʿazz properties was higher than for any other notable in Essaouira. For some years subsequent to the sequestration, the *makhzan* secured 710 ūqiya a month from the Tūfal-ʿazz properties.[117] Other properties were 'purchased' from him, that is, sold as mortgage. These mortgaged properties decreased in value, perhaps because the bailer would not look after their upkeep. Hence, rent on the house held by ʿAbd al-Wahhāb at-Tāzī was assessed at 80 ūqiya in 1872, and by 1879, after the house had been recovered, rent had decreased to 40 ūqiya.[118]

The *umanāʾ* claimed that Maḥjūb Tūfal-ʿazz continued to owe the *makhzan* 1,500 riyāl in 1871. This he disputed and instead decided to reimburse them 1,209 riyāl.[119] These problems were exacerbated by the claims of foreign creditors. Richard Grace and Christopher Lamb of London were claiming £1,664 sterling from Tūfal-ʿazz's securities.[120] His financial difficulties probably explain why his name appears on the list of *casbah* tenants in 1864, but is absent from the register in 1879.[121] It seems that indeed he sold his *manfaʿa* rights to Jacob Afriat for the big house he held in the *casbah*.[122]

The personal financial problems of Tūfal-ʿazz did not prevent him from carrying out ordinary business deals nor from rendering important services to the *makhzan*. In 1882, the Sultan ordered Qāʾid ʿAmāra to send al-Ḥājj Mahjūb to the Haha with two ʿ*adl*s to register trees, lands, and other proerties belonging to the *makhzan* which had been left from the estates of Ū Bīhī and other rural governors.[123] He was also employed in supervising the construction of the walls of Tiznit, a critically important task for the *makhzan*.[124] Essaouira's eminent Soussi *makhzan* merchant was of great use for the Sultan's plans in the south. The same year, the *umanāʾ* allocated money on the Tūfal-ʿazz house in Essaouira. His continued debt to the Sultan amounted to 1,601.4 riyāl in 1884.[125] Tūfal-ʿazz, like many *tujjār* was finding it difficult to repay the *makhzan* their monthly instalments. Yet the *tujjār* and the *makhzan* were bound together in an interdependent relationship of debt and credit. Both continued to perform services for each other in times of financial crises.

The city which historically had the most active and far-flung commerce was Fez, and to a degree, its Mediterranean entrepôt, Tetuan. Fez, which was the largest city in Morocco, was the only major city in North Africa in which Jews did not play a major role in international commerce.[126] Most of Essaouira's principal Muslim merchants were from either Fez or Tetuan: Būhillāl al-Fāsī, ʿAbd ar-Raḥmān al-Labār al-Fāsī, Mawlāy aṭ-Tāʾī al-Qādirī at-Tiṭwānī, and Sīdī Aḥmad al-Labādī at-Tiṭwānī. Of all these families, Būhillāl was the most prominent. The early development of Essaouira began attracting the Būhillāls away from their traditional stronghold in the Eastern caravan trade and the trans-Saharan trade via Fez to commerce with Europe on the coast. Yet it was only after 1844 that the first groups of Fasi and Tetuani merchants arrived in Essaouira. The most prominent among them was aṭ-Ṭālib Ibn al-Ḥājj al-Makkī Būhillāl, probably the son of the leading Fasi merchant trading with Timbuktu.[127] Together with his son Aḥmad, the Būhillāls were among the principal merchants shipping gums, almonds, olive oil, and other products from the south to London, Gibraltar, and other places in Europe.[128]

The Būhillāls, like Tūfal-ʿazz, were appointed as *umanāʾ* in the port,[129] positions which could be particularly remunerative. Administrative reforms in 1862 excluded the *umanāʾ* from trading during their service. Nevertheless, aṭ-Ṭālib Būhillāl continued to play an administrative role in Essaouira as a commissioner (*wakīl*) appointed to intercede in matters involving foreigners.[130]

Despite his former position as *wakīl* for the *makhzan*, aṭ-Ṭālib Būhillāl gradually became entangled in numerous disputes with foreigners. Increasing British pressures on the *makhzan* to settle foreign claims led to the creation of a commission. A *makhzan* official, Idrīs b. Muḥammad Idrīs, was sent to Essaouira as *wakīl*, and aṭ-Ṭālib Būhillāl was made to appear before the commission for debts owed to the British merchants, Curtis and Renshaw. According to the British vice-consul, Būhillāl refused to submit to the tribunal and was imprisoned, but was released soon after without the matter being settled.[131]

Foreigners continued to impose their own prerogatives, which denied people like Būhillāl their former advantages. At the end of December 1880, an old conflict between Abraham Cohen, a British merchant, and Būhillāl resurfaced when Cohen's children apparently sold a disputed house. Consequently, Būhillāl sought redress for the injustice through a traditional form of protest: he took sanctuary at the shrine of a noted saint, the *zāwiya* of Mawlāy ʿAbd al-Qādir al-Jillālī, and invoked a decision in his favour which had come before the ulama of Marrakesh.[132]

The Būhillāls found it increasingly difficult to compete in commerce. They did not have the kind of extensive outside capital which gave the Afriats and foreign merchants the edge. Although continuing to trade in the principal commodities – almonds, gums, wool, and olive oil in exchange for cotton goods, sugar, tea, and iron[133] – their reliance on the *makhzan* loan was a serious impediment to expansion.

In 1870, aṭ-Ṭālib Būhillāl had to hand over his assets as security to the *makhzan* to pay off his debt.[134] In fact, financial difficulties were general for the *tujjār* at that time, caused by a slump in trade and a high rate of inflation. The next year, six *tujjār*, including Aḥmad Būhillāl, petitioned Muḥammad Bannīs against a sharifian order to increase monthly repayments on the royal loan.[135]

The difficulties of aṭ-Ṭālib Būhillāl continued. In 1873, he was still unable to pay back the *makhzan* on his original debt or on the new loan, though his nephew Aḥmad was solvent. aṭ-Ṭālib Būhillāl's properties were still being held as security by the *umanāʾ*.[136]

al-Ḥājj Aḥmad continued to receive monthly loans until 1884; in fact, they were higher than those of other *tujjār* (see table 6). Yet commerce was slackening during this period and he became insolvent. To recover his debt for 6,650 riyāl, the *umanāʾ* were ordered to sequester his property in town – houses, shops, etc. – as legal collateral (*rahn ash-sharīʿi*) and to have it assessed by competent authorities. This came to a total of 1,224 riyāl which was, as al-Ḥājj Aḥmad's bailiffs pointed out, 'insufficient for what he owes'; they further added that 'he has no other property besides that indicated'.[137] He died later that year, still owing the 6,650 riyāl to the *makhzan* and an untold sum to European creditors who were making various claims against his estate.[138]

aṭ-Ṭālib Būhillāl as well was never able to make repayments to the *makhzan*, either for the 'old debt' or the 'new loan'.[139] When he died a few years later, the Sultan ordered the *umanāʾ* to appraise his property in Essaouira. The *umanāʾ* of Rabat and Salé were directed to allow the children of Būhillāl to sell the property in Rabat bequeathed to his wife and son. His property in Essaouira was valued at 4,495 riyāl (a far cry from the 39,840 riyāl assessed for Elmaleh's *mellah* property in 1864!).[140]

Urban bourgeoisie in the age of European expansion

The problems facing the five merchant families examined in detail – Corcos, Elmaleh, Afriat, Tūfal-ʿazz and Būhillāl – resembled those facing other merchants of the elite in Essaouira. All five began their careers as privileged merchants of the Sultan. Their involvement in foreign trade allowed them to make considerable profits, which were partly invested in urban property. While these five merchant families continued officially to be commercial agents of the Sultan, *tujjār as-Sulṭān*, their relationship to the *makhzan*, and indeed, to Moroccan society as a whole, had changed because of their new connections with Europe.

The rising importance of merchants was a major factor in nineteenth-century Moroccan history. In both the coastal towns and Fez, the position of merchants was strengthened. With the growth of foreign trade, merchants began to play a role in the administrative reforms of the *makhzan*, and the administrative class became involved in commerce.[141] Yet unlike in Europe, the merchants were unable to effect a significant political transformation. Certain individual merchants may have had an influence in the reforms of the *makhzan*, but as a social group, the merchants never evolved into a class with articulated interests or a power base. Laroui pointedly asks the question: can one speak of a 'Moroccan bourgeois class' in the nineteenth century?[142]

Ostensibly, the similarities between the development of the urban merchants of Essaouira and merchant capitalism in Europe are there. The indigenous merchants begin to extend their capital into the surrounding countryside. Yet put into perspective, the scope of these developments was limited. The social and political structure of Morocco had not transformed to the degree required for capitalist agriculture to develop. In comparison to other parts of the Middle East, capitalism made few inroads in Morocco. Neither the *makhzan* nor the merchants were able to alter the productive forces of the country in the way that, for example, the Egyptian government or the entrepreneurs of Beirut and Aleppo were able to do in the same period.[143]

The absence of the kind of social and agrarian changes needed for capitalist development certainly restricted the growth and power of the merchant elite. For the Swiri merchants involved in foreign trade, the most secure kind of investment involved the export of capital by depositing money in foreign banks or buying shares in foreign enterprises.[144] Though banks were established in Tangier towards the end of the nineteenth century, they mostly served foreign merchants and their protégés and their operations were limited to deposits, cheques, and exchanging currencies.[145] Merchants were able to establish economic ties which were independent of the *makhzan*, but they were subservient to foreign business houses. To the degree that the merchants continued to operate in their native framework, they still remained bound to the Sultan in credit and debt. The fortunes of the merchants were therefore tied to the economic prosperity of the state. In the second half of the nineteenth century, *makhzan* finances were in crisis because of foreign intervention and the growing costs of running the state. The crisis of the *makhzan* became, in most cases, the crisis of the merchants. Many lost or mortgaged their land and property. Even the Corcos firm had to offer their six houses in the *mellah* as collateral security in 1896 because of the claims of foreign creditors. As a consequence, they soon lost their status as American protégés and in 1900, Meyer and Aaron Corcos were forced into bankruptcy.[146] Both the Būhillāl and Tūfal-ʿazz legacies, as we have seen, were in decline. The fortunes of Elmaleh were waning.[147] Almost all the major merchant firms of Essaouira went bankrupt, or were on the verge of collapse.[148]

Only a few merchants of Essaouira were able to operate continuously on a large scale. The Afriats were the most noted example. The stability of their wealth, however, lay not in land holdings in Morocco, but in foreign investments. Most other merchants also became involved in a number of capitalist ventures, such as participating in the formation of steamship companies,[149] but none had spread their investments abroad sufficiently to avert the crises in the way that the Afriats had done. The Afriats' foreign connections, together with their familiarity with the inland markets, made them the most prosperous merchant house in Essaouira in the latter half of the nineteenth century, and well into the twentieth century as well.

The nature of the Jewish merchant elite

From the late eighteenth century until the last decades of the nineteenth century, Essaouira's Jewish elite reached its pinnacle in wealth and influence. It followed a lifestyle which combined the urbane Moroccan Jewish city culture with European bourgeois manners. This image contrasts sharply with the portrayal of Jews in Islamic countries by Bernard Lewis, whose description suggests that the Jews living in Islamic countries from the late eighteenth century to the end of the nineteenth were at the low ebb of their existence.[150] Lewis suggests that this decline was evident all over, though the Jewish communities living in the lands of the Islamic periphery – Iran and Morocco especially –

appeared to suffer the most hardship. Though the poverty and degradation of the masses of Moroccan Jews was at times intense,[151] the growth of a Jewish bourgeoisie belies this general picture of decline. In the coastal as well as the inland cities, both Muslim and Jewish merchants prospered from the development of commerce with Europe. Lower level intermediaries also benefited from this surge in trade. New and prosperous Jewish communities began to spring up along the inland caravan trade routes, and Jews continued to serve the *makhzan* as *tujjār* and tax-farmers.

The decline of many of the Jewish merchant elite families was precipitated by the political and economic crisis in the decades leading up to the establishment of the French Protectorate in 1912. The undermining of the power of the *makhzan* and its inability to meet the challenge of colonialism led to the ruin of many Jewish merchants who were closely tied to the Palace. With the advent of colonialism, a new westernized generation of elite Jewish merchants was to emerge, fostered by the French colonial economy.

Foreign commerce gave a boost to Moroccan traders, but this is not specifically a nineteenth-century phenomenon. Merchants had always played an important role in cities of the Muslim world, though they were generally excluded from political power.[152] A native bourgeoisie, involved in international commerce, was to be found in all the major cities of the Middle East and North Africa before the age of European expansion and colonialism.[153] It has been shown that the bourgeoisie of Fez, for example, began to emerge at the end of the eighteenth and the beginning of the nineteenth century before the opening of Morocco to Europe.[154] The growth of the merchant elite in the nineteenth century also needs to be understood in a Moroccan context, and not solely as a function of the integration of Morocco into a European-centred, world market system.

European influence was nonetheless important in the coastal towns of nineteenth-century Morocco. External manifestations of foreign culture became symbols of power and a strategy of the Jewish elite. A Spanish traveller noted in 1803 that the Jewish elite of Essaouira was allowed to wear European clothing, a privilege not extended to other Jews in Morocco. Thus they became part of the wider corps of merchants which also included foreigners.[155] 'Notwithstanding the imbecile prejudices of the native Barbary Jews', wrote a British traveller, 'such of them who adopt European habits, or who mix with European merchants, are tolerably good members of society, always endeavouring to restrain their own peculiarities.'[156] European clothing became a symbol of prestige for a few Jewish merchants who could afford the privilege. But increasingly it was seen as a challenge to the sovereignty of the Sultan. A Swiri Jew was alleged to have appeared before Sultan Sulaymān's court in European garb at the beginning of the nineteenth century, causing the Sultan to issue a decree that Jews must wear native Jewish clothing. This order was invoked by Sultan ʿAbd ar-Raḥmān as increasing numbers of Jews of Moroccan origin, returning to Morocco from Gibraltar as British subjects, donned their European garb. The Sultan decided that Jews coming from Gibraltar would have to adopt Moroccan Jewish dress within one month after their return.[157] Such restrictions, however, were not well-enforced, and except for a period of time under Sulaymān's reign, they do not seem to have been applied in Essaouira. European clothing was not the only expression of status or prestige among the Jewish elite of Essaouira. Side by side with foreign garb, elegant Moroccan clothing was worn. Wealthy Jewish men dressed in elaborately embroidered woollen tunics with coloured sashes, silk handkerchiefs on their heads, and black slippers. Women wore wide muslin shirts with fine needlework and a wide waistcoat fastened by a girdle. Women who were married wore flowing silk handkerchiefs and all the women of the wealthy class adorned themselves with necklaces of precious stones and gold and silver jewellery.[158] In Moroccan society, status was displayed by wearing one's bridal wealth. Lavish jewellery and clothing were given to the bride. The bridal-price could vary a great deal, but considerable sums were always given by the wealthy.[159]

The influence of Europe on the culture of the merchant elite in Essaouira was significant, but it was also absorbed in a Moroccan context. Foreign textiles (especially British), clocks, and other European material objects began to find their way into the homes of the Moroccan elite.[160] From the 1820s onwards, the consumption of British imported tea and sugar became popular, and soon spread to all segments of the population.[161] But the cultural forms which the tea drinking habit took were specific to Morocco, and a curiosity to foreigners:

> Putting a good handful of the herb into the previously-warmed teapot, he pours in hot water which he leaves just long enough to take the deleterious surface colouring off the tea-leaves, and then pours away on to the ground. Then he breaks off a huge lump from a loaf of white sugar, which he jams into the mouth of the teapot, pours hot water slowly on the sugar, melting it gradually away into the tea leaves below. When the pot is full he lets it stop a short time to draw, puts a little fresh green mint, or aniseed, or some other herb to flavour it – sometimes a morsel of ambergris, if he be a rich and luxurian musulman swell – and then the scalding hot, exceedingly saccharine, bright golden coloured beverage is handed around – without milk of course – on one of the beautifully chased brass trays, which are a quaint and pleasing speciality of Moorish manufacture.[162]

The physical surroundings of the elite merchant families changed but minimally. The layout of their houses in the *casbah* resembled the houses of the bourgeoisie elsewhere in Morocco, or for that matter, in other Middle Eastern cities.[163] The streets of the *casbah* were extremely narrow and dark and the houses were virtually closed off from the street, concealing the elaborate decoration on the inside. The characteristic structure of all the houses was the interior courtyard encircled by a gallery on the upstairs level, and sometimes there were two floors above the ground level. The ground floor often had storerooms for merchandise. The upper floor would be inhabited by the merchant's family, while on the terrace there might be light constructions to house the servants. It was not uncommon to find two parlours for receiving guests: one would be decorated with European furnishings and objects (e.g., a piano, a portrait of Queen Victoria, European chairs), and a second laid out in the Moroccan fashion: low, cushioned sofas lining all sides of the wall, elaborate ceramic designs, and objects engraved in brass.[164]

At the same time it was becoming increasingly clear that success in international trade required more than a superficial veneer of European trappings. From the very early period of Essaouira's existence, Jewish merchants began sending their children to England to receive an English education.[165] By mid-century when regular steamlines between Essaouira and Europe were introduced,[166] visits to Europe became much more frequent. In the second half of the nineteenth century, schools of the Alliance Israélite Universelle, the English Board of Deputies, and the Anglo-Jewish Association in Essaouira began to form new cadres of westernized Jews.[167] A new type of western-trained merchant began to appear on the local scene.

Despite these European influences, the Jewish elite was still rooted in Moroccan bourgeois culture. Until the end of the nineteenth century, there were two roads for acquiring an education. While some elite merchants sent their children to Europe for an education, others were sent to Jerusalem to study.[168] Most of the leading merchants were still educated in a Moroccan milieu. Abraham Corcos, for example, never knew English or French even though he was the American vice-consul. Joseph and Reuben Elmaleh corresponded with the Alliance Israélite Universelle in an educated rabbinical Hebrew. The leading merchants exchanged all their commercial correspondence in colloquial Moroccan Judeo-Arabic. If one takes the reports of the Alliance Israélite Universelle at face value, then the picture of Moroccan Jewish culture that emerges is one of total ignorance, a situation which could only be uplifted by western civilization. 'Living in a milieu of a profoundly backward and fanatical Arab population, speaking their language and practising their customs, the Jews of Mogador have acquired the predominant vices of their Muslim compatriots: ruse and hypocrisy', states the Alliance director of Essaouira in his annual report to Paris in 1892.[169] The Alliance directors were even contemptuous of the Arabic language spoken by the Jews, which was also the language of instruction in primary education.

The Moroccan Jewish merchants did see the utility of having children educated in Europe. Yet among the elite *tujjār* of Essaouira, westernization in the nineteenth century did not come at the expense of the native bourgeois culture. While the Moroccan merchants needed to learn about European commercial practices, they still had to operate in the Moroccan environment, with all its complexity.

Chapter 4

Port and bazaar

From harbour to bazaar

A foreign trader coming to Essaouira caught his first glimpse of the town as his ship sailed between the island and the port where the harbour was located. The ship would then anchor and wait for the lighters operated by either the Banī ʿAntar or Ahl Agādīr boatmen. In winter months anchorage would sometimes be hazardous for those in sailing ships, particularly if caught in western winds.[1] Otherwise, the bay would be fairly calm and the visitor would promptly set foot at the landing and proceed through the port gate, Bāb al-Marsa. To the right of the gate were storehouses belonging to customs where merchandise was stored, sometimes in lieu of paying duties in specie. Merchants would also store goods there which had cleared customs prior to shipment. Continuing towards the town, the traveller would probably pass numerous sacks of goods, camels, brokers, and porters unloading merchandise or assembling caravans for the long journeys to the Sous. Together with the merchandise and a porter, he would then move into the *mashwar*, the area adjacent to the *makhzan* palace used for horses and gunpowder, games and other festivites,[2] and enter Bāb Muḥammad Ū Masʿūd, proceed to the large square at the centre of the *casbah*, and finally enter the customs house (*dār al-aʿshār*) where a 10 per cent *ad valorem* duty would be assessed by the customs officials for any goods imported.

Goods were moved between the port and the *casbah* either by the Banī ʿAntar or the Ahl Agādīr porters. Their monopoly in the porterage of the port was considered cumbersome to the merchants.[3] The porters allegedly pilfered the merchandise at times. The *makhzan*, aware of losses caused by theft and contraband because of the distance between the harbour and *dār al-aʿshār* in the *casbah*, decided to construct a new customs house close to the harbour in 1885.[4]

Once the goods had cleared customs, they were then conveyed down the streets of the *casbah* to the merchants' storerooms, generally on the ground floor level adjacent to the interior courtyard. Most of the storage on the ground floor was for items of export – sacks of almonds, casks of

4 Landing for the lighters, port of Essaouira, 1913

Courtesy of Monsieur Samuel Levy

Ships had to anchor some distance from the landing. All goods and passengers were transported to and from the ships by lighters.

5 Loading goods in the *ḥaddāda* (street of the smiths), 1914

Courtesy of Monsieur Samuel Levy

olive oil, bundles of goat skins – awaiting shipment at a propitious moment. Camels and other beasts of burden would sometimes enter into the central courtyard.[5]

The *casbah* was surrounded by formidable ramparts, partitioning it both from the exterior and the interior of the town. At least until the completion of the new *casbah* in 1869, which partially enclosed the *mashwar* and extended the walls of the city, the gates of the *casbah* were shut at night. It was a symbolic barrier more than a real obstacle for those who wanted to venture into the *medina* after dark. In fact, the wealthy Jewish and foreign merchants of the *casbah* never really needed to set foot in the other quarters of town, for purchases of daily necessities could be made by their brokers and servants. To a degree, the connection of the import and export trade with the local market was limited. Cotton goods, tea, sugar, hardware, and other import commodities sent to the interior by caravans left the *casbah* and were assembled outside Bab Sbaʿ, circumventing the town's bazaar. Likewise, goods destined for export were spread out in front of Bāb Sbaʿ where brokers approached the owners of camel loads directly on the beach.[6]

It could be argued that the local market of the *medina* on the one hand, and the import and export trading sector on the other, constituted two different, even autonomous, spheres of economic activity, as Polanyi's paradigm might suggest.[7] Administratively they were independent to some extent: in the port the *umanāʾ* were concerned primarily with the business of the wholesale merchants, while in the *medina* the market provost (*muḥtasib*) regulated the day-to-day business of the market place. There were also two different monetary exchange systems, one fixed by the government for customs and the other fixed at the current negotiable rate at the market. While silver coins were the primary currency used at customs, copper coins and barter were the main mediums of exchange at the market-place.[8]

Yet it would be misleading to over-emphasize this separation. The market also imposed its priorities on the administration of the port. Imported merchandise was supposed to be assessed according to the local market price. The merchants insisted that the *umanāʾ* abide by this practice and merchant interests were certainly taken into consideration by the authorities. 'If the price goes up', says a letter from an *amīn* to Bannīs, 'we should go up with it; if it goes down, we should go down with it'.[9] Likewise, the weights and scales at the *diwāna* (the buildings attached to customs at the port)[10] were regulated by the *muḥtasib*, who also regulated and controlled the town markets.

Administrative separation, which was only partial anyway, did not imply that *casbah*/port and town/market were economically wholly separate units. Merchants did not always distinguish between long-distance and local trade. Many items destined for export, such as almonds and olive oil, were consumed in the town. Only a small part of the imports found its way to local shops, but nonetheless, the inhabitants of Essaouira heavily consumed foreign goods, particularly tea, sugar, and textiles. Local, regional, and long-distance trade were all interdependent parts of the economic system.

Growth in the local retail trade

No sector in town was more connected to foreign trade than the retail market. For some towns in Morocco the impact of foreign trade can be gauged by examining traditional industries and the role played by cheap, manufactured imports in undermining traditional crafts.[11] The influence of foreign imports on Essaouira, with its limited industries, is more difficult to judge, but it was nevertheless affected by the influx of foreign commodities. This was most noticeable in the expansion of shops and the diversification of retail commodities.

The shop (*ḥanūt*, pl. *ḥawānit*) was the traditional work place of artisans, although they were generally required to peddle their trades in the markets, either themselves or through intermediaries.[12] Much retail trade was undoubtedly transacted in the town markets, closely controlled by the *muḥtasib*. The increased import trade with Europe and the broadening of the distribution network in Morocco must have been an impetus for diversifying the retail trade and creating new shops in town. The most apparent manifestation of the expansion of retail trading was the 'new market', *sūq al-jadīd*, for foreign imports, mainly Manchester textiles. Markets referred to by this term were found not only in the coastal towns but in the cities of the interior as well.[13] Essaouira's *sūq al-jadīd* was established as *ḥubus* by Sultan Sīdī Muḥammad b. ʿAbdallāh in the eighteenth century, though some of the shops belonged to the *makhzan*.[14] It formed a small square on the main thoroughfare of the bazaar, surrounded by a colonnade under which successive shops of drapers were located. The square was shut at night.[15] It is revealing that the predominantly Jewish retailers of European textiles were at the very centre of Essaouira's local trade, at the heart of the bazaar. *Sūq al-jadīd* had far more shops than any other market in Essaouira.

The other important market selling European imports was *sūq al-ʿaṭṭārīn*, the perfume / drug / spice market.[16] The druggist, *al-ʿaṭṭār*, already dealing in diverse items, was in a good position to become the general retail trader, selling not only his traditional goods, but new import products as well: cooking utensils, hardware, paper, glassware and other consumer wares.[17]

The development of these two types of retail trades in Essaouira might suggest a comparison with the growth of shops in Europe – the evolution from workshops to retail stores in which middlemen operated between producer and consumer. The shop in the *ʿaṭṭāra* might be compared to the general store in Europe, the merchant in the drapers' bazaar to the more specialized retailers in European towns. The causes for such expansion in Essaouira were also similar to Europe: a growth in the distribution network, a population increase in the town, and the development of credit because of the increase of wholesale trade.[18] The central difference was that this development in Essaouira was tied uniquely to foreign trade and did not involve the same kinds of social changes as in Europe. The shopkeepers in Essaouira did not develop into a *petite bourgeoisie* with separate corporate interests. Instead livelihoods of the shopkeepers were regulated by traditional patterns of administration, and administrative reforms did not seek to modify urban institutions as such, but rather were aimed at increasing the revenues of the *makhzan*, often to the detriment of the shopkeepers who never solidified into a special-interest group.

Warehouses and *funduq*s

Two types of urban institutions in Essaouira which reflected this mesh of international and local trade were warehouses and *funduq*s. The growth in the former was due to the development of the wholesale trade; the latter was an age-old institution connected to the caravan trade. Both institutions were influenced by the increasing scale of foreign trade.

The growth of foreign trade and the arrival of new merchants after the commercial treaty with Britain in 1856 created a severe shortage in housing and warehouses in town. Some merchants in the 1860s began to store their goods in flimsy sheds at the central square of the *casbah* and along the wall separating the port from the beach. A British merchant from Gibraltar, J. S. Ratto, agent for the newly-created French steamship company, built two sheds as coal depots along the wall near the beach. Another shed at this location, containing empty casks, rags, etc., belonging to the British merchant Grace, was burned down, allegedly by arsonists.[19]

The Moroccan government, under pressure from merchants and obligated by the 1856 commercial treaty to provide foreign merchants with premises, decided to erect a new *casbah*. In 1863 the first constructions were under way.[20] Two years later, the Jewish notables, backed by the foreign consular corps, also sought more housing and demanded that the overcrowded *mellah* be expanded. Housing in the so-called 'new *mellah*' was to be constructed for the poor. This was never realized, and instead the *makhzan* built shops in the new *mellah* to meet the demands of the Jewish merchants.[21] Key rights for 30 additional shops were auctioned: 'for each shop, 5,000 ūqiya and this is benefit (*manfa'a*) for the Sultan'.[22]

Places of business in general had become increasingly cluttered with merchandise. Merchants continued to place their goods pell-mell around the town, actually causing delay in the construction of the new *casbah* which was being built for their benefit. 'The happy *mashwar* in Essaouira used to be neat and tidy', write the *umanā'* in a letter to Bannīs. With the new constructions, the *mashwar* was now wedged between the old *casbah* and the new one being built. The letter continues

> The merchants have taken it [the *mashwar*] as their goat skin market [*manshara*]* which is visible to the governor, and it faces his [place of] government. We spoke to him about having this stopped, but he retorted 'that's the way it is and it's always been that way'. This is contrary to what the people of the town claim and attest. He [the governor] is involved with those who are spreading out [the skins] there, despite the well-known fact that for a long time past the *manshara* had been outside the town.[23]

The governor and the *umanā'* were both right. Perhaps the *manshara* had always been at or next to the *mashwar*, but before the construction of the new *casbah* it would have been clearly outside the town.

The construction of the new *casbah* sought to alleviate some of these problems. The largest houses and stores of Essaouira were subsequently to be found in this new quarter, but nevertheless there was still insufficient space. Native Jews and Europeans began to acquire warehouses in the *medina*, an area where they had not been allowed in the past. Previously, non-Muslims were leased shops only in the bazaar part of the *medina*, not in the residential district. Yet by 1878, all the *makhzan* warehouses in the *medina* were in the hands of foreigners or Jewish protégés, except for one Muslim, Sīdī Muḥammad al-Asfī (see table 10).

The construction of the new warehouses hardly altered the way business was conducted in Essaouira. The appearance of the city seemed unaffected by the pressures of foreign trade, and the additional warehouses did not lead to foreign innovations. Wheeled carts were still unknown and the constant congestion of pack-animals and goods was in no way eased by the additional storage facilities provided by the *makhzan*. The skin market where, according to one resident of Essaouira in 1891, up to 4,000 skins were sold a day,[24] was kept outside the walls of the town. Yet some of the skins were washed inside the city, a health

*literally, place of 'spreading'. The skins were spread out to dry before shipment.

Table 10 *Warehouses of the* makhzan: *1296/1878–9*[a]

Quarter	Holder[b]	Rent in ūqiya
medina	Moses [Corcos]	80
medina	Ben Messan	80
medina	Hāʾimi	80
medina	Juan Damonte	80
medina	The *Hazan*	80
medina	Sīdī Muḥammad al-Asfī	80
medina	Ben Zagury	50
medina	Bensaude	50
medina	Ben Garrab	50
medina	Son of Ben Hadd[an]	50
medina	Daniel al-ʿAllaf	50
medina	Ibrahim Ben Sasu	40
medina	Ibrāhīm Amlūl	10
medina	Shalom Corcos	60
Old *mellah*	Hanu	30
Old *casbah*	Grace	19.5
New *casbah*	Bolelli	76
New *casbah*	Jacquetty	184.25
New *casbah*	Jacob Afriat	173.25
New *casbah*	John Grace	379 (2 warehouses)
New *casbah*	Perry	238.25
New *casbah*	Coleman	195
New *casbah*	Messod Turgaman	141

[a] Listings of houses inclusive of warehouses are omitted in the table.
[b] Names are rendered in their European spelling when identified; otherwise they are transliterated.
Source: K[93].

hazard in the minds of foreign residents.[25] Beyond the southern gate of the city where the large caravans assembled, the buying and selling for the merchants was transacted by crowds of brokers. The merchandise was transported in small loads to the merchants' warehouses inside the town.[26]

The most important institution which dealt with the continual traffic of people and merchandise in the city was the *funduq*, often broadly translated as caravanserai. Its architecture has been described on countless occasions by the observers of Moroccan cities.[27] The same kind of structures were found throughout North Africa and the Middle East, though the name sometimes varied.[28] Essentially, the *funduq* was a two-level rectangular structure which surrounded a courtyard and contained small rooms on each floor. The ground floor was for the beasts of burden and merchandise, while the upper floor was for lodging people. In Essaouira, the size of the *funduq*s varied considerably as did their functions.[29] Some were set up to lodge the caravan drivers, beasts, and their merchandise, while others were primarily entrepôts for storing particular kinds of commodities. The rooms in some *funduq*s, instead of serving a transient clientele, were rented by merchants who transacted their business on the premises. Other *funduq*s combined functions as caravanserai and entrepôt. Sometimes the upper rooms may have been occupied all the year round, while at other times they may have served as cobblers' workshops.[30] In Essaouira, actual ownerships of the *funduq*s was rather complicated, but the evidence suggests that they were divided up fairly equally between *mulk*, *makhzan*, and *ḥubus*. Individual *funduq*s might be partly freehold and partly *makhzan* or *ḥubus* property. Unlike other towns, where *funduq*s mostly belonged to the *ḥubus* – the original owners having made them into religious endowments some centuries back[31] – Essaouira's *funduq*s were mainly *makhzan* or freehold.[32] A few *funduq*s were owned as private property by the principal merchants, such as Corcos, Elmaleh, and Tūfal-ʿazz. The reason why more *funduq*s belonged to the *makhzan* than to the *ḥubus* was that the town was new and closely administered by the central government. The *makhzan* sometimes constructed new *funduq*s and then saw to their maintenance.[33] During the great famine of 1878–9, the authorities used several *funduq*s to house the starving migrants.[34]

Regardless of who actually owned the *funduq*, much of the profit went to the merchant who controlled it. Key rights for *ḥubus* or *makhzan* *funduq*s were auctioned, and subsequent rents were either collected by the superintendent of the *ḥubus* (*nāẓir al-aḥbās*), or the *amīn* of *makhzan* properties. Akkan Corcos, the well-connected Jewish merchant from Marrakesh, held a *makhzan funduq* in the *medina*, which was viewed as a nuisance by the Muslims of the quarter. In 1875, one of the *qāʾid*s of Shiadma, Mubārak b. ʿAmr ash-Shiyāẓmī, complained to the Sultan that the *umanāʾ* had constructed two apartments for Akkan Corcos in a *funduq* where the Shiadma tied up their livestock. The *qāʾid* claimed that the gate belonging to Corcos extended into the street, obstructing both the door to the mosque and private residences. Corcos continued to expand the activities of the *funduq*, constructing a wall to enclose an olive oil refinery. 'This is causing harm to the mosque', said the *qāʾid* in a report to the Sultan 'since it is impossible to pass in the street because of the congestion caused by all the camels, pack-loads, and caravans of olive oil'. Inquiries into the matter were fruitless: 'nothing has been done about it and nothing has changed'.[35]

Additional *funduq*s, like the warehouses, did not resolve the problem of storage which seemed to be worsening as merchants kept larger stocks. The larger caravans were usually kept outside the town, but the continual influx of rural pedlars, merchandise, and animals into the town was still a dilemma. Even after the construction of the new *casbah* the delay in building a proper road was making the passage of goods difficult. In his capacity as American vice-consul, Abraham Corcos complained to the *qāʾid* that the residents of the new *casbah* 'dreaded the overcrowding from those bringing in and taking out merchandise'.[36] In the 1870s, the *nāẓir al-aḥbās* started to build an additional *funduq* in town, but due to delays, the *ḥubus* lost rent on it for two years and ended up letting its shops at an insufficient rate. The *makhzan* decided to expedite the process and ordered the *qāʾid*, qadi, and *umanāʾ* to assess the costs already spent on construction and the amount still needed for completion. They decided that when the *funduq* was finished, the *umanāʾ* would administer it – in other words, the *makhzan* decided to appropriate the *funduq* from the *ḥubus*.[37]

Craftsmen, traders, and pedlars in the bazaar

The actual space which could be called the bazaar was very limited (see map 3). A trader arriving from the south could easily look from the old Bab Sbaʿ and out through the north exit of the town, Bāb Dukkāla. Most of Essaouira's markets were located on this wide street or directly off it on small, enclosed squares. The spatial organization of the town conformed to the typical urban structure of Arab–Islamic cities: economic activities radiated out from the very centre of the town.[38] It was at the heart of Essaouira that the principal markets were located. The main street and markets were crowded with Swiri hawkers and rural dwellers attracted to the amenities of the city. Tribesmen would enter the town with their livestock from Bāb Sbaʿ or Bāb Dukkāla, which led directly on to the bazaar's main street, or from Bāb Marrakesh which intersected the bazaar's main street in the middle. Although the *funduq*s and many stables in the town may have relieved some of the traffic problems,[39] the highly-concentrated clutter of men, goods, and animals in the area must have continued from dawn to dusk.

Artisanal activity in Essaouira was rather limited, and unlike older urban centres in Morocco, there were few noted crafts. There were no industries in Essaouira which produced commodities sold on the foreign market – in fact, only one craft appears to have been connected to the export trade: barrel-making to provide containers for shipping olive oil.[40] Furthermore, Essaouira was slow to adopt foreign technical innovations, a situation common to cities of the Middle East and North Africa before the modern era.[41] Besides the crafts, the only industries were a few horse mills for grinding flour, a small number of soap, olive oil, and wax refineries, and a textile workshop. Foreign machinery was unknown until the 1870s when a steam mill was constructed for the first time; in the 1880s there were two.[42]

Artisans, therefore, constituted a fairly weak social group in Essaouira. The French consul in 1847, Soulange-Bodin, noted that most of the population could not subsist without the pension allocated by the customs authorities to the militia, the original Muslim settlers from Agadir, and various others who received official favour.[43] In other words, Essaouira still maintained a large military and 'official' sector. The working population, apart from merchants and porters, was limited. 'The artisan and industrial classes', wrote vice-consul Carstensen in response to a circular from R. Drummond Hay in 1870, 'do not exist here *as a class*.' The British vice-consul was not suggesting that artisans were altogether absent from Essaouira:

> There are, of course, to be found at Mogador, as in all Marocco towns artisans scattered over the population, but their number is so small that they cannot be said to form a separate class of the community. Amongst them may be noticed the slippermakers, tailors, saddlers, haikmakers, blacksmiths, tinsmiths, carpenters, maisons & C., who ply their respective trades in the town, but in numbers scarcely adequate to the requirements of the population. They do not occupy dwellings of a different description from those of the other inhabitants, nor do they live in a separate quarter of the town.[44]

A few crafts, such as brass-making and jewellery, were fairly noticeable and concentrated in one geographical area. But for the most part, Essaouira differed from older Moroccan cities in the sense that it lacked a strongly-identifiable artisan sector spread over large parts of town.[45]

R. Hay's circular of 1870 demonstrates that artisans represented about six per cent of the urban population of Moroccan cities.[46] A survey of Jewish professions in Essaouira by the Alliance Israélite Universelle in 1894 revealed a total of 392 master-craftsmen and apprentices, which represented about 5 per cent out of a population of 8,000 Jews. Jews, however, were not able to become blacksmiths, masons, potters, mat-makers, weavers, saddlers, and tanners (see table 11).[47]

Such statistics, however, do not reveal the true proportion of the working population connected in some way to the crafts. Women, who

Table 11 *Jewish artisans of Essaouira in 1894*

Professions	Masters	Daily salary	Apprentices	Daily salary
Jewellers	22	f3	15	f1.50
Tinsmiths	15	2	17	.50–.75
Brassmakers	23	2.50–3	3	1
Tailors	25	2–2.50	30	.75–1
Shoemakers (*babouches*)	22	1.50–2	84	.75–1
Cobblers	80	1–2		
Coopers	12	2	18	.50–.75
Joiners	11	1.50–2		
Cabinet-makers, painters	5	3–5		
Shoemakers (European style)	3	2–2.50		
Watchmakers	1	2.50–3		
Barbers	6			
Total:	225		167	

Source: A.I.U., Maroc XXXIII E 582, 22 February 1894.

were not taken into consideration in the Alliance survey, were employed in tailoring, weaving, and embroidering.[48] Women were also employed in a number of other menial jobs, such as in the cleaning of wool and gums,[49] and as domestic servants.[50] Most numerous of all were the professions that served the transient population. The greatest number of artisans were the shoemakers and cobblers, occupations which defy reliable enumeration, since although some of the shoemakers may have maintained permanent stalls in the bazaar, many cobblers were peripatetic. They not only circulated in town, but they also serviced rural markets along Essaouira's trade routes. This was probably the case for some tailors as well.[51]

Jewellers were also numerous in Essaouira, probably owing in part to the imported gold brought by the caravans of the Western Sudan. Furthermore, in the absence of banks, the purchase of jewellery was a form of investment. Gold and silver utensils, elaborately decorated firearms, and jewellery were well-known specialities of Essaouira.[52] Almost all the jewellers were Jews, though it was not unknown for Muslims to work in partnership with them.[53] Successful pedlars invested in gold and silver objects, and the women of wealthy merchants were adorned with gold and silver ornaments. The shipwrecked American

6 *Sūq al-Jadīd* (drapers' market), 1920
Courtesy of Monsieur Samuel Levy

7 *Jūṭiya* (auction square), 1981

captain, Riley, noted in the early nineteenth century that the young daughter of one wealthy Jewish trader in Essaouira wore ornaments valued at about $2,000, an amount that not more than 20 Jews could have afforded.[54]

Essaouira's artisanal sector may have been less impressive than in other Moroccan cities, but for the rural customer, the bazaar presented an array of different specialized services which were not always readily found in the countryside. Certain markets (*sūqs*), such as the *raḥba* (the grain market), the *jūṭiya* (the auction/flea market), and the livestock market were frequented predominantly by rural visitors. Essaouira served both as an outlet and as a distribution centre for the surrounding regions, the Haha and Shiadma, and much of the activity of the bazaar must be seen in this light.

The term '*sūq*' denotes all places of economic exchange: the bazaar in general, the weekly rural markets, as well as specialized crafts and retail trades (see table 12).[55] The centre of the bazaar was dominated by the drapers of *sūq al-jadīd*, who were mostly retailers for the *casbah* merchants. Several markets were found in small, enclosed squares surrounded by numerous stalls. The *jūṭiya* formed a square surrounded by some 27 shops,[56] or rather, small windowless stalls facing the square where various odds and ends were sold. Late in the afternoon, the *jūṭiya* filled up with country folk who participated in the auction or casually watched the activity.[57] Adjacent to the *jūṭiya* was the *raḥba* or grain market, whose architectural structure was the same as the *jūṭiya*, and whose clientele was also mostly rural peasants or their brokers. Both Jews and Muslims occupied the stalls surrounding the *raḥba* – artisans manufacturing haiks and spinning woollen yarns in looms, and smiths making iron tools and other items.[58] There were other smaller market squares for charcoal, the *qāʿa* for olive and argan oils, oil, soap, honey, butter and dried fruits, and market squares for several groups of craftsmen, such as utensil makers, joiners, and jewellers.[59] Some markets, such as the slave market, were held only on occasions when the trans-Saharan caravan reached town. There was not always a specific place for the sale of slaves, and instead the auctioneer would lead them through the streets taking bids. The total number of slaves sold annually was limited to a few dozen.[60]

Most buying and selling took place in these markets. While stationary retail traders and craftsmen were not inconsiderable in number, much of the hustle and bustle in the bazaar was caused by the numerous pedlars and porters. The largest section of the working population in Essaouira was either the hucksters or those who carried goods for others. At the turn of the century, the Alliance Israélite Universelle began enumerating the

Table 12 Sūqs *of Essaouira in the second half of the nineteenth century*

Goods and produce markets	Crafts and trades
Auction / flea market (*jūṭiya*)	druggists / general retailers (*'iṭāra*)
Fabrics (*sūq al-jadīd*)	smiths (*ḥaddāda*)
Yarn (*ghazl*)	shoemakers (*kharrāza*)
Salt (*milḥa*)	cobblers (*ṭarrāfa*)
Charcoal (*faḥam*)	tailors (*khiyāṭa*)
Olive / argan oil, etc. (*qāʿa*)	saddlers (*sahrāja*)
Grain (*raḥba*)	harness embroiderers (*saqqāṭa*)
Skins (*jild*)	jewellers (*siyāgha*)
Slaves (*raqīq*)	Muslim butchers (*jazarat al-muslimīn*)
Silver (*fiḍa*)	Jewish butchers (*jazarat al-yahūd*)
Fish (*ḥūt*)	
Fowl (*dajāj*)	
Livestock (*bahā'im*)	
Beef / mutton (*baqar, ghanam*)	

Sources: K.H., K[122]; K.H., K[93]; B.G., Habous, Essaouira: Léon Godard, *Le Maroc, notes d'un voyageur* (Algiers, 1859), p. 52

professions of the Jewish population of Essaouira. 'Out of a population of 10,000', wrote the director of the Alliance school, 'one would only find 150 families who live from practising their trades; the remainder include merchants, pedlars, and hucksters'.[61]

In a city where the transport of goods was so important, porters were very numerous. Most of the porters carried goods for the merchants and traders, and could be hired at the *ḥammāla*, a place near the *casbah* where they gathered together.[62] Yet the carrier, *al-ḥāmil*, who earned menial wages, may also have attempted to hawk his wares as well, bartering odds and ends when the opportunity arose. Auctioneers were also for hire. The British consul, Payton, describes one such auctioneer (*dallāl*): 'Houssain is a tall, good looking Moor, who wears a voluminous turban, a red or purple tunic, an embroidered leather belt, a handsome dagger, baggy white breeches, yellow slippers, a surtout, replaced on "high days and holidays", by a spotless white haik'.[63] These auctioneers specialized in different commodities and represented varying levels of the social hierarchy, from retail merchants in their own right to petty street hawkers.[64] Some *dallāl*s, as in the description above, dealt in relatively valuable commodities – inlaid guns and daggers, jewellery, and European manufactured goods. Others auctioned mules and cattle. Merchants would employ *dallāl*s to sell off their goods, particularly if they were having trouble finding prospective buyers.[65]

The distinction, therefore, between porter, auctioneer, and pedlar becomes blurred. An Alliance director in Essaouira noted that besides merchants, the population was divided between workers and porters.[66] Nearly 14 per cent of the Jewish workers were pedlars, according to estimates in 1913[67], and the number of Muslims employed as porters and pedlars must have been at least as high. Whatever the category – porter, pedlar, huckster, or auctioneer – the conveyers of merchandise assured the circulation of goods in the town and were part and parcel of the bazaar economy.

A final category of the population might be appropriately termed as wage-earner. In addition to the pedlars there were also numerous casual labourers in Essaouira who assisted the merchants in various menial tasks. Women workers were perhaps the most important sector among this lowest class of the population. Some were employed in cleaning wool and gums, earning half the amount made by low-level artisans.[68] Domestic servants earned even less.[69] The most important areas of wage-labour were in the seasonal goat skin and almond markets, which provided employment for several hundred workers.[70] The demand for workers in these areas depended on market fluctuations and seasonal changes. There was therefore a migrant labour force, which came into the town from the countryside when labour was in demand, but during the harvest season, when food was provided on top of wages, many rural migrants returned to their homes in the countryside. With the absence of workers during the harvest season, the cost of labour rose in town.[71] In a town which was dominated by trade, much of the population was transient.

Administration of town and bazaar

Activities in both the port and the bazaar were controlled by authorities who combined traditional institutions with new innovative mechanisms of administration. Administratively, commerce at the port in some ways became separate from the town markets. In general, the reforms of the nineteenth century led to a greater separation of administrative powers, which reflected the tensions between the foreign and domestic sectors. The roles that the actors played in the administration of the town were far from being static.

In theory, the chief administrator was the Sultan to whom all the officials of Essaouira were answerable. The local administrators themselves had a network of interconnected underlings. Power was delegated to three principal branches of authority, each independently appointed by the Sultan yet interlinked. At the centre of the town's power structure was the governor, called *qāʾid* or *ʿāmil* interchangeably.[72] He was the administrative link between port and market and had authority over the functioning of different officials. He also had overall charge of the garrison of the town and responsibility for assuring urban security. The power of the *qāʾid* was limited by the fact that ultimate authority rested with the Sultan who could appoint or remove him, and it was further constrained by the *shariʿa*, represented by the second principal authority in town, the qadi, who was also appointed by the Sultan, often through the suggestion of a chief qadi (*qāḍī al-quḍāh*) at the court.[73] The third part of the triad was the *umanāʾ*, appointed by the Sultan through the head *amīn*, or *amīn al-umanāʾ*. The *umanāʾ* were in charge of the fiscal administration of the town, but their responsibilities expanded in the nineteenth century to include, in addition to control of the port, the administration of the octroi, city markets, and tax-farms.[74]

As fiscal reforms developed, one of the *umanāʾ*, the *amīn al-mustafād* – the official in charge of town revenues – was given wide responsibilities quite apart from the customs administration of the *umanāʾ* at the port. This new official was put in charge of administering all sources of town revenue for the *makhzan*: gate tolls, market taxes, rents and the acquisition of properties. He was also responsible for using these funds for various constructions such as maintaining the city walls, repairing the aqueduct, improving houses, etc.[75] The development of this official reflected the expanding role of the state in fiscal matters.

Historically it was the *muḥtasib* who was the chief official in control of the fiscal administration of the town. He was appointed by the Sultan, often at the suggestion of the *qāʾid*, qadi, or *umanāʾ* of the town. He was usually a resident of Essaouira with intimate knowledge of the population, and he was therefore indispensable for the administration. The *muḥtasib* was the key urban official in Islamic cities who had a wide range of responsibilities, including the supervision of the professions in conjunction with the *amīn*, and management of the crafts, control of weights, measures, prices, gold and silver essayers, and in general, the moral conduct of town and bazaar. His position of authority was legitimized by his religious and legal function, called '*ḥisba*' (literally 'calculation' or 'counting'), which can be regarded as the moral and legal code of the market.[76]

Among the historical tasks of the *muḥtasib* was the collection of taxes in town, a role increasingly assumed by the *amīn al-mustafād*. Although the power of the *muḥtasib* was clearly weakening, he was still not entirely superseded by the *amīn al-mustafād*. His local knowledge was still needed for administering the town. The *amīn al-mustafād* only became necessary when the fiscality of the *makhzan* both expanded and also became more centralized. The *muḥtasib*, who relied on the *sharīʿa* and local practice, continued to supervise the sector for which the *amīn al-mustafād* had become administratively responsible.

The key officials – *qāʾid*, qadi, *umanāʾ*, and *muḥtasib* – relied on a whole gamut of minor employees to administer the town. The *qāʾid* retained official soldiers, called *mukhaznīs* to enforce the orders of the principal authorities. The *umanāʾ* and the qadi employed numerous clerks (*kātib*s) and notaries (*ʿadl*, pl. *ʿudūl*) at all levels of administration, wherever paper work was required.[77] Individual *amīn*s supervised specific markets, working directly under the *muḥtasib*, or at a later date, under the more general administration of the *amīn al-mustafād* as well. A French missionary-traveller, Léon Godard, lists *amīn*s for six different markets: grain, charcoal, the *qāʿa*, fowl, livestock, and fish.[78] It seems likely that there were more officials than those that caught the eye of Godard. As ubiquitous as the *muḥtasib* was, it would have been impossible for him to regulate personally the countless purchases and sales going on simultaneously in all the markets. The fish market, for example, was particularly active in a town where the sea was the source of a major part of the diet. The *muḥtasib* would have required a dutiful employee to oversee the sale of fish, in which the small ones were sold by weight and the large ones individually.[79] The position of *amīn* in the most active *sūq*s was of particular importance. Such was the case of the *amīn* of the vast goat skin market outside the city walls. Due to the commercial importance of hides, the *amīn*, at least on some occasions, was appointed directly by the Sultan, though it is not known to what degree this was at the suggestion of the qadi, *muḥtasib*, or *amīn al-mustafād*.[80]

Each of the main branches of the administration had specific institutionalized responsibilities which were redefined according to the fiscal needs of the *makhzan*. The overall pattern resembled other Moroccan towns of that era, and to a degree, Islamic cities in general.[81] In all the principal cities of Morocco, the *umanāʾ* assumed a key role in the administration. As foreign trade increased, the responsibilities of the port authorities developed in each of the eight Moroccan seaports of this era. At the same time, the traditional officials to be found in classic Islamic cities – the qadi, *muḥtasib* and *ʿadl* – maintained their importance in Essaouira. The *makhzan* created an administration which was embedded in traditional culture, yet responded to new fiscal needs with innovations.

Jewish self-government

The Jews were also subject to the regulations of the market, and were equally controlled by the *muḥtasib*. In disputes between Muslims and

Jews, they were also obliged to submit to the *sharīʿa*. But in some areas of commercial and bazaar life, the Jews maintained an entirely independent yet parallel administrative apparatus. The *muḥtasib* would rarely venture inside the *mellah*; it was the chief mediator between the Muslim authorities and the Jews, the *shaykh al-yahūd* (or *nagīd* in Hebrew) who was the enforcer of the moral code, regulating commercial transactions, and, in certain cases, prices inside the Jewish community. It was the *shaykh al-yahūd*, rather than the *muḥtasib*, who was responsible for upholding the general probity of the Jews of the *mellah*.[82] Like the *muḥtasib*, the *shaykh al-yahūd* had the power to enforce his control, even through imprisonment, and he was supported by the Muslim authorities who assigned to him *mukhaznī*s to collect taxes.[83] The *shaykh*'s authority, however, was curtailed by the *dayyan*s, the rabbinical judges who had ultimate authority in all legal matters between Jews, provided that they did not involve the Muslim community. In no case could the Jew appeal to the qadi to overturn a ruling of the *dayyan*s without the risk of excommunication (*ḥerem*).[84]

There were also taxes which were independent of the Muslims. These revenues were intended to support religious institutions, and above all, the poor. Similar to the *mustafād*, these taxes were subject to reform and alteration. The official responsible for their collection, the *gabai*, was parallel in a sense to the *amīn al-mustafād*. Certain kinds of taxes, such as the tax on heads of cattle slaughtered by the kosher butchers, were levied intermittently in Essaouira.[85] Another tax could be levied on sales in the goat skin market. Such a tax is described in 1891: 'In the skin market stands a *gabai* who records in a register the number of skins sold each day, and the brokers pay him what they owe, which he brings to the head of the community'.[86] Attached to all these Jewish officials were the *sōfer*s, adjuncts to the *dayyan*s; their relationship was similar to that between *ʿudūl* and qadis. Muslim and Jewish legally notarized documents look remarkably similar, with their intricately patterned signatures to prevent fraud. The texts and legal matters discussed are often almost identical. In some Jewish documents, the Hebrew text is interlaced with Arabic terms, a language more readily understood when concerning day-to-day economic matters.

At the top of the Jewish hierarchy in Essaouira were the notables, who, as we have seen, were usually the principal merchants of the town. There was always a head of the community (*rōsh ha-qehīlla*), who had almost total control over the community treasury (*qūpa*).[87] The *rosh ha-qehīlla* might also bear the title of *dayyan*, as in the case of Joseph and Reuben Elmaleh. In addition to his control of all communal revenues, the appointment of *dayyan*s, *gabai*s, and even the *shaykh al-yahūd*, was subject to his approval. Unlike the *shaykh al-yahūd*, who was appointed by the *qā'id*, the *rōsh ha-qehīlla* was elected by the Jewish notables, and his appointment was therefore strictly an internal matter of the Jewish community. In the case of Essaouira, the *rōsh ha-qehīlla*, and the notables who formed the *ma'amad* towards the end of the nineteenth century, were always among the leading merchants of Essaouira. Their administrative roles, assumed because of wealth, were of secondary importance to their commercial activities.[88]

Dawn to dusk

The ebb and flow of activities of Essaouira were determined, to a degree, by the topography of the town, and the ways in which each sector was controlled by the authorities. Yet the rhythms of activity were also structured according to culturally embedded perceptions of time, which need to be considered. The Swiri's day was punctuated by aspects of life inherent in Muslim societies, especially the Muslim's five daily prayers and the noon prayer at the mosque on Fridays.[89] Essaouira's large Jewish population meant that the rituals of Jews were of equal importance. The working day of the Jews began at dawn, after the men had completed their prayers (*shaḥarīt*) in the synagogue. The day ended, or according to Jewish custom, began with prayers (*minḥa/ma'rīb*) in the synagogue at dusk.[90] Patterns of work, leisure, and sleep, organized around the schedule of Muslim and Jewish daily rituals, were modified by the changing seasons. While the religious lives of Jews and Muslims remained strictly separate, the commercial life of each was influenced by the other's recurrent schedule of religious practices.

What particularly struck the foreign observer about daily life in Essaouira was the rhythm of artisans and workers. French Consul Beaumier wrote of the artisan putting in eight hours of work a day, beginning at six in the morning and finishing at four in the afternoon, with a two-hour rest in the middle of the day.[91] Another observer suggested that work never lasted more than seven hours. In the winter, the artisan worked from seven in the morning to three in the afternoon without interruption, except on Fridays when an hour of prayer intervened at noon. The seasonal variations of work were determined by the rotation of prayer time. Life for the day labourer was more onerous. His work began at daybreak and continued until about four in the afternoon, with a break of only a half hour for a meal. It was noticed that the women workers who cleaned wool and gum at minimal wages were given only a half hour's rest at noon.[92]

The working day left little time for leisure, but nonetheless patterns of work were interspersed with leisurely breaks.[93] It was the growing consumption of tea that most affected the daily patterns of drudgery. From the 1830s onwards, tea was drunk throughout Morocco, due largely to the Swiri importers. Henceforth work was punctuated by the beverage and leisurely social calls could not pass without the appearance of the sweet mint tea.[94] The consumption of coffee, whose popularity predated tea, was not negligible either, and although it never attained the same widespread popularity as tea, coffee imports were growing in the nineteenth century.[95] As a result of this growth in consumption, the number of cafés increased. In these meeting-houses, time was spent sipping coffee or tea snd listening to itinerant musicians, or perhaps discussing commerce.[96]

This form of leisure did not always meet with the approval of the authorities. According to the local historian aṣ-Ṣiddīqī, the *qāʾid* of Essaouira, Muḥammad Brīsha, ordered the closure of the town's cafés in the 1850s, possibly because alcoholic beverages were also consumed there. Though forbidden by Islam, a kind of fig or date *eau de vie* called *maḥyā*, manufactured mostly by the Jews, was very popular in the Muslim community. The *qāʾid* at this time decreed that those caught consuming alcohol would receive 100 lashings.[97] It is clear that Brīsha's measures were not applied after his administration ended in 1857.[98] In 1867 further orders were issued by the Sultan to close the cafés in the coastal towns.[99]

At nightfall, almost all forms of work ceased. The three gates leading out of the town were closed and guards were posted, and between nine or ten in the evening, depending on the season, the internal gates of the town were shut. The guards announced this closure by firing rifles. From that point on, tranquillity and security normally reigned in the town. Those who ventured out into the main street after dark would be liable to stumble over dogs or cows, and to awaken the sleepy guards.[100]

Almost all labour, therefore, stopped at night, except for a few marginal or ephemeral areas of employment. The larger and more valuable fish were sometimes caught by the fishermen from the outlying rocks at night.[101] Incidents of extramural contraband trade sometimes occurred at night, as a guard at the goat skin market outside Bāb Sbaʿ, the *manshara*, discovered one summer night in 1865.[102]

For Muslim and Jew, night-time delimited ethnic boundaries. During the day, the Jew maintained his shops or conducted his business in the *sūq*s of the *medina*. After nightfall, the Jew found security among his coreligionists behind the guarded gates of the *mellah*. In a sense he was moving from the profane to the sacred, from the mundane activities of the market to the exclusively Jewish world of the *mellah*.[103] It was within the

8 Market day and Saturday: early twentieth-century postcard of Essaouira
Courtesy of Monsieur Isaac Abecassis

The postcard shows the marketplace at Bāb Dukkāla. On Friday, the marketplace is extremely active. On Saturday, the Jewish sabbath, the shops are shut and the street is practically empty.

confines of the Jewish quarter, for example, that the kabbalists, members of the mystical sodality, the *ḥebrat Zōhar ha-qadōsh*, would meet at night, sometimes to continue their prayer sessions until dawn.[104] For Muslims also, the *medina* could become the scene of popular religious gatherings. During the festivals of the Ḥamādsha and the ʿAisāwa, ritual processions took place in the streets at night, and were continued later in the religious lodge (*zāwiya*).[105] In the *casbah*, however, Jews, Muslims and Christians resided in the same quarter at night. In this case, social status bridged normal ethnic divisions.

Day to day

The rhythms of the market-place had their typical daily patterns, delineated by Muslim and Jewish rituals and the divisions between night and day. Yet each day of the week had its own characteristics. In Essaouira, to a large extent, the daily activities in the market were

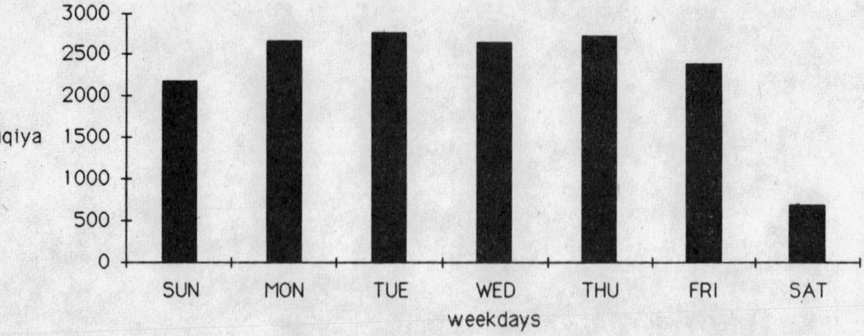

Fig. 4 Average gate and market taxes by weekday, 1301/1883–4, excluding the tax farms (*source:* K.H., K[122]).

structured by two important ritual events: the Jewish sabbath (Shabbat) and Muslim Friday (*jumʿa*).

In Essaouira there were six active market days. But, as Yaʿīsh Halewī reported in *ha-Ṣefīra*, 'on sabbaths and festivals work almost ceases, and everyone celebrates with us [the Jews]; nothing goes out and nothing comes in [the town]'.[106] This is rather overstated. There was some traffic through the town gates and in a few markets on Saturdays, but the level was greatly reduced (see fig. 4). The Jewish sabbath also affected the ebb and flow of trade at the market-place during other days of the week. The Jewish sabbath in fact begins at sundown on Fridays. On Friday mornings, Jewish beggars were likely to receive donations from their wealthier coreligionists, and at the same time, wealthy Jews contributed to Muslim beggars. Charity from the community fund (*qūpa*) was distributed to the poor, orphans, and scholars on Fridays.[107] The contributors of charity may have been on their way to market to purchase food and provisions for the Friday evening feast and for the meals on the following day. The working day for the Jews must have ended earlier than other days so that preparations could be made before the eve of Shabbat. On Friday afternoons, the Jewish cemetery outside Bāb Dukkāla became the scene of intense activity as crowds of Jewish visitors arrived there to mourn and supplicate to the *ṣaddīqs*, the Jewish saints.[108] As happens everywhere in the Jewish world, the celebration of Shabbat began at sundown. The Jewish community of Essaouira, apart from the few wealthy Jews of the *casbah*, retreated back into the world of the *mellah*, leaving behind the hubbub of the town's markets. For the Jews, the separation between the sabbath and the mundane affairs of the week was absolute.

There was nothing like this separation between the sacred and the profane for the Muslims.[109] Characteristic of Arab/Islamic cities generally, the largest mosque in Essaouira, Sīdī Yūsuf, was contiguous to all the markets.[110] It was here that the mid-day Friday prayers were held. When the prayers finished, the adherents poured out into the street where they would immediately come into contact with the Jewish artisans and shopkeepers. As can be judged by the mean level of gate and market taxes, commercial activities were average on Friday, compared to the rest of the week. After an important afternoon meal, the Muslims would return to the bazaar and resume work as on any other day.

Nevertheless, Muslim religious life did influence the rhythms of Friday. Although Friday was not a day of rest, the mid-day prayer (*ṣalāt al-jumʿa*) was attended by large numbers of men. In addition, Muslim scholars (*ṭalaba*) were paid to say special litanies after the prayer in the mosque (*al-lāṭif al-awsaṭ*).[111] Before going to prayer, soldiers in the militia would regularly parade before the *qāʾid* in official uniform.[112] The Friday afternoon meal was the most important meal of the week. The poor were taken into consideration on that day. It was the time of charity, *ṣadaqa*, and besides individual contributors, the authorities also distributed *ṣadaqa* to the poor and rations (*muʾna*) to prisoners. The poor at the sanctuary of Sīdī Magdūl regularly received olive oil, fruit, and vegetables from the authorities on Fridays.[113]

It was the confluence of Muslim and Jewish practice that created a rhythm of time peculiar to Essaouira, and probably to other Moroccan towns with large Jewish populations. The customs of Fridays and Saturdays influenced the activities of the other days of the week, which is reflected in the average level of taxes gained by the *umanāʾ*. With the convergence of *ṣalāt al-jumʿa* and the approach of the eve of Shabbat, trade slackened in certain sectors. The hide market, dominated by Jews, slowed down on Fridays and almost ground to a halt on Saturdays (see fig. 5). Jews dominated another branch of the skin trade: on the Jewish sabbath, the *umanāʾ* gained next to nothing from the cobblers' leather market. No revenue at all came from the *qāʿa* on Saturdays, suggesting that the Jews had a monopoly in the retail trade of edible oils, butter, honey, dried fruit, nuts, and other items sold in this market.[114] Even movement in the *jūṭiya*, which served large numbers of the rural Muslim population, lessened on the Jewish Sabbath (see fig. 6).

The busiest day of the week in Essaouira's markets was Thursday. This was typical of other towns in Morocco, where the people from the countryside came into the town to sell their cattle and sheep and other commodities.[115] The *umanāʾ*, on average, gained over twice as much from taxes on cattle, sheep, and the slaughterhouse on Thursdays than on any other day of the week (see fig. 6). The butchers of Essaouira also had their

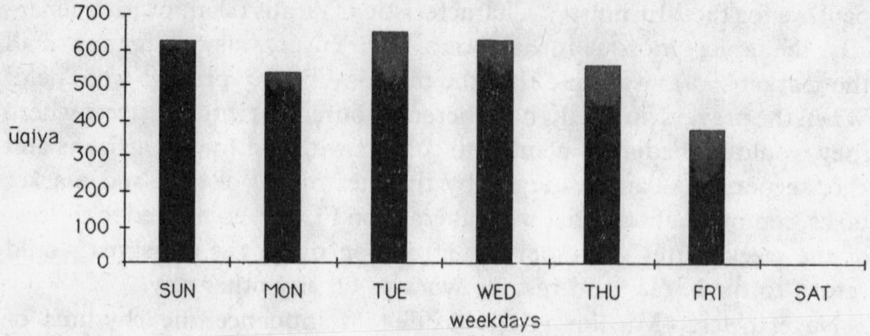

Fig. 5 Hide market: averages by weekday, 1301 / 1883–4 (*source:* K.H., K[122]).

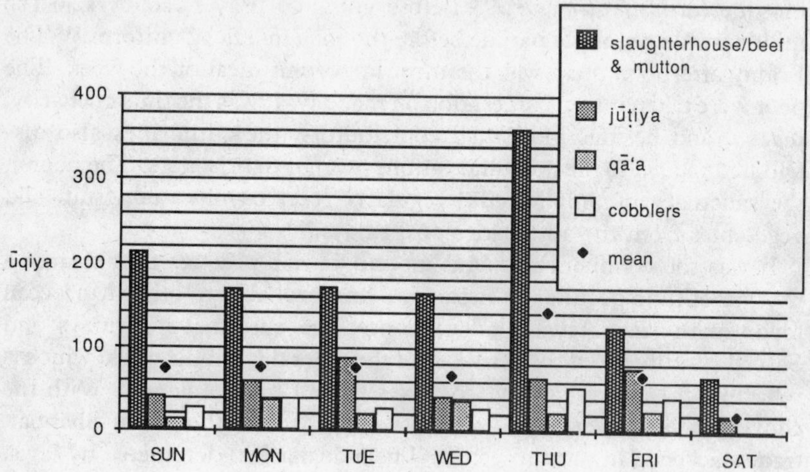

Fig. 6 Averages of the slaughterhouse, *jūṭiya*, *qāʿa*, and cobblers' market by weekday, 1301 / 1883–4 (*source:* K.H., K[122]).

busiest day of the week, since the residents of the town needed meat for the traditional Friday afternoon meal the following day, and so did the Jewish cobblers, probably by servicing the numerous traders from the countryside who came into town for the market on that day.[116] The approach of *jumʿa* and the eve of Shabbat dictated from week to week the movement in the city markets.

Much of the ebb and flow of commercial activities in Essaouira's markets depended on the relationship of the town with the surrounding countryside, and the seasonal rhythms of long-distance trade. Urban activities were intricately tied to the modalities of exchange, not only in port and bazaar, but also along the caravan routes outside the walls of the town.

Chapter 5

Beyond the walls

The approach to Essaouira from the land presents the image of an oasis. 'It bursts upon one's view like a desert mirage, for several miles of drifting sand-hills have first to be crossed and on the far side nestles the town, its white roofs and mosque towers shown up clearly by the deep blue sea beyond.'[1] Essaouira appears like most other cities in Morocco: its immediate hinterland is uncultivated.[2] Only a few gardens stretch out for a short distance beyond the ramparts. The town itself is on a promontory jetting out into the sea, so that its climate is always temperate and breezy. One has to travel only a few miles inland to enter a hot, intemperate zone. The city, surrounded by its walls, gives one a sense of isolation from the rest of the world; its micro-climate contributes to this feeling of detachment from the rest of Morocco.

And yet this physical image belies the senses. In many ways Essaouira was tied both to its hinterland and to distant inland markets. The constant stream of merchants and pedlars – of Berber tribesmen and Jews – through the town gates was another striking image of the town. This continual movement of people and goods relied on social networks which, under normal conditions, facilitated the peaceful passage of itinerant traders and caravans over distances near and far.

Pedlars

On the weight of numbers, Essaouira was pre-eminently a city of pedlars. Some, as we have seen, served as the brokers of the *casbah* merchants. More significantly, they were the essential link between town and country. This was of particular importance since Essaouira was geographically isolated and food supplies were transported over a considerable distance. Thus Essaouira appears to foreigners as a city which 'has no immediate rural connections'.[3] To the French consul Soulange-Bodin, Essaouira is an 'artificial city'.[4] Artificial, because most of the rural inhabitants lived too far from Essaouira to travel there and back in one day. This meant, according to one paradigm, that Essaouira really had no 'local trade',[5] and consequently, because of distance and the cost of transport, food prices were more expensive than in other towns.[6]

Despite these distances, most of Essaouira's connections with the neighbouring regions of the Haha and Shiadma in a sense were 'local' since, for the most part, they were not related to Morocco's import–export trade. A distinction can be made between pedlars who make the rounds in the regional markets and return at the end of the week, and itinerant traders, who leave for entire seasons.

People would come into town from the countryside for provisions and yet they were also dependent on pedlars to convey their produce. Many tribesmen preferred to travel to a weekly market in their vicinity where they would meet pedlars from town. These 'riding merchants', who went about the countryside by donkey or mule in groups of two or three, specialized in supplying the peasant with imported commodities: cotton fabrics, tea, and sugar.[7] The surrounding countryside therefore, as Yaʿīsh Halewī, a writer from the *mellah* of Essaouira described, 'was dotted with small merchants who buy merchandise with money or credit, loading their beasts and going out from the city to sell in markets'.[8]

A high proportion of these pedlars was composed of Jews. Studies have shown that in many parts of North Africa, Jewish pedlars were the predominant group which linked town and country. The very fact that the Jews were not rooted in rural society, with tribal or kinship ties, meant that they did not constitute a political threat and were therefore more trustworthy in economic matters. Paradoxically this marginality was the guarantee of a neutrality which was in the interest of all parties to maintain under normal conditions. In sex roles as well, the Jewish pedlar was both marginal and neutral. While it would be unthinkable for a Muslim man to interact with a woman outside his immediate family, a Jew, because of his inferior status, could enter the home of a Muslim woman for the purpose of trade.[9]

Scattered throughout Essaouira's hinterland were weekly markets (see map 4), protected by local *qāʾid*s and sheikhs. The small merchants, reports Yaʿīsh Halewī, 'buy merchandise with their beasts and go out from the town to sell in markets among the *gōyīm* [i.e., Muslims], and every day of the week has a *sūq* called by the name of the day'.[10] Each market was indeed called by the day it was held (*sūq al-aḥad*, *sūq al-ithnayn*, etc.). Some 34 different weekly *sūq*s have been identified in the Shiadma, Haha, and northern Ida Ū Tanān in precolonial times (see table 13).

As a study of recent *sūq*s in northern Morocco has shown, Sunday in Essaouira's hinterland appeared to command the week.[11] Only Thursday had as many *sūq*s as Sunday, which was clearly a big market day in rural as well as in urban areas. Wednesday had only one *sūq*, perhaps because it preceded *sūq al-khamīs*. Friday also had a fair number, coming right

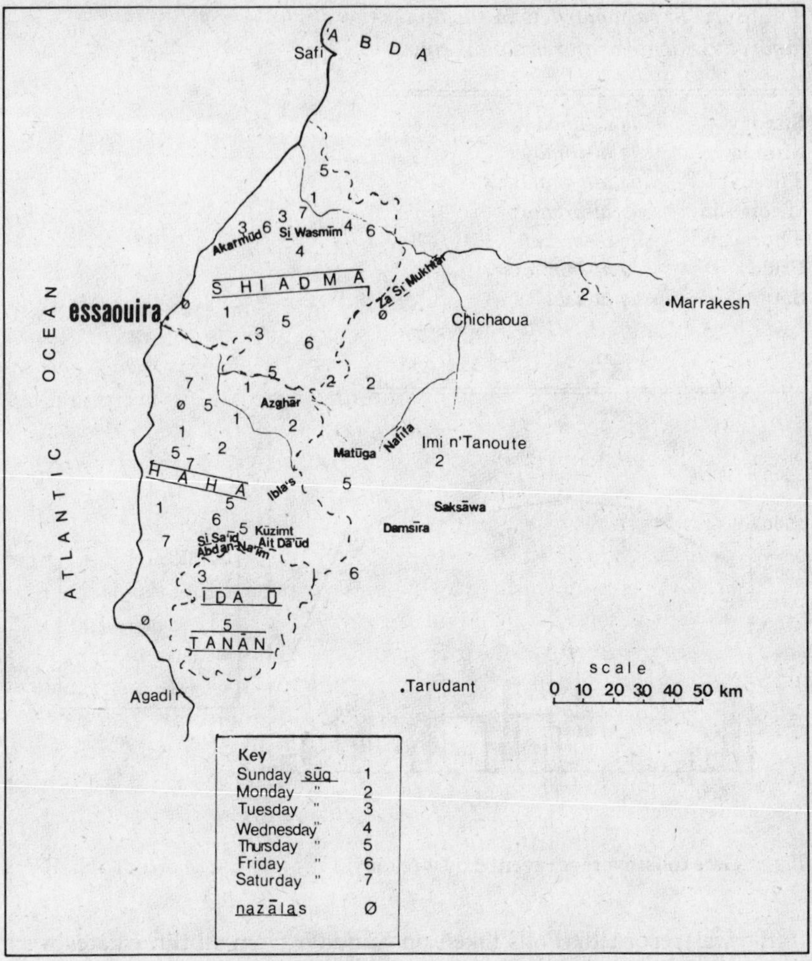

Map 4 Markets in the hinterland of Essaouira in precolonial times

before the Jewish sabbath. The Jewish pedlar who had not returned home to Essaouira after this *sūq* would have had to make camp until Sunday. Saturday was not a big day for markets possibly because Jewish pedlars predominated. And yet people in Essaouira considered Saturday a good day to travel,[12] and we do find a few 'Muslim' markets on that day.

It is possible to recapture some of the movement of the itinerant pedlars by studying the records of gate tolls for Essaouira (see fig. 7).[13] Traffic through all three gates of the city was fairly steady on each day of the week, except on Saturday, when only about 39 per cent of the average

Table 13 *Weekly markets in the hinterland of Essaouira in precolonial times*

Sunday	*sūq al-aḥad*	8
Monday	*sūq al-ithnayn*	5
Tuesday	*sūq ath-thạlātha'*	4
Wednesday	*sūq al-arbaʿā'*	1
Thursday	*sūq al-khamīs*	8
Friday	*sūq al-jumʿa*	5
Saturday	*sūq al-sabt*	3
	Total:	34

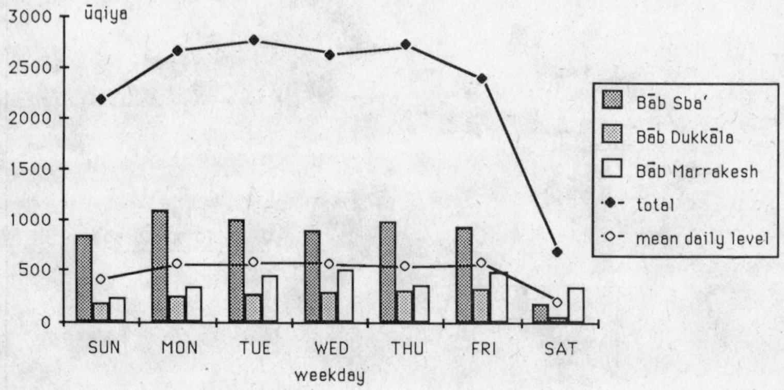

Fig. 7 Gate tolls: average revenue by weekday, 1301 /1883–4 (*source:* K.H., K[122]).

traffic was recorded. Tolls taken on Sundays from all three gates were lower than average (by about 16 per cent), probably because a less than normal number of Jewish pedlars would have returned to Essaouira with their goods so soon after leaving at the end of Shabbat. Yet already by Monday, Bāb Sbaʿ, the southern gate, had its most active day of the week. The large number of Sunday markets within a radius of 50 miles to the south and east of Essaouira would have permitted many of the pedlars to finish their business by late morning, and to reach the town by late afternoon on Monday. Traffic from Bāb Marrakesh, gateway to the capital, picked up after Sunday. Jewish itinerant traders leaving Marrakesh on Sunday morning would not have been able to reach Essaouira before Tuesday or Wednesday.[14] The Monday and Tuesday markets to the east of the town might perhaps explain the increase of traffic through

Bāb Marrakesh. On Thursday there was a drop in traffic, perhaps because many of the tribesmen would have stayed in Essaouira's *funduq*s the night before to be ready at an early hour for the big Thursday town market. On Friday, movement through Bāb Marrakesh increased, probably as a result of Jewish pedlars returning home for the sabbath. Others may have stayed at the big rural markets of Maskāla to the east, and Naknāfa slightly to the south. Traffic through Bāb Dukkāla, the northern gate, gradually increased throughout the week, reaching its peak on Friday. Jewish pedlars, coming from the north, would have returned home before the sabbath evenings. On Saturdays, practically no traffic passed through the northern gate which is contiguous to the *mellah*. Muslim traders, some of whom may have stopped in the Friday markets, would have preferred to use Bāb Marrakesh which entered into the *medina*. Similarly, traffic through Bāb Sbaʿ was greatly reduced. Much of the traffic through this gate must have been conveyed by the Jews, who brought goat skins, almonds, and other commodities from Haha to the town. It was near this gate that the predominantly Jewish goat skin market was held on every day of the week except the Jewish sabbath.

The Swiri pedlar had to plan his itinerary particularly carefully, since the distance to rural markets was considerable. The pedlar depended on mules, donkeys, and occasionally camels as modes of transport, and thought in terms of hours by foot to reach a destination.[15] For the mountainous terrain surrounding Essaouira, and certainly for parts of the Haha and Ida Ū Tanān, the mule or donkey was indispensable. The closest *sūq*s in Ida Ū Gurḍ or Ḥanshān probably lay at a distance of at least four hours by foot. Sūq al-Ithnayn at Ida Ū Issāran was a nine-hour journey from Essaouira.[16] But most *sūq*s were further than a one day's journey, which meant that the pedlar followed well-established routes. Marrakesh, as we have seen, was at least a three-day journey from Essaouira, which meant spending two or three nights out of the city. On the route to Sous, Imi n'Tanoute was considered to be 20 hours by foot. Government-created stations, called *nazāla*s, were provided to protect the itinerant traders and their goods and beasts.[17] Jews sometimes maintained semi-permanent shops at the rural *sūq*s, where perhaps they could sleep at night. While some Jewish pedlars returned to Essaouira in time for the Sabbath, some would stay away longer, living in semi-permanent Jewish communities. Furthermore, it was in the interest of the local *qāʾid*s and sheikhs to protect the itinerant traders on whom they relied for provisions.

We learn about the weekly peregrinations of the Jewish pedlars from the descriptions of the misfortunes of two brothers from Essaouira. The story of the newly-wed Salām b. Yiṣḥaq Abīḥaṣīra, and his brother Makhlūf, described by Yaʿīsh Halewī in 1891, illustrates an itinerary: On Monday, the two brothers were at Sūq al-Ithnayn of Imi n'Tlit to buy merchandise to sell on their route. That evening they went to a place called Aït Dāʾūd where they slept. The next day, the two brothers went to a place called Iblaʿs, and then circulated for three days in the district to buy products of the country. On Friday, they were due to arrive at *sūq al-jumʿa* of Aït Dāʾūd (another place with the same name in the Ida Ū Būziya). When they did not show up by evening, some of the Jews at the *sūq* went to the local *qaʾid* to see if they were there, but they failed to appear. The next day, reports circulated that the two brothers had been murdered. This was confirmed shortly thereafter. The Jews had to wait for Saturday evening (Mōṣaʾei Shabbāṭ) to send a messenger to Essaouira, because the Friday market of Aït Dāʾūd (today a Saturday market), was too far from town to allow him to reach home in time for the beginning of sabbath on Friday evening.[18]

The Muslim pedlar also had to plan in terms of the religious week. Markets were almost always held in close proximity to *zāwiya*s and other shrines for marabouts.[19] Among the two most 'popular' sanctuaries in the region were Sīdī Wasmīm in the Shiadma and Sīdī Saʿīd ʿAbd an-Naʿīm of the Ida Ū Būziya. Important Friday markets were held next to the shrines, permitting commerce in the morning before Friday afternoon prayers. The peaceful conduct of commercial affairs was guaranteed in the aura of the holy men.[20]

Safe passage

Overland trade in Morocco depended on a social network which allowed pedlars and transporters to circulate unmolested in the countryside. One source of protection was the Sultan himself. As part of the contractual relationship between Sultan and royal merchants, the sovereign was required to protect the goods of the *tujjār as-Sulṭān* along the trade routes. If the *tājir* was a Jew, the Sultan had the additional obligation of protecting his protégés (*dhimmī*s), for it was the duty of the Islamic state to safeguard the livelihood of the Jews as a legally inferior but protected community. In 1846, for example, a *qāʾid* instructs Ḥusayn Ū Ḥāshim, the marabout of Iligh, that a Jewish *tājir* of the Sultan, Sāhūl, has been sent to recover his debts owed by Jews and Muslims of Iligh and Ifrane. The Sultan has written to the *qāʾid* to assist the Jew, and the *qāʾid* asks the *sharīf* to help because 'his money has now become the money of the Sultan (may he be victorious)'. As the *qāʾid* explains, 'the Jew is one of the merchants of the Sultan, *and must be protected*, both out of respect for the sacrosanctity of the Sultan and for the sacrosanctity of the protégés [*ahl adh-dhimma*], since the Prophet (God bless him and grant him salvation) granted their protection'.[21]

While the Sultan could maintain a degree of legitimacy in regions outside his direct control,[22] in areas more closely controlled by the central government protected stations called *nazālas*[23] were provided. These stations sheltered the itinerant traders at night for a small fee, which was levied on beasts, loads of merchandise, and Jews. Between Essaouira, Marrakesh, and Safi *nazālas* were found at each stopover.[24] Some travellers regarded these stations as obstacles, because of the fees. Furthermore, it was not unknown for lodgers to be attacked.[25] But such incidents were rare, for it was in the interests of the *makhzan* to protect the trade routes leading to and from Essaouira.

For travel in southwestern Morocco, the trader needed local protection to assure safe passage, because the *makhzan* could not assure the security of most trade routes. Traders, therefore, were compelled to pay tribute to the tribesmen who ruled the regions that they crossed. A kind of passage toll called *zaṭṭāṭa*[26] – literally 'a small piece of cloth' in Berber, but in fact it could be the haik of a chief – was symbolically exchanged between client, often the sheikh or *amīn* of the caravan, and those guaranteeing safe passage (*zaṭṭāṭ*). In dissident areas, *zaṭṭāṭ* was indispensable: such was the case in the mountainous Ida Ū Tanān, where the *makhzan* was rarely able to collect taxes and install governors. During a time of unrest at the end of 1875, the Sultan acknowledged in a letter to the *qāʾid* of Essaouira, 'that you cannot pass through their tribes except with *zaṭṭāṭ*'.[27]

It was also in the interests of the tribesmen to guarantee the passage of traders. A network of patron-client relations – and such terminology is not absent from nineteenth-century sources – allowed the itinerant trader to pass unmolested over long distances. Of the Jews of the Atlas, the English doctor–traveller, Davidson, wrote in the 1830s: 'their case is one of patron and client, and all enjoy equal privileges, and the Berber is bound to take up the cause of the Jew upon all emergencies'.[28] A relationship, generally between Muslim and Jews, was established by *dhabīḥa*, a ritual slaughter of a sheep or bull by the Jew before a Berber or Arab patron (the *sīd*).[29] In practice a more exorbitant exaction may have been involved, particularly if Jews were the clients seeking passage. The sacrifice formed a bond called *mezrag* (lit. 'spear' in Berber),[30] or alternatively *al-ʿār* (lit. 'shame' in Arabic).[31] Henceforth, the client was under the protection of his patron, or for that matter, the whole tribe. Annual payments in linen or sugar would be made subsequently to the chief. These pacts were inherited jointly by the offspring of both patron and client, and were maintained rigorously. The relationship facilitated travel and commerce since the Jew was protected by his patron: an attack against the Jew was regarded as a violation against the chief or tribe assuring the protection, and violent retribution was legitimized.[32]

The most powerful patrons of all were the marabouts of the southern *zāwiya*s whose fortunes were derived from their control of the trade routes. They, like the Sultan, sought to protect the merchants who formed the basis of their political and economic power. Sheikh Abū Bakr of the Nāṣiriyya *zāwiya* of Tamgrout in the Draʿ protected caravans and Swiri merchants involved in the trans-Saharan trade.[33] His protection was given not only in the immediate surroundings of the *zāwiya*, but also throughout a vast region. The inviolability of traders was assured during the time of the pilgrimage-fairs, even during periods of considerable rural unrest. Itinerant merchants travelling to the *mawsim* of Sī Ḥmād Ū Mūsā in the Tazarwalt were assured protection all along their routes by the powerful marabout, Sīdī Ḥusayn Ū Hāshim of Iligh. When brigandage was rife, the marabout would assure repayment to the pillaged trader. Ḥusayn would seize goods at the *mawsim* belonging to the people from the territory where the robbery had taken place. This would pay for the robbery and enable the marabout to appropriate surplus goods for himself. All parties, therefore, had an interest in maintaining security during times of the *mawsim*. As the French consul of Essaouira reports in 1879, 'the numerous examples of this expeditious, and above all, lucrative justice for he who delivers it, has finally stopped the brigandage during this new truce of God'.[34]

It was through these various forms of protection that individual traders and caravans were able to traverse vast regions in relative security. Traders sought the protection of different patrons simultaneously in order to maximize their mobility. The guarantors of protection profited from traders passing through their territory. It was the thread of these relationships that facilitated travel over hundreds of miles.

Caravans

Overland travel was cumbersome. The only means of transport was by pack-animals – camels, mules, and donkey – since wheeled vehicles and roads were totally absent in Morocco.[35] Even in Essaouira itself, which became Morocco's principal steamboat port, wheeled carts were not introduced.[36]

It was by the slow overland caravan that items for exports reached the port, or that European goods, imported in Essaouira, were distributed throughout southern Morocco and parts of the Western Sudan. The size of a caravan could vary greatly: from two or three persons with their donkeys to several thousand people and camels. The caravan was called '*qafīla*', although the large annual caravan to Timbuktu was also known as the '*akbar*' (lit. 'the largest').[37]

The trip from Essaouira to Timbuktu could take 60 to 70 days,[38] but in practice the length of the journey depended on the route taken, the kinds of camels employed, the size and nature of the caravan, and the kinds of trading activity undertaken *en route*. The trip from Goulimime, one of the major points from where the caravans departed across the desert, took between 30 and 57 days, though it could take even longer if the route passed through Akka or Tindouf.[39] Mordekhai Abīṣrūr, a Jewish merchant from Akka, who was responsible for settling a small colony of Jews in Timbuktu, estimated that the caravans from Akka to Timbuktu took between 65 and 80 days.[40] The length of time also varied because the point at which the different arms of the caravan came together moved at different historical junctures. The traditional departure points of Tatta and Akka[41] shifted to Tindouf in the latter half of the nineteenth century.

In the latter half of the nineteenth century, it was generally estimated that, in the largest caravans, up to 10,000 camels headed southward from the desert town of Tindouf (approximately 17 days from Essaouira).[42] Only about 20 per cent were laden with goods since at the half-way point, Tawdenni, the rest of the camels were loaded with salt – an extremely lucrative item of exchange at Timbuktu. A significant proportion of the camels, perhaps 20 per cent, were sold at Timbuktu because the loads were lighter on the return journey. The load of a camel on the journey northward was about 150 kilograms, which was much lighter than the camel's full capacity.[43] It can be supposed that the onerous trans-Saharan journey was taken into account as well as the relay of exchange: goods were bought and sold at different stages of the route.[44] Most caravans stopped at Tindouf on their return journey, and it was there that many of the slaves were sold. Some of the less valuable goods, such as giraffe skins and camel and goat hair, were also sold in Tindouf to avoid paying the cost of long transport. Goods were passed from the large caravan to smaller ones. In addition to the large annual trans-Saharan caravan, there were a number of smaller caravans that crossed the desert, departing from a number of locations.[45] These caravans usually consisted of 100 to 200 camels, carrying various imported goods and local products (see table 14).[46]

There was also a continuous flow of traffic between Essaouira and the cities of the interior, particularly Marrakesh. Essaouira served as an entrepôt for European imports and Moroccan exports. The routes

Table 14 *Inventory of a caravan from Timbuktu, 1887*

Camel loads	Items	Kgs.	Price	Total value
40	ostrich feathers	6,000	f75	f450,000
85	ivory	12,750	8	102,000
120	giraffe skins	*180	75	13,500
30	incense	4,500	5	22,500
20	white and blue fabrics	3,000	6	18,000
35	camel and goat hair	5,250	1.5	7,875
225	gum arabic	33,750	2	67,500
45	wax	6,750	2	13,500

*600 total loads Subtotal: 694,875

added items: 520 slaves, averaging 200 Fr. francs each: 104,000
8,750 mithqāl gold powder, at
13.5 Fr. francs each: 118,125
Total value: f917,000

*error in original document

Source: A.E., C.C.C., Mogador 7, 17 March 1887, Lacoste. Lacoste's information is the same obtained by the *Times of Morocco*, 11 August 1887, and Zerbib, 'Slave Caravans', pp. 98–9.

through southern Shiadma were often filled with caravans of various sizes. Jewish pedlars travelling to Marrakesh would usually accompany these caravans as a means of security. Surplus money acquired from customs and excise was periodically sent from Essaouira to Marrakesh in armed convoys. A description of one such convoy in 1871 is typical: a total of 70,200 mithqāl were sent in six boxes, each box containing 18 sacks, each sack filled with 650 mithqāl. The convoy was accompanied by a company commander (*qāʾid al-miʾa*), eight horsemen and five footmen.[47] It appears that the camels used for transporting money did not belong to the *makhzan* but instead were put up for hire by their merchant owners. Properly trained camels were seldom found in the town or in the surrounding markets. The authorities were therefore sometimes obliged to wait for the arrival of the caravans. On one such occasion, 21 camels were appropriated from a caravan to send money to the Palace. Jewish merchants claimed that some of the camels belonged to them.[48]

Specie was not the only item sent to the Palace in convoys. *Makhzan* registers of expenditure list the regular hire of camels for sending a variety of imports. In 1860, 21 and a half camels were hired – one half of one camel's load was presumably used by the owner himself – at 65 ūqiya each for sending wood to Khalīfa al-Ḥasan.[49] In 1860, a number of large convoys of iron were sent to Marrakesh. In one instance, 1,671 bars of iron were sent on 75 camels to be followed three days later by another load carried by a further 37 camels. Hiring the first 75 camels cost 3,939 ūqiya (or 52.5 ūqiya each), saddling costs another 313 ūqiya, and the accompanying soldier (*mukhaznī*) was paid 30 ūqiya.[50] A variety of goods, such as cotton fabrics, clothing, barley, and hardware, were sent on official convoys, employing camels, mules, donkeys, and occasionally horses. Prisoners, too, were transported under heavy guard. Members of the royal family were accompanied by sizeable cavalry units. It was unthinkable for the armed government convoys to be attacked on the well-trodden route between Marrakesh and Essaouira.[51]

Fairs and festivals

The merchants of Essaouira had to organize their business activities around several coinciding cycles of events. The synchronizing of the caravans to Muslim and Jewish festivals and agricultural seasons was crucial for meeting the requirements of supply and demand.

The system of festivals is complicated because three different calendars – Muslim, Jewish, and Julian – are followed simultaneously. While Muslim 'orthodox' festivals rotate around the Islamic non-adjusting lunar calendar, taking about 34 years to return to the same Gregorian month, 'popular' religious festivals are celebrated according to the solar calendar, pointing to their pre-Islamic agrarian origins.[52] Jewish 'orthodox' festivals, on the other hand, fall in the same season each year since the Hebrew solar/lunar calendar is self-adjusting – every two to three years a month is added (Adar II). Jewish festivals can be associated with the agrarian seasons, and some, such as Succoth (Tabernacles) and Shavuoth (Pentecost), maintain specifically agricultural rites. In Morocco, both Muslim and Jewish 'orthodox' festivals are also supplemented by local religious celebrations. The Muslims call this type of festival '*mawsim*' (pl. *mawāsim*, French *moussem*) in Arabic, and in Tashelḥit, *amūggar*.[53] Literally, the word *mawsim* means 'the time of the year' or 'season', and in Morocco it is also used in the sense of harvest. Such a festival usually falls at about the same time each year. In fact, the Julian months are used in the vernacular nomenclature. In rural Morocco the Julian year is marked by a variety of rites – among them *mawsim*s – as both Westermarck and Jacques Berque describe at length.[54] The popular Jewish festivals, the *hillūla*s, are based on the veneration of a Jewish saint (*ṣaddīq*), usually of either fictional or real Palestinian origin.[55] Likewise, *mawsim*s are centred on pilgrimages to the tombs of venerated persons, the marabouts. Furthermore, Muslim and Jews shared many common saints and pilgrimage sites.[56]

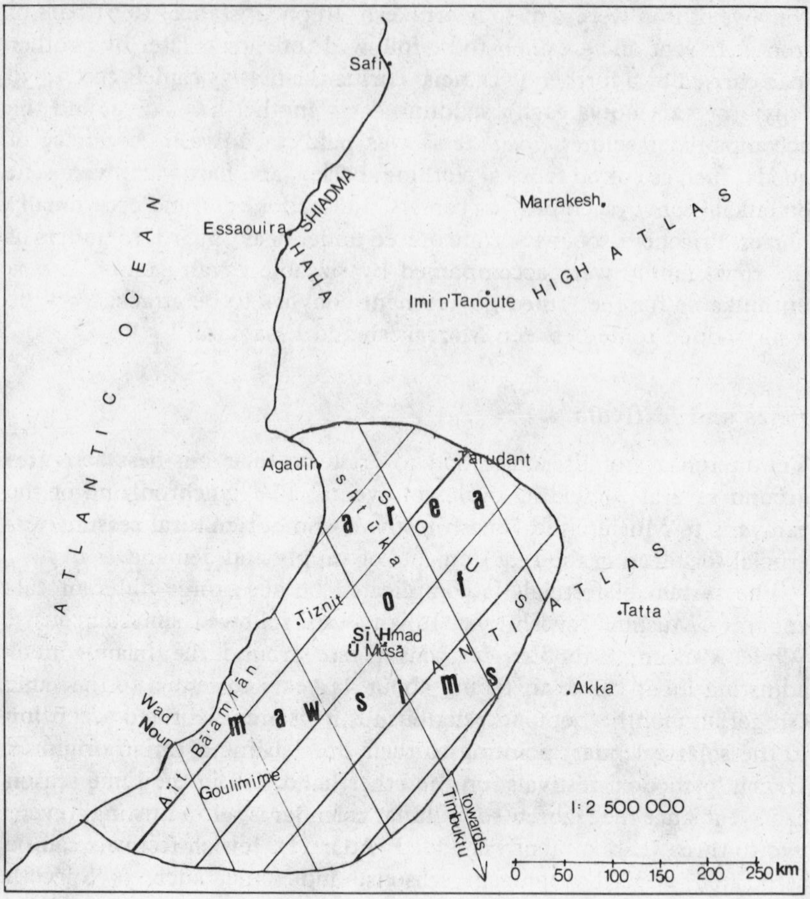

Map 5 Region of the principal *mawsims* of southwestern Morocco

The convergence of Muslim and Jewish festivals affected economic life, and the ebb and flow of commerce. While the major orthodox Muslims festivals, such as the ʿĀshūrāʾ, Ramaḍan, ʿĪd al-Fitr (ʿĪd as-Saghīr), and ʿĪd al-Aḍḥā (ʿĪd al-Kabīr) – the same festivals found throughout the Islamic world – affected commerce on a short-term basis, since they are not of agrarian origin, the major *mawsims* in southwestern Morocco, falling between March and October, combined pilgrimage with market, transforming the site of the shrine into a fair (see map 5). The *mawsims* were scheduled by the Julian calendar, corresponding to different harvests and times of commercial exchange. They also coincided with some of the most important Jewish festivals (see table 15).

Table 15 *Jewish festivals between March and October*

Festival	Hebrew date	Range in Gregorian calendar
Rosh Hashanah	1 Tishrī	beginning of September to beginning of October
Yom Kippur	10 Tishrī	mid-September to mid-October
Succoth	15 Tishrī	five days later
Passover	15 Nīssan	end of March to end of April
Lag Ba'omer	18 Iyyar	end of April to end of May
Shavuoth	9 Sīwan	mid-May to mid-June
Ninth of Ab	9 Ab	mid-July to mid-August

In addition to the orthodox Jewish festivals, which fell at about the same time as the *mawsim*s, a few popular festivals also took place when the season of Muslim festivals began. Some of the *hillūla*s commemorated the anniversary, reckoned by the Hebrew calendar, of the death of a *ṣaddīq*, but often they followed Passover or fell on the day of Lag Ba'omer, particularly if the date when the *ṣaddīq* died was unknown. Another specifically Moroccan Jewish holiday, the Mīmūna, began on the evening that Passover ended.[57] The Passover season, therefore, was a time of festivals and fairs. After the Passover celebration, Jewish pilgrims began to visit *ṣaddīq*s in the countryside. For the Muslims, this was the time of the Ragrāga *mawsim* in the Shiadma, where for 40 days pilgrims travelled from sanctuary to sanctuary to visit the numerous marabouts in the region. Perhaps pilgrimage and trade were combined.[58]

In southwestern Morocco, commercial exchange was interwoven with religious celebrations. The merchant's schedule was arranged from one festival to the next. Both Jews and Muslims structured their commercial time around the requirements of these celebrations. Take, for example, the case of Mordekhai Rbībō of the *mellah* of Ifrane, who received from Ḥusayn Ū Hāshim, the *sharīf* of Iligh, the sum of 1,257 riyāl as credit on 5 February 1875 so that he could buy ostrich feathers. The *sharīf*'s account book certifies that 'repayment of what he owes has been deferred until the coming *mawsim* of March [*mārs*], God willing'. The cycle continues the following year. On 6 November 1876, Rbībō receives credit to purchase feathers which was to be repaid at the March *mawsim*.[59]

The *shurafā*' of Iligh in Tazarwalt, the heirs of the marabout Sī Ḥmād Ū Mūsā, capitalized on the arrival of large numbers of pilgrims at the shrine of the saint in the mid-nineteenth century by turning the *mawsim* into the most important bi-annual emporium of southern Morocco.

Twice a year, at the end of March and at the end of August or beginning of September, caravans from all over southern Morocco, the Sahara and Timbuktu converged on the village where the shrine of the marabout was located.[60] Jewish traders were especially active at these *mawsims*. Though Jews were not allowed to reside in, or enter, the village of the shrine, they were consigned to an encampment on the outskirts of the village during the time of *mawsim*.[61] Itinerant traders organized their routes so that they could be present at the successive fairs held in southwestern Morocco.[62] The first large *mawsim* of Sī Ḥmād Ū Mūsā generally preceded Passover, followed by a whole series of spring *mawsims* in the Shtūka and Aït Bāʿamrān.[63] After the *mawsim* of Issig and Asrir in the Aït Bāʿamrān in April, caravans would leave Wad Noun for Timbuktu. Then, having returned to Wad Noun, caravans would head up the coast, reaching Essaouira by late spring. In June and July, the *mawsims* of Qaṣabī and Sīdī Ighāzī took place in Wad Noun. The year that the British traveller Davidson was in Goulimime, the annual *mawsim* held on Mawlid an-Nabī (*sūq al-mawlid*), the anniversary of the Prophet, took place in July, and shortly afterwards the caravans set out for Essaouira.[64] The most important *mawsim* of the year in southwestern Morocco was the giant fair of Sī Ḥmād Ū Mūsā, held at the end of August or beginning of September, just before the Jewish New Year. After the great *mawsim* of Sī Ḥmād Ū Mūsā in late August or early September, there was still the important *mawsim* of Issig in the Aït Bāʿamrān, located on the other major axis of the western trans-Saharan caravan route. There were also various other *mawsims* in the Shtūka, and finally a minor *mawsim* in the middle of October at Sī Ḥmād Ū Mūsā.[65] At the end of the *mawsim* season, with the stocks of Swiri merchants full, large quantities of goods were exported (see fig. 8).

It was in the autumn, after the festivals and fairs, that traders in Marrakesh, Tazarwalt, Wad Noun, and other points in the south prepared for the great caravan to Timbuktu. Jewish traders headed south after Succoth with European goods to give on credit in exchange for the goods which would return a few months later with the northward-bound caravans. The Jewish pedlar or itinerant trader of Essaouira, often absent for most of the year, would return home to his family to celebrate Rosh Hashanah and Yom Kippur, and then leave just after Succoth, only returning for Passover in the spring.[66] In Essaouira, therefore, it was often between the end of August and the end of October, or between the end of February and April that trading activity reached its height. The Jewish pedlar would return from the *mawsims* laden with items from the trans-Saharan caravans.

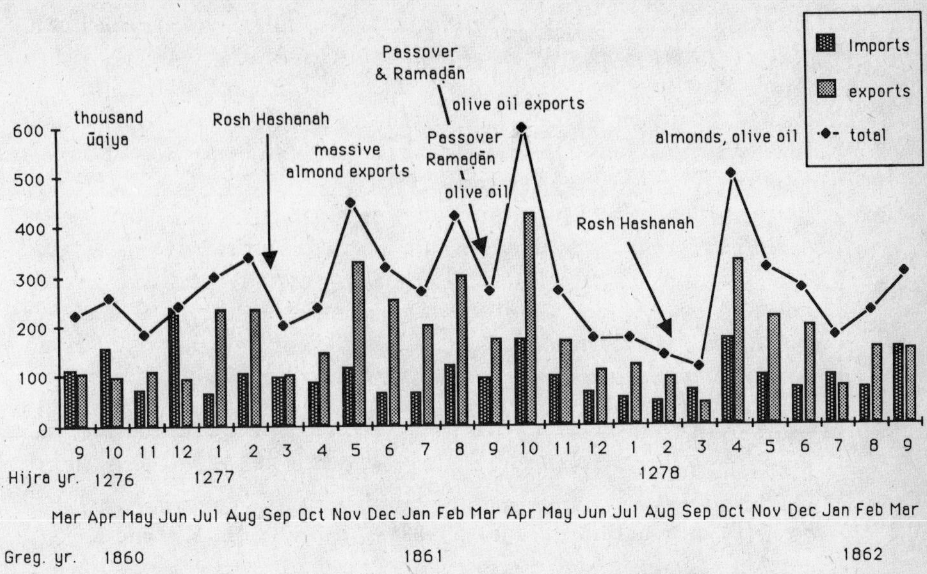

Fig. 8 Import and export duties collected in 1860–2 (*source:* K.H., K[42]).

The flow of goods into the town was also affected by the Muslim calendar. In 1884 and 1885, for example, there was a sharp upsurge in commercial activity in the *qāʿa* in the month of Ramaḍān (see fig. 9). Jews, who were the main retailers in the *qāʿa*, would certainly have profited during this period. In modern times, an intense activity in the trade of legumes, eggs, oil, spices, and dried fruit has been noted.[67] These were all ingredients which either went into the soup (*ḥarīra*) to break the fast, or were consumed with it. Most, if not all, of these items were sold in the *qāʿa* of Essaouira in the nineteenth century. Traders probably sold produce at high prices during Ramaḍān, making a greater profit on the domestic rather than the foreign market. During Ramaḍān from 1277–9 (1860–2), there were almost no exports from the port of Essaouira (see fig. 8).

In terms of the overall commercial flow into the town, Jewish festivals may have had a greater impact, because of the high proportion of Jewish pedlars who returned home for the celebrations. During the days leading up to Rosh Hashanah and the following festivals of Yom Kippur and Succoth, commercial activity in Essaouira could reach a frenzy. In 1884, the week of Yom Kippur and Succoth converged with the biggest Muslim celebration of the year, ʿĪd al-Aḍḥā, which fell on 10 Dhū al-Ḥijja. This undoubtedly gave a great boost to commerce in a season

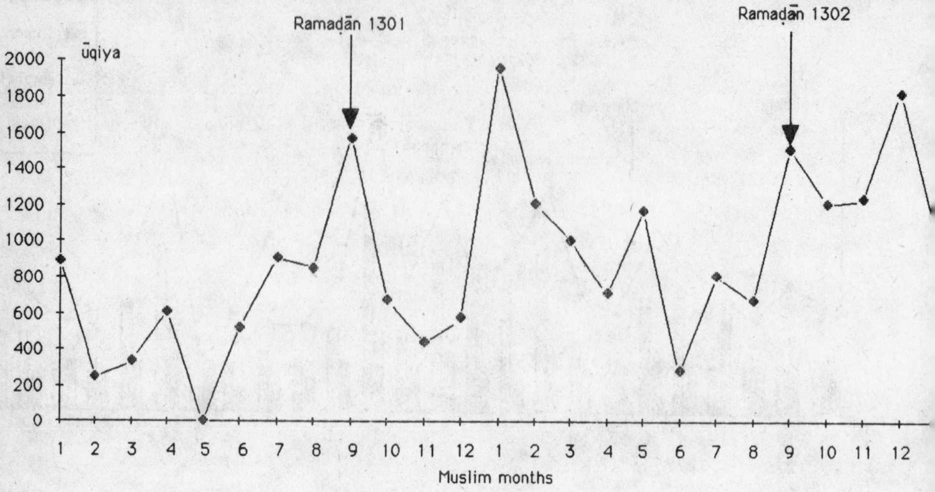

Fig. 9 Taxes from the *qāʿa*, 1301–2 / 1883–5 (*source:* K.H., K[122] and K[131]).

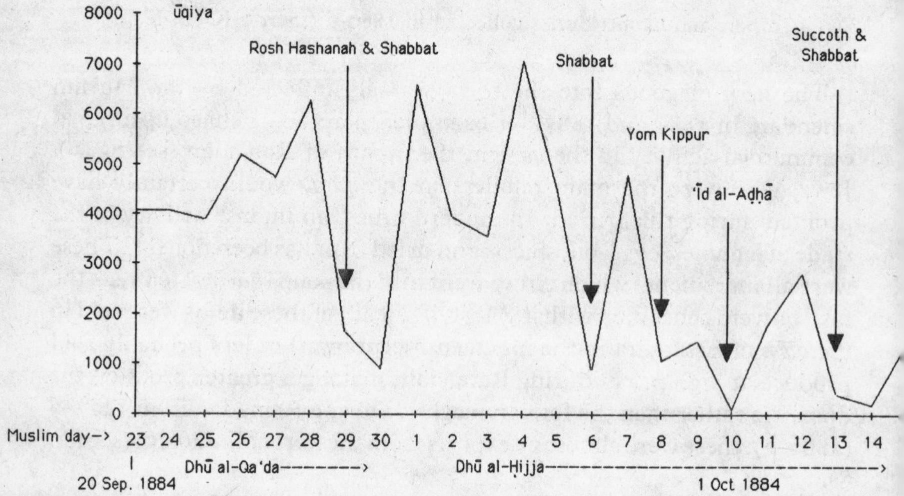

Fig. 10 Gate and market taxes during the Jewish New Year, 5645 / 1301 / 1884 (*source:* K.H., K[122]).

which was normally active anyway (see fig. 10). As Rosh Hashanah approached, traffic through the town gates and in the markets of the bazaar was the busiest of the year. Clearly Muslims were also busy providing Jews with needed commodities. Even on the New Year, which was also a Shabbat that year, when no Jew would have been found in the bazaar or on the road, some commercial activity took place. Trading during the ten days leading up to Yom Kippur, followed two days later by ʿĪd al-Aḍḥā, fluctuated dramatically. On the second day of the new year, still celebrated by the Jews, little activity appears in Essaouira's markets, but the following day there is a sudden upsurge. During the next ten days, the market is jolted by dramatic fluctuations, depending on the Shabbat and the approach of the festivals. Then, on Īd al-Aḍḥā, commercial activity comes to almost a total standstill. Not only would Muslims not work on that day, but few Jews would venture out into the bazaar area when Muslims held celebrations. Finally, after Succoth, which comes three days later, fluctuations become much more regular.

The convergence of the spring *mawsim*, the return of the caravans, and the Passover season all affected the flow of goods in the spring through the town gates, into the markets, and to the port. The Passover celebration, which lasted for a week, must annually have deprived the *makhzan* of considerable revenue. In the month that Passover fell in 1863, 1884, and 1885, the flow through the town gates dropped considerably (see figs. 11–13). The lull in exports in 1861 (see fig. 8) may be accounted for in part by Ramaḍān – the month in which Passover fell – but both imports and exports slowed down, which probably also reflected the celebration of the Jewish festival. In each case, the *makhzan* was compensated in both the month preceding and the month following the Passover celebration, when revenues taken from the town gates and markets were considerable. In 1302 (1305), revenues soared to their highest of the year (see fig. 13)[68].

Seasons and harvests

Festivals had their greatest impact on commerce only when they corresponded to the agrarian cycle. Almonds, one of the most important export commodities, were picked for much of the summer in the region around Marrakesh, the Haha, and most importantly, the Sous.[69] Probably large quantities were sold at the *mawsims* of the Sous. In August, the almonds began reaching Essaouira, and in the autumn, large quantities were exported (see fig. 14). Summer was also the season when the fruit of the argan tree ripened. The oil and flour extracted from the nut of this uniquely southwestern Moroccan tree constituted one of the chief elements in the diet, though it was not an export item. Argan served as fodder for the goats of the Haha and the Sous, and during the season when the argan was ripe, goats were found climbing the trees in the hilly regions surrounding Essaouira.[70] Argan was one of the main items sold in the *qāʿa*, and the surge in the tithe taken by the *makhzan* from this market in the autumn of 1884 and 1885 is probably an indicator of the arrival of the oil into town (see fig. 9). Certain kinds of gums exported from Essaouira were harvested in the summer. The sap of a brown gum ʿ*Ilk aṭ-*

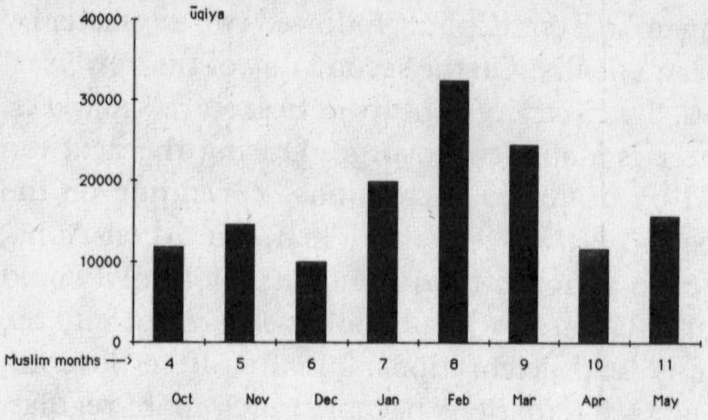

Fig. 11 Gate taxes, 1279/1862–3 (*source:* K.H., K[46]).

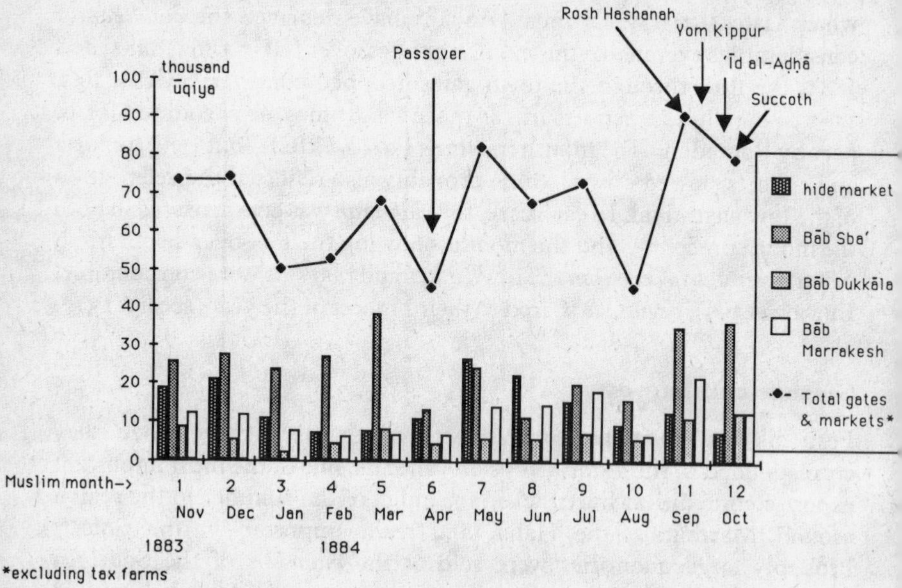

Fig. 12 Gate and market taxes, 1301/1883–4 (*source:* K.H., K[122]).

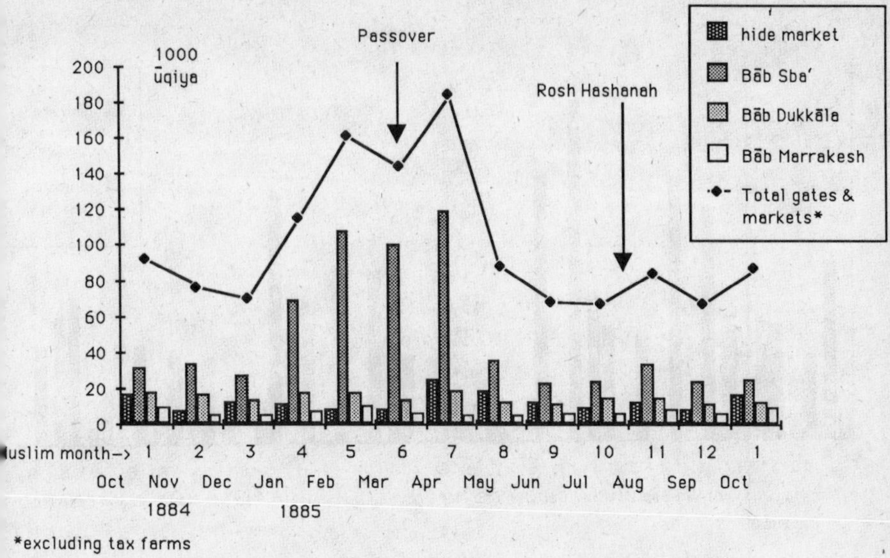

Fig. 13 Gate and market taxes, 1302/1884–5 (*source:* K.H., K[131]).

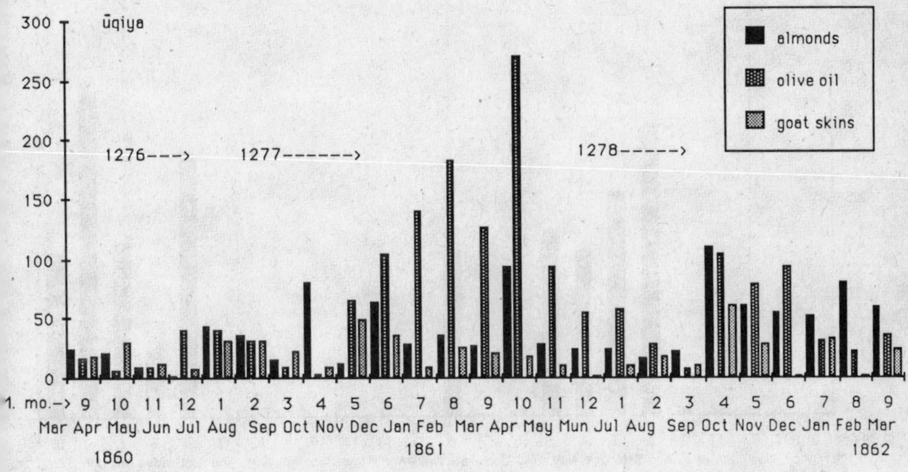

Fig. 14 Export duties collected on almonds, olive oil, and goat skins in 1860–2 (*source:* K.H., K[42]).

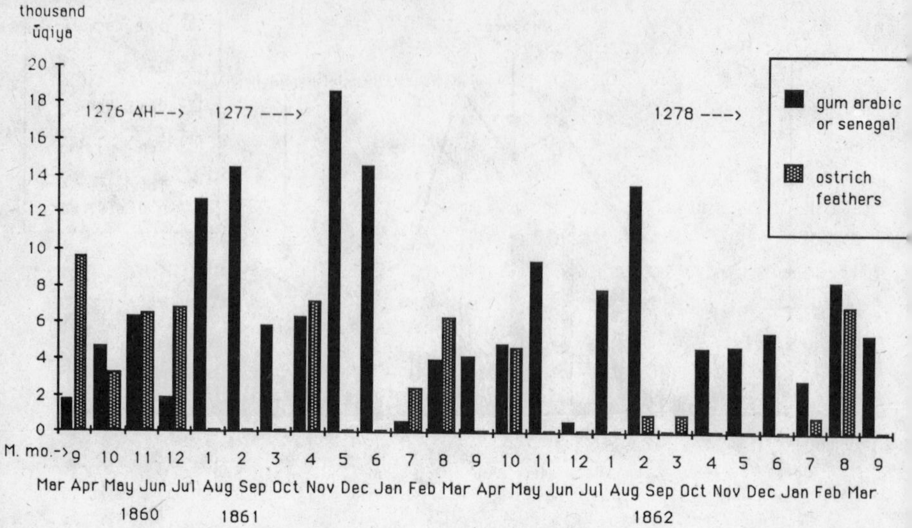

Fig. 15 Export duties collected on gum arabic, gum senegal, and ostrich feathers in 1860–2 (*source:* K.H., K[42]).

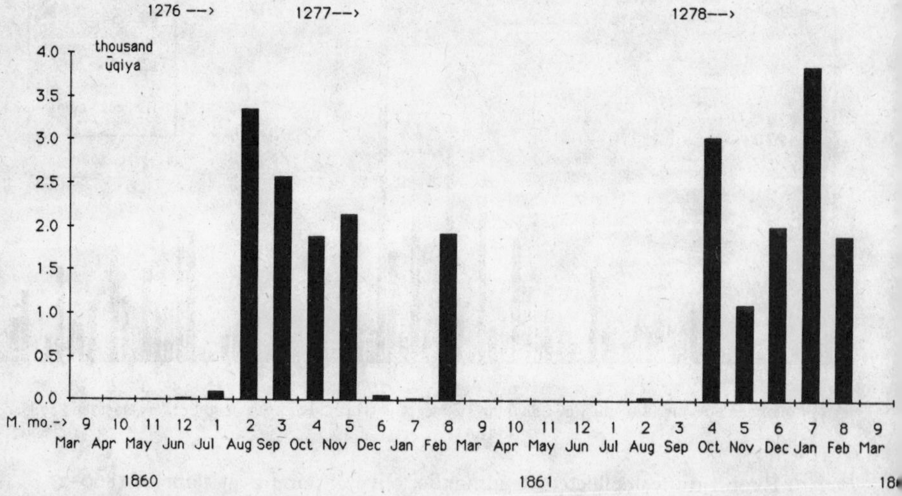

Fig. 16 Duties collected on fanegas of legumes exported (millet, chickpeas, beans) in 1860–2 (*source:* K.H., K[42]).

ṭalḥ, a variety of *acacia gummifera* (called 'gum arabic', 'gum morocco', or 'gum barbary'), was collected in the summer. Gum sandarac (colloquial, *al-grāsa*), extracted from the thuya tree, and gum ephorbium (*furbiyūn*) were also sapped in the summer. All these gums reached Essaouira in large quantities at the end of summer. Gum 'senegal', transported by caravan from West Africa, also reached Essaouira in August.[71] In the late summer and early autumn of 1860 and 1861, large quantities of gum were exported from the port (see fig. 15).

Autumn was generally a busy period for exports in the port of Essaouira. It was the period when the late grain crops, such as maize and millet, sold extensively in the market. Millet was exported in some quantity during the autumn of 1860–1 (see fig. 16). Not only did itinerant traders leave town in autumn, but also seasonal labourers as well, and consequently, with some of Essaouira's inhabitants in the interior for cultivation during the rainy season, labour became expensive in town. By December, business slowed down with few export commodities reaching the market. Calm generally reigned in the countryside, as Essaouira entered its colder and rainier months. With peasants engaged in cultivation, rural unrest and disturbances were infrequent.[72] During the winter months, the peasants devoted their energies to picking olives and ploughing the soil as the *amīn* of *makhzan* properties of Adra in Shiadma informs the Sultan in a letter dated the end of November 1885.[73] Most of the olive oil was conveyed from the Sous, and in the 1860s it was probably the most important export item. In the latter part of December, the freshly pressed olive oil would begin to reach the port.[74] In years when the export of olive oil was brisk, numerous loads of the product would have entered Bāb Sbaʿ, and this was probably the reason why revenues from the gate tolls reached a peak in January–February of 1863 (Shaʿbān 1279) (see fig. 11). The merchants might wait for a propitious moment to export the oil, but probably they did not wait very long, as is shown in 1861, when olive oil exports soared to new heights between January and April, reaching their highest level in April (see fig. 14).

The return of the trans-Saharan caravans brought new commercial activity to the port of Essaouira. While it is clear that the big annual caravans set out for Timbuktu in September or October, their return could vary from year to year. Occasionally a trans-Saharan caravan might reach the town gates as early as December, but usually they arrived between February and April.[75] The jumps in the level of tax levied at the southern gate, Bāb Sbaʿ, in 1884 and 1885, may indicate the arrival of caravans (see figs. 12 and 13). These caravans were able to convey, among other things, some of the commodities collected in the winter. December was the season when the harvest of 'senegal' gum took place, which was exported by caravan to Essaouira.[76] Both gums and ostrich feathers were sometimes exported in large quantities in the winter or early spring (see fig. 15), either with the return of the trans-Saharan caravans or before or after the first March *mawsim* of Sī Ḥmād Ū Mūsā.

Springtime, as we have seen, corresponded to the Passover season and the first of the trading *mawsims*. In rural markets, it has been observed that large numbers of animals are purchased in the rural markets in the early spring since this is the best time of the year for pasturage.[77] In spring or early summer, after the animals had been fattened, Essaouira's livestock market could be quite active. It was also the time when the largest number of goat skins were sold in the hide market (see figs. 12, 13). In the dry summer months, shepherds would want to get rid of their animals,[78] with the result that the price of goat skins dropped in Essaouira during those months.[79]

The summer months were generally quite prosperous ones for the people of Essaouira. Imports of European textiles, tea, and sugar were usually high at that time of the year.[80] May and June were the months when wheat and barley were harvested, and grain prices dropped in the market.[81] Legumes also reached the market at this time, and in some years, such as in 1860, large shipments were exported in summer or autumn (see fig. 16). Fish as well were abundant during the summer months, providing not only employment for the fishermen, but also cheaper food for the inhabitants of Essaouira.[82]

Camel versus steamboat

Until the 1860s, Essaouira's commercial activities were limited by the uncertainties of sailing ships. Shipwrecks were frequent along the southern Moroccan coast, and ships at anchor in Essaouira's harbour would frequently go ashore in a gale. Exports in general vastly outstripped imports, and though there was no lack of proposals for flooding the Moroccan market with European manufactured goods, it was only with the coming of steam transport in the 1850s and its growth in the 1860s that European imports grew extensively.[83] French and British steamship companies rapidly monopolized the transport of most of Essaouira's cargo, and sailing ships began to disappear. Consul Huet reported in 1864, that 'Steam navigation, since several regular services have been established on the Moroccan coasts, has delivered a fatal blow to sailing in these passages.'[84]

Steamboats brought about a regularization of shipping, since short of serious storm, safe winter passage was assured. Passenger traffic was also changed by the new steamship companies. Pilgrims making the hajj could rely on a much more reliable mode of travel to Alexandria by steamboat. If the overland route departing east from Fez had been severely disrupted by the French conquest of Algeria,[85] it was steam transport which made it a thing of the past.

Yet this regularization of shipping, though reducing some of the seasonal fluctuations in the shipping trade of Essaouira, had only a minimal effect on the modes of operation of the major shippers. The Swiri merchants still needed to accommodate themselves to the annual agro-religious cycle specific to southwestern Morocco. In Europe, the decline of fairs has been seen as a consequence of the replacement of peripatetic commerce with more sedentary modes of operation,[86] and it has also been suggested that the development of the wholesale trade replaced the function of fairs.[87] In Morocco, the growth of the wholesale trade did not cause a decline in the big trading *mawsim*s. On the contrary, commerce with Europe gave them a boost.

Methods of transport in the overland trade remained the same. The large camel caravans continued to cross the desert. While the seas between Morocco and Europe were harnessed, the trans-Saharan routes were almost unaffected by innovation.[88] The itinerant trader remained at the mercy of meteorological and natural catastrophes. More importantly, trade continued to operate within the context of Moroccan culture. Archaic modes of transport and exchange persisted because they were an integral part of the social fabric.

Long distance trade

The persistence of the trans-Saharan caravan in the age of European commercial expansion on the coasts intrigued European observers. As early as the 1780s, Consul Louis Chénier in Rabat writes:

> It is astonishing that despite the market at Fort Louis, these Arabs prefer to cross an immense desert – a fifty day journey by foot – to come sell their gums at Mogador. One cannot understand why, considering the low price for which this product can be purchased on our settlements of Senegal. It must be that the difference of price that they find for gums at Mogador is considerable for these Arabs to cross an immense desert where they have to subdue all kinds of hardships and fatigues. Might it not be possible for the Senegal company to prevent the export of gums [overland] to Mogador?[89]

European trade did grow along the West African coast in the nineteenth century, yet the trans-Saharan trade did not decline.[90] For both Libya and Morocco, the statistics on exports from the seaports suggest growth.[91] Miège estimates that as much as 16 per cent of the exports from Essaouira were products from the Western Sudan, and that these goods combined with those from Wad Noun accounted for about one-third of the town's exports.[92] The most important products were gums and ostrich feathers. From the mid-nineteenth century, this trade began to increase, largely because of the growth in demand for ostrich feathers. Essaouira remained one of the northern termini of the trans-Saharan trade until the last two decades of the nineteenth century, when disturbances in the south, competition with foreign markets, the development of coastal routes, and finally, the conquest of Timbuktu by the French in 1894, put a final end to the trans-Saharan trade.[93]

Long distance trade was at the heart of urban life in Morocco and in North Africa generally.[94] The two largest cities of Morocco, Fez and Marrakesh, were both at the crossroads of major trade routes. Despite the growth of the coastal towns in the nineteenth century, the inland cities of Morocco remained more important as economic centres. Essaouira served as an intermediary, and was therefore linked to a vast network of overland exchange. Because of contact with Europe, Essaouira did affect the geopolitical networks of trade, encouraging the growth of certain trade routes and the rise to power of those in control of them. Yet these geographical modifications did not change the nature of social networks which assured the vitality of a trade that spanned a vast area.

The sheer distance of the overland route might in some ways define the essence of Essaouira's long distance trade – a trade comparable to other societies of Africa and the Middle East.[95] The greater the distance, the more complex were the commercial networks, and the more lucrative the goods exchanged. The more valuable commodities, such as gold, ostrich feathers, gums, and slaves required a great degree of specialization since they were transported over the greatest distances and changed hands at several stations. Yet it was not only the distance or the nature of the goods traded that defined Essaouira's long distance trade. As Claude Meillassoux argues, the central feature of long distance trade was that the commodities defined should not compete with local production.[96] This was certainly the case in Essaouira. But in some ways it is a mute point, since Essaouira's local production was minimal anyway, and therefore, competition was not really the issue.

The idea of a 'trading diaspora', a term coined by Abner Cohen, provides a useful frame of analysis. Cohen argues that long distance trade relied on the resolution of five different problems: information on supply and demand; transport (speed); trust and the regularization of credit; a system of arbitration; and the maintenance of an authority structure. These problems would be overcome 'when men from one ethnic group control all or most of the stages of trade in specific commodities'. This ethnic group would form a 'trading diaspora', which was generally associated with a 'universal' civilization or religion, such as Islam in West Africa.[97] Such a 'trading diaspora' would be an appropriate way to describe the social network which facilitated the operation of Essaouira's long distance trade.

Trade by credit and commission

Exchanges involving valuable commodities over vast regions required an elaborate system of credit. Goods or specie might be advanced on credit in exchange for export commodities. Many merchants traded entirely on commission for European merchant houses in Marseille and London.[98] Networks of Jewish families, with representatives in various Mediterranean ports, speculated in trade with Essaouira.[99]

No banking facilities existed in Essaouira. The local agent, therefore, had to keep his principal informed about how much money and what goods to send from Europe. A British merchant of Essaouira recommends to his principal in London in 1839 to 'immediately dispatch a small vessel with a few goods and $20,000 in specie gold and silver to enable me to prepare a cargo gradually and at advantageous prices'.[100] The degree to which bills of exchange were used is hard to assess, but their circulation was clearly growing in the nineteenth century. In 1849, the French consul De Vallat reports that bills of exchange are almost unknown.[101] By 1875, times had changed. Beaumier advises merchants that bills of exchange drawn up in Essaouira are easily negotiable in London, Marseille, or even Paris though one should be circumspect in accepting them.[102]

The principal traders of Essaouira were also, in effect, commission agents of the Sultan. As we have seen, the elite merchants were able to establish themselves in town through the interest-free loan (*salaf*) from the Palace. As commission agents for either the Sultan or European merchant firms, the merchants of Essaouira had their own agents who sold their goods on commission at various levels in Morocco. This practice was so common that the word *comisario* from the Spanish, or *commission* from French or English is frequently found in Hebrew and Arabic commercial and legal documents (*kūmiṣya*).

After the wholesale merchants imported the goods on commission they in turn transferred the goods on commission to shopkeepers in town or in Marrakesh.[103] Most of the shops, which belonged to the *ḥubus*, would be leased at low rates to the merchants on long-term contracts. In this way the merchants would acquire squatters' rights (*jilsa*). We find, for example, a leading merchant, Abraham Bensaude, seeking *jilsa* for two new shops being built in the drapers' bazaar (*sūq al-jadīd*).[104] Once the merchants had acquired these commercial premises, they sublet the shops to retailers who would sell their goods on commission.[105] Sometimes credit on merchandise was extended for three to six months, but more often, goods were advanced without a fixed date of reimbursement. In the latter case, the wholesaler would collect from the shopkeeper a portion of his weekly sales.[106] The retailer, no doubt, would also extend credit to his customers. Thus, the shopkeeper – as Braudel remarks for Europe – 'lived between those who owed him money and those to whom he owed it'.[107]

More important than the local market was the distribution network in other parts of Morocco. Agents of Swiri merchants sometimes travelled to Marrakesh with goods on commission. At times, problems would arise, and the merchants would have trouble recovering debts from their agents,[108] but generally the system functioned well. Throughout the countryside, agents of the wholesale merchants of the town traded on commission. Goods were also given on commission to agents involved in the trans-Saharan caravan. The agents of Jewish merchants would sell European items, above all, cotton fabrics, in exchange for the lucrative products of the trans-Saharan caravan, and the Jewish agents for the Swiri firms would also travel to the southern markets, sometimes as far as Tindouf.[109] Jewish traders from Essaouira were to be found throughout the Sous and Aït Bāʿamrān, hiring camels to convey their merchandise.[110] Traders and transporters of the Aït Baha would travel southward from Essaouira to the edge of the Sahara, laden with textiles, which would be given on credit to the Saharan traders until the season for ostrich feathers. In the meantime, the Aït Baha traders would buy further produce at the *mawsim* of Sī Ḥmād Ū Mūsā, undertaking their own subsidiary trade. They would then return to the Ṣaḥrāwi traders, and upon receiving the feathers, would give them new goods on credit until the next season.[111]

The commercial operations at intermediate stages of the trans-Saharan trade resembled, *mutatis mutandis*, those of the Swiri merchants. As Pascon has shown, Ḥusayn Ū Hāshim of Iligh acted as banker, creditor, and financier of the caravans.[112] The house of Iligh, Bayrūk of Goulimime, and the merchant houses of Essaouira were all integral parts of the network of exchange. Many of the commission agents for the Swiri firms were also agents for the chiefs of the Sous. Masʿūd ʿAmār and his father, important ostrich feather merchants, are good examples. They traded on the capital of the Corcos house and simultaneously were loaned considerable sums by Ḥusayn Ū Hāshim of Iligh to purchase ostrich feathers.[113] The ʿAmārs of Ifrane were able to profit from their position as middlemen between Iligh and Essaouira. It was this chain of credit relationships which made the trans-Saharan trade possible.

Partnership and *commenda*

Essaouira's role in international trade was that of a commercial entrepôt – a place where deals were made, partnerships formed, and contracts signed. The successful merchant firms needed to know not only how to operate in the European arena, but also how to build up an extensive network of relations with the interior of Morocco. Merchandise was not just conveyed to Essaouira and freely sold on the open market, nor were imports generally sold for hard currency to buyers coming to Essaouira. Almost all commercial transactions connected to the import and export trade in town, whether by barter or cash, were based on legally binding agreements between merchants and their partners, agents, and brokers.

The kinds of legal associations found in Essaouira were based on Islamic principles of credit according to the Mālikī school of law prevalent in North Africa. Studies have divided these associations of credit into two types: commenda (*qirāḍ*) and partnership (*sharika*). The former involved the investment of capital by one party in another. The profits are divided up, but the supplier bears all the risks if there is a loss of the capital. In the case of *sharika*, both sides share the losses. These are the essential principles of the two forms of associations, though the ways in which such financial operations were conducted in North Africa were considerably more complex.[114] In addition to legally-binding agreements based on Islamic law, many of the legal associations involved Jews. Though economic collaboration between Jews and Muslims was common,[115] a large part of the commerce was between Jews alone. The legal forms of partnerships and associations between Jews, called *ribbit we-iqṣā*ʾ and *shūttafūt*, mirrored closely the *qirāḍ* and *sharika*.[116]

A contract between Abraham Corcos of Essaouira and Masʿūd ʿAmār of Ifrane sheds light on the way *commenda* agreements operated. The agreement, drawn up in 1863 by two *dayyan*s of Essaouira – Abraham b. Yaʿqōb Ben ʿAṭṭār and Mōshe Hakōhen – states that Masʿūd ʿAmār, the son of Yōsef b. Amzīl, a resident of Ifrane, received from Abraham Corcos 3,385 *doros* (another term for riyāl which is frequently used in Hebrew documents) in French coin. He had the right to use that money in commercial transactions for an entire year. All profits made from dealing in ostrich feathers, wax, and gold were to be divided between them, and furthermore, it was stipulated that for each day of commercial activity Masʿūd should get an ūqiya on condition that the profits of the transactions were divided. All the transactions were to be recorded in writing by Mas'ūd. The original money advanced was to be returned, but in the event of loss, so long as Mas'ūd was able to prove by the testimony of two witnesses that the losses were sustained honestly, the debt would be cancelled.[117]

The same basic principles apply in this document as had applied to the Muslim *commenda* since the Middle Ages.[118] Such an arrangement left Mas'ūd 'Amār free to operate quite independently from Corcos. It was the only way in which Swiri merchants could provide their agents with sufficient mobility to assure the flow of goods from the trans-Saharan caravan. Ifrane was on the edge of the Sahara and was one of the most southerly *mellah*s from which Jews operated. The contract was made in summer, which would have given Mas'ūd 'Amār enough time to return for the Jewish New Year. He could take with him goods purchased in Essaouira to advance to the traders going south on the annual *akbar* caravan, or use the advanced sums to purchase some of the goods sought by Corcos at the autumn *mawsim* of Sī Ḥmād Ū Mūsā. It was the French silver coin, one of the main currencies in circulation, which was used as the investment in the contract.[119] Such a contract relied on close personal ties, and depended on the agent being trustworthy, *ne'eman*, a word repeated several times in the document.[120] This contract was also suitable for long distance trade in another way, since it also agreed to pay for Mas'ūd's business expenses. As Udovitch puts it: 'In a paradigmatic *commenda* agreement, the investor contributed his capital but no time and effort, and the agent contributed his time and effort but not capital.'[121] Finally, as has been seen, expenses and transactions were to be recorded in a register book, and losses had to be attested by two witnesses. Perhaps the only difference between this contract and the Muslim *commenda* is that in our example a time limit of one year was imposed. In the medieval Muslim contract, the duration of the agreement could not be stipulated.[122] In another agreement drawn up in 1869 between Mas'ūd b. Dawid Halewī and David b. Jacob Corcos, two years were stipulated.[123]

The merchants of Essaouira also advanced capital on interest-free loans to rural chiefs. Ties of this kind with those in power along the trade routes were essential for the maintenance of exchange. Some of the rural *qā'id*s appear to have been dependent on loans from the merchants of Essaouira. At the same time, the merchants relied on these rural leaders to assure the circulation of goods and sometimes to help recover debts.[124] Loans to rural *qā'id*s by Jewish merchants were also based on personal ties and trust, like commercial contracts. Interest-free loans were extended without the stipulation of any time limit. In 1873, for example, 'Abd al-Mālik Ibn 'Abdallāh Ū Bīhī, a *qā'id* in the Haha, asked Abraham Corcos for an interest-free loan of 7,000 mithqāl (*'ala wajh as-salaf*).[125]

In a loan contract of 1869, Qāid Aḥmad b. Muḥammad as-Sūsī al-Waltītī aṣ- Ṣawīrī received 130 mithqāl from Abraham Corcos. Of course it was not stipulated when the loan should be returned.[126]

Another kind of association, and perhaps the most common, was the partnership (*sharika*). Often this might be an agreement on the trade of a specifically agreed amount for a defined commodity. For example, in 1877 we find Mawlāy ʿUmar b. Muḥammad al-ʿAlawī of Essaouira in partnership with Muḥammad b. aṭ-Ṭayyib al-Maḥmūdī of Marrakesh for 100 bales (*trāḥa*) of goat skins. Both the capital investment and the profits were to be divided up, half and half. The skins were sent to Essaouira, but a dispute arose when al-ʿAlawī claimed that he had entrusted the skins to a broker (*dallāl*) since the merchandise was not currently in demand.[127]

Similar kinds of partnership agreements, called *shūttafūt*, were made between Jews. Conflicts arising over such partnerships have produced considerable discussion among Essaouira's rabbis.[128] In one case, which involved a partnership in skins, a claimant sought payment from the heirs of his partner, apparently for debts owed to him from their joint profits.[129]

Muslim and Jewish legal norms for partnerships were similar. Both were relatively flexible, capable of resolving disputes and responding to the needs of long distance trade. This legal structure, which encompassed the entire trade route, was what enabled – to return to the term used by Abner Cohen – a 'trading diaspora' to develop.

Personal bonds and the circulation of information

The personal relations of the Jewish merchants of Essaouira with Jews in Marrakesh and the Sous were vital for the successful operation of the long distance trade. Jews could travel from one *mellah* to another, or indeed, from one country to another and find security in the home of a coreligionist. Their common jural system reinforced their social cohesiveness. The social and political separation of the Jews from Muslim society was conducive to their concentration in commerce. Their network of contacts gave them rapid access to information about supply and demand.[130]

But ethnicity is only one factor to consider. Many of the commercial relationships were interdenominational. Though it was often the Muslim who was the 'patron' and the Jew who was the 'client', this relationship could be reversed. Muslims in the countryside might perceive the Jewish merchants in Essaouira as protectors. A Muslim who had made an oath before a Jewish *tājir* could later, upon sacrificing an animal, take sanctuary in the Jew's house. Meyer Corcos gave sanctuary to some Muslims from the Shāwiya who feared imprisonment by their *qā'id*, as he explains:

As a custom in Morocco, it is wrong to turn out of the house people who bring such sign of refuge called *El Aar*. My late father has many times, and for many months Moors lodging in the house who he could not send away until they chose to go themselves, and several times my late father settled amicable affairs pending between his lodgers and the governors of surrounding districts.[131]

Mutual interest preserved a system of relative trustworthiness between Muslims and Jews. Muslims depended on Jewish brokers to market their merchandise in the countryside. Jews relied on Muslim transporters, such as the Aït Baha, to convey their goods over long distances. Goods consigned to itinerant traders and transporters, whether Muslims or Jews, were entrusted 'in God's protection' (*fi amān Allāh*).[132]

The effective circulation of news about supply and demand was an essential part of the system of exchange. The wholesale merchants of Essaouira often communicated in writing with agents or chiefs in distant regions. William Grace, a British merchant in Essaouira, wrote to Daḥmān Bayrūk of Goulimime in 1864 telling him that the market for ostrich feathers in Europe was 'cold' but good quality gum arabic was much in demand, fetching up to 20 riyāl.[133] Information about political conditions to assure safe travel was also exchanged. Agreements and deals were made between Swiri merchants and the inhabitants of the far south, such as Tajakant, to obtain certain goods or to arrange meetings at the southern markets or *mawsims*.[134]

Urgent news was sent by special courier, called *raqqāṣ*.[135] This was the principal means whereby the *makhzan* exchanged political information or sent directives to the different administrative centres.[136] Such couriers were also employed by powerful chiefs and wealthy merchants for the rapid dispatch of commercial information.[137] The *ḥazān* Yaʿqūb of Tafilalt sent a *raqqāṣ* to Abraham Corcos in Essaouira, instructing him not to sell the ostrich feathers he sent until his son had reached the port. The feathers went from Tafilalt to Fez and then to Essaouira, but their price was tied to the amount declared by Ibn al-Malīḥ, the agent of the *makhzan* in Gibraltar.[138] Here we find that the circulation of vital information – price differentials between distant regions for a particularly lucrative commodity – relied on the dispatch of rapid personal couriers.

The official correspondence of the *makhzan* was in classical Arabic, albeit with a number of terms specific to Morocco and some arabized Spanish commercial terms. Most of the commercial correspondence, however, was written in Judeo-Arabic, the vernacular Arabic written in the Hebrew script commonly found in Jewish communities throughout the Islamic world. Since medieval times Jewish traders had employed a written adaptation of their spoken Arabic dialects.[139] The Judeo-Arabic employed by the Moroccan Jewish traders, therefore, was the colloquial Arabic spoken by the Jews at the time. Whether the Jewish trader was in London, Essaouira, or the Berber-speaking regions of the Sous, correspondence in Judeo-Arabic was the means by which both personal news and commercial information was communicated. It was also the language in which the merchants kept their account books.[140]

So important was the network of Jewish merchants, that non-Jews employed Jewish secretaries and interpreters who corresponded in Judeo-Arabic on behalf of European merchants and Muslims chiefs. A certain Aharōn Wīzgān of Agadir writes to a Dutch merchant, Uhlmann, just after the foundation of Essaouira. The latter was a former merchant of Agadir who had returned to Holland, yet still active in the commerce of that port and of Essaouira. The letter contains information about the availability of almonds, wax, olive oil, gums frankincense, and other items. Wīzgān also writes of the demand for a variety of European imports.[141] The chiefs of the south also corresponded in Judeo-Arabic through their Jewish agents. A British vice-consul and merchant in Essaouira, Chaillet, wrote to Sheikh Bayrūk in 1829, asking him to procure some ostrich feathers. The response came to the consul-general, E. W. A. Drummond-Hay, in Judeo-Arabic. The Sheikh indicated that Hay should reply in the same language since his secretary was Jewish.[142] The *shurafāʾ* of Iligh also employed Jewish secretaries in addition to Muslim ones, as can be seen in their account books.[143]

Traditional patterns of trade

For Essaouira in the nineteenth century, the embedded jural patterns of exchange and credit took precedence over the foreign commercial practices which had begun to appear on the coast. Furthermore, the overland trade still had more influence on economic and social structures than did trade by sea. The persistence of traders in organizing and operating caravans seemed to be almost unaffected by sea transport. The merchants of Essaouira conformed more to the cycles of the interior than did the domestic suppliers, who adapted to the timetable of urban demands. The traders of the coast were subject to all the traditional patterns of trade in Morocco – slow and cumbersome modes of transport and exchange through networks of patron and client relations at each stage of the route.

And yet, as a maritime port, Essaouira was a catalyst for foreign influences. In a sense, the town was caught between the very persistence of its traditional way of life and the dramatic forces of change. Some of these forces, such as foreign economic penetration and war, came from the outside. But the Moroccan response to these foreign pressures followed an internal dynamic. In this light, the interior of Morocco still overshadowed the coast.

Chapter 6

The politics of trade

The bombardment of Essaouira in 1844 by the French fleet was a decisive turning-point in the history of Essaouira. The pattern of trade that had evolved gradually over the previous twenty years was threatened. Morocco had timidly initiated an opening with Europe by developing a system of royal trade over which the Sultan was able to exercise close control. Such protectionism was to crumble under the weight of foreign pressure. The capacity of Europe to impose its will was demonstrated by the events of 1844.[1] Within a period of fifteen years after the French attack, Morocco had embarked on a precipitous course towards foreign domination. Two decisive events made this inevitable: the treaty with Great Britain in 1856, and the Spanish invasion of Tetuan in 1859–60. Both of them permanently altered the relationship between the Muslim authorities and the foreigners and their protégés in Essaouira.

The revival of trade

The opening of Morocco to Europe began two decades before the war of 1844. Foreign trade was resumed by Sultan ʿAbd ar-Raḥmān (1822–59), who had spent some time in Essaouira as governor prior to his succession to the throne.[2] His interest in foreign trade was probably reinforced by his close ties to some of the merchants of the town. In contrast to the reign of Mawlāy Sulaymān,[3] ʿAbd ar-Raḥmān viewed trade with Europe as a valuable source of revenue. But as far as possible, such trade was to be contained and left in the hands of Jews, as the British merchant and vice-consul, Willshire, remarked: 'H. M. *encourages commerce* which his predecessors never did, but unfortunately support is given to unworthy and unprincipled Jews'.[4]

Royal policy was not the only factor which encouraged a reorientation towards the Atlantic through the port of Essaouira. The Eastern caravan routes were disrupted by the French invasion of Algeria in 1830. In the decade before 1844, an average of 50 to 60 ships called annually at Essaouira and the average value of annual imports was about £100,000, while exports were about twice that amount. Although other coastal ports too were to benefit from the growing Atlantic trade, Essaouira still took the bulk of the trade with Europe.[5]

The response to this growth of foreign trade can be seen in a number of administrative changes in Essaouira which foreshadowed the pattern of the coming decades. One change was in the role of the governor. Since the foundation of the town, the *qāʾid* of Essaouira had been responsible for the government of the surrounding regions, and was often himself originally from the Haha.[6] The maintenance of the *modus vivendi* between town and country was vital for successful urban administration, and the selection of a powerful mediator from the surrounding countryside could help to mitigate tensions between tribesmen and the *makhzan*. The emphasis which was placed on the development of foreign trade was to change this administrative policy. In the 1820s a Tetuani *qāʾid*, ʿAbd al-Khāliq Ashʿāsh, was appointed as governor on three separate occasions.[7] His particular responsibility was to administer the business connected to the revenues of customs at the port. He became, in effect, the *amīn* of the *diwāna*.[8] The appointment of Ashʿāsh, who was a member of an important family of administrators from Tangier and Tetuan,[9] reflected the importance placed on the development of trade in Essaouira. The *qāʾid* of the town had now also become the chief customs official. All of these *qāʾid*s were subsequently chosen from noted merchant families – usually of Andalusian origin and natives of Tetuan – who had maintained some contact with European affairs. In 1839, the Sultan pointed out to Muḥammad Ashʿāsh of Tetuan that in Essaouira 'order has become disturbed and rules corrupted'. The Sultan directed the *qāʾid* to 'choose from among our servants of the people of Tetuan a capable, authoritative, honest, and trustworthy man and send him to take up service in Essaouira'.[10]

As the volume of trade grew, the *makhzan* began to increase the number of officials in Essaouira.[11] In 1840, Delaporte noted that the eighth customs official, al-Ḥājj Muḥammad Brīsha, arrived in town and was put in charge of the port together with Sīdī Muḥammad b. Shaqrūn. Brīsha was also from an important merchant family of Tetuan. In addition to his function as *amīn* at customs, he was also a commission agent for the trade of the Sultan. Later that year, Brīsha was called to Marrakesh to take control of royal finances.[12] In 1854, he was again appointed *qāʾid* of Essaouira. The administration of the royal port of Essaouira had become a crucial policy issue for the Palace.

Brīsha was typical of a number of officials at this time – *makhzan* merchants who combined functions as royal agents and administrators. This combination of duties was open to abuse. The foreign community, for example, was particularly unhappy with Qāʾid ʿAllāl az-Zamrānī, who had been the deputy (*khalīfa*) governor of Ashʿāsh. He was removed from office in 1842 over a diplomatic quarrel with the French,[13] and replaced by al-Ḥājj al-ʿArabī aṭ-Ṭarrīs. aṭ-Ṭarrīs was closely tied to the Sultan, and highly regarded by the foreign community, who expected that conditions for foreign merchants would improve.[14] It was aṭ-Ṭarrīs who was *qāʾid* at the time of the French bombardment.[15]

The bombardment of Essaouira

In the early afternoon of 15 August 1844, the bombardment of Essaouira began. The action was part of a punitive expedition against the Moroccans for not preventing the beleaguered leader of the Algerian resistance, ʿAbd al-Qādir, from crossing into Morocco at the eastern frontier. In the early summer, a number of skirmishes took place near Oujda between the Moroccan and French forces. The army of the Sultan then mobilized at Wad Isly near Oujda. An ultimatum was delivered to the Moroccans by the French, who in fact had no intention of resolving the conflict diplomatically. The commander of the French forces in Algeria even proposed the capture of Fez. 'I believe', wrote Bugeaud, 'that the capture of Fez could compensate for a very large part of our war expenses, for the city is rich enough to pay us a big contribution.'[16] British attempts to mediate in the conflict were to no avail. A French naval squadron, under the command of the Prince de Joinville, the son of King Louis-Philippe, shelled Tangier on 9 August. A few days later, the commander of the French forces defeated the Moroccans at Wad Isly on the northeastern frontier. The *coup de grâce* followed with the bombardment of Essaouira by the Prince de Joinville on 15 August.[17]

The Moroccan resistance at Essaouira was also short-lived. After a few hours' bombardment of the island and the town, the Moroccan artillery was silenced. Shortly thereafter, the Moroccan garrison on the island was defeated by a force of 500–600 French soldiers. The Prince de Joinville wrote Bugeaud two days later: 'The island was fiercely defended by 400–500 *kabyles* who had locked themselves in houses, mosques, and batteries.' By six in the evening, the French claimed to have wiped out the Moroccan forces. The Prince de Joinville remarked to Bugeaud: 'I am sending you a hundred and some odd prisoners to show how we put the Moroccans to task from our side.'[18] The Moroccans later reported that out of a total of 314 soldiers in the garrison, some 92 were killed and another 130 were taken prisoner to Oran. In the meantime, the Moroccan authorities and soldiers fled from the town. The next morning, the French continued to shell Essaouira in order to destroy the now abandoned batteries along the ramparts, and an estimated 90 people were killed. The French force landed on the beach, but decided not to enter the city. An occupation force remained on the island until September 16.[19]

The effect of the French attack on the inhabitants of Essaouira was immediate and devastating:

> When the Christians (may God annihilate them) fired balls and volleys on the town of Essaouira (may God preserve it) [the town], the people left for safety, fearing the destruction. The tribes took advantage of the havoc by unmercifully pillaging houses, and this spread until the customs house and treasury were ransacked.[20]

As soon as the authorities fled, the town was pillaged by thousands of tribesmen from the Haha and Shiadma. Rural prisoners were set free from the town prisons. Pandemonium broke out and those who could, fled into the countryside. Almost all foreigners had escaped by ship prior to the attack. A few of the elite Jewish merchants also escaped by British vessel,[21] but most of them sought refuge in the countryside among friendly rural notables with whom they had commercial ties.[22] The common people were less fortunate. The *mellah* in particular was the target of attack by the marauders. It was reported that the Jews first attempted to defend themselves by locking themselves into the *mellah*, but the quarter was broken into and sacked.[23] The *medina* was not spared by the plunderers either, and after the *mellah* had been sacked, the pillaging spread to the other quarters. As an-Nāṣirī remarks, 'first the Jews then the others'.[24] The town was left devastated and depopulated as a result of the combination of the French bombardment and the ravages of the tribes. The Muslim population returned forty days later, only after the French had evacuated the island and authority had been restored. Most of the Jews stayed away for an even longer period, and some emigrated permanently, finding their way to Gibraltar, Algiers, and probably other Mediterranean ports.[25]

Rural rebellion became widespread in the Haha, Shiadma, Shāwiya, and Dukkāla.[26] It took several months before order was restored in and around the region of Essaouira. At the end of September, repairs began on the damaged walls, gates and watch-towers of the town.[27] Efforts were made by the Sultan to seize the goods and money which the pillagers had stolen, and which they were trying to sell in town and rural markets.[28] Qā'id al-Ḥājj al-ʿArabī aṭ-Ṭarrīs returned to resume his duties, and on the 18th of November, William Grace, a well-established English merchant of Essaouira, returned to town as the newly-appointed British vice-consul.[29] In February 1845, Grace reported that the region was tranquil and people from the countryside were bringing goods into the town. The Sultan ordered those in Marrakesh to return.[30] In April, the consul remarked that commerce was as extensive as before the war.[31] Though it took a few years before government authority was firmly established in the Haha and Shiadma, by the end of 1845 Qāʾid aṭ-Ṭarrīs was able to claim that the port 'is peaceful and tranquil, and its business is restored; likewise there is security among the tribes of the region and on the roads'.[32]

The signs of peace in Essaouira camouflaged the new situation. The ease with which the French were able to violate Moroccan sovereignty and impose a peace settlement stirred up rural dissidence, and emboldened European proponents of imperialism. Henceforth, foreign inroads in Morocco were to be a major cause of revolt against *makhzan* authority. For their part, foreign powers increasingly sought alliances with dissident tribal leaders in the south, such as Sheikh Bayrūk of Goulimime and Ḥusayn Ū Hāshim. Shortly after the war of 1844, a French writer succinctly expressed the new power relation which had emerged between France and Morocco:

> The commercial alliance which we have signed with the Sheikh of Wad Noun, the brilliant feat of arms of our navy at Mogador, and finally, the victory at Isly in which the nicest result will be to hasten the return of normality between Fez and Tlemcen, have already established our moral influence over the two far ends of this region. It is a good beginning for our future relations: it only depends on time and wisdom to develop our interests in Morocco and Algeria.[33]

Makhzan trading strategies

For Morocco, the French attack was a strain on the finances of the state. The *makhzan* initiated costly military reforms by creating a new army (*ʿaskar niẓāmī*) based on a European model.[34] Furthermore, growing European demands after the war brought new hardships to the Moroccan government. Apart from the military expenses of the war, the Moroccan government was pressed to pay reparations for damage sustained by French citizens and protégés during the pillaging of Essaouira.[35] One naturalized French citizen, Joseph Cadouch, wrote to the French consul-general: 'As a consequence of these unfortunate events, I lost 8,000 piastres (about f40,000) in property, objects, jewellery, etc., which I can prove with my marriage contract, drawn up five years before the bombardment of Mogador (not counting purchases made since that time, estimated at f4,000).'[36]

After the 1844 war, the Sultan, was no longer able to closely contain the foreign presence in Morocco. 'After the settlement was reached with the French,' writes an-Nāṣirī, 'the Sultan removed what the foreign countries used to pay [in tributes], and foreign visitors and merchants grew in the ports of Morocco, increasingly mixing and intermingling with the people.' As a consequence, 'their trade increased in merchandise which had been prohibited, opening up a door which had been closed to them previously'. The result, according to an-Nāṣirī, was that prices rose and the Moroccan currency was devalued against foreign silver coins, as foreign trade increased.[37]

The *makhzan*, nevertheless, did attempt to maintain its control over trade. Over the next decade protective tariffs were imposed, monopolies on certain commodities established, and the export of specified products prohibited. Moroccan merchants were given advantageous privileges.[38] In a sense, this was the same policy as before 1844, but what had changed was that the Moroccans were no longer masters of the situation. A floodgate had been opened, and the government was no longer able to prevent the increasing influence of foreigners in trade. The isolation of Morocco had now ceased.

The Moroccan government needed to adapt administratively to these changes. Increasingly the *qāʾid* of the town concerned himself with the daily business of the customs house – to such an extent that the British vice-consul was led to believe in December 1844 that another governor had been appointed, leaving Qāʾid aṭ-Ṭarrīs only as director of the customs house.[39] Undoubtedly a new *bāshā* of the militia, who was also called *qāʾid* and *vice versa*, was appointed at that time. The British vice-consul must have exaggerated the separation of functions. aṭ-Ṭarrīs remained the titular *bāshā* of the whole town as well as head *amīn* at the port. But his day-to-day activities were now centred in the customs house where he supervised the *ʿudūl* who recorded the transactions. The *qāʾid* was also in charge of channelling revenues for maintaining the ramparts, *makhzan* houses, and the aqueduct, paying the militia, and taking care of other general expenses. His domination of daily business was noted by the French consul, who remarked: 'his power is almost absolute'.[40]

This system kept smuggling and contraband at a minimal level, probably less than was the case in any other Moroccan port.[41] Essaouira continued to be closely administered by the *makhzan*, and the *qāʾid* of the town was considered to be one of the most important government officials in Morocco. With the death of aṭ-Ṭarrīs in 1854, Muḥammad Brīsha returned to the port as governor. Brīsha, who had travelled widely in Europe, was well-received by the foreign community who considered him to be, like aṭ-Ṭarrīs, refined and conciliatory.[42] He was also closely tied to the Palace, and served the Sultan as an important financial advisor.[43] Faced with an increasing volume of trade, Brīsha attempted to make the administration more efficient. After his arrival in Essaouira, he soon discovered that the division of tasks at the port between the *umanāʾ* and the *ʿudūl* was not operating smoothly. Consequently, Brīsha suggested that an *amīn* from Tetuan should be sent there.[44]

Merchants too were sent from the Muslim Tetuani elite. After the war, four merchants who were closely tied to Ashʿāsh and Muhammad ar-Razīnī – the latter was the Sultan's agent in Gibraltar – were sent by the Sultan to Essaouira, supplied with a large sum in Spanish riyāl to use in commerce.[45] Essaouira's trade, especially with Gibraltar, was given a boost with this new influx of capital.[46] Credit on outward duties, extended to the original *tujjār*, was suspended.[47] For a period of time, only the four merchants from Tetuan were allowed the privilege of delayed payment of duties. But even with these advantages, the Tetuani merchants were unable to gain a foothold. By 1848, two of them had given up, a third had established himself in London, and the fourth was barely able to stay afloat in Essaouira.[48] Credit on duties was again given to the other *tujjār*, often for six to ten months. Deductions or exemptions on duties were granted to Jewish merchants for import goods, and certain privileged merchants, such as ʿAmram Elmaleh, received deductions on export duties as well. These duty-free goods were sold at low prices, making it difficult for foreign merchants to compete. To get rid of accumulated goods a twenty per cent import duty was imposed. The stocks were sold on credit to the shopkeepers in Marrakesh with little chance of reimbursement.[49]

Makhzan credit to Moroccan merchants irked foreign proponents of liberal trade. The French consul, Beaumier, indicated that in 1844 the debt owed by the *tujjār* stood at 800,000 piastres (or riyāl). It was evident to the consul that in seven years nothing had entered the *makhzan* treasury, and most of the revenues were absorbed by the small garrisons of Essaouira and Marrakesh. It was, according to Beaumier, impossible to compete with the *tujjār* who had nothing to lose. The French consul pleaded for the installation of liberal trade so that Morocco could be exploited like Tunisia, Egypt, and the countries of the Levant.[50]

The constant adjustment of tariffs in this period reflected an effort by the Sultan to maintain his control over foreign trade.[51] Manchester merchants dealing with Morocco on a number of occasions sought the intervention of the Foreign Office to end restrictive tariffs. Import duties on textiles, which generally had been at 10 per cent *ad valorem*, were raised to between 35 and 75 per cent in 1845.[52] Ten years later the Manchester Chamber of Commerce was still protesting to the Foreign Office, on 'the very sudden manner in which the Government of Morocco constantly and capriciously increased duties, both upon exports and imports, to the grievous injury of British commerce to that country'.[53]

The other main method by which the Sultan attempted to control foreign trade was the imposition of the royal monopoly (*kunṭrada*). In 1844, the only monopoly reported was that of leeches – sold to a Jewish merchant, Yamin Acoca – which the merchants considered to be rather inconsequential.[54] Over the next decade, however, monopolies were imposed on numerous products: iron and steel, grain, wool, cochineal, sulphur, sugar, coffee, tea, logwood, tobacco, and most important of all, skins. Moroccan, as well as foreign merchants, objected to these measures, since they curtailed their flexibility. Coffee and sugar, for example, were usually sold for cash, and therefore were vital for the payment of duties and the monthly instalments to the Sultan.[55] The monopoly established in 1850 on goat skins, one of the most important Moroccan export items, was even more consequential. This was connected to the re-establishment of the *maks*, a general term for non-Islamic taxes. It had existed under Sultan Muḥammad III, but Sultan Sulāyman, with his reformist tendencies, had allowed only the strictly Islamic taxes.[56] The establishment of non-Islamic taxes was only considered legitimate when the Islamic state was at risk. In 1850, 'the Sultan initiated the *maks* in Fez and in other cities, first on skins (with Muṣṭafā ad-Dukkālī Ibn al-Jillānī ar-Ribāṭī and al-Makkī al-Qabbāj al-Fāsī in charge), then on cattle'.[57] What this meant was that prospective skin dealers had to pay taxes on their merchandise and sell their hides to *makhzan* agents, who had the monopoly on the foreign commerce of this item.[58] ad-Dukkālī and al-Qabbāj, who were already important tax-farmers in Morocco, gained the monopoly.[59] This measure met with considerable opposition from the ulama.[60]

Essaouira, which had the largest share of the skin trade, was particularly affected by this measure. On 17 September 1850, the *makhzan* began to seize all the skins brought in for sale.[61] The effect on the suppliers, mostly from the Aït Bāʿamrān and the Haha, was immediate. The skin traders from the Sous stopped bringing skins into the cities. The monopoly also had the same effect on the skin trade in the Rif. In Essaouira it was reported that in a forty-day period from the establishment of the monopoly, hardly 200 dozen skins, which was the equivalent to the daily amount generally reaching the town, had entered the government stores.[62] The implications of such a policy soon became apparent to the *makhzan*. A contraband trade developed and the Sultan ordered a patrol of small boats on the Rif coast.[63] The Sultan wrote of his concern to the chief *qāʾid* of the Tangier and Tetuan region, Būsilhām b. ʿAlī: 'Most of the ports export skins, and if this is disrupted the profits of the treasury will diminish and commerce will weaken.'[64] While a government monopoly might bring in some revenues, it might also reduce the income from duties on exporting skins. The Sultan clearly recognized this predicament. But did the Sultan's admission imply that the monopoly had been annulled? The subsequent evidence is contradictory. Qā'id aṭ-Ṭarrīs apparently petitioned the Sultan to rescind the order.[65] On 10 December, Grace noted that the monopoly had been abolished on goat skins while sheep and calf skins were to remain subject to the decree of 17 September.[66] Essaouira was to be made an exception. In other towns and regions, the monopoly was to remain in force.[67] Later sources suggest that restrictions on the skin trade persisted. In February 1852, Grace disclosed that the Sultan was allowing people from the Sous to bring hides to the market for sale, but a tax of 12 ūqiya per dozen sheep and goat, and 8 ūqiya per dozen calf skins was being imposed. The vice-consul feared that the duty would have the same effect as the prohibition.[68] In 1854, Grace gave notice that the Shiadma, Haha, and Matūga were to be allowed to bring skins to the market, effectively putting an end to the monopoly.[69]

By 1854, most of the monopolies had been rescinded.[70] Many of the trade restrictions had never been effective anyway. aṭ-Ṭarrīs, for example, disregarded the prohibitions on commodities, such as wool and olive oil.[71] It seems probable that the Sultan was aware that his orders were not being followed. With hindsight the Sultan appears to have been ambivalent about his trade strategy, hoping to gain revenue both from a monopoly on produce and by allowing free trade to develop to augment export duties. This uncertainty probably explains some of the inconsistencies between royal decrees and practice. The free trade option ultimately prevailed, but to a large degree this was caused by accelerated foreign pressures from Tangier. The foreign representatives claimed that their own countries as well as the Ottoman Empire prohibited monopolies.[72]

Apart from a few products, such as tobacco, hashish, and sulphur, all of the monopolies were annulled. Prohibition on the export of certain products – usually those specifically associated with the payment of legal taxes (*zakāh* and *a'shār*), such as olive oil and grains – was imposed only intermittently. With the commercial treaty between Great Britain and Morocco in 1856 the era of protective and administered trade had drawn to a close.

The treaty of 1856

The 38 article commercial treaty between Great Britain and Morocco was the culmination of foreign pressures for liberal trade in Morocco. In particular, the untiring efforts of the British Minister in Tangier, Sir

John Drummond Hay, led to the agreement between the two governments.[73] In the treaty and accompanying convention, provisions were made to protect British subjects and their agents in Morocco. Dwellings and warehouses for British subjects were to be provided. All monopolies on imported goods were abolished, except those on tobacco, opium, firearms, and a few other items. Taxes and tolls, besides export duties were prohibited. In short, the provisions of the treaty were designed to assure freedom of trade. In this way, the commercial treaty of 1856 inaugurated an era of 'liberal' trade.[74]

Already by 1848, duties on many import goods had been lowered to 10 per cent *ad valorem*. The British vice-consul in Essaouira attributed the reduction to the intervention of aṭ-Ṭarrīs. During this period, the idea of a commercial treaty had been gaining momentum.[75] The treaty unequivocally established the ten per cent *ad valorem* duty on all imports. At the same time, it also granted the Sultan the right to prohibit the export of certain commodities, but on conditions that British subjects be allowed to export any of the items that they had in stock. The tariff on exports, however, was unalterable. As a consequence, the *makhzan* established a compulsory exchange-rate at customs. Since the tariff was fixed in the currency of account, any devaluation of the mithqāl against silver would have seriously diminished customs revenue.

The commercial convention with the British became the basis for future agreements with other European countries. The *umanāʾ* applied the tariff, established for the British, to the Moroccan *tujjār* as well as merchants of all nationalities.[76] On a number of occasions, questions arose about fixing duties for items previously not exported. But by and large no innovations were made over the next few decades. This, however, did not prevent disputes. Soon after the treaty was signed, the British began to protest about transgressions of the treaty relating to taxes on olive oil entering the town gates and on skins in the market. At the time of the foundation of the town, a two per cent tax on produce, deducted by the merchants on payments to the suppliers, was in operation. This would be accounted for by the *umanāʾ* on the exportation of produce. At the end of Mawlāy Sulaymān's reign, the *makhzan* had agreed to accept seven mūzūna (4 mūzūna = 1 ūqiya) per quintal (a small quintal, Arabic *qinṭār*, generally weighed 117 English lbs., and a large one about 177 lbs.), instead of the two per cent. An additional toll of our and a half ūqiya per quintal of oil, and seven mūzūna for goat skins had been established in 1855. If the oil was being brought in for sale in the market, the vendor was to pay the fee, but if it had been brought in by an agent for a town merchant, the latter was to cover the cost.[77] After the treaty was signed, both the British vice-consul, Elton, and Hay began to put pressures on the *qāʾid* of Essaouira and the Sultan against this tax and the tax on goat skins, invoking article 3 of the convention which stipulated that besides export duties, neither tax nor toll should be levied. In the Arabic version of the treaty, the term *maks* is used,[78] a tax of dubious legality. A tax on olive oil, however, could be regarded as 'legal', since it could be considered as the tithe on agricultural produce (*al-aʿshār*).[79] The Sultan ordered that the taxes on oil and skins be continued despite the repeated protests of the British.[80]

In the final analysis, the dispute was over the question of who was to be taxed. The native vendors of oil and goat skins continued to be taxed, either at the gates or in the markets, but the merchants who had merchandise brought in by an agent could no longer be taxed according to the treaty. This system was totally exposed to abuses, since it would be difficult to determine who was the owner of merchandise entering the town.

Another dispute involved prohibitions on exports. As indicated, the treaty allowed the Sultan to prohibit the export of an item, provided that the merchants could export all that they had of that item in their possession or all that they had bought prior to the prohibition. A ban against the export of sheep skins and wool soon led to controversy. British merchants claimed that besides the sheep skins in their possession, they had contracts for more.[81] Such disputes in the period following the treaty were rarely resolved in a definitive manner.

A new generation of foreign merchants began to arrive in Essaouira during this period. Some, such as David Perry, who arrived one year before the treaty was signed, were prepared to put both Moroccan and British government to the test, by invoking the treaty at every possibility. Perry soon became embroiled in numerous disputes with the local authorities and the British consulate. In September 1858, Perry began to demand that the local authorities provide him with an escort to enable him to travel to Tarudant, allegedly to settle some accounts there. Article 4 of the treaty, which stipulated the right of the British to travel, was invoked. Hay pointed out that no Christian had visited the Tarudant area for 40 years and claimed that Perry simply wanted to prove that British interests were not adequately supported by the British representatives in Morocco. Hay defended his position to the Foreign Office, and cogently summed up what had been, and was to remain, the role of Britain in Morocco:

> Great Britain, I consider, has a very strong interest in maintaining the integrity and independence of Morocco, not only on account of the important position it occupies in the straits of Gibraltar and the Mediterranean, its fertility, productions, and extent, but also from the fact of its Eastern confines adjoining the French colony of Algiers.[82]

Hay wished to avoid diplomatic confrontations at all costs, and felt that if foreign merchants started to travel in the interior, murders and robberies would occur. The French, he feared, would consequently act with less moderation.

Foreign inroads in Morocco nevertheless grew out of hand, and this state of affairs was facilitated in part by the treaty of 1856. Trade was already on the upswing in 1855, a surge which was caused in particular by the brisk trade in olive oil.[83] New firms in Essaouira, such as Perry and Curtis, dealing in large quantities of olive oil, were largely responsible for the growing scale of exchange over the next decade. Besides a general growth in exports, imports of textiles, sugar, and tea grew substantially. It was in the decade after the treaty, as Miège points out, that foreign habits and tastes developed.[84]

The actual physical presence of foreigners and their protégés soon began to threaten the control of the town by the local authorities. By the mid-1860s, foreign merchants in Essaouira only numbered about 15,[85] yet their influence far exceeded their numbers. British merchants began to occupy space in the port area without authorization. In 1863, the British merchant, Curtis, began placing containers of olive oil at the oratory of the port used during festivals by Muslims. The authorities attempted to make him remove his goods. Soon after, other merchants at the port began to surround their goods with wooden barrels. Muḥammad Bargāsh, the *wazīr* in charge of dealings with foreigners, complained to Hay that 'the extent of the harm done will spread and merchants will rule the country'.[86]

The treaty of 1856 had obligated the *makhzan* to secure premises for British merchants. With the number of British merchants and protégés growing in town, the problem of space became critical. Foreigners and protégés, armed with the new commercial treaties, became more assertive in their demands for houses in town. The British vice-consul listed eleven large houses in the *casbah* held by people who were not trading. This, the vice-consul felt, was a reason for ejecting the tenants to make way for the newly-arrived British merchants.[87] In 1863, after several years of pressures from John Drummond Hay, the Sultan agreed to add a walled enclosure to the town for additional dwellings and warehouses.[88] The following year, the construction of the wall by some 200 workmen began.[89] The expenses of building the wall ranged between 9,000 and 18,000 ūqiya a month (or about £55–£110); even greater sums of money were spent on repairing the houses of some of the leading merchants (Perry, Bensemana, Aḥmad Būhillāl, ʿAbd al-Majīd al-Ḥarīshī, Musa Aflalo, and Mukhtār Ibn ʿAzūz) and on the British consulate.[90]

Notwithstanding these efforts, the constructions dragged on, and the foreign merchants began pressing the authorities to allow them to store goods outside the town walls. The *makhzan* did not approve of this kind of physical expansion.[91] A new and detailed account of the housing problem was compiled by the British vice-consul in 1864.[92] The following year, agreement was reached on the new housing: the lease-holder would pay in rent annually six per cent on the outlay of the construction.[93] Two new skilled contractors were appointed to supervise the constructions when reports reached the Sultan that the original supervisor was 'sluggish and lazy', and that he was not doing his task with 'energy and exactitude' (though he was not yet dismissed). In addition, the *umanā'* were ordered to see to the improvement of all *makhzan* houses when it was revealed that many were in a decrepit state. It was decided that an additional floor could be added to the houses.[94]

It was not long before the merchants began complaining of lavish expenditures on houses in the new *casbah* (since they were to pay six per cent interest on the outlay).[95] By 1869, most of the constructions were complete but many merchants withdrew their applications, considering the six per cent to be out of proportion to the value of the building.[96] In 1870, the *makhzan* proposed that it should lease the houses to merchants for eight to ten years.[97] Negotiations about the payment of the six per cent on the outlay dragged on in Tangier. In the meantime, merchants began refusing to pay rent on their houses and stores, disagreeing with the expenses incurred by the constructions. Some were also seeking reductions in rent for houses in the old *casbah*. The *umanā'* appealed constantly to Bargāsh in Tangier to intervene with the foreign representatives.[98]

A number of proposals were put forward. Hay suggested that the prospective tenant should have an overseer of his own during time of construction. The French minister insisted on a reduction of two-thirds of the six per cent. A one-third reduction was agreed upon in 1872, unless the building had been supervised by the applicant. Hay also insisted to vice-Consul Carstensen at this time that the claims put forward by the British merchants to withhold rent appeared to be 'futile' though he later decided to leave it up to the vice-consul to judge each case individually. Finally, in April 1873, the terms of the six per cent agreement were settled between Hay and Bargāsh. The applicant was to be kept informed daily of the expenditures, and the rent was to begin from the day he received the keys. The contract was to be binding for eight years.[99] After countless delays in obtaining the rent from protégés and two months after the agreement was signed, the *umanā'* were able to write that they had received all the rent.[100] As for major repairs, the *makhzan* would agree to undertake the work only on condition that the tenant paid six per cent on the outlay. This was often contested by the foreign merchants who would sometimes withhold paying their rent.[101] It should be noted that the *makhzan* often agreed to a deduction on the old debt of the *tujjār* if they undertook the work themselves.

Although the disputes on construction had dragged on for nearly a decade, the new *casbah* became a *fait accompli*. The new quarter of the town, enclosed and protected by the extended city ramparts, stood as a symbol of the expanding foreign presence.

Makhzan revenues

While the Moroccan government was unable to prevent foreign inroads, it might be argued that the *makhzan* did derive greater revenues from customs duties on the growing trade with Europe. In 1821, average customs revenue for Essaouira was estimated at 170,000 piastres per annum (about 2,295,000 ūqiya or £40,640).[102] In 1848, Beaumier estimated average customs revenues at 960,000 francs (about 3,264,000 ūqiya or £37,824).[103] This shows that there was a growth of trade between 1822 and 1848, but this was partly at the expense of lower customs duties to facilitate greater foreign exchange. Moreover, while revenues increased by about 30 per cent, the value of the currency in the same period had decreased by 25 per cent.[104] In a period of 17 months in 1858–9, total customs revenue equalled 7,856,876.5 ūqiya or about 5,546,030 ūqiya per annum (see app. C). In a decade, customs revenue had increased by about 41 per cent, but the value of the riyāl had again fallen by 25 to 28 per cent.[105] Despite the increased volume of trade the overall growth in customs revenues, therefore, was minimal. Gains may have been somewhat greater had not the prices of many import and export items dropped. In this respect, the fall in the price of cotton goods, the most important import item, was particularly noticeable.[106]

The increase in foreign trade also required the expansion of government apparatus. This meant an increase in government expenditure. The marginal increases in *makhzan* revenues could hardly compensate for the growing costs of the Moroccan state. A Spanish source from the 1850s estimated the total annual revenue of *makhzan* at 47,557,000 ūqiya. Essaouira's contribution from customs revenue was estimated at 1,700,000 ūqiya. Though this was higher than any other port, it still only represented about 3.6 per cent of the total revenue of the *makhzan*. Customs duties from all the ports represented about 11 per cent of state revenues.[107] This source may be questionable, but it does suggest that Essaouira's contribution to the *makhzan* coffers was moderate. Even in the best years, it seems extremely unlikely that customs revenue from the seaports would have constituted more than, let us say, 15 per cent of the revenues of the *makhzan*.[108]

In a period of 17 months in 1858–9, customs duties in Essaouira accounted for about 27 per cent of the total revenues of Essaouira (see app C). The *makhzan* derived the bulk of its revenue from the reimbursements from the *tujjār*'s debts. These figures, however, are deceptive if expenditures are not taken into account. About 87 per cent of what the *makhzan* gained from the *tujjār* was remitted in credit to them. Furthermore, Essaouira was expensive. General expenses for the military, repairs to the town walls, salaries to port officials, etc., amounted to nearly 40 per cent more than the amount gained from customs duties.

If the *makhzan* expected to gain revenues from increased duties derived from foreign trade, this hope was dashed by a new and more serious violation of Moroccan sovereignty: Spain's occupation of Tetuan and the indemnities imposed on the Moroccan government. The people of Essaouira were stunned by these events. Morocco was plunging into a pattern of foreign domination.

Chapter 7

Foreign intervention and domestic reforms

In the decade following the Spanish Moroccan war of 1859–60, foreign intervention led to the transformation of the Moroccan state. Morocco was compelled to empty its treasuries to pay a war indemnity. There were insufficient funds to pay the Spanish, so payments continued for years to come. During the reign of Sīdī Muḥammad b. ʿAbd ar-Raḥmān (1859–73), Morocco attempted to consolidate its position. Administrative and fiscal reforms were initiated to increase the revenues of the *makhzan* in order to meet the costs of an expanding state apparatus.

War and indemnities

Soon after the peaceful succession of Sīdī Muḥammad b. ʿAbd ar-Raḥmān – proclaimed in Essaouira on 30 September 1859[1] – Morocco was threatened by a Spanish invasion. Domestic difficulties in Spain had pushed the Spanish government towards an imperialist adventure in Morocco. Agitation by the Rif tribes against the Spanish enclaves of Melilla and Ceuta provided the excuse for the invasion. The Spanish also considered invading Essaouira, which was still the most active seaport of Morocco. When attack on Essaouira appeared imminent, many Swiris began to flee the town, fearing a repetition of the events of 1844. Some of the elite left by sea for Gibraltar. About 220 Jews, mostly women and children, left on board a steamer with the departing British community.[2] Some Swiris who had the means, such as Aaron and Abraham Corcos, Dinar Ohana, Moses and Judah Afriat, and Moses Assor, made their way to London.[3] The less fortunate escaped into the countryside, seeking a perilous refuge in the surrounding regions. Conditions worsened for these victims, who began to die from famine and exposure.[4] The cost of hiring animals to convey goods and property rose to exorbitant rates,[5] and prices of essential foodstuffs were greatly inflated.[6] Houses belonging to some of those who fled from the town were plundered.[7]

War was proclaimed on 22 November 1859. Tetuan was rapidly occupied, sparing Essaouira from attack. A peace treaty was signed in the spring of 1860 after Morocco had agreed to pay Spain a twenty-million piastre indemnity by the end of the year.[8] This amount the Moroccan government was unable to pay. Popular resentment in Essaouira against the Spanish was reported when a commission arrived in September to collect an instalment on the indemnity. The Spanish delegates had to enter the town under the protection of Qāʾid ʿAbd al-Qādir al-ʿAṭṭār because of the hostile mob. A month later, the commission arrived again, but was this time preceded by a Spanish warship. The commander claimed that the money was to be sent through Muḥammad Brīsha, the former *qāʾid* of Essaouira who was now the head *amīn* of the Moroccan treasury. Qāʾid al-ʿAṭṭār, however, claimed that he did not have the authorization to hand over the money. After several months of fruitless negotiations between the Spanish and the Moroccan authorities, threats ensued. The Spanish sent two armed ships along with a steamer and, according to the local historian, aṣ-Ṣiddīqī, threatened to destroy the town. The *qāʾid* handed over the first instalment, amounting to five million of the twenty-million piastre indemnity.[9]

The treasury of the Moroccan government was now depleted of all its reserves, so the Spanish occupation of Tetuan continued. Negotiations proceeded through Spanish and French mediators. Spain offered to relinquish Tetuan in exchange for the occupation of Essaouira. The British, however, were opposed to foreign occupation and became the principal intermediary between Spain and Morocco. The negotiations dragged on. In June 1861, the level of tensions rose when the Spanish made a naval demonstration before Essaouira.[10] But finally, a compromise was reached at the end of October, whereby another three million piastres were to be sent to Spain immediately in exchange for the evacuation of Tetuan. The *makhzan* was unable to collect that amount, so the British agreed on a loan of £426,000 to be paid back in twenty years with interest. With the help of the loan, the *makhzan* managed to pay back half of the total indemnity.[11] The ten million remaining piastres were to be repaid to Spain by allowing them to take half of the customs duties from Morocco's eight ports, which were supervised by Spanish officials.[12] A British official was to receive repayment on the loan semi-annually from the other half of the customs revenues. Finally, an entrepôt was to be ceded to the Spanish on the southern Moroccan coast.[13]

The Spanish officials at the ports (*recaudadores*) remained for over 20 years. Their chief function was to collect half the revenues from customs each month, but they also influenced the running of commercial affairs. Merchants in Essaouira complained that the Spanish officials intervened in matters which did not concern them.[14] But for the most part, foreign merchants profited from the presence of the Spanish. A few months after their arrival in Essaouira at the beginning of 1862, the French consulate reported that fraud had been eliminated and that the governor was no longer able to favour indigenous merchants by exempting them from paying duties. It had previously been difficult for the foreign merchants to compete, when the natives could, in the words of the French consular agent 'inundate the market with merchandise at a very low price and thus ruin, or at least, seriously impair the business of other merchants, their competitors'.[15] Three months later, it was further noted that the business of native merchants had been cut in half, since unlike in the past, the local merchants were now obliged to pay in cash. This gave the Europeans the advantage, with their greater capital resources, and enabled them to expand their business to an unprecedented level.[16] The British merchants Curtis and Perry became the two most important traders of Essaouira, to judge by the amount of duties they paid.[17] Moreover, the fortunes of a number of Jewish merchant families, most notably Shriqi, sprung from their service to the Spanish agents.[18]

The loss of an important part of the income of the ports seriously impaired the finances of the State. This came at a time when the cost of the state was rising. Morocco, like other countries of the Middle East and North Africa, was unable to raise sufficient revenues to repay its debts, meet the cost of rising military expenditures, and in general, pay for the reforms which were initiated over the next decades.[19] The problem of growing expenses was worsened by the fact that one-half of the income from customs was paid to Spain for over twenty years. The major jump in trade in the 1860s was insufficient to compensate for the debt and indemnities. In the boom year of 1865–6, customs duties amounted to slightly over twice those of the year before the war.[20] Half of these revenues were paid to the Spanish. Another large part of the surplus was sent to the English in Tangier to pay off the loan, either directly or via the treasury in Marrakesh, where money was exchanged for the appropriate currency.[21] The *makhzan*, therefore, could not expect to make substantial gains, even in the best years. Only after the departure of the Spanish from the customs house at the end of 1884 was a large surplus from customs revenues possible. In the three years prior to this date, no surplus money entered the treasury. At the end of 1884 and beginning of 1885, the situation had improved. An excess of 50,586 ūqiya over expenditure for a period of three months was reported.[22] In 1885, a boom year in trade because of the revival of the export of olive oil, nearly 8,400,00 ūqiya were collected, as compared to 3,500,00 in 1884.[23]

The war with Spain was a turning-point for Morocco. The *makhzan* undertook fiscal and administrative reforms to defend itself against foreign encroachments and to increase the revenues of the state.

Port reforms

The presence of the Spanish agents in the Moroccan seaports required changes in the port administration. In 1862, Sultan Muḥammad decided that two *amīn*s were to be appointed to each port. One was to be native to the town, and the other was to come from outside; the former was to earn 60 riyāl a month, the latter 90 riyāl. These *umanāʾ* were to work independently of the governor and were forbidden to engage in commerce. Muḥammad Bannīs was appointed director of the port *umanāʾ* (*amīn al-umanāʾ*). The various other officials in the port – the captain *qabiṭān ar-rasā*), his deputy, and the *ʿudūl* – were also to receive regular salaries so that trading activities would be unnecessary.[24] The Sultan clearly hoped to curtail corruption and to encourage the development of a professional civil service.

In the period before 1860, the *qāʾid* had become the chief official responsible for the operation of customs at the port, a responsibility which was combined with his functions as the *bāshā* in charge of the town's security. In practice, the *qāʾid*'s functions became too diverse with the growth of trade. His involvement in the affairs of the port – the *qāʾid* himself had also become a merchant – may have been an indirect cause for the discontent within the ranks of the garrison of Essaouira. In 1859, there was resentment in the town when Qāʾid al-Ḥājj Muḥammad b. ʿAbd as-Salām Ibn Zākūr, of Fez, in office for a little over a year, refused to distribute uniforms to the troops. Subsequent protests by the military led to his dismissal.[25] His successor, al-Ḥājj ʿAbd al-Karīm ar-Razīnī, held office only briefly, leaving after the death of Sultan ʿAbd ar-Raḥmān a few months later. aṣ-Ṣiddīqī suggests that the *qāʾid* asked to be dismissed because he feared the local militia as a result of what had happened to his predecessor, Qāʾid Ibn Zākūr.[26]

A few months after the appointment of Bannīs as *amīn al-umanāʾ*, the *de facto* governor of Essaouira, al-Ḥājj ʿAbd al-Qādir al-ʿAṭṭār, who was acting for his brother al-ʿArabī – the successor of ar-Razīnī – was replaced by Qāʾid al-Mahdī b. Buʿazza Ibn al-Mashāwrī, who came from the military ranks.[27] The replacement of al-ʿAṭṭār may be understood as part of the plan to separate administration from commerce. The acting *qāʾid*, ʿAbd al-Qādir al-ʿAṭṭār, was one of the established *tujjār* of the town, and owed the Sultan 182,441 ūqiya in 1865, a debt already compounded for some years.[28] After his dismissal from office, he continued trading for some years, and even became a protégé of the Spanish,[29] but he never resumed administrative functions. Ibn al-Mashāwrī, on the other hand, represented the more military aspect of the *qāʾid*'s functions. The *makhzan* was certainly concerned with avoiding conflicts between the *qāʾid* and the troops, which had proved to be dangerous in the time of Ibn Zākūr. More important was the need to separate responsibilities, and to create a more effective port administration.

The *qāʾid* still represented the principal authority of the town, and though he no longer sat at the customs house as in former times, he had to settle the numerous disputes arising between the merchants. His authority, therefore, still sometimes overlapped with that of the *umanāʾ*, despite the attempt by the Sultan to separate their functions. The chief *amīn* of the port, ʿAbd al-Wāḥid Aqaṣbī, complained in 1865 about a Sharifian letter which alleged that the *umanāʾ* were interfering in the decisions of Qāʾid al-Mahdī Ibn al-Mashāwrī, and which he denied: 'We are occupied with that which we've been assigned, namely, the business of the port: imports, exports, expenditure for constructions, etc.', he wrote.[30] When disputes arose between the merchants and the port authorities, the Sultan would ask the *qāʾid* to intervene, as happened, for example, when allegations of fraud and negligence by the boatmen and porters were mounting.[31]

The two *amīns* assigned to the port were insufficient for Essaouira's needs – not only because Essaouira's import and export trade was more active than in any other Moroccan port, but also because all the fiscal concerns of the town were administered by them. It was not long before the numbers of officials increased. In 1865–6, Essaouira had four *umanāʾ* at the port. Their salaries were slightly lower than the 90 riyāl a month suggested in the *dahir* of 1862, perhaps because the increase in officials required greater expenditure (see table 16). Other port officials on the *makhzan* payroll included the captain of the port, a *faqīh* who probably acted as chief ʿ*adl*, and *ṭalaba* who worked as clerks. The salaries of these principal port officials, fixed in silver currency (riyāl), remained approximately the same for the next few decades. The salaries of other minor officials – guards of the port, builders for lighters and their supervisor, etc. – were fixed in mithqāl, the money of account, which meant that their real income was to fall considerably over time.[32]

The same categories of officials had worked at the port before the reforms of 1861, but their salaries had not been regularized. This had encouraged local merchants, such as Tūfal-ʿazz and Būhillāl, to become *umanāʾ*, since such positions combined with commerce could be extremely remunerative. The port authority reforms of 1861 gave birth to a new type of public official. The *amīn* had multiple duties as customs' agent, and tax and rent assessor.

Most of the daily dealings of the *umanāʾ* were with the merchants, and therefore, the smooth operation of the port required the judicious

Table 16 *Salaries of the principal port authorities, 1281–2/1864–6*

Name or title	Function	Salary (in riyāl)
ʿAbd al-Wāḥid Aqaṣbī	chief *amīn*	85.5
ʿUmar b. ʿAmr al-Awsā	chief *amīn*	85.5
ʿAbd ar-Raḥmān b. al-Ḥasan	native *amīn*	46.5
Muḥammad Amillāḥ	native *amīn*	46.5
aṭ-Ṭayyib Būjayda	construction foreman	40
qabiṭān ar-rasā	captain of port	22.5
Muḥammad b. ʿAbd as-Salām	*faqīh* (chief clerk?)	20
al-Ḥajj Qāsim	official in customs house	6
4 *ṭalaba*	clerks	76
	Total	428.5

Source: K.H., K[295].

administration of the former and the co-operation of the latter. As a result, the merchants took an active interest in the conduct of the *umanāʾ*. Abraham Corcos, in particular, served as an informal advisor to Bannīs. After the complaints were raised against Aqaṣbī, for example, Bannīs assured Corcos that the situation had been rectified: 'He improved his conduct, actions, and relations with the people, praise God, and it is our desire that he should conduct himself well [so that] the commoners and elite will praise it [his conduct].'[33] The merchants of Essaouira took a direct interest in the appointments of the *umanāʾ*. In 1866, Aqaṣbī, then chief *amīn* of Essaouira, was replaced by al-Ḥājj Bujnān al-Bārūdī (who died after three months in office). Regarding his appointment, Bannīs explained to Abraham Corcos:

> You have written to us concerning the appointment of the *amīn* who will be in your (joyous) port . . . With the guidance of God (may he be exalted), we nominated a good, humble, and judicious man for you who handles business with adroitness . . . He has been an *amīn* in the port of El Jadida.[34]

His replacement, al-ʿArabī ash-Sharrāṭ, was highly praised by Beaumier.[35] Corcos not only took an interest in appointments, but he might also be asked to instruct a new appointee in his tasks. When, for example, Muḥammad Bannīs secured the royal appointment of an uncle, al-Ḥājj al-ʿAyashī Bannīs, as *amīn* of Essaouira, he asked Corcos to assist the latter in his new post:

We would like you to inform him on matters with which he is not familiar, and to guide him so that he will be competent and successful. We have entrusted you with this task . . . for it is due to the affinity between us that your counsel has been sought in this matter.[36]

The central administration adopted a number of new methods to improve the functioning of the port authority. One important area of improvement was in the procedure for book-keeping, which led to a better defined division of labour among the port officials, and at the same time, a more complex system of control and supervision by the central government. In 1865, the Sultan ordered the *umanāʾ* to send in the ships' manifests accompanying the monthly accounts of the port. These manifests listed the cargo in weight or number, and the names of the consignees, all of which were translated in Arabic.[37] It was on the basis of the quantities listed that the *umanāʾ* calculated the 10 per cent *ad valorem* duty. The introduction of this procedure enabled the central administration to double check the calculations. The English complied with the order, but the French and Spanish at first refused to hand over the manifests for their ships.[38]

The presence of the Spanish agents may have induced the *umanāʾ* to keep more regular accounts. When errors were made, the *umanāʾ* sometimes double checked with the Spanish records. The fact that half the duties were paid to the Spanish produced other bureaucratic changes in the port as well. The Gregorian calendar, for example, was used alongside the Muslim calendar.[39] The amount of paper-work also multiplied. Progressively greater numbers of account books (*kanānīsh*) were kept, and English register books were imported.[40] A special *ṭālib* was responsible for registering the various accounts in the *kanānīsh*; one such *ṭālib* was reprimanded by the *umanāʾ* in 1871 for laziness and told to work harder.[41]

Increasingly the authorities realized that the kinds of entries in the registers had become too varied, making it difficult to check accounts. Rents on *makhzan* property were simply recorded together with other revenues of the port. In 1871, the *umanāʾ* were instructed to record in greater detail the revenues from the rent of *makhzan* properties and to separate them from the listings of other revenues. In the future, these details were to be sent to the *makhzan* together with the monthly accounts.[42] The *makhzan* at this time was having difficulty collecting rents and wanted to find a means to keep a precise account. Two years later, the *muḥtasib* of the town, al-Ḥājj al-Hāshimī, was given the responsibility of collecting the rents, for which he was to be rewarded 25 mithqāl each month.[43]

Further reforms of the port administration were undertaken during the reign of Mawlāy al-Ḥasan. Since 1873, the *muḥtasib* al-Hāshimī had been the principal official in charge of *makhzan* rents, but there were various officials at the markets and gates, known as *umanāʾ al-mustafādāt*, who also assisted in the collection of taxes.[44] All these officials came under the financial control of the *umanāʾ* of the port. It was only in about 1880 that a new *amīn al-mustafādāt* was delegated with wider responsibilities: all town revenues excluding customs, and all taxes collected in the hinterland, were to be under his direction. This official and his assistants were granted a house of residence.[45] The *muḥtasib* was still essentially in charge of collecting rents, but the *amīn al-mustafādāt* had a supervisory role in the collection of all urban taxes and rents (apart from the *ḥubus*).

The task of the port authority had become more complex, and the *makhzan* had to devise ways of checking on the port's activities. Absenteeism, for example, was to be reported directly to the Sultan.[46] Officials involved in misconduct were to be dismissed. In 1866, the *umanāʾ* reported that insolent boatmen and porters had been involved in thefts. Goods stolen from merchants were being sold in town. When the *umanāʾ* tried to intervene, under pressure from the foreign consuls and merchants, the boatmen responded with insulting language. This, according to the *umanāʾ*, they did 'in the presence of Governor al-Mahdī, who did not get them to change nor scold them – rather, he gave them his support'.[47] It may have been that the *qāʾid* who, like the boatmen, came from the military ranks, wished to undercut the growing role of the *umanāʾ*. But the port authority took precedence in this case and the Sultan ordered the governor to arrest eight of the sailors who had defied the *umanāʾ*, including the captain, and to send them to Prince Mawlāy al-Ḥasan, who was *khalīfa* in Marrakesh at the time. Their arrest caused 'the town to shake with fear and alarm from the power of carrying out the authority of the Sultan (may God give him strength) . . . not one boatman returned to work at the port'.[48]

During the reign of Mawlāy al-Ḥasan (1873–94), numerous reforms were adopted in an effort to create a more centralized system of government. A new *amīn al-umanāʾ* was appointed, Muḥammad at-Tāzī ar-Ribāṭī, who was responsible for general reforms. On February 22, at-Tāzī arrived in Essaouira to inspect the receipts of the customs house. A number of port officials were replaced.[49] A few years later, the *umanāʾ* were instructed to keep a special register book for recording all ships, specifying whether they were steam or sail, where they came from, their destination, tonnage, the dates of their journey, and a number of other details. The various commodities were to be precisely enumerated in seven columns, together with their tax.[50] Most of these items and categories were already recorded in one register or another, but this new procedure increased the paper-work by having the register exclusively for the ships and their contents.

Such improvements in the bureaucracy meant more efficient control over the activities of the *umanāʾ*, but they were probably inadequate as a means for totally stamping out the undoubtedly universal problem of the corruption of customs officials. The salaries of the *umanāʾ*, though higher than most other *makhzan* officials, remained relatively low. Miège refers to Mawlāy al-Ḥasan's vain attempt to eradicate corruption by raising the salaries of officials, especially the *umanāʾ* of the ports.[51] In fact, their salary in 1884 was one riyāl less than it had been in the mid-1860s, quite apart from the question of inflation, which certainly devalued their earnings to a degree.[52] Bearing this in mind, the motivation for cheating the *makhzan* must have been high. The *umanāʾ* reportedly paid a high price for their position, and by manipulating the accounts, were able to make large profits by the end of their service. Park's meticulous study of duties on imports and exports for 1301/1883–4 has shown that possibly up to two-thirds of the potential revenues from customs were stolen. This amount would have increased dramatically when the Spanish officials finally left the ports at the end of 1884.[53]

It is difficult to assess how often such large-scale corruption occurred. The *makhzan* certainly created any number of checks on the activities of the *umanāʾ*, and corrupt officials could be dismissed. One check in Essaouira was the balancing of the two chief *amīn*s between one Rabati and one Fasi, each from well-known merchant households. In 1865, ʿUmar b. ʿAmr al-Awsā, the Rabati *amīn* of Essaouira, complained about his colleague, Aqaṣbī the Fasi. The two *amīn*s of El Jadida were also having some differences. According to an administrative letter, this conflict did not involve 'a division between the people of Fez and the people of Rabat'.[54] A few months later, however, the two *amīn*s of Essaouira reported to Bannīs that everything was operating smoothly at the port and that suggestions of differences were untrue: 'No one proceeds without the other in any matter, except after consultation and negotiation.'[55] The local *umanāʾ* also could be a check on the power of the head *amīn* of the town. After reports circulated that Aqaṣbī had been monopolizing all the business at customs for himself without allowing other *umanāʾ* to take part, Muḥammad Bannīs wrote to the port officials in Essaouira asking them to declare the validity of such accusations. They categorically denied the accusations: 'very little is done except in the presence of the *umanāʾ* as-Sayyid al-Ḥājj ʿAbd ar-Raḥmān b. al-Ḥasan, in most cases with the two local ʿ*adl*s, and the Spanish agent in charge of recording with us'.[56] Another check was to limit the term of office, which rarely lasted more than three years. The assumption was clearly made that by appointing members of respected merchant families who were strangers to the town, and limiting the time of their service, it would be possible to keep corruption and the incentive for involvement in local business affairs to a minimum. The fact that Spanish officials were simultaneously recording the duties was an additional check on potential illegal profit.

The two local *amīn*s had similar tasks to those of the chief *amīn*s. The term of office of the local *umanāʾ*, however, was much longer, giving them more opportunities to take advantage of their positions for personal gain. Amillāḥ and ʿAbd ar-Raḥmān b. al-Ḥasan both served for many years. Amillāḥ was appointed in 1863, serving until 1872, when he was arrested for squandering public funds. One of his main tasks had been to collect money from various taxes in town, and hence he was sometimes referred to as the 'superintendent of collection' (*amīn al-qabḍ*). Suspicions arose when Amillāḥ was unable to provide accounts of dirham he had collected as *amīn al-qabḍ*.[57] Several years later, Amillāh was arrested and imprisoned in Fez (where he died shortly afterwards) for misappropriating *makhzan* funds, and his assets were sequestered and sold by auction. His house in the *medina*, near the Bawākhir mosque, was said to have been one of the nicest houses in Essaouira of that era, constructed by builders that Amillāh himself had hired from Fez.[58]

After Amillāḥ's death in 1872, only three *umanāʾ* remained at the port. There were still two 'foreign' *amīn*s, while the third position was continued to be held by the veteran Swiri *amīn*, ʿAbd ar-Raḥmān b. al-Ḥasan.[59] Efforts were made by the *makhzan* to improve the management of funds and to create greater checks on the activities of the port authorities. In 1874, the Sultan gave explicit instructions to Qāʾid ʿAmāra:

> We ordered the *umanāʾ* to bring into the treasury (may God make it prosper) all surplus funds they have each month, and you are to be present when it is deposited. Likewise, when something is taken out with authorization, you are to take the keys and keep them by you, and to put a register book inside the treasury to certify all that goes in and all that comes out . . .[60]

Qāʾid ʿAmāra, therefore, was given a much more supervisory role in the port than his predecessors. Under the close supervision of the central government, he began to monitor the activities of the *umanāʾ*.[61] He was made responsible in particular for cracking down on contraband.[62]

In addition to the administrative reforms, projects to improve the physical facilities at the port were also initiated. An English engineer, James Craig, arrived in Essaouira at the end of 1862 to undertake the construction of a jetty at the harbour for the lighters. He was also hired by the Sultan for a number of other engineering works. Five years later, and after substantial payments were made, the project was abandoned with the pier as yet unfinished. Disputes between Craig and the *umanāʾ* were blamed for the failure.[63]

In the view of the merchants, facilities at the port remained inadequate.[64] But despite the failure of the port works, the administrative reforms were able to create a bureaucracy which responded to the new situation brought about by the Spanish presence and the increasing scale of foreign trade. It has often been argued that the bureaucracy created was rudimentary, and it has even been suggested that the *makhzan* totally lacked any archives.[65] This was not the case. While the reforms were not a remedy for the *makhzan*'s financial problems, they did meet the specific administrative needs of the port.[66]

Monetary control and revenue

The growth of foreign trade, indemnity, and debt together created a new monetary situation in Morocco. Export duties at the ports were fixed in ūqiya (1 mithqāl = 10 ūqiya). The mithqāl originally was a silver coin of 29 grams, but in the latter part of the eighteenth century it became exclusively a money of account. What this meant was that payments on the mithqāl/ūqiya tariffs were translated into silver currency at the current rate of exchange. Had the *makhzan* permitted this system to continue, it would have lost considerable returns from customs duties as monetary inflation increased. Considering the fact that the Moroccan government was hard-pressed for money, and that monetary inflation – hitherto almost unknown in Morocco – was growing, the *makhzan* had to be innovative in its control of the monetary system.

The direct cause of the accelerated depreciation of the ūqiya (see fig. 17) was the constant counterfeiting of copper coins (literally *fals*, pl. *fulūs*, colloquial, *fils*, *flūs*), especially in the Sous.[67] In theory, there were 24 flūs in an ūqiya, though there were various denominations of bronze coins which all were proportionally related to the standard flūs.[68] It was with copper coins that goods were bought in the market, rural taxes were assessed, and soldiers and many *makhzan* officials were paid.[69] But the silver riyāl was used as the main medium for commercial transactions. Under Sultan Sulaymān, the Spanish piastre (also called the piastre, the hard dollar, and the Spanish *real* – hence the *riyāl* in Arabic), became the principal coin used in commerce,[70] and the reference currency for the monetary system.[71] The Spanish piastre continued to represent the silver standard for Morocco throughout the nineteenth century, though the net

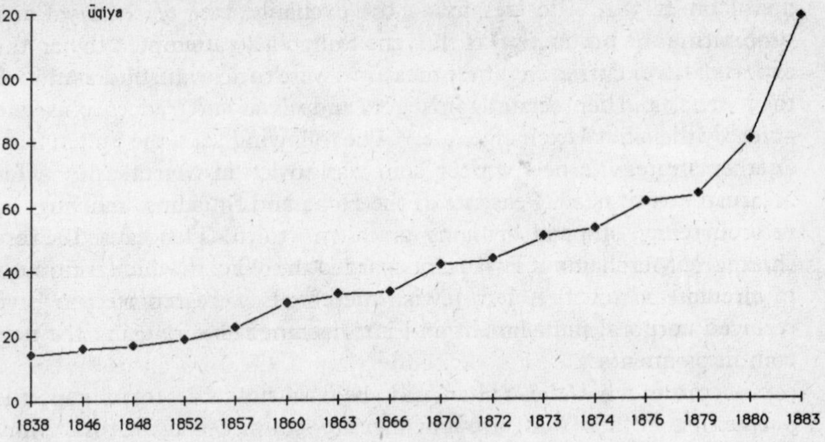

Fig. 17 Rate of exchange for the 5f (French riyāl).

weight of the coin altered. According to one source, it decreased from 27.06 grams in 1772 to 25.96 in 1854–64.[72] Until 1860, the Spanish piastre remained the principal silver currency used in Essaouira, but after 1830 and particularly in the 1850s, the French five-franc piece (5**a**), came increasingly into use.[73] Moroccan silver coins (*dirham sudasī, dirham rubaʿī*)[74] or gold coins of lower alloys (*bunduqī*), were hardly in evidence in Essaouira. Sultan ʿAbd ar-Raḥmān had made a number of unsuccessful attempts to melt down these coins and produce a new Moroccan mint.

The growth of foreign commerce disrupted the Moroccan bi-metal system of bronze and silver, since copper coins could not be used in foreign exchange. As foreign silver riyāl imposed itself more and more on the Moroccan system, the ūqiya began to inflate. Hence, more flūs were counterfeited, further reducing the value of the ūqiya. This problem was exacerbated between 1845 and 1851, when drought went from bad to worse. Silver specie was exported to purchase grain from abroad.[75] As prices began to rise, the production of copper coins increased, and starting in 1846, the Sultan repeatedly had to prohibit the striking of flūs.[76] The growth of flūs, and the virtual disappearance of silver coins from the market, jeopardized Moroccan commerce. Those merchants who had silver coins were obviously hoarding them, speculating on the further depreciation of the ūqiya. To control the problem, the Sultan attempted to fix the exchange rate in 1848. The French and Spanish silver coins were fixed at 17 and 18 ūqiya respectively; the quarter riyāl (*dhū al-madāfi*) was to be exchanged at 4.5 ūqiya, and the *basīṭa* (*peseta caro*) at 3.5; and the gold *bunduqī* was established at 34 ūqiya and the doubloon at 384.[77] Besides fixing the exchange rate of the riyāl and prohibiting the production of flūs, the Sultan also attempted to ban the export of silver currency. These measures were to no avail: flūs continued to be struck and depreciate against gold and silver, and traders refused to abide by the official exchange rate.[78] The following year, the Sultan tried another strategy: a new copper coin was struck in Marrakesh.[79] This measure was resisted. Peasants in the Haha and Shiadma, refusing the new currency, stopped bringing grain into town. This caused severe shortages. Merchants of Essaouira hoarded the old coin which continued to circulate in town. A few Jewish merchants were reported to have received corporal punishment and imprisonment for refusing the new coin in payments.[80]

No matter what the Sultan did, he was not able to prevent the production of flūs. With drought in 1849–50, prices again rose. More copper coins were struck. The Sultan pointed out that 'time and time again' the production of coins had been prohibited, and ordered the arrest of those involved in illegal production. Riyāl seized in contraband were to be melted down for minting a new dirham, and shortly thereafter, Spanish piastres too were taken out of circulation for the same purpose.[81]

The treaty of 1856 and the growth of trade hastened the process of monetary inflation. In 1852, the Spanish piastre had been fixed by *dahir* at 20 ūqiya and the 5**f** piece at 19,[82] but its average exchange in 1857 for purchasing imports in Essaouira was 24 ūqiya and exports between 21 and 23.5 ūqiya.[83] As the market value of bronze against silver continued to depreciate, the *makhzan* decided to fix the 1852 rate of exchange (the 20/19 ratio) at customs. This was the only way for the *makhzan* to maintain its level of revenues since it could not longer readjust the tariff.[84] By the time of the agreement with the Spanish in 1861, the 5**f** had reached 32.5 ūqiya, and the Spanish dollar had gone up to 34.2. These new rates of exchange were fixed by the *makhzan* for the whole country, though it tried to maintain the 20/19 exchange at customs. But in 1862, foreign pressures forced the Sultan to raise the customs exchange in conformity with the rest of the country, causing a plunge in the returns from customs, and a rise in prices.[85] This new rate of exchange was initially disadvantageous, but as the ūqiya continued to inflate at market rates, the maintenance of a fixed system of exchange became essential for avoiding a serious reduction in *makhzan* revenues.[86]

The Spanish riyāl continued to be the principal reference currency, and it was probably maintained because of the need to divert substantial revenues to pay the monthly instalments on the indemnity. To help facilitate the exchange of different currencies, a new accounting system was developed whereby the Spanish riyāl, the reference currency, would translate into 20 '*bilyūn*', and the 5f at 19, and other currencies would follow proportionally.[87] Money was sent to the Spanish and English either directly from Essaouira, or after it had been exchanged in the treasuries of Marrakesh. Furthermore, due to the fact that almost all coins were of foreign origin – and indeed, the *recaudadores* refused any other coins – the *makhzan* found it necessary to send two agents abroad to deal in foreign specie: al-Ḥājj aṭ-Ṭāhir b. al-Malīḥ went to Gibraltar and Muḥammad Ibn ʿAzūz went to London for this purpose.[88]

This fixed rate for international currencies, however, did not prevent the continued inflation of the ūqiya at the market rate of exchange. Counterfeiting of flūs continued, particularly because of the rising demands for imported goods and increased taxation. The Sultan was unable to control the exchange rate of the ūqiya in the market. Consequently, a practice eventually developed in which the *makhzan* translated taxes and debts paid in bronze to the current market exchange rate of the ūqiya against the riyāl. This meant that taxes and payments to the *makhzan* increased commensurate with the rate of inflation. While the units of money of account remained the same, there were two concurrent systems: one floated in the market and the other was fixed by the *makhzan* for foreigners or merchants dealing with foreign exchange.[89]

Monetary controls by the *makhzan* often came into conflict with the merchants. In 1863, a copper coin called the *tazlaght*[90] began to flood the market and depreciate the value of the acceptable currency, to such an extent that the *umanāʾ* were ordered to seize the coin. The *tujjār* received explicit instructions: 'Pay what you owe in the currency presently circulating, providing that it is in silver, not copper.'[91] The merchants were undoubtedly having difficulty meeting their obligations because of bad harvests in Europe and Morocco, the depreciation of the currency, and a concurrent rise in prices.[92]

The effort to recover some of the losses sustained by the imposed 1862 rate probably explains why the rents of *casbah* houses were raised in 1864 (see table 9). The merchants paid rent for their *casbah* houses in riyāl (though accounts were kept in mithqāl/ūqiya), and demanded that they should pay at the market exchange rate. 'I did not obtain [the Sultan's] agreement . . . but in [times of] difficulty, a lower exchange rate for riyāl against mithqāl would be granted', wrote the *wazīr* Bū ʿAshrīn to Abraham Corcos.[93] The merchants claimed that the rent increase would cause them harm, but in fact the *makhzan* augmented rent by only 25 per cent, compared to a 41.5 per cent loss between the 1856 and the 1862 exchange rate (i.e., from 20/19 to 34.2/32.5).

The new exchange imposed on the *makhzan* and the presence of Spanish agents who prevented the extension of credit on duties, gave foreign merchants advantages over Moroccan *tujjār*. Despite the fact that prices of imports were dropping generally in Morocco, foreign goods, especially Manchester textiles, still commanded much higher prices in Essaouira than in Europe. This must have been one of the reasons why the *tujjār* were having trouble paying both duties and the monthly instalments.[94] After the boom year of 1865, there was a slump in trade and the merchants had to delay payment of debts, and, unable to pay duties, had to leave their merchandise to rot in the customs house.[95]

The depreciation of the ūqiya at the market exchange continued for the same chronic reasons. Locusts in 1866–7 devoured the almond and olive crops. This disaster was followed by drought. Specie was again exported, and food prices went up. As a consequence, counterfeiting of flūs was unstoppable.[96] In 1869 the ūqiya was estimated at 38 against the Spanish riyāl.[97] This depreciation prompted the government to melt down both silver and copper coins and reissue new flūs and dirham coins at lower standards of weight. The Sultan ordered that customs should be paid half in new dirham and half in riyāl. The British vice-consul advised British merchants not to abide by the order, claiming that it was in contravention of the treaty.[98] The *tujjār* naturally preferred to pay off customs with the debased dirham, but the Spanish would accept only riyāl. Once the *umanā'* had collected the dirham from the merchants, it was sent to Marrakesh to be exchanged for riyāl in order to pay the Spanish.[99]

The *makhzan* could find no solution to the problem through traditional methods. Counterfeit silver from Europe, Algeria, and the Sous began to circulate, defeating attempts to reissue the new coin.[100] A more radical measure was adopted in February 1869: the Sultan ordered that for customs the 5**f** was to be exchanged for 19 ūqiya and the larger dirham for 9 mūzūna (or 2.25 ūqiya).[101] This re-established the duties fixed by the tariff of exports in the treaty of 1856. The government justified its actions by pointing out that merchants would not suffer since prices would fall just as they had risen in 1862.[102] This new rate of exchange was never implemented, though the British were willing to go along with it. The other consulates protested and the merchants argued that an unfavourable exchange would bring commerce to a grinding halt. The *makhzan* relented, and the order was rescinded in November.[103]

The *makhzan* adopted another strategy at the same time that the attempt to re-establish the 20/19 exchange rate at customs was initiated: the dirham was re-established in a new accounting system of one dirham to one ūqiya, as had existed in the time of Sultan Sīdī Muḥammad b. ʿAbdallāh. All Moroccans in the city and the countryside were to abide by this exchange. The *makhzan* hoped to reconstitute a dirham system which could be used, among other things, for the payment of customs duties at the fixed rate of exchange for the ūqiya just like the foreign riyāl.[104] The attempt by the *makhzan* to restore the Moroccan silver currency was unsuccessful for the most part. Counterfeiting hastened the devaluation of the dirham against the foreign riyāl. Furthermore, since the dirham was established at the fixed rate of exchange, it was only natural that the merchants would rather pay duties in the debased coin. A year and a half after the dirham reform, the *amīn* al-ʿAyāshī Bannīs reported that 'no riyāl are entering the diwāna'.[105] While the market value of the legal dirham (*dirham sharīʿ*) was only about seven per cent higher than the official exchange rate at customs, the 5f was 20 per cent higher, now exchanged at 41.5 ūqiya.[106] Naturally, as al-ʿAyashī Bannīs observed, the merchants would rather hoard their foreign riyāl, and pay customs in dirham.[107]

The dispute between the merchants and the *umanāʾ* points to an underlying problem of monetary controls that the *makhzan* faced. The 1856 tariff was fixed on the assumption that the exchange rate of bronze against silver was stable. It had emerged that this was not the case. The *makhzan* was therefore in the process of defining the relationship between the fixed exchange of currencies for international exchange, and the domestic value, a distinction, as Park terms it, between the ūqiya and the 'pseudo-ūqiya'.[108] The *tujjār* began to argue that they were taking into account the mithqāl value of export commodities in relationship to the bronze values established in mithqāl by the tariff of 1856. The *umanāʾ* were saying that the tariff was now being redefined in silver since the exchange rate was fixed and unalterable. Furthermore, the *makhzan* insisted that the merchants had to settle in both dirham and riyāl at a customs exchange rate, regardless of the market value of silver. This was the *makhzan*'s prerogative in safeguarding revenues in the face of inflation.

The merchants were compelled to accept this arrangement. The payment of export duties henceforth was fairly straightforward. The commodities were assessed by weight and charged according to the tariff. Payment was made at the fixed rate of exchange. The merchants would only squabble over which currency they used to settle their accounts, or perhaps over the accuracy of the scales (which were periodically regularized to the correct standard).[109] Import duties, however, were another matter. Imports were assessed by value rather than by weight, and the value was determined by fluctuating local prices which varied. Not surprisingly, the merchants often disagreed with the *umanāʾ* on the valuation of merchandise. These kinds of disputes increased when there were slumps in trade at Essaouira, such as in 1870–1. The central government felt that merchandise was under-assessed since it sold for much more in Europe. The merchants claimed that when they had merchandise auctioned in the market, it sold for less than the amount assessed by the *umanāʾ*. This, according to the *umanāʾ*, was because the merchants obtained goods from their creditors cheaply to exchange in kind. Prices were therefore higher in other parts of Morocco: 'the price for merchandise in Essaouira is not like the price in Fez', they claimed.[110]

The *umanāʾ* were therefore caught between the pressures of the merchants and the demands of the *makhzan*. Three months later, the *amīn* al-ʿAyāshī Bannīs wrote to the *amīn al-umanāʾ*: 'The Sultan has written to us a number of times reprimanding us for leniency in the valuation of merchandise, and he did not accept the reasons we gave for this.' The *umanāʾ* continued to assess the merchandise at current prices. To increase the amount of duties, the Sultan arranged for a list of rates to be sent from the *umanāʾ* of Marrakesh and ordered the *umanāʾ* of Essaouira to apply those rates when assessing the merchandise. This the merchants refused to accept, since the list was based on prices in bronze which were high in Marrakesh. The Swiri merchants were stuck with the disadvantageous customs exchange rate. The *umanāʾ* gave the merchants two choices: 'either the duties should be paid on the basis of that list or the duties on merchandise should be paid in kind as is practised by the *umanāʾ* of Tangier', but this proposal was not accepted by the merchants. The English consul suggested that three merchants be appointed to assess the merchandise, a suggestion which was obviously unacceptable to the *umanāʾ*: 'How can [it be expected that] the merchant make the valuation for himself [if] prices are high?'[111] The list of prices was probably only applied for a short period of time, if at all. When disputes arose, the goods were deposited in the stores of the *diwāna*. The *umanāʾ* were instructed to settle at the end of the month, taking a higher sum if the price of the commodity had risen on the market.[112] Often, however, the goods ended up being auctioned by the authorities in the market.

In making these periodic adjustments, the *makhzan* was less affected by inflation than the merchants. Furthermore, the *makhzan* made the *tujjār* pay for the continued depreciation of the Moroccan bronze and silver currencies. In 1870, rent on dwellings and warehouses in the old *casbah* were raised by 30 per cent, the second major increase since 1862.[113] In the following years *makhzan* properties were again reassessed. In 1874, the *umanāʾ*, under the supervision of the *qāʾid*, was carefully to register all *makhzan* properties.[114] The task was accomplished in 1296/1878–9. The investigation revealed that in the two *casbah*s where rent was paid in riyāl, monthly rents amounted to 24,663.75 ūqiya which equalled 758.88 riyāl at the 32.5 exchange rate charged. Readjusted at the market rate of exchange (now at 62 ūqiya the riyāl), a total of 47,050 would have been collected.[115] This was to become the new rate for *makhzan* property. Almost all the houses in the two *casbahs* were held by foreigners or protégés, and therefore the *makhzan* had to charge rent at the customs rate of exchange since any alteration would not have been acceptable to the foreign community. In addition, foreigners and protégés often withheld rents, first demanding settlements of outstanding claims they had against the Moroccan government.[116] Some merchants also stopped paying rent to force the *makhzan* to undertake repairs on their premises. In 1878, the *muḥtasib* reported that 1,166 riyāl were owed on rent of six properties for a period of 38 months.[117]

The only means, therefore, for the *makhzan* to maintain its revenue was to periodically adjust its rents in the two *casbahs* as it did in 1296/1878–9. In 1301/1883–4, incomes from rents averaged at about 59,800 ūqiya a month (they varied because at times the merchants withheld payment),[118] which represented an increase of only 21 per cent, while the ūqiya in the same period had risen by 100 per cent against the riyāl. The *makhzan* also raised rent on *ḥubus* property by 50 per cent to recuperate amounts lost through inflation. The foreign consuls vigorously protested, claiming that their protégés already paid a high price for the key rights, and *jilsa* which were auctioned off in the market. The *makhzan* and the consuls argued over the legality of this rent increase. The Sultan conceded that the poor occupying *ḥubus* property should only pay a 30 per cent increase.[119]

The monthly instalments on debts was another area affected. In 1871, the Sultan decided to demand that repayment of the total debt be increased – from 0.5 per cent to 0.75 per cent. The *tujjār* petitioned that they were unable to pay the additional amounts, due to the slump in trade, and asked that if the increase were implemented, they should be allowed to pay off their debts in dirhams.[120] At this stage, the dirham exchange had dropped to 33 ūqiya, that is, only 1.5 per cent more on the market than the customs exchange rate. The riyāl, on the other hand, was still climbing. By 1870 it was being exchanged for 41.5 ūqiya; by 1872, it had climbed to 42–43.[121] The *umanā᾽* insisted that the duties be paid only in riyāl. Some merchants left their goods in the customs stores rather than acquiesce.[122]

The continued depreciation of the riyāl during the reign of Mawlāy al-Ḥasan forced the Sultan to adopt new measures. The influx of counterfeit flūs from the Sous in 1879 had contributed to further inflation. an-Nāṣirī remarks that while the riyāl was being exchanged for 63 ūqiya in Marrakesh, in Fez the exchange was at 53. People in Marrakesh hoarded the bronze currency in order to later obtain a better exchange for silver elsewhere.[123] Flūs began to disappear from the markets of the interior.

The Sultan probably felt that this would be detrimental to trade because if exchanges were sluggish in the interior, gate and market taxes would diminish. He therefore decreed that the market exchange for the riyāl was to return to 32.5 ūqiya. If such a measure was successful, the merchants, who were the main sector of the population dealing in foreign silver currency, stood to lose. This is exactly what occurred, according to an-Nāṣirī: 'The merchants were harmed from the devaluation of the riyāl, just as the poor were hurt by the lack of flūs.'[124] At the same time, the *makhzan* applied the old market exchange rate of 63 ūqiya the riyāl at the gates and markets. Rent of *ḥubus* property, which were fixed in ūqiya, went up in proportion to the new exchange.[125]

With hindsight, such draconian measures had little chance for success. The forced depreciation of the exchange rate by nearly 100 per cent may have encouraged petty trade in the interior, and hence increased gate and market tax revenue, but it threatened to diminish the profits of the merchants dealing in foreign currency. The merchants and the consuls of Essaouira put pressure on the Moroccan government to abrogate the decree, claiming that in other parts of Morocco the exchange persisted at 60 ūqiya. It was not long before enforcement of the regulation was abandoned.[126]

The riyāl depreciated by another 100 per cent in the following years, as prices rose during the worst drought of the nineteenth century (1878–82).[127] Toward the end of 1883, the market of Essaouira was again swamped by counterfeit coins:

> The coinage of the very basest sham copper money was continued apparently without any attempt at repression so that by the end of the year good *floos* had entirely disappeared from the market, and the quality of the bad became so wretched that a sample of coins sent to England was pronounced, it is said, not a sufficient percentage of copper to repay the cost of smelting.[128]

The situation became so bad that the authorities posted guards at the gates to seize the coins. Commerce came to a standstill. The riyāl was being exchanged for 150 ūqiya, and, as in 1877, legal flūs coins disappeared from circulation. Attempts to regulate the problem led to serious differences between the *amīn al-mustafādāt* and the *umanā*ʾ of the port when the latter tried to take the counterfeit coin out of circulation. The *amīn al-mustafādāt* who had the keys to the room where the counterfeit coins had been placed, took the base coins out. The *umanā*ʾ feared that the riyāl would rise to an exchange rate of 200 ūqiya![129] Consequently, the authorities fixed the exchange rate in the market at 125 ūqiya for the legal bronze coins, though initially they had little success in enforcing this rate. Those who had hoarded the good coins exchanged them for 80 or 90 ūqiya the riyāl. Eventually, however, the base coins disappeared from circulation, and the exchange rate was stabilized.[130]

In 1881, fresh attempts were made to restore a Moroccan system of silver coinage. A contract was signed with the French to mint in Europe twenty million francs worth of a new silver coin (*ar-riyāl al-Ḥasanī*) between 1881 and 1884.[131] The coin was to be based on the legal dirham system and equal intrinsically to the French riyāl: the one riyāl piece was to weigh ten legal dirham, equivalent to the French riyāl standard, and smaller denominations were to be valued proportionally by weight to this dirham accounting system.[132]

The introduction of the new coins at the end of 1883 was justified in a *dahir*, which circulated around the country, as an effort to re-establish a strictly legal system of exchange, based on what were perceived as Islamic principles for the denominations of silver coins, namely, that the 'legal' dirham should weigh 55 grains of barley in order to implement an Islamic system of taxation: 'The kings of old (God be merciful upon them) were free from the increase and decrease in the weight [of coins] . . .' The coins were struck on the basis of five units: ten, five, two and a half, and one-half dirham *sharʿī*. These coins were to be circulated in the markets, and any coins deviating from these weights were to be seized.[133] The *qāʾid* of Marrakesh, Aḥmad Amalik, suggested to the Sultan that the changes should be applied at customs in the ports.[134] When the *umanāʾ* tried to put the new system of denomination into effect at customs, all the merchants protested 'in one tongue', claiming that the riyāl (i.e., foreign silver coin), which was the only coin accepted in the Sous, would disappear if they had to pay customs in the new currency. This was because, as the letter seems to imply, most imports were sold in Marrakesh and if the merchants needed to sell their products there in the new currency, they would obtain an insufficient supply of riyāl to make their purchases in the Sous. This, the merchants complained, would be detrimental to commerce. The *umanāʾ* were therefore unsuccessful in implementing the new measure.[135] Orders were again issued to circulate the new coins struck in Europe.[136] Although the coins became a common currency on the market, this attempt to recreate a stable Moroccan currency – based more on ideology than a grasp on monetary realities of unequal exchange – failed as it had done in 1869. The new coin depreciated in value a few years later.[137]

Apart from the effort to re-establish a stable Moroccan currency, the monetary measures adopted by the state met with a modicum of success. By creating a dual system, whereby two exchange systems were allowed to co-exist – one for international exchange, and the other for the domestic market – the Moroccan government was able to avert excessive losses in customs duties due to inflation. Inflation itself was more moderate than has sometimes been assumed. Between 1862 and 1887, Park estimates an inflation rate of about 4.9 per cent.[138] Where Morocco failed was in developing a monetary system which could cope with the inequitable exchange with Europe. All efforts at re-establishing a sound Moroccan currency were doomed to failure, and Morocco slipped more precipitously into a relationship of dependence on Europe.[139] More importantly, the finances of the state were faced with insurmountable difficulties. The *makhzan*'s traditional fiscal structure was incapable of bearing the costs imposed by the new situation. Payments to Spain and England, and the costs of reforms designed to create a strong centralized state required revamping the finances of the state. As a consequence, new types of taxes were imposed to increase the revenues of the Moroccan government.

Taxes and tolls

In July 1860, the Sultan decided that given the dire circumstances, a gate tax was to be established. The octroi, classified as *maks*, could only be legitimate if the Islamic state was threatened. The justification in this case was the necessity to pay the Spanish who were still occupying Tetuan.[140] By the end of 1860, the gate tolls appear to have been put into effect in Marrakesh. At the same time, the goat skin, hide, and fruit markets were farmed out in Marrakesh for 1,000 mithqāl each, according to the British vice-consul in Essaouira.[141] By late February, or early March, 1861, orders were received by the governor of Essaouira to impose an octroi on the sellers of merchandise (see table 17).

In the period immediately following the imposition of the new gate and market taxes in Essaouira, the gate tolls, the tax on olive oil at the scales of the *qāʿ*a, livestock, the skin market, and silversmith market appear to have been initially administered by *makhzan* officials.[142] The concession of tobacco, hashish, and other items that were smoked (*aṭ-ṭarqa*) was farmed for 80,000 ūqiya.[143] Records of revenues from 16 Ramaḍān 1276/17 April 1860 through Shawwāl 1278/9 May 1862 for the gates, including the tax on olive oil, equalled 94,857.5 ūqiya.[144] Considering that the octroi was established only in March 1861, this probably represents 14 months' revenue, at an average of 6,775.5 ūqiya per month. This figure seems particularly low since we know that a few years later, the gates of Essaouira were contracted for 200,000 ūqiya a year. In the period following – Rabīʿ II 1279/September 1862 to Dhū al-Qaʿda 1279/April–May 1863 – revenue from the gates and the *qāʿa* amounted to 17,736 ūqiya.[145] This growth can be explained by the jump in trade. In

Table 17 *Taxes and tolls established in 1861*

Item	Amount levied
Goat skins (per ½ dozen)	6 ūqiya
Hides (per quintal)	40 ūqiya
Large camel load of oil	12 ūqiya
Small (Sous load) of oil	9 ūqiya
Mule load of oil	7 ūqiya
Camel or mule load of grain	1.5 ūqiya
Charcoal per camel, mule or donkey load	1 ūqiya
Lime, salt, bricks or firewood per camel, mule or donkey load	2 mūzūna
Wood for beans, etc., per camel, mule or donkey load	5 ūqiya
Large bullock	4 ūqiya
Small bullock	3 ūqiya
Calf	2 ūqiya
Sheep	3 ūqiya

Source: F.O., 830/2, 2 March 1861, Elton to Hay.

1863, Essaouira's export trade in 1863 almost tripled that of 1862.[146]

Usually, however, the gates were farmed out to the highest bidder, establishing a monopoly or 'contract' (*kunṭrada*) for a defined period of time. To assure maximum profits, the *makhzan* might give the concession to a higher bidder if the original tax-farmer was unable to equal the amount of his competitor.[147] This guaranteed the *makhzan* income from the gates, and gave the tax-farmer the opportunity to make a large profit. But it also involved great risks for the tax-farmers who often had difficulties meeting the obligations of the contract. In 1863–4, the gates of Essaouira reverted to the tax-farmers. The tax-farmer responsible for contracting the concession was a Marrakshi, Wild al-Ḥājj al-Makkī Ghazīl. He soon became involved in numerous disputes with the merchants of Essaouira. Apart from the fact that he had trouble administering the gates, his difficulties were undoubtedly compounded by the drop in trade in 1864. Unable to meet his obligations, Ghazīl's position was usurped only twenty days after his contract began, when he was outbid by some Swiris.[148] The *wazīr*, Muḥammad b. ʿAbd aṣ-Ṣaffār, wrote to Abraham Corcos, that this change in contract to the Swiri tax-farmers met with the Sultan's approval 'since they will know how to deal with the people of their region'.[149]

Local businessmen may have been more adept than outsiders, but such contracts were not always remunerative. Not only might drought befall the unfortunate tax-farmers, but political circumstances might prevent them from obtaining the amount envisaged. One main reason for the difficulties of the tax-farmers was the refusal of foreign protégés to pay the tolls. This was not accepted as an excuse by the *makhzan*, as the *amīn* of the treasury of Marrakesh indicated: 'they knew this when they entered into the contract'.[150]

High risks were involved in tax-farming. For this reason the *makhzan* wanted to ensure that contracts would be made with people who had substantial means. Early in 1867, the *kunṭrada* for Essaouira (as well as Demnat and Tamlalt) expired. Some new bidders proposed to pay 35,000 mithqāl per annum, which was 7,000 more than the amount being paid. The deal might have been concluded except, as Mūsā b. Aḥmad noted to Khalīfa Mawlāy al-Ḥasan, 'the *umanā*ʾ reported that the first ones were people of wealth while the other ones were not'. The Sultan decided that if the new bidders could not cover the amount in cash 'then the sale should be made with the wealthy ones'.[151]

The uncertainty of the *makhzan* receiving the agreed amount on the one hand, and the tax-farmers' risks of suffering losses on the other, may explain why another course of action was adopted in 1868. Agreement was reached with the merchants of Essaouira who selected eleven Jewish *tujjār* of the town to obtain the concession of the gates of Essaouira for three years at 60,000 mithqāl.[152] At 20,000 mithqāl a year, this was considerably lower than the 35,000 bid a little over a year previously. In addition, the tax revenues of Agadir were sold, but for a much smaller sum (probably 10,000 mithqāl a year). A twelfth merchant, Judah Bensemana, became a shareholder in the company for the final year of the contract by order of the Sultan.[153]

The passing of the contract to the 11 merchants came only after tense bidding and proposals. The company formed by Haim Corcos – the uncle of Abraham Corcos – made a higher bid for the gates than the *tujjār* of Essaouira, which was not accepted. The company then proposed to take over the concession if the merchants were to sustain losses, but this also was unacceptable. It can be inferred from the somewhat abbreviated correspondence however, that the Corcos house in Essaouira agreed to underwrite the new contract with the company of Swiri merchants. Bū ʿAshrīn justified to Abraham Corcos why the various other bids for the gates were unacceptable: 'It is understood that you would only be interested in the gates if the numerous proposals to the *makhzan* cease.'[154] Proposals nevertheless continued. A few months later, Abraham Bensaude wished to join the group of tax-farmers. This was not allowed, as Bū ʿAshrīn made explicit, 'because it [the *kunṭrada*] was by agreement with the corps of *tujjār* who appointed from among themselves a total of eleven to be conceded the sale . . . after that, discussion should not persist'.[155]

The merchants were given three months to come up with the total sum of 60,000 mithqāl, which as it seems, Abraham Corcos was responsible for sending to the *makhzan*. One of the purchasers of the gates, Jacob b. Adi (Delevante), wrote to the *makhzan* saying that he was unable to pay his share for the three years, and asked instead if he could pay in three months' instalments. From the warning that Bū ʿAshrīn sent Abraham Corcos, the answer appears to have been negative: 'You know what to do with him and with others in that case.'[156]

Six months after the contract began, the money was remitted to the *makhzan* by Abraham Corcos.[157] It is unknown whether he was able to obtain all the shares from the controllers, or whether some of them remained in debt. In any event, the *makhzan* found a temporary solution to its difficulties in recovering debts owed for the gates. By getting a wealthy, if not the wealthiest merchants of Essaouira, to underwrite the contract for the shareholders, the *makhzan* did not have to take the risk of the tax-farmers not being able to recover the amount owed by the actual income of the gates. It is true that the Sultan closed the door to further bidding for a three year period, but it has already been seen that certain speculators would bid far beyond their means and then find themselves incapable of paying their dues. Thus, it was better to sell the gates at a lower rate – 20,000 instead of 28,000, and certainly not 35,000 mithqāl! – for a fixed term. The merchants, for their part, could see it as a long-term investment. Some months were more profitable than others. In some years the traffic slackened in Essaouira, but in others, the town witnessed a brisk trade.

After the three years had expired, however, the merchants claimed to have suffered losses, and in 1871, they asked for an extension of four months. The total amount paid for the gates of Essaouira for 43 and a half months equalled 658,333 ūqiya. The *makhzan* seems to have been lenient in this instance since an average of 7,777.7 ūqiya a month was paid as opposed to the average rate of 16,666.6 ūqiya during the three year period.[158]

The difficulties of the Swiri *tujjār* may explain why the gates of Essaouira and Agadir were granted to a group of Jewish merchants from Marrakesh at the beginning of 1872, this time for 85,000 mithqāl for three years.[159] The *umanāʾ* had some difficulties recovering the sum owed for the three and a half months prolonged after the initial four months accorded by the Sultan.[160] Although initially the Sultan agreed to renew the contract, in the end negotiations for its renewal failed. The Swiri group offered 63,000 for the three years, undertaking to discharge the losses,[161] but they were probably unable to prove their solvency and were outbid by the Marrakshi Jews who made an offer of 85,000 mithqāl. The Marrakshi Jews, however, fared no better in administering the gates and were soon asking the *makhzan* if they could wait until each month elapsed before paying their instalments.[162] Less than a year later, the Marrakshi Jews gave up the *kunṭrada* because of the losses they had sustained.

The exemption of foreigners and their protégés was the main reason why the tax-farmers could not make ends meet. The transporters were avoiding tolls by claiming that the merchandise belonged to these exempted merchants. To get around this, in 1873 the Sultan decided to impose gate tolls on the owners of pack-animals.[163] Such a measure transferred the burden to rural pedlars coming to the market, and must have been one of the major causes for the uprising of the Ida Ū Gurḍ, the tribe to the south of Essaouira, in 1873. The people of the Haha initially refused to pay and the *qāʾid* of Essaouira was ordered to clamp down on their disobedience. The continued rural dissidence effectively closed down the gates for three months.[164]

In January 1874, the Marrakshi tax-farmers returned to the gates and the local authorities allowed them to reinstate the tolls, albeit reluctantly, since they feared rural reactions. But this time there was little resistance to paying the augmented rates, even though they caused prices on staples to rise sharply.[165] The *makhzan* was determined that the taxes should be collected. Guards from Marrakesh were posted at the gates and watch towers and further constructions to strengthen the town security were ordered.[166]

After two months of poor administration, Akkan Corcos, Jacob Corcos, and Dinar Ohana outbid the Marrakshi tax-farmers and obtained the contract of the gates for 340,000 mithqāl for a term of three years.[167] This was four times as high as the three-year contract signed before the increase in the rate of duties during the summer of 1873. No mention is made of a down-payment, though these three merchants must certainly have been known as men of capital. Clearly they were gambling for high stakes. According to Beaumier, the three had bid an additional 20,000 mithqāl for the contract, as well as paying 5,000 to 6,000 to obtain the offer.[168] Bidding was also a device to force the original tax-farmers from Marrakesh to increase the rate of their contract. Only a month later, it was agreed to return the contract to the Marrakshi company of Saʿdān Wild al-Qalʿāwiyya, and to release one of his partners, Maymūn Mīmrān, who had been imprisoned for debts owed on the contract.[169]

The Jew Saʿdān Wild al-Qalʿāwiyya complained before the Sultan (exalted by God) on how he was harmed by taking away from him the contract of the gates of

Essaouira. He asked to have the right of pre-emption over the merchants who have it now. The Sultan (may God protect him) signed the contract with al-Qalʿāwiyya and his company for the price that Akkan Corcos and his company had it for: namely, 340,000 mithqāl for three years.

Akkan Corcos and his partners had lost in the gamble, still owing the *makhzan* 6,296 mithqāl – less than one month's rate – for the gates of Essaouira. They claimed exemption from paying another sum of 3,777·7 mithqāl for Agadir since the governor of Agadir had administered the gates for two months after the death of their agent there.[170] Akkan Corcos and his partners had controlled the gates for a period of only five months.[171]

What is evident is that large profits were not being made from contracting the gates of Essaouira. Protégés found ways to convey goods without paying taxes.[172] The irony of the situation was that the new Swiri tax-farmers were protégés themselves.[173] Beaumier hoped that they would be more likely to respect the commercial treaties regarding exemptions of foreigners from tolls,[174] but his hopes were soon dashed since the new tax-farmers persisted in collecting a goat skin tax of six ūqiya per half dozen (i.e. an ūqiya a skin) from protégés and natives entering the gates. This would have augmented their revenues considerably. Some 1,135,956 skins were exported in 1874, all of which would have entered through the gates of Essaouira. The tax on these skins alone would have recovered the annual amount paid on the gates, but instead of paying the tax, the merchants abandoned their skins. The consuls went to the *qāʾid* and invoked the treaties of commerce in protests. The skins piled up at the gate. Merchants sent messages to their agents in the interior telling them to refrain from sending the skins to town. This situation continued for several months, but finally foreign protests paid off. In August, Muḥammad Bargāsh, the chief *wazīr* in charge of foreign affairs, ordered that the goat skin tax at the gates be annulled, though native traders were still subject to the tax at the skin market.[175] Yet the *makhzan* even had difficulties collecting taxes from the native skin dealers. In 1875, the tax-farmers complained to the governor that 'people from the countryside are bringing skins to the market, and by attaching themselves to protégés, they sell them without paying anything'.[176] Ostrich feather dealers also attached themselves to protégés. In 1875, for example, a trader from Wad Noun sold some feathers for 30,000 riyāl, and, claiming that he was associated with some Jewish protégés, refused to pay the tax. The feathers had been stored at Wad Noun for two years until the two protégés, who themselves were natives of Wad Noun, Abraham Afriat and Messan Knaffo, arranged to have them conveyed to Essaouira under cover of their protégé status. The Sultan ordered the detention of the man until the due was paid.[177] Traders would stop at nothing to avoid payment of the tolls. It became common for the transporters to claim that even their pack-animals belonged to foreigners, and hence should be exempt from the new tolls established in 1873.[178]

A more lucrative enterprise appears to have been contracting some of the markets in town. Periodically, a variety of markets in town were farmed out by the *makhzan* when it seemed profitable to do so. The market for items that were smoked, *aṭ-ṭarqa* was constantly farmed out as a monopoly. In 1861 it was selling for 8,000 mithqāl; ten years later it was selling for about 10,000. In 1869, Akkan Corcos wrested control of the monopoly when he offered an increase of 19,000 a year. The Sultan accepted on the condition that one-third more a month be handed over.[179]

The *makhzan* developed a flexible system, combining tax-farming with direct administration through the *umanā*ʾ (see table 18).[180] Competition between the merchants over contracts for the more lucrative markets could only have increased the *makhzan*'s revenues. The two tax-farm companies belonging to al-Qalʿāwiyya and Akkan Corcos competed for the concessions. al-Qalʿāwiyya managed to take over the tobacco and hashish concession held by Akkan Corcos. The gates, however, seem to have been a chronic risk for speculators, and it appears that after the three-year contract of al-Qalʿāwiyya and company for the gates had expired, the *umanā*ʾ decided to administer the gates directly. During the years of drought, the tax-farmers were probably unwilling to take the risk of buying the concession. Only a few of the markets deemed to be still profitable in times of hardship were auctioned.

Tax-farmers may have made substantial profits from the markets of Essaouira, but in comparison to the major cities, the *makhzan*'s earnings for the *mukūs* of Essaouira were relatively small. Despite the 50 per cent payment to Spain, customs duties were still the most important source of surplus revenue from Essaouira. In 1281 / 1865–6, the income from duties in Essaouira mounted to about five times the revenue derived from other sources in town.[182] This was over 17 times the amount derived from farming the gates of Essaouira at the 200,000 ūqiya per year contract. Nevertheless, through the system of tax-farming the *makhzan* invested little in the administration of the gates and markets of Essaouira. Furthermore, the contracts were fixed in the money of account, translated at a later date to the market exchange rate. It was therefore not the *makhzan* but the tax-farmer who risked losing from either inflation or slow traffic.

It is difficult to judge if the income derived from the new *maks* for the

Table 18 *Gate and market taxes in 1296/1878–9*[181]

Administered by the *umanā'*	Administered by tax-farmers	Price paid by tax farmer(s)
Bāb Sba'	tobacco/hashish, etc (*at-ṭarqa*)	270,000 ūqiya
Bāb Marrakesh	livestock market	
Bāb Dukkāla	slave market	
Grain market	old clothes[a]	36,000
Olive/argan market (*al-qā'a*)	new clothes[b]	
Beef and mutton	yarn market	
Unworked skins	coffee grinder	5,200
Cobblers' leather market		
Sulphur		
Silversmiths' market		

[a] In the *jūṭiya*.
[b] In *sūq al-jadīd*.
Source: K.H., K[80].

whole of the country compensated for the loss of revenues to the Spanish, but it seems unlikely that this was the case. A growing number of protégés were escaping the new taxes, depriving the *makhzan* of the revenue it hoped to gain. When the foreign powers met in Madrid to regulate the question of consular protection in Morocco, taxation was a major issue. The treaty of Madrid established that foreigners should no longer be exempt from the payment of taxes. Although the settlement regarding the payment of agrarian taxes remained a dead letter, the Moroccan authorities did not relinquish their insistence that foreigners and protégés should pay gate tolls in accordance with the Madrid agreement.[183] New gate tax rates were established in 1881 for pack-animals leaving and goods entering the town gates. These tolls were to apply to foreigners and protégés as well as to natives, and were fixed in riyāl.[184]

More important was the social impact of the new taxes. The cities had previously enjoyed a privileged status with respect to taxation. The town dwellers were now being asked to pay for the difficulties of the *makhzan*,[185] which must explain, in part, the opposition of the urban ulama to these non-Islamic taxes. But it was above all the rural poor who were saddled with the burden of the new tax. Suppliers from the countryside also had to pay the taxes when they brought their goods through the gates to sell in the markets of the town. Discontent therefore grew in both the urban and rural sectors.

This discontent was too heavy a price for the Moroccan government to pay. In 1885, the Sultan decided to suppress the octroi. A moratorium on the payment of gate tolls was put into effect. an-Nāṣirī writes that when the decree was promulgated, 'the people rejoiced, and from their purest desire, prayed for the victory and triumph of the Sultan'.[186] The *dahir* was sent to all the towns.[187]

It was above all the rural sector that the *makhzan* sought both to tax and control. One should bear in mind that at least 90 per cent of the population lived in the countryside, so that much of the attention of the central government was therefore turned away from the cities. Foreign merchants too cast their eyes on the hinterland of Essaouira and the lands to the south, since most of their trading interests lay in these rural regions. Their efforts to expand outside the confines of the ports threatened the stability of the Moroccan government and thrust Morocco precipitously down the road to chaos and foreign domination.

Chapter 8

The struggle for the southwest

For the Europeans, Essaouira was an opening to the interior of Morocco. It was the gateway to all the lucrative markets of Marrakesh and the southwest. For the *makhzan* as well, Essaouira was an outlet to the Sous. Quite apart from the increments gained from customs duties, Essaouira's commercial role was of great geopolitical importance for the central government. It made potentially dissident regions dependent on a town closely controlled by the central government. This became a crucial strategy in counteracting foreign inroads in the lands to the south.

Southern chiefs

The development of Essaouira greatly contributed to the rise to power of Sīdī Hāshim of Tazarwalt and Sheikh Bayrūk of Wad Noun. Both chiefs had agents in Essaouira who in turn marketed their goods in Europe. A French consul in Essaouira estimated that Bayrūk's annual profits amounted to about 610,000 piastres.[1] The rising power of these southern chiefs presented the central government with a predicament. On the one hand, it was in the interests of the *makhzan* to preserve the commercial importance of these local powers in the Sous to assure the flow of traffic, but on the other hand, they also needed to curtail their influence. Yet efforts to reduce the influence of Bayrūk, and particularly, his more powerful rival, Sīdī Hāshim, tended to disrupt trade with Essaouira which ultimately worked against the interests of the *makhzan*.

The biggest threats to the *makhzan* were European imperialist aims in the southwest. On several occasions, Bayrūk entertained the possibility of establishing independent commercial ties with Europeans along the southern littoral. This led to the mission of John Davidson in 1835–6,[2] and the efforts of Delaporte in 1837–41,[3] which both ended in failure. The French tried again in 1845. This time, Bayrūk's principal agent, Buʿazza b. al-ʿAwwād aṣ-Ṣawīrī, guided a French ship from Marseille to the coast of Wad Noun. The ship anchored on the coast for two months but was unable to land. When the Sultan heard of the ship, he sent one of his sons to Bayrūk and wrote to Sīdī Hāshim's successor, Ḥusayn, for help. Ḥusayn claimed that he went to the coast and averted Bayrūk and the people from loading the ship. The ship broke anchor and went to Essaouira. Būʿazza was arrested and sent to prison in Marrakesh.[4] Not to be outdone by the Europeans, the American consul-general in Tangier proposed to the President of the United States in 1848 that direct commercial ties should be established with Sheikh Bayrūk.[5] Manchester merchants as well saw trade there as a potential outlet for British goods in the interior of Africa: 'A difference of opinion exists amongst the travellers and traders as to the best means to be adopted, in order to secure a safe, permanent and progressive intercourse with the natives of the interior – but all agree in the importance of the subject, and in the certainty of finding a fruitful field for the employment of British capital.'[6]

All these attempts at establishing independent commercial relations on the coast of the Aït Bāʿamrān were doomed to failure because in the end Bayrūk backed out, fearing both the reaction of the *makhzan* and his rival in Iligh. Furthermore, the British and French governments were unwilling to lend full support to the initiatives for two reasons. First, they were not persuaded that Bayrūk could provide security to a European establishment since he was at times beleaguered by the Aït Bāʿamrān, the tribe stretching along the coastal region where the foreign port (Assāka) was destined to be built. Second, it was desirable for cordial relations with the Moroccan government to be maintained, if only because of rivalries between the powers. Such initiatives created difficulties for the British and the French in their dealings with the Moroccans. Thus, the aims of the foreign merchants were not always in accordance with those of their governments.

Nevertheless, these ventures were serious enough to alarm the *makhzan*, because they called into question the legitimacy of the Sultan's rule over the Sous, and potentially jeopardized the whole system of royal trade at Essaouira. The Sultan therefore pursued a policy of placating the southern chiefs, through a combination of force and concessions. Bayrūk was granted the right to export at one-quarter of the normal tariff. Apparently he was reimbursed with two-thirds to three-quarters of the duties paid by the merchants to whom he sold produce. He was even given a house in Essaouira where one of his agents collected the duties.[7] Ḥusayn Ū Hāshim soon sought similar favours,[8] which Sultan ʿAbd ar-Raḥmān acknowledged in 1852: 'Concerning the favour in duties you asked for the *zāwiya* of your blessed ancestor on [items] you sell in the town – an additional favour to that given to the *zāwiya* by our predecessors (may God have mercy on them) – you know very well that commerce at the port of Essaouira has diminished.' The Sultan added that unless commerce improved he would be unable to fulfil the request.[9]

Ḥusayn Ū Hāshim, now reaching the height of his power, was clearly manœuvring for concessions. The next year, the Altaras brothers of Essaouira and Marseille and David de Léon Cohen of Marseille began making contacts with the local powers in the Sous, and particularly with Ḥusayn. The Marseille merchants suggested that goods could be bought 50 to 60 per cent more cheaply if they traded directly with the southern regions. According to French consular reports, Ḥusayn began dispatching secret emissaries to the French, via Altaras in Essaouira. The *sharīf* proposed that he be recognized sovereign prince by the Emperor Napoleon. With a supply of arms, he could occupy Agadir and open it as a port of trade exclusively for French commerce. Products would be exported at a low price. Altaras claimed to have proposed to Ḥusayn that a ship or two could be loaded at the southern coast and that Ḥusayn had responded that he was willing to meet the ship, but that he would require an alliance with France before he would risk the danger of establishing a port which would provoke the Sultan. The French seized on rumours from marabouts that the ʿAlawid dynasty was approaching its end, that the far Sous (Sūs al-Aqṣā) was virtually independent, and that Ḥusayn, possessor of many *zāwiya*s, was the most powerful potentate there.[10]

Imperialist aims such as these were based on a failure to understand the intricacies of dynastic loyalties and the economic interconnections between the Sous and the regions to the north. The Sultan continued to grant Ḥusayn important concessions, such as selling him sulphur from Essaouira and granting him a house in town.[11] These concessions also tied the interest of Ḥusayn to the trade of Essaouira. It was for this reason that the *makhzan* played a more important role in the southern regions than was admitted by the foreign powers. Furthermore, the network of trade all along the routes created a balance of interests, since many parts of the network were interested in maintaining the system. The growth of trade in the 1850s increased the volume of the Saharan and trans-Saharan trade which ultimately passed through Essaouira. A new relay point was established further to the south when Tindouf was expanded in 1852, in part eclipsing the role of Akka and Tatta.[12] The south was both unwilling, and unable to break away from the ʿAlawid dynasty.

Haha *qāʾid*

The government sometimes resorted to force in controlling the Sous. In particular, the *makhzan* used the *qāʾid*s of the Haha as an instrument of power. The *qāʾid*s of the Haha, as well as the Shiadma, were usually appointed directly by the Sultan and were often resident in Essaouira and granted rent-free *makhzan* houses in town.[13] Because of their rural connections, the *qāʾid*s often could assure the security of the town and of the region.[14] But even more important, the *qāʾid*s of the Haha were instruments for the control of both the Haha and the Sous. The domination of the Haha in the Sous is reflected in the oral tradition of the southwest.[15]

al-Ḥājj ʿAbdallāh Ū Bīhī of the Haha (like his father and ancestors) was the *makhzan*'s main instrument to control the Haha and the Sous in the 1840s and 1850s. As Robert Montagne writes: 'In the coastal region, the champion of the *makhzan* is al-Ḥājj ʿAbdallāh Bīhī, *qāʾid* of the Haha; the enemy of the Sultan is the marabout of Tazarwalt.' According to Montagne, ʿAbdallāh Ū Bīhī succeeded in controlling for the *makhzan* all of the Haha, Matūga, the Ida Ū Tanān, Tarudant and the Shtūka.[16]

ʿAbdallāh Ū Bīhī seems to have been appointed *qāʾid* in 1843, after the disgrace of Aḥmad Agūnī. With an army he was able to subdue part of the Sous and to collect taxes there.[17] In the aftermath of the bombardment of Essaouira in 1844, ʿAbdallāh Ū Bīhī had difficulty keeping order in the Haha, though he did induce some of the dissident tribes who had been involved in the pillaging to come to Essaouira and attest their allegiance to the government.[18] A fine was imposed on the Haha tribes by the Sultan for their role in the pillaging. However the *qāʾid* of the Haha was unable to collect the fine of 30 mithqāl for a married man and 20 mithqāl for a single man. This fine was reduced to 20 and 10 mithqāl respectively when the Nāṣirī sheikh, Abū Bakr b. ʿAlī, who had a considerable following among the Haha, mediated.[19] ʿAbdallāh Ū Bīhī continued to serve as an instrument of the Sultan in the Sous from the *makhzan* stronghold in Tarudant. In 1848, the appointed *qāʾid* of Tarudant, Bū Mahdī, was under siege. He was replaced by ʿAbdallāh Ū Bīhī, who combined the administration of Tarudant with the Haha.[20] He returned to Essaouira after ten months in Tarudant, where he had failed to gain recognition of his authority, though a *khalīfa* was left behind there.[21] Over the next few years, he embarked on a number of expeditions to the Sous, in order to collect taxes.[22] Having completed his task for the *makhzan*, he went on a pilgrimage to Mecca with a group of Swiris, and returned three years later in 1858.[23]

In the 1860s, ʿAbdallāh Ū Bīhī's activities were centred in the region of Essaouira. He managed to subdue rebellion in the Matūga and keep the Haha tribes firmly under his grip.[24] Locusts, followed by drought in 1866–7, were probably causes of discontent in the region. Rebellion in 1868 was countered by the *qāʾid* cutting down trees in dissident regions. For months ʿAbdallāh Ū Bīhī, with his Haha followers, laid waste the Ida Ū Tanān, cutting down trees and setting fire to much of the land. Hundreds of deaths were reported in the fighting. As this was going on, famine prevailed in the countryside.[25] ʿAbdallāh Ū Bīhī died later that year in Marrakesh, leaving the Haha in an ungovernable state.[26] Incessant rebellion in the Haha in the following years threatened the town of Essaouira itself.

In its effort to control the southwestern part of the country, the central government used a carrot and a stick. Concessions were granted to southern chiefs to build up their dependencies on the *makhzan* and the port of Essaouira. Military expeditions were sent to collect taxes and to subdue rebellious regions. The ability of the *makhzan* to control the region also depended on extraneous circumstances. Drought, for example, a perennial problem in Moroccan history, was usually a cause of rural unrest, but in addition, a new situation had emerged which was to undermine the capacity of the *makhzan* to govern. Foreign encroachments in the interior began to challenge the legitimacy of the Moroccan government, and to induce rural tribes to rebel.

Imperialism by treaty

The victory of free trade by the treaty of 1856 was a catalyst. The treaty assured the right of travel and residence in the interior. The existence of such a clause was ominous for the *makhzan*, because it constituted a challenge to governmental control of foreign movement in the interior of Morocco. The Spanish invasion in the north of Morocco in 1860 impelled the Europeans to make further demands. After the arrival of the *recaudadores* in Essaouira, the Spanish demanded that they be allowed a resident consul in Marrakesh. While technically the Sultan could not oppose the demand, it was made explicit that he would not be responsible for the consequences if anything were to happen to the consul.[27]

The number of foreigners who actually travelled or resided in the interior was limited. More importantly, their native brokers (*simsār*s) were used increasingly as a means of penetration. These native protégés enjoyed extra-territorial rights by extension of the special status granted to foreigners resident in Morocco, which were similar to the Capitulations granted to the Europeans by the Ottomans.[28] These rights were fiercely defended by the foreign consular agents on the coast. One of the major privileges enjoyed by the protégés was exemption from paying taxes and tolls, an obvious advantage used to the full by the foreign merchants. The proliferation of protection began after the war with Spain when the *makhzan* was attempting to raise funds through the *mukūs*. The increase in the number of protégés was, as the Sultan put it, 'causing harm to the treasury and to [Morocco's] sovereignty because of the loss of jurisdiction over her subjects'.[29] The various governors would be unable to assert their authority if protégés stopped paying taxes. It was not only the foreign consuls who had protégés, but also the foreign merchants, many of whom were native Moroccans who had acquired foreign nationality after a short sojourn abroad.

The Sultan sought to regulate the problem, which led to negotiations with the French and the Béclard agreement of 1863. This agreement was subsequently sanctioned by the other foreign powers.[30] Although the convention limited the number of *simsārs* to two per merchant firm, the problem spread because the right to extend protection was now sanctioned by an international accord. The convention recognized for the first time the right of agricultural association between foreigners and farmers (coll., *mukhlāṭs*).[31]

Foreign nations with only marginal interests in Morocco employed the principal merchants of the town as consuls. The latter in turn granted protection to other merchants and their families. The British merchant, William Grace, in his capacity as consul of Belgium and Denmark in Essaouira, granted protection to nine agents. As a British merchant, he also employed two *simsārs* who were registered at the British consulate. His son, John Grace, registered Antonio Bolelli as an agent. Bolelli was a long-standing Italian merchant in town who was consular agent not only for Italy, but also for Norway, Sweden and Portugal. Joseph Elmaleh and other relatives were protected by one or another of Bolelli's consular agencies. Elmaleh himself registered his agents as protégés of the Austro–Hungarian Empire. No sooner had Abraham Corcos been appointed United States vice-consul than he began to extend protection to his principal associates – first to his nephew Dinar Ohana (probably the most important ostrich feather merchant in Morocco) and to his brother Jacob, and then to two *simsārs*, Dawid Hallāwa in Tarudant and ʿAbdallāh Shtūkī in the Aït Baha. Some consular agents from countries with few interests in Morocco appointed the chief native merchants of Essaouira as interpreters (*turjumāns*), which afforded them protégé status. Such was the case of Isaac Coriat, the *turjumān* for the U.S. vice-consulate. The Spanish selected al-Ḥājj ʿAbd al-Qādir al-ʿAṭṭār, the former *qāʾid* of Essaouira as their *turjumān* and Muḥammad Raghūn as his successor. The British and French had the most protégés. Apart from the various agents serving the British consulate, the eight principal British merchants in town – David Perry, William Grace, John Grace, James Curtis, John Damonte, Moses Messiah, Yamin Ferache, and George Broome – together registered another 11 agents as protégés. The French consulate in Essaouira maintained the most protégés, registering some 41 persons in 1866.[32]

The number of protégés was still relatively limited, and some of the foreign powers, such as Great Britain, maintained some restraint in extending protection to new agents.[33] But many of the native Jewish merchants of Essaouira were British subjects anyway, having obtained their naturalization papers in Gibraltar or England some years previously.[34] In 1871, the British vice-consulate listed some 172 British subjects, many of whom were naturalized Jews of Moroccan origin.[35] In the period following the Béclard agreement of 1863, as many as half the leading shippers were either foreign merchants or protégés. After another decade had passed, every important merchant had the protection of one foreign state or another. Similarly, many of the *tujjār* in debt to the *makhzan* became protégés. Among the largest debtors were Jacob b. Adi Delevante, an Italian protégé, Saul Cohen-Solal, a French protégé, ʿAbd al-Qādir al-ʿAṭṭār, a Spanish protégé, and Musa Aflalo, a Spanish protégé. One could also add Elmaleh, Corcos, Coriat, and others who were both debtors and protégés at the same time (compare table 1).

One of the major problems that this posed for the *makhzan* was the collection of taxes. No sooner had the gate taxes been established than conveyers of merchandise began to claim that the goods they were carrying belonged to foreigners and protégés.[36] A large quantity of the goods passing through the town gates were certainly destined for export by protected merchants. Likewise, most goods leaving the town gates would have been imported by foreigners or protected persons. This situation was prejudicial to the Muslim and Jewish *tujjār* of the town who were not protégés, thus increasing the incentive to obtain the protection of a foreign consulate. In 1863, the unprotected merchants complained to the Sultan about this situation, claiming that it was causing them great losses. In order to give them equal opportunities, the Sultan ordered the *umanāʾ* to ensure that the unprotected *tujjār* would not be taxed.[37] By putting the *tujjār*, who did not enjoy protection, on an equal footing with the foreigners and protégés, the *makhzan* was depriving itself of potential revenues. Yet had it a choice? No matter what action was taken, practically all Muslim and Jewish *tujjār* who had not obtained protection already were to become protégés within the next decade.

The growth in the number of protégés not only threatened to deprive the *makhzan* of revenues from the gates of Essaouira, but from the gates of interior towns as well. In the 1860s, the number of *simsār*s representing Swiri firms in Marrakesh increased. The principal agent of the British in Marrakesh, Sīdī Bū Bakr, was able to acquire considerable wealth through this protection.[38] The first foreign merchants also began to settle in the southern capital, which threatened to diminish the gate tax revenues even further. Early in 1867, the *khalīfa* ordered that taxes were to be taken from goods passing through the gates of Marrakesh, with no exception being made for Europeans' property. The receipts accompanying the goods of foreign merchants, issued by the *umanāʾ* of Essaouira to exempt foreign-owned goods from taxes, were to be considered null and void. Pressures from the British led the Sultan to order the return of these gate tolls to British merchants in 1868. In 1870, it was reported that gate tolls were again being levied on goods brought in from the interior by agents for the accounts of foreigners. In Tarudant, agents were taxed both on entering and leaving the gates.[39] Many, in any event, were finding ways to undermine the system. In Marrakesh protégés were reported to be purchasing goods, which should have been sold in the town, at a lower price outside the ramparts, and providing the sellers with papers which stated that the goods belonged to the former. The goods would then enter the gates in the protégés' names without payment of tolls.[40]

Who then was left to pay taxes? One might guess that it was the poorer Muslim and Jewish pedlars dealing mostly in local or regional trade. These small traders, particularly the Jewish ones, also sought foreign protection. Beaumier noted how this contributed to a migration of Jews towards Essaouira which, as he believed, tended to push Muslims out to rural areas.[41] The system was open to fraud even by those who failed to obtain protection, as the Sultan pointed out to Bargāsh: 'Any [Moroccan] subject who wanted an exemption from paying taxes would go to one of them [protégé or foreigner] who would give him a receipt that the load belonged to him [the protégé or foreigner].'[42] This evasion of taxes meant that the burden of taxation fell principally on the poor, which was certainly one of the major causes of rural protest and rebellion in the latter half of the nineteenth century.

The Béclard convention of 1863 had recognized agricultural association between natives and foreigners. Foreigners had been particularly interested in acquiring this right because it had enabled them to invest in the interior, further capturing the Moroccan market. Agricultural associations thus became another instrument of foreign penetration in the interior, further destabilizing the relationship between town and country. Foreigners and protégés began extending credit to local traders and investing in crops and cattle in the interior. Contracts attested to by *ʿudūl* were drawn up between the two parties in the association. The merchants would advance credit, to be repaid by a portion of the harvest.[43] This was a form of veiled usury – money advanced on credit in exchange for goods at a later date. Profits, according to Hay, could range from 25 to 60 per cent.[44] The consequence of this kind of speculation was that many debtors became insolvent and subsequently alienated their property to the merchants. This kind of usury, leading to the acquisition of real estate, was not a new phenomenon specific to the nineteenth century.[45] What was different was that property was being acquired by foreigners and protégés who were outside the jurisdiction of the Moroccan government. If disputes over property transfers were to arise, the authorities would not be able to resort to the traditional methods of mediation, but instead would be subjected to diplomatic pressures and consular harassment. This disrupted the delicate balance between the town authorities and the rural population.

It also led to numerous disputes over urban real estate. Foreign merchants who advanced money in credit to agents in the interior often made a contract through a guarantor in town. Sometimes agreements would be made with rural notables who possessed urban real estate. Muslim merchants would offer their houses and property as collateral to creditors. Often the recipient of foreign credit was already a debtor to the *makhzan*, and this led to numerous legal disputes between protégés, defended by their consulates, and the authorities. The Muslim authorities invoked the *sharīʿa*. The consulates claimed that they were outside Muslim jurisdiction. The settlement of outstanding debts, therefore, dragged on for years.[46]

The problem in these cases was compounded by the fact that many of the debtors to the Europeans were rural *qāʾid*s and sheikhs. It would have been dangerous for the security of the town for the *makhzan* to act too severely. Nevertheless, foreign pressures on the *makhzan* led to the commission of al-Ḥājj Idrīs b. Muḥammad b. Idrīs, who was delegated to Essaouira in 1869 to settle outstanding debts. The scope of the commission was limited, according to Corcos, since the *makhzan* would not interfere in debts owed by governors and sheikhs.[47]

There were ample incentives for rural dwellers to establish associations with foreigners and protégés. Though the native farmer might have to cede a large part of his profits, those lands or flocks declared to be held in partnership would not be subject to taxation. Foreign protection extended to him would also apply indirectly to other peasants employed on the farm. Yet the end result was that the rural population became increasingly dependent on the foreign sector, and property fell into foreign hands, because the Europeans often made contracts with persons already in debt to the *makhzan*. Furthermore, serious drought in the 1860s made it difficult for native partners to fulfil their engagements with the Europeans. Hay accused the Europeans of underhand methods in obtaining land transfers.[48]

The more the Europeans extended credit to the countryside, the more unpaid debts accumulated. This problem was exacerbated in times of drought. To recover debts, foreign merchants often sought the intervention of the *makhzan*. For debts owed in the Sous, the authorities would write to the *qā'id* of Tarudant for assistance. In a letter to Khalīfa al-Ḥasan, for example, Bannīs suggested that 'a sharifian letter should be sent to the governor of the Sous to [have him] take firm action for the *dhimmī* and *tājir* Abraham Corcos to recover money from his debtors there'. Mawlāy al-Ḥasan replied immediately: 'We have written to the governor of the Sous.'[49] The validity of some of the claims were questioned by the *makhzan*. The foreign merchants not only held the *makhzan* responsible for recovering debts, but also for alleged thefts.[50] Where the merchants had more influence, they might appeal to the rural *qā'id* directly. A *qā'id* of Shiadma, ʿUmar b. Aḥmad al-Ḥanshāwī, wrote to Abraham Corcos in 1867 saying that he would spare no efforts in helping him recover the debts owed by a certain ʿAbd ar-Raḥmān al-Mashīshtī.[51]

The demands of foreign merchants on their debtors became more and more onerous. A British merchant, Thompson, claimed 7,000 riyāl from a sheikh, ʿAbdallāh Ū Sulaymān, of the Aït Baha. Carstensen insisted that the sheikh pay interest on his debt, and threatened to sell his house in Essaouira by auction. This obliged the sheikh to come to Essaouira to settle the debt.[52] The foreign merchants held the rural *qā'id*s and the governors responsible for recovering the debts, but as claims grew in Marrakesh and other regions, the Sultan found that this was an unacceptable procedure. In 1866 orders were issued to the governors that claimants had to appear personally before the *qā'id* of the area for a decision to be made on the case. But this was for regions where it was possible for the claimants to go.[53] For more distant regions, Hay made an agreement with Bargāsh which authorized vice-consul Carstensen to settle British claims against dissident tribes of the Sous by seizing the movable property of these tribes when they came to Essaouira. In 1866, Carstensen seized two Muslim tribesmen and six loads of Buenos Aires hides for claims of the British merchant, Curtis, against the Ida Ū Bakīl. The vice-consul alleged that they were harbouring a Jew heavily indebted to Curtis.[54] This procedure soon led to disputes with the authorities who were opposed to the idea of arresting the fellow kinsmen or protectors of insolvent debtors. Furthermore, it was felt that if the debtor had fled to areas outside his tribe, arresting his fellow tribesmen might not help the merchant recover his debt.[55]

Such reasoned arguments fell on deaf ears. Growing foreign pressures forced the authorities to take the more drastic step of having debtors arrested and sent to prison in Essaouira, pending settlement of the claims. Many debtors took sanctuary at the many religious shrines scattered along the coast, or at Sīdī Magdūl, the patron marabout of

Essaouira a short distance to the south of the town.[56] Most of the incarcerated debtors were soon released by the authorities, on the grounds that they were insolvent. This was often the subject of protest by the consuls.[57] Although agreement was reached that the insolvency of debtors had to be certified, the Europeans complained that this was not being practised. They further complained that the authorities in Marrakesh and the interior were refusing to send debtors from Marrakesh or other regions to Essaouira to settle claims.[58]

Spurious claims, fraud, and above all, usury were challenging the authority of the *makhzan* to govern. In 1869, the Sultan ordered that no contracts were to be drawn up between foreigners and Moroccans in town unless the *ʿudūl* could certify that the latter were not in debt to the *makhzan* and were known for their integrity; if they were natives of the interior, they would be required to produce written evidence from the regional authorities of their solvency and honesty.[59] In 1873, the Sultan wrote to Qadi Ḥamīd al-Banānī of Essaouira saying that if a debt were to be contracted for over 50 mithqāl, it should be notarized by two *ʿadl*s and only after the qadi had examined the terms of the contract. But even if the load involved a smaller sum, the two *ʿadl*s required to notarize the contract were to be scrupulous regarding its legality. Furthermore, the decree stated: 'The sale or mortgage of a property should not be notarized except with the authorization and agreement of the governor . . . taking into account the terms contracted.'[60] A few months later the Sultan ordered the governor of Essaouira to have the qadi appoint two *ʿadl*s to notarize any money confided by the merchants to their agents for trade in the interior.[61] This seems to merely have been a repetition of an arrangement made in 1866,[62] showing that such legal controls were difficult to enforce.

Claims for the restitution of debt and compensation for theft grew in the following years. Increasing numbers of murders were reported along the trade route. If the victim had any association with foreigners or protégés, consular demands for indemnities were made. The murder of Jewish pedlars in the Haha and Shiadma in 1874 elicited the response of the Anglo-Jewish Association and the Alliance Israélite Universelle. Both organizations sought the intervention of the consulates. The Muslim authorities were circumvented altogether. In their appeals for support, little mention was made of the general state of brigandage prevailing in the hinterland during this period.[63] Consul Beaumier felt compelled to stress that such attacks were not directed against Jews exclusively. Robbery was the prime motive: 'You can be certain that these unfortunate people were not murdered *because they were Jews*, but simply *because they were carrying quantities of money which tempted the robbers.*'[64] As the number of murders increased, pressures on the authorities for compensation of the victims grew steadily. A commissioner was appointed in 1875 to settle the cases of murders of Jewish pedlars in the Haha, Shiadma, and Dukkāla.[65]

During the years of drought and famine in 1878–9, claims for compensation were compounded enormously, and the government had little success in settling them. Some of their efforts may have been half-hearted, but, considering the intensity of the famine, and the continued fighting among the tribes, foreign claims could hardly have been adequately dealt with, even with the best intentions. Roads were frequently cut and caravans pillaged. Rural suppliers, ruined by the ravages of the drought, had little hope of settling with the city creditors. The claims of merchants grew as conditions in the countryside deteriorated.

In 1878, Abraham Corcos was seeking payment on debts in the Ida Ū Gurḍ and the Ida Ū Tanān from Mubārak Anflūs, who controlled the roads between Essaouira and Agadir. Between January and June of that year, the repeated appeals of Corcos to Anflūs and complaints to the *makhzan* on the *qāʾid*'s failure to act, were to no avail.[66] Both Corcos and Abraham Afriat put forward their claims against the Banī Tāmar in August; by then the famine had become intense. Mūsā b. Aḥmad wrote to Corcos and Afriat, insisting on the need for patience in such dire circumstances:

> We received your letter concerning your claims against the Banī Tāmar and we know [from your letter] Qāʾid Mubārak Anflūs is still asking for patience in expediting the [other] half, and [i.e.,] deferring [payment of] the rest for another time. You asked that he be required to settle with you . . . The *mukhaznī* sent to deal with the case [i.e., recover the money] returned with nothing. He [Anflūs] wrote pleading that his tribe was in disarray due to the famine.[67]

Other merchants took more drastic steps to pursue their debtors. The British merchant, Broome, went into the interior to recover money and gum sandarac owed to him. The Sultan explained to Bargāsh why Broome would have little hope of settling his claims: 'The Haha tribe is not behaving rationally and its people are not answering to claimants, for the famine has reached the point of bringing misery to its people – the land has left them destitute, their cattle have perished, their strength has been broken, and their poverty has intensified.'[68] Settlements of claims in the drought years were therefore difficult to obtain. Constant pressure by the foreign representatives led to a commission at the end of 1880, sent to Essaouira and Agadir for settling claims in the Haha and the Sous. One French merchant in Essaouira, Jacquetty, claimed f21,175 for advances on almond and gum sandarac harvests in the Haha. al-Mahdī b. aṭ-Ṭayyib b. al-Yamānī (the son of Būʿ Ashrīn), the commissioner sent to Essaouira for settling the claims of merchants against Anflūs, was unable to find a solution.[69] The French consulate in Essaouira accused al-Mahdī of being inept, but considering the devastation caused by the famine, even the most able mediator would have an impossible task. How could the *makhzan* succeed in recovering debts for the merchants, as the Palace explained to Abraham Corcos, in view of 'the great rise in prices, the sweeping death, and the extreme misery'?[70] Many debtors had actually perished in hard times. The sons of Būhillāl sent a *wakīl* to Anflūs to recover a debt from the heirs of a man who had died in the famine. They were unsuccessful in this initiative.[71]

After the drought had subsided in 1883, new diplomatic efforts by John Drummond Hay led to another commission. Some debts were settled, but other claims continued to be scrutinized between 1884 and 1886.[72] The unrelenting consular pressure on the authorities forced the *makhzan* to settle the claims of foreigners and protégés. *Qāʾid*s in the Haha and Shiadma were ordered by the Sultan to settle the claims of English merchants.[73] It is probable that Hay, concerned with the advancing penetration of other foreign powers in Morocco, was as interested in settling claims as the *makhzan*. But protégés continued to abuse their privileges regardless of who was the protecting power.

Reports reached the *makhzan* that many Jewish merchants had stopped the practice of recording with *ʿudūl* goods and money which had been entrusted with their agents and sent to the countryside or to other towns. Some of these agents, protégés of foreign merchant firms, were allegedly travelling with unrecorded sums, or even with no money at all, and later claiming that thousands of riyāl had been stolen. A new measure was adopted. Qadis in each locale were to appoint four *ʿudūl* to register all goods and money with which Jews were travelling. Claims of theft were henceforth to be considered only if the Jews could produce appropriately notarized documents. But it was revealed that the problem not only involved Jews. On receiving the *dahir*, Būshtāʾ b. al-Baghdādī, the governor of Fez, pointed out that there were also Muslims who were agents of foreign and Jewish merchants, though some of the Muslim traders had no foreign protection. 'Shall we proceed with the same practice for all, or shall we limit it to the Jews', he asked the Sultan.[74]

These reforms were little more than palliatives. The instability of the countryside, combined with mounting consular pressure on behalf of protégés, prevented the *makhzan* from implementing effective government. This instability was greatly increased by the encroachments of foreigners and their protégés into the countryside. In particular, this involved the further acquisition of rural real estate during the years of hardship. The right of agricultural association between foreigners and natives had been only the first step. Foreigners saw the right to own property as the next step. This right was officially recognized by treaty at the international conference to regulate the problem of protection, held in Madrid in 1880. The Madrid agreement, rather than limiting the spread of protection, further legitimized its expansion by officially recognizing what up until this point had been only *de facto* categories of protection.[75] The right of foreigners to own land was conceded in exchange for the *makhzan*'s right to impose a universal tax on Moroccans, foreigners, and protégés alike. Muḥammad Bargāsh, who was the Moroccan negotiator, was urged by the Sultan to resist ceding this right, but to no avail: 'The foreign [ministers] will not agree that their subjects pay taxes on gates, etc., except on condition that they should have [the right to own] houses and lands.'[76]

Foreign merchants had been acquiring property for some time before the Madrid agreement, but armed with an official sanction, this practice spread rapidly. The right to acquire property coincided with times of severe hardship. Numerous peasants in partnership to town merchants in land or cattle defaulted. Rural lands were sought by creditors. The alienation of peasants from their land and absentee ownership combined to make the land less productive. Hence, the *makhzan* stood to lose considerable sums from the agrarian tithes, which were now being more vigorously imposed. Furthermore, the land owned by foreigners could not be taxed, since diplomatic pressures in 1881 had forced the Moroccans to abandon the agricultural tax on foreigners and protégés.[77]

The *makhzan* had little other recourse than to adopt measures to make the transfer of property to foreigners and protégés difficult. As previously, strict control of debt contracts by *ʿudūl* was proposed to prevent the transfer of real estate. The measures taken were not a defence against foreign penetration alone. During time of drought, urban merchants – native as well as foreign – purchased land at low prices. Transfers of real estate to urban merchants were effected by the heirs of deceased debtors. The *makhzan* attempted to control these transfers by delegating the *umanāʾ* to purchase domains left by deceased rural landowners. Revenues accruing from the production of these lands were henceforth to be gained by the *makhzan*.[78]

During the years of hardship, many agricultural associates (*mukhlāṭs*) sold their partners' land, which sometimes led to disputes.[79] The *makhzan* found land transfers that had been effected to foreigners, Jews, and protégés as a result of agricultural associations even more worrisome. Qāʾid ʿAdī b. ʿAlī an-Naknāfī of the Haha wrote to the Qāʾid ad-

Table 19 *Partnerships of foreigners and protégés with natives in the Ida Ū Gurḍ, 1883*

Name of merchant	Locale	Numbers of partners
Ratto	al-Ghazzan	2
Ratto	Būkhū	5
Ratto	Tazart	10
Ratto	Būzamūr	8
Ratto	Flūst	2
Ratto	Tadwart (in Banī Ballāla)	4
Jacquetty	Agar (in the Aït Maryah)	3
Bolelli		8
Bolelli	the Aït ar-Ramal	1
Broome	Ḥarārtha	1
Brauer	Ḥarārtha	1
Yule	the Aït Tahālla	3
Coriat	Aʿzāmna	3
Alharar	Aʿzāmna	2
Ferache	Aʿzāmna	2
Bensaude	Aʿzāmna	3
Knaffo	Aʿzāmna	1
	Total	59

Source: K.H., 1 Rabīʿ I 1301/31 December 1883, an-Naknāfi to Sultan.

Dawbilāli in 1883 asking him to arrange for the consuls in Essaouira to register the merchants who had associates in the Ida Ū Gurḍ, the district adjacent to the town (see map 6). The investigation revealed that there were some 59 rural partners to foreigners and Jewish protégés in the Ida Ū Gurḍ alone in 1883 (see table 19). an-Naknāfi attributed the growth in partnerships to the shortage of cattle. One can infer by the *qāʾid*'s suggestion, that with the peasants' loss of numerous animals in the drought, the incentive for entering into partnership or contracting debts with rich city merchants increased.

It had been agreed in Madrid that the right to own property should be subject to the Sultan's approval. But there were soon numerous abuses. When loans were made to rural dwellers, their lands were often held as securities. The intrigues between rival merchants and rural authorities contributed to the transfer of property to foreign merchants in Essaouira. Such was the case when the activities in the Ida Ū Gurḍ of a British merchant, Pepe Ratto, prompted the authorities to undertake the general

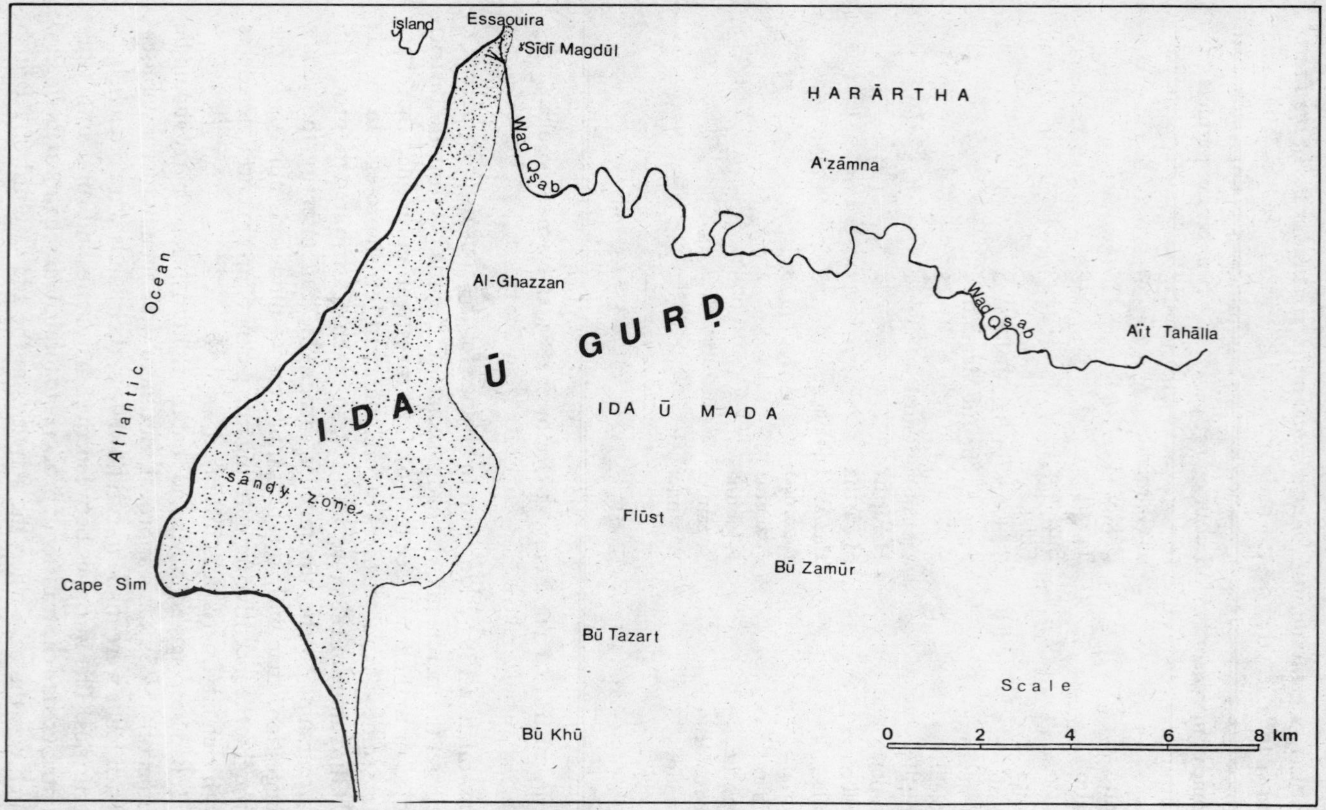

Map 6 The Ida Ū Gurḍ: the lands bordering Essaouira

investigation of agricultural associates referred to above. The investigation revealed that Ratto had 31 associates in the Ida Ū Gurḍ and adjacent regions. His activities in the surrounding countryside had already aroused considerable controversy in 1881, when some of the followers of Anflūs had tried to raid Ratto's cattle.[80] A new controversy erupted when Zerbib, a French missionary of Algerian–Jewish origin who resided in Essaouira, 'purchased' a house at Tagwadīrt in the Ida Ū Gurḍ which Ratto claimed to hold as a mortgage. Ratto therefore protested, claiming that the sale was illegal. In defence of Zerbib's claim, the French consul and the whole French community of Essaouira went out and pitched a tent on the property. The camp was then attacked by some tribesmen. The French alleged that Ratto was directing the action with the consent of Qāʾid an-Naknāfī. Subsequently, Ratto took over the property and the seller of the house was arrested.[81]

Whatever the truth was in the Ratto case, it appears evident that the *makhzan* would spare no efforts to prevent foreigners from purchasing property in the countryside. A letter to the Palace stated:

> As for the matter of merchants purchasing properties in the district of Qāʾid ʿAdi . . . we and the *qāʾid* have exerted the utmost effort in this, and not one merchant persists in buying property in our district whatever it may be (in compliance with the sharifian decree issued on this matter) . . . but for those who have already bought property in the past, we should give up trying to expel them.[82]

To avoid further demands for property, the Sultan ordered an-Naknāfī to make concessions to the claims of the merchants. But property sales continued, even when the conveyance was made through the consulates.[83] Furthermore, rural qadis and *ʿudūl* clearly profited from drawing up the conveyance. In 1886, some rural *ʿudūl* were dismissed in the Shiadma and Hashtūka for alleged irregularities. The local *qāʾid*s claimed that things had been set right, except that the qadi of the Hashtūka was 'still disdainfully drawing up usurious documents and executing sales between native subjects and protégés'.[84] At about this time the rural authorities were ordered to delay transactions – sales, loans, repayments, etc. – until they had been validated by documents in Essaouira. A rural *qāʾid* noted that 'most of the transactions of the people of our region are of these types'. The *qāʾid* pleaded that it would be difficult for the people to travel such distances, 'every day and at all times', and appended plaintively to his letter that 'we people of the mountains are weak and humble'.[85]

Clearly the acquisition of urban and rural property by foreigners and protégés had advanced significantly during these years. Abusive credit and usurious loans, legitimized by international agreements under the guise of 'protection', led to numerous land transfers. The crises of the late 1860s, and 1878–82, gave numerous speculators, often with limited capital, great opportunities as poor debtors fell insolvent. This had the effect of destabilizing the Moroccan authorities' capacity to rule. The Moroccan government was challenged even further by the increasing support that foreigners gave to dissidents and rebels.

Foreign intrigues

The biggest challenge to the local authorities and legal system came in 1867–8, in the case of Masʿūd b. ʿAbd al-Qādir at-Tallāwī ash-Shiyāẓmī. The case unfolds as a sordid dispute over a debt between the American and British consulates, involving an agent of Abraham Corcos who had dealings with the *qāʾid* of the Matūga, and Masʿūd ash-Shiyāẓmī, a British protégé. All three legal systems were employed in the case. Affidavits and counter-statements were drawn up in preparation for the case. Foreigners testified in the consulates, Jews signed their affidavits before the rabbis, and Muslims went before the qadi.[86]

What appeared to be just another typical consular dispute, emerged as an affair of much graver consequences. As it turned out Masʿūd b. ʿAbd al-Qādir at-Tallāwī was the brother of the former *qāʾid* of the Shiadma. The latter died in Fez in 1861, but Masʿūd had apparently made off with considerable sums of money belonging to his brother, obtained through exactions and illegal means. Masʿūd, pursued by the *makhzan*, took refuge in a *zāwiya* in Marrakesh. From there he went to Essaouira. Qāʾid al-Mahdī Ibn al-Mashāwrī received orders from the Sultan to have him arrested, but to everyone's astonishment he produced a patent of protection as a *simsār* for a British merchant, which had been granted by the vice-consul Carstensen. The *qāʾid* claimed that Masʿūd owed about 168,000 riyāl, a sum of substantial proportions. The implication was that Masʿūd had used the illegal money to purchase his protection. Even more serious were allegations that he had used the money for inciting a rebellion in the Shiadma against Qāʾid ʿUmar b. Aḥmad al-Ḥanshāwī between August and September 1867 by providing the rebels with arms and supplies. Affidavits were drawn up accusing Masʿūd of harbouring rebels in his house. Counter-statements were signed denying that he had any involvement in the Shiadma revolt. The case came before the British consulate during November and December 1867, and not surprisingly, Carstensen decided in favour of Masʿūd. In March 1868, the case went to Tangier for appeal. Masʿūd, in the meantime, fled the country, ending up in quarantine because of the cholera epidemic in Gibraltar. He later seems to have reached Wad Noun. With Masʿūd's departure from Essaouira, his protection was no longer considered valid. Bargāsh ordered the *qāʾid* of Essaouira to seize all Masʿūd's property and to warn the British vice-consul not to meddle.[87]

This was more or less the end of the affair for the consulates, and it seems that Corcos was able to recover the money he claimed.[88] But the ramifications of the case had stretched too far not to concern the central government. In April, Qāʾid al-Mahdī Ibn al-Mashāwrī was summoned to Marrakesh for a review.[89] Abraham Corcos, it seems, had kept his allies in Marrakesh closely informed about the proceedings of the case and about the activities of Masʿūd, and had informed the *makhzan* that 'his brethren [of the same tribe] and companions were gathered together with him [at his home] in a seditious manner'.[90] The *qāʾid* of Essaouira had been constrained to act against Masʿūd and his band, who threatened to have the routes to Essaouira cut and to put the town under siege. The rebels were left free to roam about town.[91] There were also suggestions that the *qāʾid* of the Haha was aiding the rebels.[92]

At the end of April, Abraham Corcos went to Marrakesh with the *tujjār* to pay tribute to the Sultan. He returned, in his words, 'after having had a most flattering reception by H.I.M. the Sultan'.[93] It seems likely that the case of Masʿūd ash-Shiyāẓmī was discussed. The day after his return to Essaouira, a newly-appointed governor arrived in town. Qāʾid al-Mahdī Ibn al-Mashāwrī had been imprisoned in the meantime.[94] The former *qāʾid*, according to Corcos in a letter to the U.S. consul-general, had been 'disgraced and removed for irregular proceedings and none [sic] performance of the proper duties of the office confided to him'. Corcos refers coyly to the tamperings of 'a certain European official in town'.[95]

But the *makhzan* was unambiguous about the reasons for the *qāʾid*'s removal: it was because of his involvement in the Masʿūd ash-Shiyāẓmī affair! The new *qāʾid*, al-Ḥājj ʿAmāra b. ʿAbd aṣ-Sādiq, was delegated to undertake an unprecedented task, which amounted to no less than the cleaning out of the entire legal establishment in town.[96] All those who testified in the case were removed from office. Two of the four *ʿudūl* at the port were dismissed. One of them, ʿAlī at-Tanānī, had been acting qadi of the town for about fifteen months after the death of Qadi Ibn Yāḥyā, and before the appointment of al-Mazmīzī. The latter was also removed in the overhaul.[97] Two *ʿadl*s from Marrakesh were appointed to the port. Almost all the *ʿudūl* in the town proper were also dismissed. A few months later there was talk of removing the other two *ʿadl*s at the port. At least one of them, ʿUmar b. ʿAbd as-Salām Amāhu, was dismissed, despite the fact that he denied having testified in the case.[98]

Such measures appear drastic, particularly since the *ʿudūl* were viewed as respectable members of the ulama. They were also men of considerable means as a result of the fees they received for the performance of various private legal services. ʿAlī at-Tanānī, for instance, held a house in the *casbah* together with the elite merchants.[99] It should be noted that some of these officials were later restored. ʿUmar Amāhu was reinstated at the *diwāna*, though he died shortly thereafter. The *umanāʾ* also considered reinstating ʿAlī at-Tanānī in his place, though they feared that because of his involvement in the Masʿūd affair, the Sultan would not approve his appointment.[100] He was nevertheless reappointed ʿ*adl* at the port, and then after the death of the Sultan later that year, he became qadi of Essaouira.[101] As for Qāʾid Ibn al-Mashāwrī, he seems to have been released from prison and employed in the Palace until the Sultan's death in 1873. He then returned to Essaouira with a pension and rejoined the military ranks.[102]

Despite the leniency toward a number of these well-established Swiri officials, the gravity of the Masʿūd ash-Shiyāẓmī case was not forgotten. In the eyes of the *makhzan*, Masʿūd was an unscrupulous rebel, first gaining the protection of the British, then obtaining the complicity of the legal establishment, and finally securing the complacency of the *qāʾid vis-à-vis* activities which threatened the town's security: namely, the revolt in the Shiadma.

In the case of Masʿūd ash-Shiyāẓmī, the Moroccan authorities were able to gain the upper hand because the administration of Essaouira was still under the direct control of the *makhzan*. In areas further to the south, foreign intrigues were more difficult to counter. Abraham Corcos and the British consulate maintained intimate ties with rural chiefs. The French consul Beaumier kept a close association with Ḥusayn Ū Hāshim of Iligh.[103] More dangerously, the Europeans renewed efforts in Wad Noun to establish a port which would be independent of *makhzan* control. After the death of Sheikh Bayrūk, his son Ḥabib resumed contacts with foreign vessels along the coast. In 1861, Ḥusayn Ū Hāshim – the 'enemy of the Sultan, according to Montagne – reported to the Palace about a Spanish ship communicating with Ḥabīb on the coast. The Sultan sought Ḥusayn's cooperation, which might explain why the *makhzan* agreed to send Ḥusayn sulphur from Essaouira and El Jadida.[104] The following year, another three foreign ships were reported at Wad Noun, where Ḥabīb Bayrūk had prepared some 30 camel-loads of merchandise and provisions to sell. His brothers, Muḥammad and Daḥmān, were opposed to the deal and attacked Ḥabib's party with some tribesmen from the Aït Bāʿamrān. Ḥabīb fled into the Sahara, and the tribes of Jazūla and Takna were warned by the Sultan not to have any further dealings with the Christians.[105] In 1864, fresh rumours about intrigues between Ḥabīb

Bayrūk and the Christians reached the Sultan.[106] In 1865, secret negotiations took place on several fronts. Beaumier reported in 1866 that Ḥabīb Bayrūk had travelled to Tenerife and Cadiz to discuss commercial relations with Spain. He was alleged to have returned with a plan to open up a port, and to have begun negotiations with the British vice-consul.[107] When these allegations reached the Palace, warnings were issued to the Sous regions. Sultan Muḥammad simultaneously sent letters to the Aït Bāʿamrān, Ḥusayn Ū Hāshim, and to the tribes of the Sous in general ('particularly those [tribes] beyond Wad Ulghās, and most specifically the ulama, marabouts, and notables [*aʿyān*] there'). The three letters repeated the same advice: 'It is obvious that anyone who has a grasp of reason and religion will not get involved in this [venture] which would bring calamity onto Muslims and particularly onto the people of the Sous region.' To the Aït Bāʿamrān, the Sultan added: 'Essaouira is your port, and the road to it is close to you . . . in the event that harm befalls you on its road, raise the matter before our sublime presence (exalted by God) in order that we may eliminate it [the problem].'[108] The illegal port was, after all, intended for the coast which the Aït Bāʿamrān tribes controlled.

The Sultan's stern warning ensured that the tribes in the area would oppose Ḥabīb's ventures. Moreover, two of the sons of Sheikh Bayrūk, Daḥmān and ʿAbdīn, were opposed to the plans to open the port. The latter hoped to restore some of the privileges enjoyed by his father under Sultan ʿAbd ar-Raḥmān: namely, the reduction in duties, particularly in ostrich feathers, and the use of a house in Essaouira for commercial purposes. Both these concessions had been taken away because of the intrigues. The *khalīfa* dispatched some soldiers to Tarudant and then to Iligh to obtain more information.[109] But Ḥabīb persisted again in the following year and the Sultan wrote to Ḥusayn Ū Hāshim calling for steps to be taken.[110]

Efforts by the Europeans to trade directly with the Sous ultimately failed in this period for the same reason as before: the economic links of the Sous with Essaouira were too strong. In fact, it was in this period that the trade of Essaouira generally, and the trans-Saharan trade specifically, reached its highest level.[111] The chiefs of the south, and particularly the marabout of Iligh, Ḥusayn Ū Hāshim, had much to gain from this growth of trade through Essaouira.

By 1873, the situation had changed. Though the trans-Saharan trade was still active, it was now clearly in decline. The continuous disturbances in the Haha jeopardized this trade, which was why the Sultan placed such a high priority on subjugating the Haha. Controlling the Haha meant controlling the Sous.

Rebellion in the Haha

After the death of ʿAbdallāh Ū Bīhī, the rebellion of the Haha tribes continued for some five years. The government was unable to impose its authority. Foreign inroads were certainly one cause of rural instability, and the imposition of the octroi at Essaouira another reason for rural discontent. It was above all the poorer traders from the countryside who were saddled with this tax since almost all the important town merchants had become protégés and were thus exempt. Furthermore, in the reorganization of the rural tax system in 1862, canonical taxes were almost exclusively levied in badly needed cash instead of in kind, as had formerly been the case, which must have intensified resistance against *makhzan* control.[112] This discontent was exacerbated by drought and severe hardship in the late 1860s. Finally, there was considerable dissatisfaction with Muḥammad U Bīhī, who was appointed *qāʾid* of the Haha on the death of his father in 1868. A rebellion was first led by the former *khalīfa* of ʿAbdallāh, who pillaged the Ū Bīhī stronghold of Azghār during Muḥammad's absence. Muḥammad reasserted his control, but his authority was again challenged by a rebellion of the Banī Tāmar just north of Agadir, led by Laḥsan Ū Tagrazīn. The Ida Ū Tanān threatened to join the revolt.[113]

From this time on, trade with Essaouira was constantly disrupted. Discontent remained widespread and brigandage was prevalent throughout the southern provinces. Abraham Corcos alerted Bū ʿAshrīn of 'the fear, the anarchy, and the plundering of caravans on the Agadir road'.[114] The Sultan ordered the *qāʾid* of the Haha to re-establish control, but little could be done against the brigands in a province suffering from such severe shortages.

In the spring of 1871, the simmering dissidence in the Haha exploded again in all-out revolt. The Matūga tribe joined in the uprising. Azghār, the residence of the detested *qāʾid* was razed.[115] The town of Essaouira itself was soon threatened by the uprising. A group of tribesmen from the Haha came to Essaouira at the beginning of June, threatening to cut the water supply if their kinsmen, imprisoned in town, were not released. The prisoners, most of them undoubtedly incarcerated for debts owed to foreigners and protégés, were freed.[116] Lacking troops, the governor of Essaouira was unable to act against the rabble filling the town. A few weeks later, a deputation of about 100 Haha tribesmen entered Essaouira and sacrificed three bullocks before the different town authorities, attesting their loyalty to the Sultan and assuring the merchants that their property would be protected in transit. At the same time they insisted on being freed from the rule of Muḥammad Ū Bīhī.[117]

The control of the Haha was a high priority for the *makhzan*. Not only did the security and prosperity of Essaouira, and ultimately the control of the Sous, depend on it, but furthermore taxes had to be collected. It had become evident that Muḥammad Ū Bīhī could not govern the province. In addition, the Palace received reports that the *qā'id* of the Haha was misappropriating *makhzan* funds, possibly diverting the money to dissidents in the South. Muḥammad Ū Bīhī was removed permanently from power.[118] This seems to have calmed the province temporarily. The central government now needed to forge new alliances and to play one local power off another. There were some twelve tribes of the Haha, and each one seemed to be governing itself by following its own local leader. It was to take a few more years before the *makhzan* could wrest control of the province, and in the meantime, Essaouira was threatened on several more occasions.

The appointment of a new *makhzan qā'id*, Muḥammad b. aṭ-Ṭāhir ad-Dawbilālī, proved to be little more than a stop-gap. Troubles continued in the region north of Agadir. With the routes cut and Agadir under siege by followers of Ū Tagrazīn, the *makhzan* called for reinforcement from the Sous army and from Essaouira's garrison.[119] The general unrest in the Haha spilled over into Essaouira itself. In March 1872, disturbances broke out during the *ʿĀshūrā'* celebrations in town. Throngs of rural dwellers were reported to have come to town, breaking into houses and insulting Jews. The *qā'id* was unable to act, and the militia of the town remained inert during the affray. The *qā'id* of the Haha also remained immobile. His continued presence in town, and his incapacity to quell the disturbances in the Haha, were regarded as a threat to Essaouira.[120] Intermittent troubles continued during 1872. Further disturbances in the Haha were reported only two hours from town. The soldiers sent by the *qā'id* to seek reconciliation between the warring parties were repelled.[121]

By 1873, it had become apparent that the situation in the Haha needed to be stabilized. In May 1873, the Khalīfa al-Ḥasan began actively campaigning in the Haha for an agreement between the fighting factions.[122] A new *makhzan qā'id* was appointed, ʿAbd al-Mālik Ū Bīhī, another son of ʿAbdallāh, but it was also clear that the *makhzan* was going to have to make alliances with the local chiefs, who had emerged as the most formidable local powers in the Haha: Anflūs, Laḥsan Ū Tagrazīn, and to a lesser degree, Bū al-ʿAshrāt. This was essential if taxes were to be collected, contributions exacted for the royal military encampment of the *khalīfa* (*maḥalla*), and order restored.[123]

The Sultan died in Marrakesh in September 1873, when his son, Mawlāy al-Ḥasan, was at Bū Rīqī in the Haha. There, he was proclaimed

Sultan by the chiefs of the Haha, and returned to Marrakesh to succeed his father. According to Montagne, the Sultan promised to appoint the principal sheikhs of the Haha as *qāʾid*s before his return to Marrakesh.[124] Revolt broke out in the Shiadma on 15 October,[125] followed by an uprising of the Ida Ū Gurḍ. The revolt of the Haha was apparently sparked off by the Sultan's decision to divide the Haha between the four sheikhs: ʿAbd al-Mālik Ū Bīhī, Anflūs, Ū Tagrazīn, and Bū al-ʿAshrāt. The four *qāʾid*s entered the town, but when the Haha tribesmen heard of these appointments, the town was put under siege. Soon the number of insurgents grew, and the town was blockaded. Anflūs and Tagrazīn left town and returned to their rural homes. Troubles continued for several days before order was restored by the town authorities.[126]

The policy of vesting power in rural chiefs led to the emergence of new and often dissident leaders in the Haha. The dominant force in the region was Mubārak Anflūs, and soon most of the Haha came under his rule. The other *qāʾid*s had less of a following, and Bū al-ʿAshrāt died later that year.[127] When ʿAbd al-Mālik Ū Bīhī imprisoned the Haha tribesmen in Essaouira immediately following his appointment, Anflūs threatened to cut off the town.[128] Some kind of agreement was reached by the two *qāʾid*s about a week later, but the complaints continued against Anflūs. Qāʾid ʿAmāra of Essaouira informed the Sultan in 1876 that the brother and children of the late Qāʾid Bū al-ʿAshrāt of the Ida Ū Gillūl were being intimidated by Anflūs.[129] Anflūs also began to encroach on some of the districts assigned to Tagrazīn in 1875.[130] Claims and counter-claims of the theft of camels, cattle, sheep, firearms, and equipment reverberated between Anflūs and Tagrazīn in 1877.

Banditry continued in the countryside. Rural insecurity also jeopardized Essaouira. Vagrants from the countryside, often connected to brigands in the Haha or the Shiadma, filled the town, and orders were sometimes issued for their arrest.[131] Essaouira, like all ports, attracted the riff-raff, the dispossessed peasants lured to the city in the hope of living off the surplus. The Haha tribesmen serving in the garrison in town were sometimes involved in supplying arms to outlaws from their tribes.[132] Furthermore, Qāʾid Anflūs would put pressure on the governor of Essaouira to obtain the release of fellow tribesmen imprisoned in town.[133] Security was further jeopardized by the followers of Anflūs in town who, as Qāʾid ʿAmāra reported, 'filled their houses with gunmen from the provinces joined by country vagabonds'.[134] The rural *qāʾid*s themselves, as we have seen, maintained town residences which in some circumstances became centres of sedition.

What one can say about the general causes of banditry,[135] is also true of the Haha. The revolt was a reaction to worsening poverty under the burden of heavy taxation, a protest against the state and the new political order it tried to impose, an expression of hostility towards the town and the usurious dealings of the wealthy merchants. Moreover, the Haha reflected wider movements of social unrest in Morocco at the time. In 1872, urban discontent erupted against the authorities in Marrakesh, forcing the city markets and gates to close for several days.[136] In the following year, the tanners of Fez rioted, their anger directed toward Muḥammad Bannīs and his detested skin tax.[137] This kind of protest was certainly not a new phenomenon in Moroccan history. Nevertheless, these movements emerged out of the new situation engendered by foreign intervention. The cost of the war with Spain had led the Moroccan government to impose new and cumbersome taxes on the population, which heightened discontent. Furthermore, the growing encroachment of foreigners and protégés challenged the authority of the Sultan, and encouraged the dissident tribes of Morocco to rebel.[138]

Taxing the southwest

In an attempt to gain control of the countryside, and to increase the revenues of the state, Sultan al-Ḥasan embarked on the most ambitious fiscal reform of the nineteenth century. A network of *umanāʾ* were sent to rural areas to collect the canonical taxes, *al-aʿshār* and *zakāh*. This was the first time that government officials were permanently stationed in rural regions as tax-collectors. Formerly, it had been the responsibility of local notables and sheikhs to send in the dues from their regions. Although their assistance was still needed, the rural *umanāʾ* now took charge. Furthermore, tax-collectors were assigned to *zāwiya*s, which eliminated the tax exemption that these religious lodges had enjoyed in the past.[139] Apart from being a port of international trade, Essaouira assumed a growing importance as a regional administrative centre during the reign of al-Ḥasan. Bearing in mind that the population of the Haha and Shiadma was much more sizeable than the town of Essaouira, the imposition of a universal rural tax promised to bring in much greater revenue than the gate and market taxes in the town proper.

Umanāʾ were first delegated to the Shiadma in 1879 and to the Haha in 1881.[140] Not only were they assigned to collect the agrarian tithes, but they were also in charge of appropriating domains for the *makhzan* from the rural holdings of deceased *qāʾid*s, such as ʿAbdallāh Ū Bīhī, Laḥsan Ū Tagrazīn, or Bū al-ʿAshrāt al Gallūlī.[141] Henceforth the produce from trees on these lands was collected by the *makhzan*. In general, *makhzan* properties in Shiadma and the Haha were registered and appraised by the rural *umanāʾ* with the assistance of local sheikhs.

Essaouira became the administrative centre for this new taxation system. The *a'shār* of Shiadma and the Haha was sent to the *amīn al-mustafādāt* in town. This official was responsible for the sale of produce when taxes were collected in kind. The produce from *makhzan* property in the countryside was also sent to the town officials. Furthermore, city officials such as the qadi and his appointed *'udūl* supervised the collection of produce from rural *makhzan* properties, and assisted in its sale in town.[142] These functions enhanced the influence of Essaouira's administrators. In particular, the *amīn al-mustafādāt* emerged in this period as the most important financial official in town.

A further reform, known as the *tartīb* (lit. an administrative system), was initiated in 1884. This reform stemmed from the 1880 treaty of Madrid, where it was agreed that foreigners and protégés would also pay agrarian taxes. The stipulations about the taxation of livestock and agricultural produce, of which the regulation on gate taxes was a part, were agreed upon in 1882. Yet subsequent resistance by foreigners prevented the *makhzan* from implementing what was designed to be a universal tax. Marabouts, *shurafā'*, and other beneficiaries of quasi-feudal royal privileges (*tawqīr* and *iḥtirām*) would no longer be exempt. Foreigners and protégés, as we have seen, escaped the new system, but major reforms were nevertheless initiated in 1884, involving both administrative and fiscal changes. This is a point on which foreign sources are silent.[143] Lists of families and other units were drawn up as an aid in assessing the amounts of taxes to be paid (*al-khirṣ*).[144]

Already by 1883 the collection of taxes from the *zāwiya*s was assiduously pursued, though not without encountering considerable resistance. Qā'id ar-Ragrāgī ad-Dawbilālī, who became governor after the death of 'Amāra in 1883, reported, in 1884, of two marabouts from Zāwiya Amzīllat who protested when an official had come to collect taxes the year before. 'They produced *dahir*s they had from the Sultan's ancestors (may God sanctify their spirits) together with a *dahir* of the [present] Sultan (may God protect him), [stating] that the *zakāh* and *a'shār* are taken from their rich and given to their poor.' The plea of the two marabouts was not accepted so they took sanctuary in the Qādiriyya *zāwiya*.[145] Numerous marabouts of Ragrāga *zāwiya*s began producing letters of *tawqīr* and *iḥtirām*.[146]

Severe measures could be taken to assure that rural taxes were successfully collected:

The sharifian decree has reached us, brought by a commander (*qā'id al-mi'a*) and ten cavalry – [this unit formed] a dragoon [which was to remain in operation] until the tribe had paid its dues in *al-a'shār* to Essaouira. We have obeyed the Sharifian order, and during their tour they went around to the homes of all the people from the tribes who had not paid their *al-aʿshār* until nothing was left [to be paid in taxes], except for the amount assessed on those who kept residing in town during the period of tax-assessment (*al-khirṣ*) . . . and after they were assessed on what they had [that was taxable], they moved back to their homes in the country.[147]

Harka to the Sous

For the Sous, where control was less direct, the central government was not able to employ a system of regular taxation. Nevertheless, for the Palace, control of the Sous remained an important priority, and foreign intrigues on the coast of Wad Noun were an added impetus for the Sultan to assert his authority in the far south. In 1863–4, the Sultan sent Khalīfa al-Ḥasan on an expedition (*ḥarka*) to the Sous to collect taxes, the first such expedition there for five years. The *ḥarka* – also called *maḥalla*, though the latter term referred more to the encampment – was the principal means used by the Sultan to bring dissident tribes within the fold.[148] Khalīfa al-Ḥasan was accompanied by a large number of tribesmen from the Haha and Shiadma.[149] Taxes were collected from Tarudant and the tribes and regions of the Sous which the *makhzan* could penetrate – the Tiyūt, Damsīra, Nafīfa, Shtūka, Raʾs al-Wād, Masgīna, al-Jabbāla, etc. (see map 7). These taxes also included tributes (*hadāyāʾ*), fines (*dhaʿīra*), and poll tax (*jizya*) from the Jews of Tarudant, the Shtūka, and Raʾs al-Wād. A total of 3,587,624 ūqiya was collected.[150]

The principal motive of the *ḥarka* must have been to collect money, which was desperately needed after the war with Spain. At the same time, it was imperative to make a show of force to avert dissidence and contraband in the more distant parts of the Sous. To Sūs al-Aqṣā – the deep Sous – the *khalīfa*'s expedition would not venture.[151] The only means of deriving some revenue from the brisk trade taking place in the parts of the Sous outside *makhzan* administration was still through customs duties at Essaouira.[152]

Increasingly, however, foreign intrigues were perceived as a threat to this system and a challenge to the Sultan's sovereignty in the southern regions. The first was the protracted case of Jacopo Butler, a Spanish merchant, and a vice-consul of El Jadida, who travelled to Wad Noun to conduct secret negotiations with Ḥabīb Bayrūk. The three were imprisoned by the sheikh when they failed to reach an agreement, and it took eight years of prolonged negotiations between several foreign consulates, merchants, Soussi chiefs, and the Moroccan government before they were ransomed for 27,000 riyāl in 1874. The *makhzan* was forced to reimburse a large part of the sum to the Spanish.[153] The case

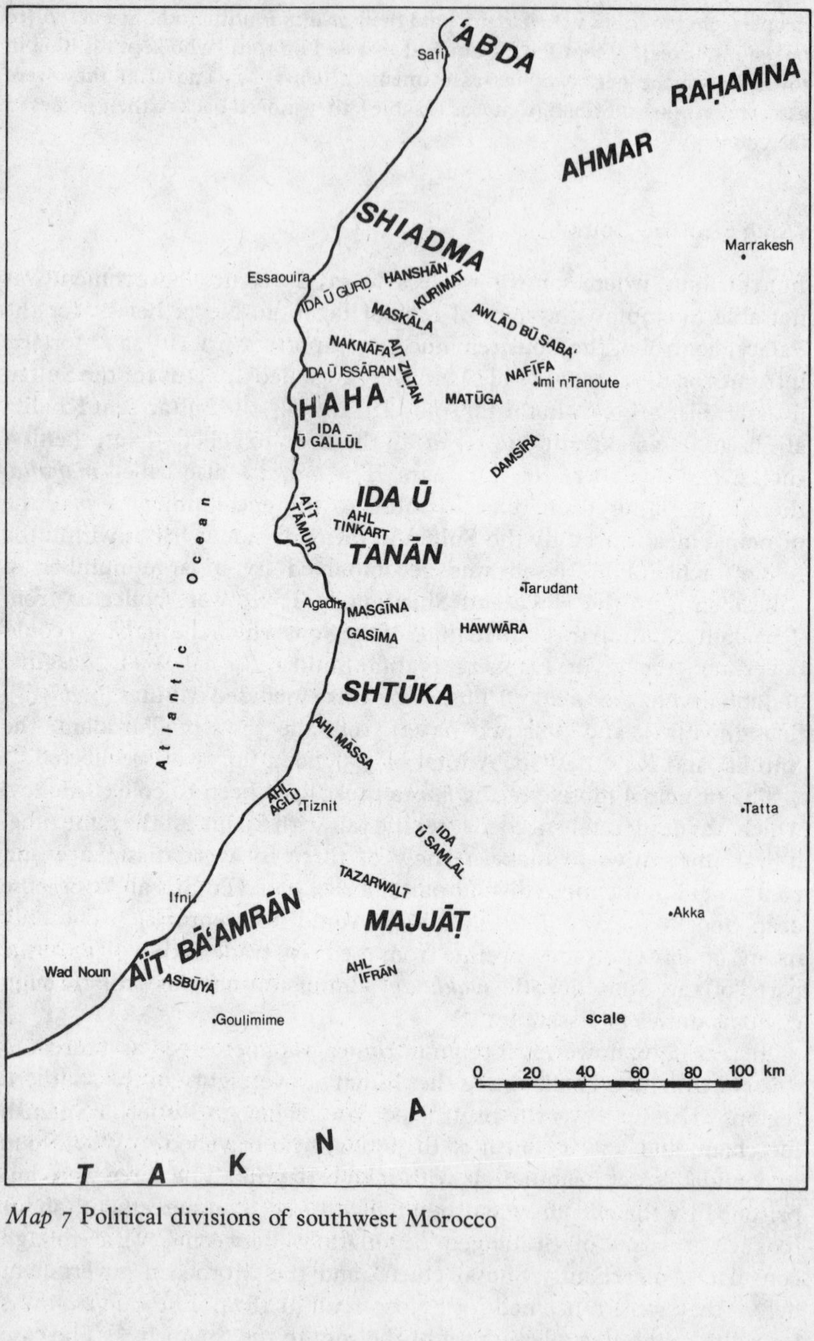

Map 7 Political divisions of southwest Morocco

demonstrated that the Sultan had little power over the Aït Bāʿamrān, and furthermore, the incident had risked direct Spanish intervention in the Sous. Foreign efforts to gain a foothold on the southern coast intensified after the Butler affair.

In 1878, the Spanish sent a ship along the coast to find a location for their fishing entrepôt, theoretically ceded by the Moroccans in the Treaty of Tetuan after the war of 1860. Landing at Ifni, the expedition began communicating with the native inhabitants.[154] Sīdī Ḥusayn Ū Hāshim immediately wrote to both the *makhzan* and Awlād Bayrūk, and, according to the British consul in Essaouira, incited the Aït Bāʿamrān to burn down houses belonging to the inhabitants of Ifni. Emissaries were sent throughout the Sous by Ḥusayn to resist the Spanish.[155] The Spanish consul in Essaouira asked Ḥabīb Bayrūk to stop repelling the Spanish, claiming that Sultan Sīdī Muḥammad had conceded a strip of land to them. Sultan al-Ḥasan, replying to Bayrūk's queries, vehemently denied that this was true.[156]

In 1879, the route between Essaouira and the Sous had become extremely hazardous as a result of famine and rural disturbances. Caravans travelling through the treacherous Ida Ū Tanān had to be accompanied by about 200 armed men. Even with such protection, stragglers were being shot at and robbed by brigands.[157] The claims of Swiri merchants multiplied against the people of the Sous, and other districts along the routes.[158] Ḥusayn Ū Hāshim also began to accumulate claims, demanding from the Sultan 55,000 riyāl as compensation for the murder of five Jews who were conveying his goods. The Sultan instructed his mediator, ʿAbd al-Wāḥid al-Mawwāz in Agadir, to reach a settlement with the tribes on the route to Essaouira.[159]

These difficulties induced the Marseille merchants to contact Sīdī Ḥusayn with the hope of establishing a *comptoir* on the southern coast. The establishment of the entrepôt of Cape Juby at Tarfāya by an English merchant in 1879 (see below), added to the urgency of the French initiative. Cohen, Julien and Cie of Marseille had correspondents in Essaouira, particularly Joseph Elmaleh and Mordecai Bensaude, who served as Ḥusayn's agents. It was this firm which began to solicit the support of the French foreign ministry for their project. The steamship 'Anjou' was sent to the coast with the intention of establishing direct commercial relations. According to foreign sources, the Sultan sent money to Ḥusayn and offered him a house with stores in Essaouira, as well as credit on customs duties for his agents. The chief of Iligh was hesitant in trading with the French without the Sultan's sanction, however, so the mission of the 'Anjou' failed. The following year, when an agent of Ḥusayn went to Essaouira to claim the concession, the *umanāʾ*

said that they had not received instructions from the Sultan. Consequently, communications with the French were resumed. But once again, Ḥusayn withdrew from the overtures, fearing the reaction of the Sultan. Jacquetty went to the Quai d'Orsay, but failed to gain the French foreign ministry's recognition of Ḥusayn as an independent sovereign.[160]

The *makhzan* began to plan more drastic measures to avert what it perceived as the partitioning of Morocco. An English merchant, Donald Mackenzie, began seeking the support of the British government and Chamber of Commerce for a proposed port at Cape Juby. Such a port, Mackenzie argued, could capture almost all the lucrative trade of the Western Sudan.[161] He was allegedly ceded a piece of land by Muḥammad Bayrūk in an agreement signed in April 1879. Operations from Cape Juby soon commenced. By the end of the year, the enterprise formed into the *Northwest African Company*.[162]

The reaction of the Sultan was swift. 'If we do not hurry up . . . serious harm will be caused to the port of Essaouira and all of Morocco.' The British representatives in Morocco, while hesitating to give the venture their full support, claimed that the territory was outside Moroccan jurisdiction. This was unacceptable to the *makhzan* which was intent on pressing the British to 'close the detrimental door that Mackenzie opened by his initiative in this region'. The British proposed that Agadir be opened to commerce, an idea that the Forwood Steamship Co. (a Liverpool line that had a service to Morocco) and the Manchester Chamber of Commerce had been advocating for years. At this juncture, the proposal was rejected by the *makhzan*. 'Inform them that Agadir is a village on a rock surrounded by forest in the midst of the tribe of the Ida Ū Tanān who are highlanders and accept no laws . . . do not let them achieve their aim with it [opening of Agadir] because it is Essaouira that has command over it [Agadir].'[163] Delegations were sent to frustrate the initiative. A wooden structure built by Mackenzie was burned down. The resistance of the neighbouring tribes had been invoked.[164]

The overtures of certain factions of the Aït Bāʿamrān to open a port for French commerce were probably due to the fear that Mackenzie's entrepôt would deny them access to the profits of the caravan trade. The French merchants sought the support of Ḥusayn Ū Hāshim. Daḥmān Bayrūk, a rival to his brother Muḥammad, was also involved in the project.[165]

Finally, some merchants in Essaouira – Curtis, Brauer, Yule, and Broome – formed what was known as *The Sus and North African Trading Company*, with the aim of opening a port at Arksīs between Wad Nūn and Wad Māsa. The company claimed to have signed a treaty in 1880 with the sheikhs of the Aït Bāʿamrān, and with the sanction of Ḥusayn Ū Hāshim.

If Ḥusayn actually supported the project, he was quick to withdraw. Preparations by the Sultan for an expedition to the Sous had begun.[166] These initiatives failed to gain the strong backing of either the British or French governments. Hay was totally opposed to the newly established *Sus and North African Trading Company*. Likewise, as we have seen, Jacquetty failed to gain the support of the Quai d'Orsay. These failures made no impact on the Sultan who saw the initiatives in the Sous as a real threat. As far as Morocco was concerned, the foreign governments had given their tacit support to these intrigues.[167]

These combined foreign intrigues in the southwest gave the Sultan the justification to organize an expedition to the Sous.[168] The expedition can also be seen in the wider context of Mawlāy al-Ḥasan's military and administrative reforms, as part of an effort to control the countryside effectively, to raise needed revenues, and finally to assert the sovereignty of the Sultan in areas where it had been questioned.[169]

The *ḥarka* of 1882 was an attempt to bring the Sous back into the fold by a combination of concessions and co-optation. Assāka was to be opened for shipping, and *dahirs* were promulgated which stated that the new port was to be created to facilitate trade for the tribes of the Aït Bāʿamrān and Takna. Food was to be imported to those regions which had suffered from four years of drought. Agadir was officially opened to import supplies for the *maḥalla*, but the expedition was hampered by the lack of victuals, and was unable to advance beyond the region of Tiznit and Aglū. Amid hunger and desertion, the *ḥarka* had to turn back.[170] Mawlāy al-Ḥasan was therefore unable to march as far as Goulimime or Majjāṭ and placate the southern chiefs, nor was he able to get rid of Mackenzie's settlement. The Spanish continued to claim their entrepôt.[171] Nevertheless, the *ḥarka* of 1882 was the first step in bringing the Sous back into the fold. To be sure, the numerous appointments of *qāʾids* and qadis in Aglū and the Aït Bāʿamrān did little more than recognize the existing political structure,[172] yet by receiving the *makhzan* investiture, chiefs such as Daḥmām Bayrūk had, to a degree, compromised their autonomy. Furthermore, by rallying the Aït Bāʿamrān to the cause of the *makhzan*, the hopes of Curtis and *The Sus and North African Trading Company* were soon to be dashed. Finally, the town of Tiznit was fortified in the process, becoming the principal *makhzan* stronghold in the Sous.[173] In this sense, the *ḥarka* of 1882 was just the first phase in the subjugation of the southwest to the Sultan's rule.

Foreign intrigues, however, had still to be eliminated from the southern littoral. Soon after the Sultan's army left the Sous, the tribes resumed trade with Mackenzie's settlement, now considerably more fortified. Early in 1883, a number of sheikhs in the region of the fortress signed an agreement with the settlers.[174] A scramble for the southern coast began again. Despite the warnings of British officials, Curtis hastened to establish his claims at Arksīs among the Aṣbūya. Curtis and Andrews arrived at the site by steamer. They gained the cooperation of the native inhabitants by unloading some 8,000 bags of rice and barley. The ship was loaded with produce and departed, leaving the two at their settlement. The Sultan sent down a nephew, Mawlāy al-Kabīr b. Muḥammad b. Sulaymān, and Buʿazza as-Sarīfī. Both had been assigned to the area in the recent *ḥarka*. The two British merchants were arrested and escorted to Essaouira. Andrews claimed that the *makhzan*'s opposition to their settlement was induced by Spanish bribes.[175] Indeed, a few months later, Daḥmān Bayrūk arrived in Essaouira together with a number of *makhzan* officials in order to proceed to the southern coast in a Spanish ship to take possession of the port.[176]

The *makhzan* response to the threat of foreign settlement was to strengthen its position in the Sous. Provisions continued to be supplied to Agadir, and constructions in Assāka were expedited,[177] but these intensified efforts did not deter Curtis. He allegedly continued to bribe the people of Aglū and the Aït Bāʿamrān. Agents of Curtis, whom he sent from Essaouira to the Sous to recover debts, were arrested (Curtis had substantial claims involving stocks left at Arksīs, worth some £8,954). Such claims were considered illegitimate by the *makhzan*, who regarded the goods as contraband. Furthermore, Buʿazza as-Sarīfī was arrested when it was revealed by the British that he had agreed to allow Curtis to unload the provisions.[178] The Moroccan authorities effectively put an end to the activities of Curtis in the Aït Bāʿamrān. Moreover, by consolidating its power in the Sous, the *makhzan* was able to prevent the tribes from trading with Cape Juby, and in 1884, trade with the entrepôt came to a standstill.[179]

In 1884, preparations began for the second expedition of the Sultan to the Sous, some two years in advance of the actual *ḥarka*. Essaouira became the financial centre for the *makhzan*'s operations in the Sous. Customs duties from the port and the new rural taxes imposed in the Haha and Shiadma were used to support the new regular army (*al-ʿaskar al-jadīd*) stationed in the Sous. In 1883, expenditure exceeded revenue from customs duties by 476,520 ūqiya.[180] In one month alone in 1884, 7,201 ūqiya were sent for the construction of the walls of Tiznit and another 6,568 were sent for provisions to the two *amīn*s in charge of the work. The ʿaskar in Tiznit, who numbered 235 soldiers and eight *qāʾid*s, were paid 46,911 for provisions, and the provisions for the *maḥalla* in the Sous – the *muʾna* or special purveyance – amounted to 32,123 ūqiya. Another 3,711 ūqiya were sent to cover the cost of transporting 1,000 uniforms to the Sous. These expenses amounted to about 74 per cent of the total expenditure for the month. Expenses exceeded the total revenues by over 20,000 ūqiya.[181] Not only was money sent from Essaouira, but also engineers and supplies to the Soussi regiment.[182] Taxes from Essaouira's hinterland were of great importance to the *makhzan* preparations for the second *ḥarka*. With increased agricultural production in 1884 and 1885 because of the good harvests, considerable amounts of grain were exported to France.[183] It can be inferred that grain collected from the *aʿshār* was sold to merchants in Essaouira. The *makhzan* would then gain further revenue from export duties, assessed at a riyāl the fanega for wheat, and half a riyāl for durra, barley, and other grains. Some of the cash gained from duties and sales was undoubtedly expedited to the Sous, and some of the cereal was sent directly to the Sous in preparation for the *maḥalla*.[184] The grains sent were stocked up in silos in the Sous.[185]

The tribes of the Haha and Matūga played a pivotal role in the *ḥarka*, supplying both material and manpower. In the spring of 1884, the *umanāʾ* of the Ida Ū Issāran and Qāʾid Aḥmad b. Mubārak az-Ziltanī were ordered to begin preparations for the *ḥarka*.[186] Early in 1885, az-Ziltanī had begun operations among the Aït Bāʿamrān. With some of the soldiers (called *ḥarrāk*) for the expedition already in the Sous, the *ḥarka* had actually begun.[187] Soon the other *qāʾid*s of the Haha – al-Maḥjūb b. Aḥmad al-Gallūlī and ʿAdī b. ʿAlī an-Naknāfī – together with the *umanāʾ* of the province, began, with some difficulty, to collect camels and horses for the Sous.[188] In the spring of 1885, ʿAdī b. ʿAli an-Naknāfi was ordered to go on *ḥarka*.[189] At this stage, Aḥmad b. Mubārak az-Ziltanī was still actively attempting to reconcile disputes between the tribes of the Aït Baʿamrān.[190] Gallūlī too was now playing a leading role in the *ḥarka*, also trying to put an end to unrest between various rival factions in Sūs al-Aqṣā.[191]

The fighting between the tribes was partly the result of the appointment of *makhzan qāʾid*s to the Sous during the expedition of 1882. This had led to a number of rebellions soon after the departure of the Sultan.[192] Aḥmad al-ʿAbūbī, the *khalīfa* of the *makhzan* in Tarudant, was in charge of establishing authority in the Jazūla. Muḥammad, the son of Ḥusayn Ū Hāshim of Iligh, was appointed to the Samlāl and Ifrane.[193] Throughout 1884, fighting was widespread in the Hawwāra and Shtūka.[194] Suggestions were made that Ḥusayn Ū Hāshim had been inciting the troubles,[195] but nevertheless, attempts were made to use the marabout of Iligh as a mediator in the disputes.[196] Ḥusayn's difficulties increased as fighting in the Majjāṭ and the Aït Bāʿamrān grew during 1885 – the tides had turned against him.[197] Considering the relative weakness of Ḥusayn's position, it is little wonder that the chief of Iligh decided to work for the Sultan. Rewards were granted to those who were willing to collaborate. In January 1886, Muḥammad, the son of Ḥusayn, was informed that a house was to be made available to him in Essaouira.[198] In a period of four years, the power of Ḥusayn Ū Hāshim of Iligh was significantly reduced. From nearly autonomous rulers, the house of Iligh, for the time being, became representatives of *makhzan* authority in the Sous.[199]

The policy of manipulating rivalries and divisions in the Sous had successfully paved the way for the second expedition in 1886. This time, the problem of supplies was carefully planned. Provisions of grain were stocked up along the intended route of the *maḥalla* – in the Haha, Shtūka, Tiznit, Gasīma, and the Aït Bāʿamrān – through a network of government *umanāʾ*.[200] On 3 April 1886, the Sultan entered Essaouira on his way to the Sous.[201] The passage to the Sous went smoothly since Aḥmad b. Mubārak az-Zilṭanī had made sure that all the *qāʾid*s and notables of the Aït Bāʿamrān had made preparations for the Sultan's arrival.[202] In June, the port of Assāka was officially opened. Goulimime was reached without delay.[203]

The only onerous part of the *ḥarka* took place in July, during the return from the Sous through the Ida Ū Tanān. Considerable fighting broke out in the mountains there. The various *qāʾid*s on the *ḥarka* were able to subjugate the region in a few weeks.[204] The *khalīfa* of az-Zilṭanī reported to the Sultan that his men had marched on the dissident bands of the Tinkart tribe: 'We have set fire to their houses, scattered their grain, burned their trees, and plundered their money.'[205] *Makhzan qāʾid*s were appointed in the Ida Ū Tanān for the first time. A month later, the *qāʾid* of Essaouira was able to report that the region had been successfully quelled. 'Joy and happiness overwhelmed us and the people of the town on this clear and unsurpassed victory . . . we dutifully attended to all kinds of celebration – taking out cannons, decorating *sūq*s – and all things related to that for a period of three days.'[206]

The second *ḥarka* of 1886 was a firm assertion of the central government's authority in the Sous. The power of Iligh and Goulimime was, at least provisionally, dismantled. The Sultan prudently appointed Muḥammad b. Ḥusayn Ū Hāshim and other influential chiefs as *makhzan qāʾid*s, also granting them houses in Essaouira.[207] Mackenzie's enterprise, though not completely eradicated, no longer posed any significant threat, and disappeared altogether several years later.[208]

The fractionation of powers in the Sous influenced Essaouira's relationship to the central government. No longer was the trade of Essaouira the principal key for *makhzan* control of the Sous. Military and administrative control was henceforth to be exercised through the fortified bastion of Tiznit. Furthermore, the dismantling of regional power upset the triangular balance between Marrakesh, Essaouira, and the southwest. The flourishing trading *mawsim*s, under the patronage of the *shurafāʾ* of Iligh and Bayrūk of Goulimime, were in decline after 1886. As we have already indicated, the trans-Saharan trade, the basis for the wealth of the *mawsim*s, came to a standstill after the French conquest of Timbuktu in 1894. In the end, the *ḥarka* failed to eradicate the brigandage in the Haha and the Sous. As soon as the *maḥalla* left the Ida Ū Tanān, for example, the tribes killed the newly appointed *makhzan qāʾid*.[209] The trade routes between Essaouira and the Sous and Wad Noun were therefore still being disrupted.

The flourishing trade passing through the Haha and the Sous up until the mid-1870s had rested on a balance of powers between the central government and the venerated leaders of the southwest. There was a *de facto* recognition of each other's limitations. The threat of opening a port was the lever applied from the Sous to gain favourable concessions from the Sultan. The actual realization of such a project would have disrupted this balance. In fact, the balance was undermined by the settlements of Curtis and Mackenzie on the coast. Foreign intervention, therefore, followed by the dismantling of the power of southern chiefs, finally upset this structure.

Chapter 9

The people of Essaouira in precolonial times

The people of Essaouira in the latter half of the nineteenth century were affected by dramatic forces which were changing Moroccan society as a whole. Some of these forces, such as war and economic penetration, were of foreign origin, while others, such as the expansion of governmental powers and new kinds of taxes, originated within Morocco itself. But no force was as important as the dramatic recurrence of natural calamities. Seen in conjunction with other events of the nineteenth century, these natural disasters take on new dimensions.

Urbanization, and in particular, urbanization in the coastal towns, has been seen as a major consequence of Morocco's contact with Europe in the nineteenth century. Most striking of all was the increased number of Jews. Miège estimates that the Jewish population on the coast grew from 19,900 in 1832–6, to 24,800 in 1856–7, 31,000 in 1866–7, and to about 38,000 in 1900.[1] The absence of any census and the contradictions in foreign estimates, make these figures unreliable. Nevertheless, there was clearly a steady, though not dramatic, rise in the Jewish population in coastal towns. From the mid-nineteenth century onward, large numbers of Jews, particularly from the Sous, settled in Essaouira. It can be determined tentatively that the Jewish population grew from about 4,000 out of a total population of 12,000 in 1844, to 7,000 out of 14,000 in 1875, and then slowly climbed to about 8,000 out of a total of 18,000 inhabitants towards the end of the century (see app. B).[2] The Soussi Jews became the majority of the Jewish community, and in some respects, the most important element of the entire population of the town. What propelled them northward to Essaouira? Montagne suggests that the exodus from southern regions resulted from the concentration of trade in Essaouira and the disruption of local trade caused by European imports.[3] And yet, as we have seen, the population of some southern centres grew because of the stimulus of trade centred in the royal port. Estimates of population for Goulimime, for example, range from about 800 at the beginning of the century, to about 4,000 in the latter half,[4] and the same point could be made for Iligh. In its heyday (about 1879) the Jewish population of Iligh may have been as high as 500, but after 1882, and the years of drought, this figure was probably halved.[5]

The serious drought from 1878 to 1882 in southern Morocco appears to have been an extremely significant factor in nineteenth-century population movements. Migrations from southwestern Morocco, therefore, were not linked solely to the effects of foreign trade at Essaouira. Periodic rural crises were as important as the specific economic conjuncture of the nineteenth century. The perennial south–north movements, in which the south can be characterized as a human reservoir in Moroccan history,[6] is fundamental for our understanding of the period.

Drought and Epidemic

In a hundred-year period from 1795 to 1895, there is evidence of some 40 years of scarcity or drought in southern Morocco. In approximately 8 per cent of these years, starvation led to numerous deaths.[7] A population weakened from hunger was more susceptible to disease.[8] Every 10 to 20 years the population was decimated by a major epidemic. Years of abundance were rare and even periods of average harvests seemed to have been disrupted by the onset of bad years. Serious hardship for the common man, therefore, rarely relented in nineteenth-century Morocco.[9]

Foreigners in Essaouira made efforts to change the traditional system of hygiene. Consular pressures induced the authorities to adopt sanitary and preventative measures. With the advance of cholera in the Mediterranean in 1848, the consular corps interceded and the town was sanitized by the local authorities for the first time.[10] Again, as cholera spread in 1865, pressures from the foreign representatives in Tangier prevented a ship of pilgrims returning from the East from landing at the port.[11] The pilgrims were quarantined on the island of Essaouira.[12] The quarantine on the island was used intermittently for the next several decades. In the cholera epidemic of 1868, sanitary measures were taken and a quarantine on travellers imposed.[13] Pressures on the Moroccan government by a committee of foreign consuls in Tangier, the *Conseil Sanitaire*, usually forced the reluctant authorities of Essaouira to comply with such measures, but despite these measures, conditions of public health probably deteriorated because of overcrowding.[14] Furthermore, some of the measures taken were probably counterproductive. For example, many returning pilgrims incarcerated on the island in 1865 died from privation rather than epidemic.[15] Sewage canals which were installed in the 1860s due to foreign pressures may have worsened conditions of hygiene in town, as a traveller observed in 1888:

One of the unique distinctions of Mogador is its possession of a partial sewage system, which means that instead of the good old Moorish plan of having sewage deodorised and rendered innoxious in the open air, and occasionally washed away by rain or carried off by scavengers, it is now collected for a whole year in typhoid-breathing drains along the streets, from which it is extracted once a year.[16]

Cholera struck the town in 1835, 1855, and 1868. The epidemic of 1855 was more deadly than the one of 1835. An estimated 500 to 800 perished in the town as opposed to an estimated 200 in 1835.[17] This increase may have been because social conditions had deteriorated. However, in 1868, only 300, or two per cent, of the population perished in the cholera epidemic, according to Beaumier. In all other coastal towns, between four and 14 per cent of the population died.[18] While in 1855, more Jews than Muslims were probably the victims,[19] in 1868 the ratio was reversed, despite the increasingly overcrowded living conditions in the *mellah*.[20] Beaumier attributes this lower mortality rate to the preventative measures in hygiene undertaken by the local authorities at the request of the consuls, and to the aid given by a French doctor, Thévenin. In Tangier, where sanitary measures were also in force, deaths were lower than in most other ports with only four per cent succumbing to the disease.[21] In Essaouira only three years before, the *mellah* had been thoroughly cleaned and a hospital established there by Dr Thévenin (which closed down in 1869). A report dispatched on 11 September, states that owing to Thévenin only 15 out of 100 Jewish cholera cases had been fatal.[22] Evidence from the Jewish cemetery shows that the community must have been harder hit later in the month.

Whatever progress in sanitation might have been made, it was soon counteracted by the influx of rural migrants. In the years preceding the famine and epidemics of 1878–9, large numbers of Jewish migrants began to arrive from the interior.[23] New arrivals would cohabit with relatives: whole families living on rooftops and in courtyards were reported in the *mellah*.[24]

The drought and famine of 1878–9 was the most lethal of the nineteenth century. Some estimates say that one-fourth to one-third of Morocco's population perished, while as many as half the population of the Haha and the Sous died.[25] While these sources may well be exaggerated, there can be little doubt that the country was ravaged by the famine. Foucauld's account of some of the largely depopulated villages of the Sous testifies to the devastation.[26] During the famine large numbers of Swiris were carried away by disease, and as various foreign and local charities began to distribute food to the famished, numerous refugees, disease-ridden and emaciated, flocked into the city.[27] The town's normal population of about 16,000 was probably inflated to about 27,000.[28] Scores were dying in the streets, having succumbed to smallpox and chloera. Dysentery and typhus, epidemiological consequences of starvation, were no doubt taking their toll of human life. The *makhzan*

9 Jews in the *ḥaddāda* pray for rain in 1922
Courtesy of Monsieur Samuel Levy
Masses of Jews pray publicly for rain during the drought of 1922. Jews are seen in both Western and traditional garb. The four chief rabbis are near the front of the crowd to the right with the long beards (one is wearing sunglasses).

provided *funduq*s for the refugees, but since many were at the brink of death, their chances of survival were probably worsened by their confinement to these *funduq*s, where disease was rife. Between July 1878 and February 1879, about 600 to 800 Swiris died, and the majority of refugees, at least at the height of the famine, probably also perished.[29]

The urban population as a whole suffered from a high mortality rate. New immigrants continued to stream into the town, probably replacing the numbers of those who died during the epidemics. Squalor and overcrowding in the *mellah* was already intense in the years before the famine, and although a decrease in population, caused by the high mortality during the famine, might have helped alleviate some of these problems, immigrants rapidly took the place of the victims. Famine prevailed again in the Sous in 1882, impelling survivors to move northward. Many villages in the Sous were depopulated, and scores of Jews moved to Essaouira.[30] In the conditions of impoverishment, overcrowding and deteriorating hygiene, smallpox epidemics constantly took a heavy toll of lives, especially those of children, despite a programme of vaccination which had been initiated in the 1870s.[31]

European medicine may have been effective in protecting the wealthy of the *casbah*, but the poor were mostly left to their fate. Cholera and smallpox were above all diseases of poverty and privation. The town simply could not keep up with the demographic pressures, nor could traditional Muslim and Jewish charities alleviate the conditions of the destitute. A new vocal group of Swiri Jewish activists, influenced by philanthropic and liberal ideas from Europe, began pushing for social reform.

Reform and the Jewish lower classes

European Jewish philanthropy in Morocco dates back to 1844, when reports reached London of the pillaging of the town and the flight of the Jews into the surrounding countryside. The leader of the British Jewish community, Sir Moses Montefiore, presided over a *Committee for the Relief of the Sufferers at Mogador* to raise charitable subscriptions for the victims.[32] Foreign Jewish philanthropic activity, however, only became a permanent force in Swiri Jewish society after the 1859–60 war with Spain. Subscriptions for the *Morocco Relief Fund* to aid the refugees had reached some £12,812, largely because of the contributions by American Jews. A leading member of the Jewish community of London, Moses Haim Picciotto, was sent on a commission to Morocco to help determine what to do with the surplus funds.[33] Picciotto was responsible for publicizing for the first time the abject poverty of the Jewish masses of the *mellah*, and the indifference of the wealthy of the *casbah* to the fate of their poor brethren.[34] On Picciotto's recommendations, a school was established and an allowance of £10 to £12 a year to clean the *mellah* was allocated from the fund.[35]

The Picciotto mission was followed by the journey of Sir Moses Montefiore to Morocco in 1863–4. Montefiore managed to obtain a *dahir* from the Sultan which promised the Jews of Morocco equality, justice, and an end to corporal punishment.[36] The promulgation of the *dahir* had important ramifications in Jewish society in Morocco. Henceforth, many Jews in Morocco viewed European Jewry, rather than the Moroccan authorities, as their protectors.[37] Montefiore had stayed in Essaouira in the house of Abraham Corcos on his way to Marrakesh. The problem of the poverty and overcrowding of the *mellah* was brought to his attention. Montefiore requested from the *wazīr*, Bū ʿAshrīn, new housing for the Jewish poor, an idea supported by the British consul of Tangier, Reade, who went to Marrakesh with the Jewish leader.[38] Abraham Corcos also used his influence in the court to have the *mellah* enlarged, but a plan to expand the living area of the *mellah* into the Shabanāt quarter never materialized because it threatened to arouse Muslim resentment.[39] A decade later, R. Drummond Hay made another attempt to expand the *mellah* into the Shabanāt quarter, but to no avail.[40] But the initiatives of foreign reformers were not without effect. The Montefiore visit was followed by the efforts of the Alliance Israélite Universelle, a Jewish organization founded in Paris in 1860 which sought to improve the status and social conditions of Jews around the world.[41] The combined pressures of Anglo-Jewish and Franco-Jewish philanthropists, actively supported by the British and French consulates, who were anxious to spread their influence locally, led to a number of public works in town: sanitary measures were adopted, a public fountain was erected in the *mellah*, the sewage drain was constructed, improvements to houses were undertaken, and an Alliance school was founded and a hospital for the poor established.[42]

The Moroccan authorities saw the growing intervention by foreign Jews as a challenge to the sovereignty of the Islamic state. Montefiore and the Anglo-Jewry may have felt that the *dahir* of Sultan Muḥammad had changed the legal status of Moroccan Jewry, but this was largely an illusion. The Sultan, in effect, only gave his assurance that Jews would be protected, but this was perfectly in accordance with the *dhimma* pact of protection. Nevertheless, the Montefiore *dahir* was invoked whenever alleged injustices were committed against Jews. The situation was not so much that Jews had obtained a new status, but rather that increasingly they were able to escape Moroccan jurisdiction, facilitated by the system of protection.[43] In some cases popular resentment may have been aroused, in other cases local officials may have acted against the Jews.[44] The reforms were largely for the benefit of the Jews of the elite. Those Jews who managed to obtain foreign protection were exempt from paying the head tax (*jizya*). As the numbers of protégés increased, the poorer Jews of Essaouira had to pay a larger part of the annual sum of 1,000 mithqāl imposed on the community as a whole.[45] By the mid-1870s, the *makhzan* was no longer able to collect the *jizya*.[46]

Some of the heads of the Jewish community also questioned the benefit of these foreign-induced reforms. Though support was initially given to the school and hospital by the community through the establishment of a meat tax, the tax was annulled because of the hardships caused by drought and epidemic coupled with traditional resistance to foreign Jewish influence. By 1869, both the hospital and the school had to close down.[47]

In 1875, the Alliance opened its doors for the second time, but once again it did so for only a few years, shutting because of the famine of 1878–9, and not reopening until 1888.[48] With the formation of the Anglo-Jewish Association in London in 1871, new activities began in Essaouira. Jews of Swiri origin in England began furnishing the new society with information. A smallpox vaccination programme was inaugurated by the A.J.A., and demands were made through the British consulate to expand the living quarters of the *mellah*. An initiative to establish a branch organization of the A.J.A. failed at this stage, owing to divisions among the elite of the Jewish community.[49] These foreign Jewish organizations posed a direct threat to the authority and position of the Jewish oligarchy. Despite the avid support of the foreign consular corps, the A.J.A. and the Alliance initially failed to establish a firm foothold in the Jewish community. This prompted them seriously to criticize the wealthy notables for exploiting the poor. These criticisms coincided with the deterioration of living conditions in the *mellah*, caused by the large influx of Jews from the Sous. The attention of the new group of social reformers was drawn to the problems of housing, hygiene, medicine, and the distribution of food to the poor.

Both the consular corps and the Alliance criticized the Jewish elite for charging the poor of the *mellah* high rents. In their view, the elite of the *casbah* maintained a callous attitude towards the poor. As one Alliance official put it, the gap between the *casbah* and the *mellah* involved 'two totally distinct races'.[50] He was echoing the words of Picciotto some 15 years previously, who had seen the division of the community into two 'castes'.[51] The expansion of the *mellah* conceded by the Sultan at the time of the Montefiore visit failed, according to Beaumier, because of the intrigues of landlords of houses in the *mellah*.[52]

The plight of the Jewish poor increasingly caught the attention of foreign Jewish organizations. The rural exodus caused by famine in 1869 and 1878–9 led to deplorable overcrowding. The *mellah*, which formed an eighth or ninth of the area of the town, had to sustain nearly 40 per cent of its population (see table 20).[53]

The constant attention of foreign Jewish organizations toward the Jewish poor of the *mellah* had given birth to a group of social reformers in Essaouira. A number of local Jewish charitable societies were established. In 1874, the *Ḥebrat Meshībat Nefesh* was set up to aid the sick, followed by the establishment of the *Ḥebrat ʿŌz We-Hadar*, a society founded with the aim of forming a girls' school. In 1875, an A.I.U. branch was established in Essaouira.[54] A tax on meat was the traditional means of raising funds for the poor, rabbis, and other dependents on the community. With the epidemics of 1878–9, this fund was used in part for improving sanitation in the *mellah*.[55]

Table 20 *Population of the* mellah *in 1875*

Jews	5,198
Families	1,127
Houses	147
Rooms	1,164
Average family size	4.6
Average numbers per room	4.5

Source: Adapted from *A.J.A. Annual Report*, 5 (1876), 59.

The crisis years interrupted most of the activities of these charitable societies as the community became dependent on foreign distribution committees. Even the *ma'amad* of the community was in disarray. Of the members, Joseph Elmaleh wrote: 'Some left town, others died, and some were ruined (Heaven forbid!) in the years of hunger and epidemic (Heaven forbid!)' However, in 1882, the *ma'amad* was reconstituted with Joseph Elmaleh at the head.[56] One of the principal correspondents of the A.J.A. and A.I.U., Judah L. Yuly, accused the oligarchy of forming the branch for the sole purpose of diverting any funds sent through the French consulate. Furthermore, he raised the issue of the misappropriation of the communal funds: 'It is (also) to be regretted that from the selfish measures adopted by the Elders and merchants, there are hardly now funds to succour the starving people.'[57]

A growing number of local reformers began accusing certain members of the *casbah* elite of obstructing their projects to ameliorate conditions in the *mellah*. The latter, the reformers charged, were making high profits by subletting houses at exorbitant rates to the poor. Jewish merchants who encountered difficulties in commerce, seemed partly to compensate for their losses by taking advantage of their urban holdings, as Ya'īsh Halewī noted in 1891:

> God has favoured them [the Jewish elite] with abundant houses and courtyards from which they earn more than from commerce. Apart from privately owned property, they also have holdings which they rent from the Sultan cheaply and sublet expensively. In this way they make good profits without working.[58]

Charges of misappropriating the communal fund (*qūpa*), were also levelled against the community leaders.[59] The Jews of the *mellah* themselves learned to appeal directly to foreign Jewish organizations. In 1882, for example, 150 artisans appealed to the A.I.U. for aid to alleviate their hunger.[60] They obviously were not beneficiaries of the pauper fund allocated by the *casbah* oligarchy.

The traditional Jewish leaders, therefore, were no longer the sole actors running the *mellah*. Foreign Jewish organizations and their westernized agents in Essaouira had become arbiters in the Jewish community. This new element of influence challenged the hitherto unquestioned authority of the *casbah* elders, and sowed deep divisions within the community, which were further aggravated by tensions and rivalries within the elite itself, caused by commercial competition. Some of the traditional Jewish leaders, faced with diminishing profits from commerce, increasingly turned to their urban property as a source of income. Other merchants, often protégés of rival foreign powers, began to challenge the domination of their competitors over the issue of social reform.

Nevertheless, there were social stirrings in the *mellah*. The poor became more aware of their exploitation, and this is reflected in the writings of a group of reformers from the *mellah* of Essaouira.[61] Yet was there evidence, as Miège's analysis suggests, of a mounting struggle of 'social classes'?[62] It would be misleading to view the increasingly vociferous, occasionally violent, clashes between the Jews in the 1880s and 1890s as manifestations of class struggle alone. Such terminology at least needs to be qualified, because it conjures up analogies with European industrial society in the nineteenth century. Social conflict within the Jewish community did not really involve the growing consciousness of a working class as such. Lateral ties of both patronage and kinship between *casbah* and *mellah* prevented the total restructuring of the community. Disputes were rooted in the specific conjuncture of late nineteenth-century Morocco, in which foreign merchants, consular agents, and European Jewish organizations had become important arbiters in the Jewish community, thus undermining the traditional pattern of communal leadership. However this traditional leadership was not replaced by some other form of social organization, in which social classes played a major role. All of these problems were exacerbated by clashes between wealthy rivals, vying for power and foreign protection. The social reformers of the *casbah* often sought the support of their allies in the *mellah* to advance their causes against their rivals.

Profiteers and the poor

The relative lack of opportunities in commerce on a major scale, the absence of sound investment possibilities in Morocco, and the financial troubles of the *makhzan*, meant that only a few merchants in Essaouira could make large fortunes from trade. Some were able to profit greatly from the upswing in trade in the 1860s, but there were many who went bankrupt. It was an era of high competition and commercial speculation, in which high risks were taken.

Yet neither the scale of trade, nor the prosperity of the merchants necessarily reflected the general conditions of the town. From 1867 to 1869, severe drought pushed food prices up to unprecedented levels. In Essaouira, wheat prices climbed from 100 to 600 ūqiya the kharūba (about one-third of a bushel) in 1868. Thousands of animals either died in the drought or were killed by hungry peasants.[63] Consequently, skins were numerous and sold cheaply at the market in town. A brisk trade developed with Marseille, the chief customer of goat skins. In return, large quantities of grains were exported to Essaouira.[64]

Speculators were able to make handsome profits amid widespread misery, and some of the merchants exploited the hardships of the poor. Grain had become a lucrative commodity. In 1870, prices remained high, despite the fact that the drought had relented somewhat during that year. One reason for the high prices was the hoarding by foreign merchants and protégés. The Sultan issued orders which were communicated to the consulates: 'No one should buy any wheat or barley in the grain market (*raḥba*), except that which one needs for sustenance.' The *umanāʾ* were instructed to buy what grain they could, and to store it up for the poor. 'Some of the wholesalers have left nothing in the *raḥba* for the poor . . . instead they take away anything they find in the *raḥba* and the people are left destitute.'[65]

During the famine of 1878–9, profiteers again speculated in grain. Opportunistic foreign companies trading with Essaouira extended credit in grain to numerous small traders, often, according to Consul Payton, quite imprudently: 'For instance, in the famine year of 1878–9, the agent of a Manchester firm turned numbers of brokers, little shopkeepers and other 'small fry' into 'merchants' by entrusting them with large quantities of foodstuffs, resulting in a mass of bad debts, some of which are still owing in 1887, while others have been settled.' The consulate was astounded at the way in which local entrepreneurs continued to operate: 'It is surprising how the Barbary Moor or Jew manages to get credit in London and Manchester which would not be given to many a much more respectable Englishman.'[66]

It was not really so surprising. Local brokers were still needed by foreign companies if they were to expand their commercial activities in Morocco. Native merchants were more in touch with supply and demand in the interior. Those who speculated in Morocco during droughts knew that they were taking a gamble. It was implicit in the rapid rise of some merchants during the crisis years that others would fall just as quickly. These were the risks that European companies took in extending credit in distant lands where commerce was conducted by different standards and procedures.

Some merchants, therefore, suffered losses during the famine years. But it was the poor who were most dramatically affected. During years of hardship, when grain, olive and argan oil prices rose, the poor had trouble coping since their stocks were minimal or non-existent. This problem was also related to international commerce since profiteers hoarded grain imports, much of which they received on credit.

But what were the lives of the poor like during normal years? Any judgement on the living standards of the common people of Essaouira, or for anywhere else in Morocco in the nineteenth century, is hampered by the serious lacunae in sources. Few references to the prices of basic commodities and wages can be found. A few scattered indications of salaries of officials and prices can be compiled from different parts of Morocco,[67] but comparisons with other towns and regions are equally problematic. Prices and wages in Essaouira tended to be higher, a consequence of the relative separation of the town from the hinterland. The price of barley, which constituted the principal cereal consumed by the population, was substantially higher there than in many other regions.[68] Comparisons are further hampered by the variations in the size of weights and measures in different regions. A kharūba of barley in Essaouira might differ from a kharūba in Marrakesh.[69] Finally, prices are cited in various currencies: mithqāl, riyāl, peseta, French franc, pound sterling, etc.

What can be determined from the scattered references to wages? Those on the pay-roll of the *makhzan* – the only reliable source on wages we have – whose salaries appear unaltered over time, almost certainly had other sources of income. The *qāʾid* of Essaouira, whose earnings amounted to 30 riyāl a month, clearly needed to supplement his official salary with other resources. An important official like the *muḥtasib* received only 90 ūqiya a month in 1875.[70] At three ūqiya a day, his salary would have been much lower than that of the average wage-earner. It was obviously expected that such an important official would supplement his income through his services. The salaries of important officials rarely changed in the *makhzan* registers, and thus provide us with little insight about their standard of living.

As for those on the lower end of the *makhzan* pay-roll – the soldiers serving in the militia for example – it might be argued that they endured a continual fall in their standard of living since their salaries were fixed in ūqiya, and remained the same from the 1840s to the 1890s.[71] A single soldier receiving 20 ūqiya a month, even in the 1860s, could barely support himself, let alone his family. It was noted in 1866 that the poor who received alms at 30 ūqiya a month could not subsist on that amount.[72] At 20 ūqiya a month a soldier might be able to purchase over half a kharūba of barley during prosperous years in the 1860s (a kharūba of barley could range anywhere from 150 to 320 pounds), but even less if at the same time he purchased olive or argan oil, also essential staples. The price of a kharūba of barley in the good years of the 1860s averaged at 34–38 ūqiya, but in the 1880s, after the drought, when grain prices skyrocketed, it averaged at over 200 ūqiya. Taking into account the inflation of the ūqiya – from about 33 the riyāl in 1865 to 125 in 1885 – the real price of barley was perhaps over 60 per cent dearer.[73]

What is certain is that no militiamen could have survived on 20 ūqiya a month, a sum which would have allowed him to purchase, let us say, 30 pounds of barley and nothing else. No wonder that desertion was such a common problem in Morocco.[74] Soldiers in the *ʿaskar al-jadīd* – the new regular standing army – as well as construction workers building the walls of Tiznit, were receiving in the 1880s 15 ūqiya a day, paid from Essaouira, almost the monthly wage of the militiamen.[75] The militiaman in Essaouira, therefore, clearly had other sources of income. The salaries of boatmen were also kept at 20 ūqiya a month throughout this period, since they were on the army pay-roll. In their case, they received fees for their services at the port at rates per load which were periodically adjusted. In 1873, the *umanāʾ* informed Abraham Corcos of the increased rates: 'You (also) know of the poverty of their situation and the paucity of their means.'[76] Later that year, the captains of the port went 'on strike' at the Sultan's residence in Essaouira (*dār as-Sulṭān*) – they went to pay their respect (*iḥtirām*) in the language of the document – until they received an increase in wages and a promise that the *umanāʾ* would write to the consuls (for it was principally the foreign merchants and the protégés who would pay for their services at the port). The *umanāʾ* again wrote to Corcos: 'Certainly they are justified, as you are well aware of their situation.'[77]

The militiamen were therefore probably also artisans or labourers in town.[78] It was often remarked anyway that most of the militiamen, numbering about 2,000, took up arms only periodically. In 1884, only 31 soldiers were manning the garrison. It was apparent that many of the soldiers joined the ranks to be clothed and fed, and when uniforms were not distributed, discontent brewed in the army ranks. The *qāʾid* became concerned with this problem, which he reported to the Sultan: 'Clothing has still not been found, and each time we spoke to the *umanāʾ* about this they replied that they will look into it . . . certainly our Highness is well aware that it is the clothing which gets people to join the army.'[79]

In 1867, Beaumier attempted to assess the cost of living and the wages of artisans and workers. Translating his figures into ūqiya, an average artisan family would spend 4.5 ūqiya a day on food, or about 135 ūqiya a month. Annual expenses, which would include housing, food, clothing, etc., were estimated at f350 or 2,646 ūqiya. A worker at the low end of the pay-scale might earn a franc a day (7.5 ūqiya), but never more than 15 ūqiya. A master craftsman's daily wage might be 38 ūqiya a day.[80] In 1870, the British carried out a survey of all the ports. A worker in Essaouira during harvest time, when labour costs were higher in town, was paid about 17 ūqiya a day, a menial salary but certainly enough to subsist on.[81]

Yet can we speak of increasing pauperization for the years examined? Certainly during drought, poverty intensified. With grain prices inflating five or six times, such as in 1868–9, starvation came rapidly. This, however, was a perennial problem in Morocco, rather than one specific to the nineteenth century. In a good year, such as 1889, the wages of labourers were estimated at 31–9 ūqiya, and the earnings of artisans may have been at least 62.5 ūqiya a day. These wages were not as low as they seemed, according to Payton: 'With the low prices of the simple food required by the temperate workman, who can live on barley broth, bread, and oil, with a little fish or meat occasionally, pays wonderfully low house-rent, and uses hardly any furniture, the above wages may be considered good.'[82]

If the above figures can be believed, then it can be inferred that between 1867 and 1889, the earnings of labourers rose commensurate with inflation. The same figures would suggest that the wages of artisans, as opposed to day labourers, had fallen by about 50 per cent between 1867 and 1889. But it should be borne in mind that rents paid by artisans to the *ḥubus* or *makhzan* were kept extremely low, perhaps even dropping in real costs over these years.[83] The standard of living of artisans, therefore, did not necessarily drop in these years.

In many respects, the lives of the common people of Essaouira remained the same in normal years. While the fortunes of the merchants rose and fell, and while the sovereignty of the Moroccan government was being undermined by foreign inroads, the lives of the poor were still dictated by the basic need to find their daily bread.

Chapter 10

The end of an era

Essaouira's pre-eminent position as the royal port of Morocco began to decline in the 1870s. While other ports in Morocco were enjoying a boom in trade because of the large increase of imports and brisk exports in wool and grain,[1] Essaouira was descending from its plateau. Not only was the market for some of its commodities slackening,[2] but internal factors also need to be considered in the commercial decline. Disturbances in the Haha and the general insecurity both disrupted trade routes and pushed up food prices. The inflation rate grew. In 1873, the year in which the Haha tribesmen besieged Essaouira, the exchange had climbed to 50 ūqiya against the riyāl,[3] a high point in Moroccan history.

While some speculators profited from these changing circumstances, many of the merchant families were having difficulties or collapsed during the crisis years. Others, such as Tūfal-ʿazz and Būhillāl lost their properties. The property belonging to the *tājir* Boujnah was appraised at 378,625 ūqiya (equalling about £2,300), to be sold to some Jews from Marrakesh in order to pay off debts owed to the *makhzan*. The *umanāʾ* were not sure that taking over the property was a good idea: 'If this property were to be appropriated for the *makhzan*, more will be spent on it than its value, because of its decrepit condition.'[4] Jewish and Muslim merchants from among the elite of Essaouira – including Messan b. Pinhas Toby, Būhillāl, Tūfal-ʿazz, Bensemana, Judah Levy, and Solomon Amar – were close to collapse and finding it difficult to pay the *makhzan* their dues.[5]

Increasingly it was the foreign merchants and those protégés who managed to obtain the backing of European capital who were able to stay afloat. Merchants who totally relied on royal credit were the most jeopardized. A few, such as Akkan Corcos, were able to profit from government monopolies, but other tax-farmers were not so successful. As we have seen, tax-farming was a risky business, particularly since growing numbers of protégés were escaping taxation. Finally, there were those merchants who had made great profits with the help of their ties with the chiefs of the Haha and the Sous. That too was precarious because of the unrelenting brigandage of the 1870s. Indigenous entrepreneurs who traded in large quantities of goods often did so recklessly and at high risks. Fierce competition pushed down the prices of imports, severely reducing most merchants' profit margin.[6] As a consequence, some of the most solid merchant firms were to go bankrupt in the next two decades. Swiri merchants who managed to stay afloat were doing so increasingly at the expense of poor urban tenants, rural debtors, and modest pedlars taxed at the gates of markets of town.

Miège argues that the crisis beginning in 1878, while imperilling some firms, was a major turning point for the growth of the capitalism, dominated by Jews.[7] Indeed, we have seen how some profiteers made small fortunes in speculating in grain imports, and others accumulated numerous pieces of both urban and rural property. However, most of these 'capitalist' enterprises which developed during the crisis were not on solid foundations. Even some of the largest firms lacked the capital for any kind of expansion in this period. The Corcos firm, already requesting a 16,000 riyāl loan from the Palace in 1875 when the bottom dropped out of the goat skin market in Europe,[8] sought further funds from the Sultan in 1880 because of losses incurred during the drought. They blamed their financial difficulties, in part, on their inability to recover debts in the countryside.[9] In 1884, Meyer Corcos complained that the *qā'id* was not actively pursuing debtors who had property in town, a charge that the latter denied: 'How can this be called inertness when the debtors are still in prison and their properties are still in the hands of the broker . . . what else could be done to them after that?'[10] In 1888, Meyer Corcos proposed that the 19,000 riyāl owed by Abraham and Jacob Corcos (both now deceased) to the *makhzan*, be deducted from the 40,000 riyāl in debts claimed.[11] As we have seen, by the turn of the twentieth century, the Corcos firm had gone bankrupt.

What was true of Corcos was also true of many, if not a majority of, other firms. The downfall of Mukhtār Ibn ʿAzūz was even more rapid. In a sense, Ibn ʿAzūz was a prototype Moroccan 'capitalist'. As the Sultan's financial agent in London and agent for a number of European firms in Essaouira, Ibn ʿAzūz seemed to portray the new type of Muslim *tājir*. But problems began to appear in June 1878 (if not earlier) when, pressed by foreign creditors, his house and stores in Essaouira and Fez were seized by the *makhzan*. As a *tājir*, he was in debt to the Sultan, and the *makhzan* used this as a pre-emptive right against foreign claims, always causing the foreign community to protest. In 1885, French creditors had Ibn ʿAzūz imprisoned, but his properties were still held by the Sultan. Vehement protests by British creditors continued for several years.[12]

Mukhtār Ibn ʿAzūz was not the only merchant in Essaouira to go bankrupt in Essaouira during these years. Aḥmad Būhillāl was also unable to pay his debt to foreign creditors. As in the case of Ibn ʿAzūz, the *makhzan* pre-empted their claims.[13] A number of other merchants – Levy and Moses b. Abraham Cohen, Michel Moïse (of Cohen Hermanos and Co.), Bonnet, Turgaman, Penyer, Broome, and Brauer – either went bankrupt or suffered serious losses between 1878 and 1882. Some of the foreign merchants were only saved from bankruptcy because they had European partners.[14]

Some merchants, such as the Afriats, Elmaleh, Bensaude, Dinar Ohana, Akkan Levy, Zagury, Attia, Akkan Corcos, al-Warzāzī, H. Cabessa, Jacquetty, Botbol, Coriat, and Bitton, continued to prosper in commerce (see table 5). Yet there is little reason to believe that in Essaouira there was an accumulative growth in wealth after the crisis years. As we have seen, the greatest profits from trade were made between 1850 and 1877. Much urban property had been acquired at even earlier periods – such was the case of Corcos who had purchased some thirteen houses and mortgaged another four between 1845 and 1861. The Elmalehs as well accumulated much urban property in the early decades of the nineteenth century.[15] Some merchant families, such as the Aflalos, probably acquired most of their eleven houses during the period when the family was prosperous in the eighteenth or early nineteenth century.[16] The fact that there were numerous real estate transfers in the years of crisis is not evidence by itself that modern capitalism was growing rapidly in Morocco. Urban property owned by merchants was certainly not always capitalist property. Some of the merchants who acquired urban real estate in the later period were simply taking over houses from other merchants in trouble. Musa Aflalo mortgaged some of his properties to Akkan Corcos in 1875, because of his debts to the *makhzan*. The *makhzan* was going to expropriate his other properties until Abraham Corcos successfully intervened on his behalf. He was allowed to continue letting his property to enable him to improve his situation.[17] By the 1880s, therefore, some of Essaouira's elite had little left but their urban properties which they continued to let at increasingly exorbitant rates to the poor.

What this picture might suggest is that there was neither significant growth nor decline in the accumulation of wealth between 1875 and 1886, at least not in Morocco itself. Some merchants may have made small fortunes during the years of crisis, but they were probably simply outflanking their less successful rivals. Furthermore, the increasing acquisition of rural properties could not readily be converted into wealth. The merchants of Essaouira did not have the capacity to turn their holdings into capitalist properties, except in limited ways, or to alter the mode of production in such a way that significant profits could be made.

What the frequent mention of land appropriation in the archives does reflect is that the question of land transfers to foreigners and protégés had become a vexing political problem for the *makhzan*. Morocco saw foreign penetration into the countryside as a serious threat to its own control of the hinterland.[18]

Many foreign merchants believed that the appropriation of rural property was a good investment, and that land could be made more productive. In some coastal regions, though probably not in the vicinity of Essaouira, there is some evidence to suppose that peasants had begun to increase production of cereals and legumes for the export trade in the period before the drought.[19] Some of Essaouira's merchants were known to have acquired lands in the more fertile regions to the north – for example, Delevante and Corcos were alleged to have held extensive domains in the ʿAbda.[20] In the Dukkāla and Gharb as well, protégés were acquiring extensive rural holdings.[21]

But from Essaouira, with its relatively unproductive agricultural hinterland, the export of legumes and grain remained limited. It is clear that in the Haha and Shiadma, disturbed by incessant rebellion and banditry, land was actually becoming less productive. Furthermore, the drought devastated much of the land in the region. The increasing alienation of peasants from their lands because of debts to city merchants also caused the productivity of the Haha and the Shiadma to diminish. Rural holdings of merchants in Essaouira, therefore, hardly brought in extensive wealth in this period.[22]

Finally, one should bear in mind that hoarding and usurious loans had been characteristics of merchants in Morocco for centuries. These were features of commerce in countries where capitalism was yet undeveloped, where facilities for credit, exchange and investments remained rudimentary at best. Enrichment through hoarding, usury, and the appropriation of immovable property during periods of crisis were not, in and of themselves, manifestations of developing capitalism.[23]

Nevertheless, Essaouira owed much of its wealth to international trade which was tied to European merchant capitalism. This was true in the eighteenth as well as the nineteenth century. What had changed in the 1860s, and accelerated in the 1880s, was that protégés were increasingly taking advantage of, and being used by, foreign merchant firms.[24] Their fortunes, however, were subject to rapid rises and falls, their positions more unstable than solvent. In these circumstances, it might be more instructive to categorize these merchants as a 'protégé' class, compradors rather than capitalists.

Much of Miège's thesis hinges on the hypothesis that a capitalist economy developed in the coastal towns, that the growing trade imbalance of imports over exports was catastrophic in economic, and especially, monetary terms, and that the integration of Morocco into the world economy engendered a social crisis. In short, Essaouira and other coastal towns are seen as catalysts in the economic transformation of traditional Morocco. What this further implied, was that the social gap was growing, at least in the coastal seaports.[25] Ayache and other historians have argued that monetary inflation led to the collapse of the Moroccan economy and increasing hardship for the poor.[26]

There is some evidence to suggest that foreign trade, especially the importation of cheap manufactured commodities, challenged certain traditional crafts, such as textiles. This appears to have been the case in Salé.[27] But there is also evidence – for example, in Fez – that some traditional crafts were expanding during this period because of local demand, and possibly stimulation by foreign trade.[28] The production of Essaouira's crafts, as we have seen, was limited and therefore, European imports posed no threat to the artisans. In fact, the most enduring and noted craft in Essaouira today – woodworking – developed only in the 1890s.[29]

In Essaouira the imbalance in trade did not worsen after the 1860s. Until the treaty of 1856, exports indeed generally outstripped imports. After that date, the value of imports and exports was roughly equal (see app. D). In the case of Essaouira, therefore, the trade deficit *per se* was not a significant factor.[30]

Undoubtedly the poor were hit periodically by sharp changes in the exchange rate of the ūqiya caused by the suppression of a particular bronze coin, the expropriation of counterfeit flūs, or the introduction of new coins in the market. Yet the source of their woes in the long run was not of a monetary nature. Seen over a long stretch of time, inflation rates, except for a few crisis years, were relatively moderate, as Park has shown.[31] The lives of the poor were gravely affected by the steep rises in prices during droughts, but this was a perennial problem in Moroccan history, and not specific to the latter half of the nineteenth century.

European inroads did ultimately have an adverse effect on the common people. The rape of the treasury by the Spanish led the *makhzan* to levy increasingly heavy taxes, with the poor bearing the brunt of these taxes as the number of protégés escaping taxation grew.

This might suggest that protégés increased their fortunes at the expense of the poor. The latter paid the most taxes and fell prey to urban loan-sharks – in short, a widening social gap. This was partly the case. But it was equally true that the fortunes of merchants were tied to an unstable economic situation. Having pecuniary links to a bankrupt monarch was a hazardous position to be in, to say the least. While a fair number of smaller merchants entered the arena of international trade during the drought years solely on the basis of foreign credit, the old and established merchant firms still remained tied to the Sultan in a chronic relationship of credit and debt.

The consequence was that very little capital was to be found in the late 1880s. Nevertheless, numerous small Jewish traders were able to obtain loans and goods on credit from London or Manchester companies. In 1891, as a result of a continuing commercial crisis, there was a virtual suspension of payments to Manchester companies, with little hope of reimbursements in the near future. The commercial situation was described as one of 'veiled bankruptcy'.[32] In 1893, the French consul wrote:

> This place, in effect, exists only by credit. One can mention a single English firm which is creditor of this market for more than one-hundred thousand pounds sterling, close to three million francs.

At this stage, Essaouira had few powerful merchant firms with capital at their disposal. Commerce had become monopolized by small Jewish merchants trading on foreign credit. The major entrepreneurs were found in other ports.

In a sense, the social disparity between rich and poor became more glaring in the late nineteenth century. The migration of Jews to Essaouira worsened conditions of poverty. Some merchants took advantage of the housing shortage by parcelling out smaller and smaller tenements at increasingly exorbitant rates.[33] Despite these conditions, the commercial activity of the port did effect social change in the interior, but the extent of change was still very limited. Compared to the growth of some of the Middle Eastern ports in this period – for example, Alexandria and Beirut – the influx of a few thousand Jews and an even smaller number of Muslims can hardly be seen as the outcome of a major alteration of social structure in Morocco.

By the end of the nineteenth century, capitalist penetration was making greater headway in the seaports to the north: Safi, El Jadida, and most of all, Casablanca. It was this latter city that was to become Morocco's most important port for international trade.[34] The nature of Essaouira's trade remained virtually the same for the next several decades – exporting the products of Haha and the Sous, such as almonds, goat skins, gum sandarac, and olive oil in exchange for textiles, tea, and sugar from Europe. The incessant circulation of pedlars between Essaouira and its rural markets – the ebb and flow of daily life – must have given the town an almost timeless appearance.

Conclusion

The history of Essaouira as the royal port of Morocco was both brief and dramatic. Within a decade after its foundation, Essaouira had become the leading Moroccan seaport, and reigned in its position of privileged royal port for a century. But almost as rapidly as it rose, external factors posed a threat to its status. The town witnessed in these years the steady growth of foreign pressures, which undermined the Moroccan state. Morocco could no longer control its external relations, and Essaouira lost its prominent position as the guarded port of the Sultan.

Essaouira, like all seaports, maintained a core of elite merchant families. Ten to twenty merchant houses ran the bulk of the import and export business of the port. In the most active years, in the latter half of the nineteenth century, some of these merchants made substantial profits. But even in the port's heyday in the 1860s, the fortunes made in Essaouira were limited and restricted to a small number of individuals. Competition was therefore stiff, and many merchant firms were unable to sustain their business activities. By the end of the 1880s, many had either gone bankrupt or had relocated to other cities.

Essaouira, therefore, never developed into an important international seaport. The reasons that such a development never occurred are related to the era in which the town lived. Essaouira, in a sense, was already an anachronism when it was founded – an imperial city founded by a sultan during the last phase of the empire's independence. An equally important reason is that the town never developed into a major city through economic imperialism, despite the fact that it was for a century the principal seaport of Morocco. The small-scale development of Essaouira reflected the aims of the *makhzan* – commerce with Europe was to remain at a minimal level, and it also reflected European aims – Morocco was of negligible interest in the overseas trade of Europe. Great Britain, Morocco's most important trading partner in the nineteenth century, had only minor commercial interests in Morocco. In the minutes of the Manchester Chamber of Commerce meetings, the question of Morocco was rarely raised.[35] Discussion of Egypt, India, China, and other countries of crucial importance for capitalist expansion, dominated the meetings of European commercial bodies. Most of Morocco's exports were of minor economic importance to Europe. There was no cotton or silk, as in Egypt and Syria, to furnish European industries with raw materials. Though Morocco may have been viewed as an El Dorado by some of the more high spirited or adventurous foreign merchants, the European powers were unwilling to take the forceful steps required for converting the country into a market for exploitation. Morocco was too impenetrable and the foreign powers too divided for this to occur.

There were other factors inhibiting Essaouira's growth. The town was created in a relatively infertile region, its importance depended on its special status as royal port for trade with Europe, and its own regional market remained relatively small. Hence the impetus for greater urbanization was absent. While the major inland cities of Morocco, nestled in agriculturally productive regions, were surrounded by numerous markets, Essaouira was relatively isolated from its immediate hinterland. In the absence of greater expansion in foreign trade, Essaouira did not have the capacity to sustain major urbanization. While the coastal cities in Morocco today are still growing rapidly as a result of the rural exodus, Essaouira's population still barely extends beyond its eighteenth-century ramparts.

In the nineteenth century, the internal dynamic continued to be the central propelling force in the history of Morocco. It is in this light that the history of Essaouira has been interpreted. Far too much emphasis has been placed on the importance of Moroccan seaports in the nineteenth century. Though the coastal towns did sustain a limited growth, the major inland cities, such as Fez and Marrakesh, continued to be the most important centres of exchange in Morocco. The domestic market still greatly overshadowed the trade with Europe. Moroccan history in the nineteenth century is often considered solely in terms of the integration of the country into the world economy. The degree to which this process took place still needs to be studied, but this would require an examination not only of the coastal towns, but also of Morocco's interior, the major inland cities and their surrounding markets. Even more important, the whole question should also be reversed. Moroccan culture as a whole was able to withstand the impact of western economic imperialism by restructuring these external forces into a local context.

It has been argued in this study that the persistence of the overland trade helped assure the continuity of economic and social structures. The constant movement of caravans in a country where the wheel was yet unknown, seemed somehow more important than the steamship which began to ply the Moroccan coast regularly in the 1860s. Trade remained linked to patterns of time embedded in the cultural milieu of southwestern Morocco: the rhythms of Muslim and Jewish rites and festivals. The organization of this trade conformed to deeply rooted jural patterns of exchange and credit, and of patron and client relations at each stage of the trade routes. Urban institutions themselves – *funduq* and *sūq* – were still organized according to indigenous patterns of social organization.

The fact that urban society maintained most of its traditional institutions and patterns of life in the nineteenth century does not deny that the seaports were major agents of change in Moroccan history. Essaouira, like all maritime ports, was a recipient of foreign influences. In the age of economic imperialism, the *makhzan* was unable to contain this influence. Essaouira was the most important opening for European expansion in Morocco, and in particular, the southwest, and this expansion increasingly challenged Moroccan sovereignty. The forceful military, administrative, and fiscal reforms undertaken during the reigns of Sultan Muhammad IV, and, in particular, Sultan al-Ḥasan I, aimed at defending the country against foreign inroads by asserting the Sultan's authority over the countryside and strengthening the state's resources. The growing number of native Moroccan protégés of foreign powers frustrated these aims. Despite the reforms, the Moroccan state was too weak to prevent foreign encroachments. In the decades preceding the establishment of the protectorate, Morocco entered an age of political and social turmoil, because the Sultan was unable to arrest the growth of European expansion which challenged the legitimacy of Islamic state. In this sense, the seaports were catalysts of change because they paved the way for colonialism.

This study has examined the interplay of external and internal forces through the response of the merchants and pedlars of Essaouira. The traders of Essaouira spread their risks by seeking alliances with the three poles of influence in Essaouira's commerce: the Europeans, the *makhzan*, and the chiefs of the southwest. Some merchants, in their positions as middlemen, managed to reap considerable profits, yet were themselves unable to become a powerful social group. In all their alliances and dealings, they remained dependent and therefore had but minimal effects on social change in Morocco. The importance of the merchants lay, above all, in the fact that by consular protection they received and their relations with foreign companies, the seeds of colonialism were sown.

Essaouira's prominence had been created by royal policy in the eighteenth and nineteenth centuries. This underscores both the importance and limitations of the city in Moroccan history. Essaouira was constructed to serve as the royal port of Morocco, where a fairly limited and closely controlled trade with Europe could be conducted. The central aim of the *makhzan* in this trade was to maintain control of the Sous, and in this respect, the Moroccan government achieved a large measure of success. Yet failure was also inherent in this success. Essaouira was the gateway for foreign encroachments in Morocco. The ability of the *makhzan* to control the countryside was undermined by the European presence at the port. For one hundred years, Essaouira served as the principal seaport of the Sultan, a symbol of the last period, before the French protectorate, in which the Moroccan government still controlled its own destiny.

Appendix A

Corcos collection: nineteenth-century Arabic documents (1843–83)

Letters sent to members of the Corcos family Name of sender	Quantity
aṭ-Ṭayyib b. al-Yamānī (Būʿ Ashrīn)	63
Idrīs b. aṭ-Ṭayyib b. al-Yamānī	9
Mūsā b. Aḥmad	56
Aḥmad b. Mūsā	1
Muḥammad b. al-Madanī Bannīs	14
Muḥammad b. al-ʿArabī b. al-Mukhtār	6
Idrīs b. Muḥammad b. Idrīs	5
Mafḍāl Gharrīṭ	4
Muḥammad b. ʿAbd ar-Rḥamān (the *khalīfa*)	2
Mubārak b. Muḥammad Anflūs	5
Various	24
Total	189
Other documents	
dahirs or copies of *dahirs*	8
Legal documents (property transfers)	7
Misc. letters	11
Total	26
Total documents	215

Appendix B

Population estimates of Essaouira

Year	Source	Total	Jews
1770–1	Corcos		1,875
1785	Corcos		6,000
1799	P.P. report	9,000	
1800–plague	P.P. report	(1,500)	
1799	Bache	8,000	
1800–plague	Bache	(4,000)	
1799	Jackson	10,000	
1800–plague	Jackson	(5,500)	
1809	Jackson	10,000[a]	
1815	Riley		6,000
1830	Chaillet	15,000	3,000
1834	Gråberg di Hemsö	16,500	4,000
1835	Arlett	9,500	4,000
1842	Beuscher	12,000	
1843	Richardson	14,000	4,000
1844	F.O., military report	12,000	4,000
1844	Calderón	16,500	4,000
1844	*Jewish Chronicle*		3,412
1845	French consular report	8,000	4,000
1847	Soulange-Bodin	12,000	
1847	Beaumier	12,000	4,000
1849	Darondeau	16,500	
1852	Almanach Didot-Bottin	12,000	
1854	Swedish consular report	10,000	
1854	French naval report	15,000	
1855	Beaumier	15,000	
1856	Grace	16,000	4,000
1857	British consular report	17,000	
1857	Belgian consular report	11,500	
1858	Elton	16,035	
1860	Cohn		4,000
1860	Picciotto		5,000
1860	Godard	20,000	
1860	Fernandez	15,000	4,000
1861	Rohlfs	11,000	
1864	McCulloch Dictionary	20,000	
1865	Gay		5,500
1866	Beaumier		6,000

year	source	total	Jews
1866	Almanach Didot-Bottin	14,000	
1867	Balansa	12,000	
1867	Beaumier	12,000	6,000
1868	Beaumier (citing Thévenin)	15,000	
1869	Carstensen		6,000
1870	Almanach Didot-Bottin	18,000	
1872	Cohen		5,000
1872	Leared	15,000	6,000
1872	Beaumier	13,000	
1873	Hirsch		8,000
1873	Leared	14,000	
1873	Almanach Didot-Bottin	18,000	
1875	A.J.A. report		7,000
1875	Beaumier	17,500	10,000
1875	Ollive	18,500	
1875	French consular report	18,000	10,400
1875	Spanish consular report	18,000[b]	7,500
1876	Alvarez Pérez	18,000	7,492
1878	R. Hay (citing French consulate)	20,200	11,000
1878	French consular report	17,500	11,500
1878	Castellanos	16,000	7,900
1879	A.I.U. report		6,500
1880	Ginsburg	25,000	10,000
1880	A.I.U. report		6,000
1880	Leclerq		7,000
1881	A.J.A. report		4,750
1882	Spanish consular report	20,000	
1882	Bonelli	20,000	4,000
1882	Breuille	20,000	
1883	Stutfield	15,000	7,500
1883	Erckmann	13,500	
1886	Campou	22,000	8,000
1886	Jannasch	17,000	4,000
1888	Spanish consular report	20,000	
1889	Stähelin	15,000	
1889	Bliss	20,000	
1889	De Kerdec	20,000	
1891	Elmaleh		10,000
1891	Halewi		10,000
1891	Payton	15,000	
1891	A.J.A. report		8,500
1893	Times of Morocco	17,000	
1893	A.J.A. report		8,000
1895	Almanach Didot-Bottin	18,000	

year	source	total	Jews
1895	A.I.U. report		8,000
1896	George Broome	15,000	7,500
1897	A.J.A. report		8,500
1897	Spanish consular report	18,000	
1899	Al-Moghreb Al-Aksa		7,000
1899	A.J.A. report		10,000
1900	Almanach Didot Bottin	25,000	
1900	Larras	20,000	

[a] Jackson did not modify his figure in his book published after the plague, despite the high mortality rate that he himself admits to.
[b] The Spanish and French consulates give the same total figure, but with the Muslim/Jewish ratio reversed. The Spanish are probably more correct.

Reference notes:

1770–1 Corcos, *Studies*, p. 113.
1785 *Ibid.*
1799–1800 *Journals of the House of Commons*, 1799–1800, LV, p. 498 (reports that 7,500 died and 1,500 remained).
1799–1800 Bache, 'Souvenirs', p. 87, reports that 4,000 died in the plague and 4,000 remained.
1799–1800 Jackson, *Account of Timbuctoo*, p. 160 (estimate of 4,500 deaths in the plague, p. 170n).
1809 Jackson, *Account of the Empire*, p. 26.
1815 Riley, *Authentic Narrative*, p. 397.
1830 R.G.S. MS, fol. 63.
1834 Gråberg di Hemsö, p. 61 (16,000–17,000).
1835 Arlett, "Survey of some of the Canary Islands", p. 290.
1842 A.E., C.C.C., Mogador 2, 19 February 1842.
1843 Richardson, *Travels*, vol. I, p. 256 (13,000–15,000).
1844 F.O., 99/23, 2 October 1844.
1844 M.G., Maroc 3H1, dos. VIII, May 1844 (16,000–17,000). *Jewish Chronicle*, 13 September 1844.
1845 Miège, III, pp. 16, 27.
1847 A.E., Maroc, M.D. 4, December 1847.
1847 A.E., Maroc, M.D. 10, March 1867.
1849 Miège, III, p. 16.
1852 Miège, III, p. 14.
1854 *Ibid.*
1854 A.N., BB^4 1026 M^{12}.

1855	Beaumier, 'Le choléra', p. 300.
1856	P.P., 1857, p. 503.
1857	Miège, III, p. 16.
1857	*Ibid.* p. 35.
1858	P.P., 1859, XXX, p. 487.
1860	Cohn, 'Voyage', p. 701.
1860	Picciotto, *Jews*, p. 24.
1860	Godard, *Description*, p. 36.
1860	Fernandez, 'Mogador', p. 262 (14,000–16,000).
1861	G. Rohlfs, *Adventures in Morocco*, p. 312.
1864	Miège, III, p. 16.
1865	A.E., C.C.C., Mogador 4, 18 July 1865 (5,000–6,000).
1866	A.I.U., France VIII D 42, 19 May 1866.
1866	Miège, III, p. 16.
1867	A.E., Maroc, M.D. 10, March 1867.
1867	Balansa, 'Voyage de Mogador', p. 314.
1868	Beaumier, 'Le choléra', p. 299.
1869	F.O., 631/4, 29 March 1869.
1870	Miège, III, p. 16.
1872	A.I.U., Maroc XXXIV E 601, 15 February 1872.
1872	Leared, *Marocco*, p. 70.
1872	Beaumier, 'Tableau', pp. 312–13 (12,000–14,000).
1873	*B.A.I.U.*, 1e sem. (1873), 142–3 (800–1,000 in *casbah*, 7,000 in *mellah*).
1873	Leared, 'Mogador as a Winter Resort for Invalids'.
1873	Miège, III, p. 16.
1875	*A.J.A. Annual Report*, 5 (1876), 59.
1875	Beaumier, 'Mogador', p. 119 (17,000–18,000).
1875	Ollive, 'Géographie', p. 370 (18,000–19,000).
1875	Miège, *Une mission*, p. 328 (7,500 Muslims, 10,400 Jews, 214 Europeans).
1875	*Ibid.* (10,400 Muslims, 7,500 Jews, 146 Europeans).
1876	Alvarez Pérez, p. 506 (10,362 Muslims, 7,492 Jews, 146 Europeans).
1878	F.O., 99/182, 3 November 1878.
1878	Miège, *Une mission*, p. 328.
1878	Castellanos, *Descripción histórica*, p. 123 (900 Jews in *casbah*).
1879	*B.A.I.U.*, 1e & 2e sem. (1879), 41.
1880	Ginsburg, *Account*, p. 4 (two-fifths Jews).
1880	*B.A.I.U.*, 1e sem. (1880), 31.
1880	Leclerq, 'Mogador', p. 403.
1881	*A.J.A. Annual Report*, 11 (1882), p. 69 (4,500–5,000).
1882	Miège, III, p. 462.

1882	Bonelli, *El Imperio de Marruecos*, p. 210.
1882	Miège, *Une mission*, p. 99.
1883	Stutfield, *El Maghreb*, p. 462 (7,000–8,000 Jews).
1883	M.G., Maroc 3H21, fol. 253 (12,000–15,000).
1886	Campou, *Un Empire*, p. 248.
1886	Jannasch, *Handelsexpedition*, p. 37.
1888	Miège, IV, p. 398.
1889	Stähelin, 'Mogador', p. 613.
1889	Miège, IV, p. 398.
1889	*Ibid.*
1891	A.I.U., *Maroc* III C, 10 December 1891, R. Elmaleh.
1891	Halewī, (1891), p. 311 (2,000 families × 5).
1891	P.P., 1892, LXXXIII, s. 183.
1891	*A.J.A. Annual Report*, 21 (1892), 26 (8,000–9,000).
1893	*Times of Morocco* (16 February 1893).
1893	*A.J.A. Annual Report*, 23 (1894), 33.
1895	*B.A.I.U.*, 1e & 2e sem. (1895), 91.
1895	Miège, IV, p. 398.
1896	N.A., R.G. 84, 27 April 1896.
1897	*A.J.A. Annual Report*, 27 (1898), 38.
1897	Miège, IV, p. 398.
1899	*Al-Moghreb Al-Aksa* (2 September 1899), (6,000–8,000 in the *mellah*)
1899	*A.J.A. Annual Report*, 29 (1900), 31.
1900	Miège, IV, p. 398.
1900	Larras, 'La population', p. 347.

Full references are found in the bibliography.

Appendix C

Balancing revenue and expenditure: accounts of the port

Revenue	Amount in ūqiya
Export duties	5,629,242
Import duties at 10% *ad valorem*	2,227,634.5
Tax on vendors of skins coming from tribes of the Sous, Haha, Shiadma, Matūga	188,037

Revenue	Amounts in ūqiya
Sale tax on skins in Essaouira	210,877
Amount received from tax the vendor pays on olive oil production	121,741.75
Profits from sale of sulphur	59,267.5
Profits from sale of gunpowder	750
Revenue from royal properties	110,916.5
Amount appropriated by the Treasury from property left without heirs	1,000
jizya for four years	4,000
Revenue from tobacco	110,199.5
Profits from the *iṭūrn[o]* appropriated from Bensaude	10,400
Amount received from mortgaged properties	7,700
Amount received in tobacco left by aṭ-Ṭālib Muḥammad al-Ḥājj	4,584
Amount received in *ṣilla* [allowance of sultan] for 'Īd al-Aḍḥā	1,903.5
Revenue from royal orchards	680
Revenue from grain market (*raḥba*) for 7 months	2,100
Tax on silversmiths	2,253
Amount left by aṭ-Ṭālib Muḥammad al-Ḥājj from the *'itrīya* Market	167,986.5
Amount left in sulphur	45,351.75
Amount reimbursed from debts of *tujjār* up to the end of Sha'bān 1274	20,081,208
Total	29,024,032

Expenditure	Amount in ūqiya
Amount sent to Sultan in silver currency	8,080,000
Amount sent to Sultan in copper [flūs]	532,000
Amount remitted to the servant al-Ḥājj al-'Arabī al-Aṭṭār in:	
silver currency	446,922
copper [flūs]	144,647
in merchandise	1,035,057
General expenses (*sā'ir*) [military salary, etc]	10,238,626
Expenses on quarters, walls, and the aqueduct	1,184,163.5
Credit owed by *tujjār* for old debt up to Muḥarram 1276	17,517,601.75
Amount of sulphur left [i.e., by outgoing amīn]	27,412.5
Amount left by the servant, al-Ḥājj 'Abd al-Qādir al-'Aṭṭār[a]	4,144
Total	29,024,032

[a] This represents a summary of a register book kept by the amīn (who was also governor), al-Ḥājj Muḥammad b. 'Abd as-Salām. His successor was al-'Arabī al-'Aṭṭār, but sometimes 'Abd al-Qādir was acting governor.

Source: D.A.R., Essaouira misc., Ramaḍān 1274-Muḥarram 1276/1858–9 (17 months).

Appendix D

Trade statistics for Essaouira

The statistics of imports and exports provided by the different European consuls varied considerably by consular agency. The basis for assessing the value of trade in the consular reports is usually not specified, but it can be assumed that customs house registers, and possibly bills of lading, were used. In theory, after 1856 there would have been less of a problem estimating the value of imports since duties were assessed by weight, and therefore each consul might make his own assessment of the value of the commodities exported.

Several precautions should be taken in using these statistics. Overall figures sometimes exclude specie, but at other times it is not specified if it is included. Furthermore, translating the different currencies into pounds sterling presents another difficulty. In 1862, the Moroccan treasury fixed the pound sterling at 162.5 ūqiya. This assumed that **f**25 were exchanged for the pound (i.e. 32.5 = 5**f**, 6.5 = **f**1), The exchange in London and Paris fluctuated slightly, generally a few fractions above 25 francs to the pound.[a] Morocco, however, stuck to the 32.5/162.5 exchange rate. In my calculations below, I have therefore translated **f**25 into £1.

From 1851 to 1858, British consular reports give the following total value of imports and exports, probably including specie (I have added the average):[b]

Year	Imports	Exports
1851	£109,842	£115,265
1852	101,478	148,517
1853	120,350	223,940
1854	73,796	106,174
1855	167,718	284,078
1856	333,905	336,513
1857	357,971	363,717
1858	183,170	236,824
Average	£181,029	£226,879

Miège gives the following estimates for 1859–1866, excluding specie (which I convert into pounds sterling):[c]

Year	Imports	Exports
1859	£ 95,252	£183,279
1860	129,570	142,592
1861	166,684	224,863
1862	174,790	172,540
1863	247,609	334,158
1864	152,007	188,270
1865	290,504	346,763
1866	232,008	287,206
Average	£186,053	£234,959

Miège's figures, mostly based on French sources, diverge somewhat from British estimates of the period; the latter are slightly higher.[d]

Consul Beaumier provides a summary of the total value of imports and exports from 1865 to 1874. We can probably assume that his estimates include specie. Converted into pounds sterling, Beaumier's statistics appear as follows:[e]

Year	Imports	Exports
1865	£350,526	£377,915
1866	240,730	287,206
1867	261,163	212,389
1868	263,973	215,817
1869	308,622	380,583
1870	297,387	302,986
1871	297,911	314,045
1872	311,803	293,258
1873	273,153	297,726
1874	276,044	347,292
Average	£288,131	£337,694

After 1876, British consular statistics published in the *Parliamentary Papers* are generally quite complete, specifying the value of imports and exports for each commodity and the amount of specie. British estimates for 1876–1886 are the following:[f]

Year	Imports	Exports
1876	£246,686	£207,558
1877	301,813	227,425
1878	235,165	233,797
1879	230,000	151,901
1880	137,839	169,072
1881	272,144	172,167
1882	195,949	126,918
1883	100,966	119,183
1884	112,975	125,911
1885	174,285	245,603
1886	244,571	305,765
Average	£204,763	£189,573

These trade statistics can really only be viewed *grosso modo* because of the discrepancies. Several observations can nevertheless be made: the commercial treaty of 1856 brought an increase in the volume of imports and exports (though disrupted during the Spanish-Moroccan war of 1859–1860); the value of exports increased proportionally to the value of imports, and thus, the commercial treaty did not tip the balance in favour of imports; between 1865 and 1874, the average value of Essaouira's trade reached its highest level, with exports rising slightly more than imports; in the last period, the value of imports increased over exports, though the trade deficit was still not very high; the overall value of the export trade declined in the period of 1876–1886.

A final note should be added: the total quantity of imports greatly increased but prices decreased steadily from the mid-century onward.

[a] The exchange rates at London and Paris for 1857–1872 are found in P.P. 1873, XXXIX, pp. 162–88.
[b] P.P., 1857, XVI, p. 504; P.P., 1860, LXV, p. 502.
[c] Miège, III, p. 64n.
[d] Miège also cites the amount of specie imported for 1859–1866. *Ibid.* Adding this to his statistics of imports without specie, we can contrast these figures with British estimates (which apparently include specie) for 1861–5:

	Miège	*British*
1861	£202,949	£208,263
1862	196,949	228,737
1863	306,340	309,324
1864	175,405	230,312
1865	299,226	349,559

British Consular statistics are found in P.P., 1863, LXX, p. 238; P.P., 1864, LXI, p. 178; P.P., 1866, LXX, p. 183.

[e] Beaumier, 'Mogador', p. 105. The discrepancy between the figure found in Beaumier and Miège for 1865 and 1866 can be explained by the inclusion of specie in the former's report. However, in adding specie imported to general goods exported in Miège's figures, the sum of f7,822, 565 is obtained, constrasting to the f8,763, 143 of Beaumier. For 1866, the figures of Beaumier and Miège correspond by this method. Unfortunately, Miège is not precise about the sources used in his tables.

[f] Adapted from the table found in Park, 'Administration', p. 60.

Notes

1 Introduction

1 Leila Tarazi Fawaz, *Merchants and Migrants in Nineteenth Century Beirut* (Cambridge, Mass., 1983), p. 1.

2 David S. Landes, *Bankers and Pashas* (Cambridge, Mass. 1958), p. 85.

3 Abdallah Laroui, *The History of the Maghrib* (Princeton, 1977), p. 276.

4 See Edmund Burke, *Prelude to Protectorate in Morocco* (Chicago and London, 1976), pp. 19 ff.

5 These views permeate Miège's work, but are summed up in vol. IV, pp. 395 ff; cf. Jean Brignon, *et al.*, *Histoire du Maroc* (Casablanca, 1967), pp. 311–12.

6 See David Seddon, *Moroccan Peasants* (Folkestone, Kent, 1981), p. 46.

7 See Magali Morsy, *North Africa 1800–1900* (London and New York, 1984), p. 92. On Egypt, see Gabriel Baer, *Studies in the Social History of Modern Egypt* (Chicago and London, 1969), p. 153.

8 Kenneth L. Brown, *People of Salé* (Manchester, 1976), pp. 119 ff; Janet L. Abu-Lughod, *Rabat: Urban Apartheid in Morocco* (Princeton, 1980), pp. 95–110 *passim*; Aḥmad Tawfīq, *al-Mujtamaʿ al-maghribī fī-l-qarn at-tāsiʿ ʿashr. Īnūltān (1850–1912)* (Rabat, 1967), vol. I, pp. 317–24; Paul Pascon, *Le Haouz de Marrakech* (Rabat, 1977), vol. II, pp. 415–33.

9 The most noted examples of this type are: Jacques Caillé, *La ville de Rabat jusqu'au protectorat français*, 3 vols. (Paris, 1949); G. Deverdun, *Marrakech, des origines à 1912*, 2 vols. (Rabat, 1959–66).

10 Le Tourneau, *Fès avant le protectorat* (Casablanca, 1949); cf. Le Tourneau, *Fez in the Age of the Marinides* (Norman, Okla., 1961). See the comments of Brown, *People*, p. 5.

11 André Raymond, *Grandes villes arabes à l'époque ottomane* (Paris, 1985), pp. 39 ff.

12 Cf. Roger Owen, *The Middle East in the World Economy* (London and New York, 1981).

13 Cf. Rhoads Murphey, *The Outsiders: the Western Experience in India and China* (Ann Arbor, 1977). The point being argued here is that port cities in Asia and Africa, at least until late in the confrontation with the West, were more resistant to change because of the strength and stability of the local culture. On port cities in Asia generally, see Dilip K. Basu (ed.), *The Rise and Growth of the Colonial Port Cities in Asia* (Lanham, Md. and London, 1985).

14 Karl Polanyi, 'Ports of Trade in Early Societies', *Journal of Economic History*, 23 (1963), 30–45; Rosemary Arnold, 'A Port of Trade: Whydah on the Guinea Coast', in K. Polanyi, *et al.*, *Trade and Market in Early Empires* (Glencoe, Ill., 1957). Polanyi's model has been applied to Essaouira by D. S. Ponasik, 'The System of Administered Trade as a Defense Mechanism in Preprotectorate Morocco', *International Journal of Middle Eastern Studies*, 9 (1977), 195–7. It appears to be a useful paradigm for Bali. See Clifford Geertz, 'Ports of Trade in Nineteenth Century Bali', *Research in Economic Anthropology*, 3 (1980), 109–22. Polanyi's theory of an 'archaic economy' where the administration of trade predominates over supply and demand has been abandoned by many Africanists because it fails to view economic behaviour in conjunction with socio-economic institutions structuring society. Cf. Paul E. Lovejoy, 'Polanyi's "Ports of Trade": Salaga and Kano in the Nineteenth Century', *Canadian Journal of African Studies*, 16, 2 (1982); Philip D. Curtin, *Cross-Cultural Trade in World History* (Cambridge, 1984), pp. 13–14, 58–9.

15 Murphey, *The Outsiders*, pp. 81, 104–5.

16 Morsy, *North Africa*, p. 92. On growth in Fez during this period, see Norman Cigar, 'Socio-economic Structures and the Development of an Urban Bourgeoisie in Pre-colonial Morocco', *The Maghreb Review*, 6:3–4 (1981), 55–76.

17 There are no Moroccan censuses in the nineteenth century. Foreign estimates vary greatly, but a reasonable conjecture might be a population of about 40,000–60,000. See the estimates cited in Deverdun, *Marrakech*, pp. 597–8. The first serious attempt to count Morocco's population was at the turn of the twentieth century. Marrakesh's population was estimated at about 57,000 in 1900. Larras, 'La population du Maroc', *La Géographie, B.S.G.*, 13, 2e sem. (1906), 347. The population of Fez was estimated at 95,000 in 1900.

18 Foreign estimates of Morocco's population from the 1770s to the end of the nineteenth century range from 2–25 million. See M. El Mansour, 'Political and Social Developments in Morocco during the Reign of Mawlay Sulayman, 1792–1822', Ph.D. thesis (London, 1981), pp. 46–7. In 1895, one observer estimated a population of between 15 and 24 million. Auguste Mouliéras, *Le Maroc inconnu* (Paris, 1895), vol. 1, p. 27. On the basis of Leo Africanus, it has been suggested that Morocco's urban population must have been between 5% and 6% in the sixteenth century; see Daniel Noin, *La population rurale du Maroc* (Paris, 1970), vol. 1, p. 240. At the turn of the twentieth century, an urban population of between 10% and 12% was estimated; see Larras, 'La population', p. 347.

19 From diverse sources, I have suggested that the population of the Haha could have ranged anywhere from 100,000 to 200,000 in the nineteenth century, while the population of Shiadma could have fluctuated between 55,000 and 140,000; 'Merchants and Pedlars of Essaouira: A Social History of a Moroccan Trading Town (1844–1886), Ph.D. thesis (Manchester, 1984), pp. 43, 45. The first thorough population survey of the Haha was in

1905. René de Segonzac, *Au cœur de l'Atlas: Mission au Maroc 1904–1905* (Paris, 1910), pp. 400–7; for Shiadma, he only counts recruitable soldiers (p. 121 n). Cf. Noin, *La population*, vol. I, p. 251.

20 On the Maghreb generally, see the comments of Lucette Valensi, *Le Maghreb avant la prise d'Alger* (Paris, 1969), pp. 41–3.

21 Na'īma Harrāj at-Tūzānī, *al-Umanā' bi-l-Maghrib fī 'ahd as-Sulṭān Mawlāy al-Ḥasan (1290–1311/1873–1894)* (Rabat, 1979), p. 191.

22 This has been studied in detail by D. Jacques-Meunié, *Le Maroc saharien, des origines à 1670* (Paris, 1982), vol. II, pp. 629–42, 653–9, 666–79, 729–30. On the dynasty of Bū Damī'a in Tazarwalt, see Paul Pascon, 'Le commerce de la maison d'Iligh d'après le registre comptable de Husayn b. Hachem, Tazerwalt 1850–1875', in Pascon, *et al.*, *La maison d'Iligh et l'histoire sociale du Tazerwalt* (Rabat, 1984), pp. 46–8. On the economic ties between the Essaouira and the southwest, see Robert Montagne, *Les Berbères et le Makhzen dans le sud du Maroc* (Paris, 1930), pp. 103–4.

23 Cf. Murphey, *The Outsiders*, p. 103.

24 For Asia, cf. Basu, *Rise and Growth*, p. 152.

25 A meticulous study of Essaouira's hinterland has shown the uneven penetration of the capitalist economy. Thomas K. Park, 'Administration and the Economy: Morocco 1880 to 1980. The Case of Essaouira.' Ph.D. thesis (Wisconsin, 1983), pp. 390 ff.

26 Wallerstein, *The Modern World System* (New York, 1974), pp. 347–57. Wallerstein's 'world economy' model, with Europe at the centre, is the point of departure in an eloquent study by Fernand Braudel, *The Perspective of the World* (London, 1984), 69–70.

27 Eric R. Wolf, *Europe and the People without History* (Berkeley, Los Angeles, and London, 1982), p. 23.

2 The royal port

1 Pierre Flamand, *Quelques manifestations de l'esprit populaire dans les juiveries du sud-marocain* (Casablanca, n.d.).

2 P.P., 1847, XVI, 503.

3 Aḥmad b. Khālid an-Nāṣirī, *Kitāb al-istiqṣā' li-akhbār duwal al-Maghrib al-Aqṣā* (Casablanca, 1956), vol. VIII, p. 54.

4 According to a local historian, Diabet was built only three years before the foundation of Essaouira. Muḥammad b. Sa'īd aṣ-Ṣiddīqī, *Īqāẓ as-sarīra li-tārīkh aṣ-Ṣawīra* (Casablanca, n.d.), p. 40.

5 Descriptive accounts of Haha are found in Charles de Foucauld, *Reconnaissance au Maroc* (Paris, 1888), pp. 185–6; Edmond Doutté, *En Tribu* (Paris, 1914), pp. 292 ff.

6 André Jodin, *Les établissements du roi Juba II aux îles purpuraires (Mogador)* (Tangier, 1967).

7 aṣ-Ṣiddīq ibn al-'Arabī, 'Safaḥāt min tārīkh aṣ-Ṣawīra', *Majallat al-Manāhil*, 11 (1978), 314–15. P. de Cenival states that the fortress was seized in 1510 by the surrounding tribes; *E.I.*[1], s.v. 'Mogador'. But apparently the

Portuguese were still active on that part of the coast several decades later. Cf. Paul Pascon, *Le Haouz de Marrakech*, (Rabat 1977), vol. I, pp. 189–91.

8 This point is emphasized by the nineteenth-century historian, an-Nāṣirī, *Kitāb al-istiqsā'*, vol. VIII, p. 20. This tradition has been maintained in the Sous. See René Basset, *Relation de Sidi Brahim de Massat* (Paris 1883), pp. 26–7; Muḥammad al-Mukhtār as-Sūsī, *Illīgh qadīman wa-ḥadīthan* (Rabat, 1966), pp. 233–4; as-Sūsi, *Khilāl Jazūla* (Tetuan, n.d.), vol. IV, p. 85; aṣ-Ṣiddīqī, *Īqāẓ*, pp. 15–16.

9 F. Stambouli and A. Zghal, 'Urban Life in Pre-colonial North Africa', *British Journal of Sociology*, 27 (1976), 2–3.

10 Both French and local historians recount the tradition of Cournut: Fernand Benoit; *L'Afrique méditerranéene, Algérie – Tunisie – Maroc* (Paris, 1931), p. 69; Henri Terrasse, *Histoire du Maroc* (Casablanca, 1950), vol. II, p. 299; P. de Cenival, *E.I.*[1], s.v. 'Mogador'; aṣ-Ṣiddīqī, *Īqāẓ*, pp. 16, 38. The contemporary French account was published by Henri Froidevaux, 'Une description de Mogador en 1765', *Annales de Géographie*, 2 (1893), 394–8, citing B.N., MS Français, Nouvelles Acquisitions 6236, dated 1765. Another lengthy manuscript on Essaouira (in Italian), preserved in Madrid at the Archivo Histórico Nacional (Estado, legajo 4818, num. 3), apparently makes no mention of Cournut. The manuscript is discussed in Angel Gonzalez Palencia, 'Un Italiano en Mogador en 1783', *Africa*, (July–August, 1948), 29–32. I was unable to locate any plans for Mogador, which were allegedly deposited in the French Naval archives. The idea that the inscription at the *sqāla* should read Uharū was suggested to me by the director of the museum of Essaouira, Boujemâa Lakhdar.

11 Henri Terrasse, *Histoire du Maroc* (Casablanca, 1950), vol. II, pp. 299–300.

12 Benoit, *L'Afrique*, p. 69.

13 Raymond, *Grandes villes*, pp. 172–4; see also, Raymond, *The Great Arab Cities in the 16th–18th Centuries: An Introduction* (New York and London, 1984), p. 10; Valensi, *Le Maghreb*, p. 52.

14 The question of the naming of the town is discussed by two local historians: Aḥmad b. al-Ḥājj ar-Ragrāgī, *ash-Shamūs al-munīra fī akhbār madīnat aṣ-Ṣawīra* (Rabat, 1935), pp. 10–11; aṣ-Ṣiddīqī, *Īqāẓ*, p. 19. It is noted that the town is also called *Ṣwayra* (or *Ṣuwayra*) in Shiadma, meaning 'one is putting on airs'. Park, 'Administration', p. 95, n 1. On aṣ-Ṣawîrat al-Qadīma on Wad Qṣab, see Paul Berthier, *Les anciennes sucreries du Maroc et leurs réseaux hydrauliques* (Rabat, 1966), vol. I, pp. 18n, 93n, 157.

15 H. de Castries, 'Le Danemark et le Maroc: 1750–1767', *Hespéris*, 6 (1926), 343; '*Observations on the Western Coast of the Morocco State during my Journey from Mogador to Tangier in July and August 1830; Memorandum Respecting the Foundation of Mogador, its Trade, etc.*', R.G.S., MS 1828, fol. 47. The manuscript was sent to the R.G.S. by the vice-consul Chaillet. The author is anonymous, but I would guess that it is Willshire, the only British merchant in Essaouira during this period.

16 Cenival suggests that constructions began in 1760 ('Mogador'). In December 1763, the British consul Popham refers to a ship sailing from

Mogador; F.O., 25/1, Gibraltar: 2 December 1763. In March he refers to Mogador as 'a new port he [the Sultan] is fortifying to carry in prizes', (23 March 1762). By August 1765, many of the fortifications had been completed; Froidevaux, 'Une description', pp. 394–8. Contemporary Arabic sources refer to the year 1178/1764–5. See Abū al-Qāsim b. Aḥmad az-Zayānī, *at-Turjumān al-muʿrib ʿan duwal al-Mashriq wa-l-Maghrib*, trans. O. Houdas, *Le Maroc de 1631 à 1812* (Paris, 1886), p. 141. One source suggests that the Sultan went to Essaouira towards the end of December 1764 (Jumādā II 1178) to supervise the constructions and stayed there for two months. Muḥammad al-Qādirī, *The Bodleian Version of Muḥammad al-Qādirī's Nashr al-Mathānī: The Chronicles*, ed. Norman Cigar (Rabat, 1978), p. 94.

17 Ahmad b. al-Mahdī al-Ghazzāl, *Kitāb natījat al-ajtihād fī al-muhādana wa-l-jihād*, (1179/1765–6), B.N., fond arabe, 2297 fol. 5.

18 M. El Mansour, 'Political and Social Developments', pp. 221–3.

19 Castries, 'Le Danemark', p. 345. The British report that the port of Mogador was also given to the Danes, (Public Record Office, State Papers 71/9, Safi: 22 July 1751), but there is no evidence that the latter ever established themselves there.

20 On the *ribāṭ*, see *E.I.*[1], s.v., '*ribāṭ*'; see Jamil M. Abun Nasr, *A History of the Maghrib* (Cambridge, 1971), p. 93n; Jacques Berque, *L'Intérieur du Maghreb: XV*^e^*–XIX*^e^ *siècle* (Paris, 1978), p. 178.

21 an-Nāṣirī, *Kitāb al-istiqṣāʾ*, vol. VIII, p. 49.

22 K.H., 10 Shawwāl 1199/16 August 1785.

23 On the original formation of the *ʿabīd* under Mawlāy Ismāʿīl, see Magali Morsy, 'Moulay Ismaʿil et l'armée de métier', *Revue de l'Histoire Moderne et Contemporaine*, 14 (1967), 101–4.

24 an-Nāṣirī, *Kitāb al-istiqṣāʾ*, vol. VIII, p. 49.

25 The author was probably an eyewitness of the event. Muḥammad b. ʿAbd as-Salām ad-Duʿayyif, *Tārīkh*, B.G., MS D 660, folio 185. The *ʿabīd* had been regrouped from all over Morocco in the citadel of Agdāl in Rabat as part of the Sultan's unsuccessful efforts to capture Melilla. Ramon Lourido-Díaz, *Marruecos en la segunda mitad del siglo XVIII: Vida interna: política, social y religiosa durante el Sultanato de Sīdī Muhammad b. ʿAbd Allāh (1757–1790)* (Madrid, 1978), pp. 176–8.

26 F.O., 52/10, Tangier: 10 April 1793, Matra.

27 F.O., 830/3, 3 February 1856, Grace to Hay; James Richardson, *Travels in Morocco* (London, 1860), vol. I, p. 95.

28 James Riley, *An Authentic Narrative of the Loss of the American Brig Commerce* (New York, 1817), p. 423.

29 F.O., 174/28, 29 December 1829, Chaillet to E. W. A. Hay.

30 On the slave trade in this period, see El Mansour, 'Political and Social Developments', p. 148. On black slaves used in sugar plantations, see Berthier, *Les anciennes sucreries*, vol. I, pp. 241–5.

31 A.E., Maroc, M.D. 2, 1775, fol. 447; Louis Chénier, *The Present State of the Empire of Morocco* (London, 1788), vol. I, p. 47; Chénier, *Un chargé*

d'affaires au Maroc. Le correspondance du consul Louis Chénier: 1767–1782, ed. P. Grillion (Paris, 1970), p. 496 (the letter cited is dated 15 February 1777).

32 David Corcos, *Studies in the History of the Jews of Morocco* (Jerusalem, 1976), pp. 114–15.

33 In an account of the Edraʿī family, the move is noted. Mōshe b. Yiṣḥaq Edraʿī, *Yad Mōshe* (Amsterdam 5569/1808–9), fol. 4.

34 A.E., Maroc, M.D. 4, December 1847, Soulange-Bodín.

35 ar-Ragrāgī, *ash-Shamūs*, pp. 10–11.

36 K.H., K[56], 10 Ṣafar 1281/15 July 1864.

37 Shmūʾel Rōmānellī, *Massāʾ ba-ʿarab* (first published in Berlin in 1792), ed. Ḥayyim Schirmann, in *Ketabīm nibḥarīm* (Jerusalem, 1968), p. 118.

38 K.H. K[56]. It is difficult to say if they were descendants of the original settlers. Renegades were employed in the creation of new army units, when modern reforms were undertaken in the mid-nineteenth century. Wilfrid J. Rollman, 'The "New Order" in a Pre-colonial Muslim Society: Military Reform in Morocco, 1844–1904', Ph.D. thesis (Michigan, 1983), pp. 562–5.

39 Abū al-ʿAbbās Aḥmad Ibn al-Ḥājj, *ad-Durr al-muntakhab al-mustaḥsan fī baʿd maʾāthir amīr al-muʾminīn Mawlānā al-Ḥasan*, K.H., MS 1920, fol. 152.

40 Muḥammad ad-Dukkālī, *Taqāyīd tārīkhiyya*, Bodleian Library, Oxford, MS collection, Arab C 79, fol. 197; Aḥmad Akansūs, *al-Jaysh al-ʿaramram al-khumāsī*, B.G., MS D 339, fol. 224, cited by N. Cigar, 'An Edition and Translation of the Chronicles from Muhammad al-Qadiri's Nashr al-Mathani', D.Phil. thesis (Oxford, 1976), p. 637.

41 Riley, *Anthentic Narrative*, p. 423.

42 ar-Ragrāgī, *ash-Shamūs*, pp. 11–12.

43 aṣ-Ṣiddīqī, *Īqāẓ*, p. 22.

44 al-Qādirī, *Nashr al-mathānī*, p. 94.

45 K.H., K[56]

46 ad-Duʿayyif, *Tārīkh*, fol. 171; F.O., 52/9, Tangier: 28 February 1783; F.O., 52/7, 29 June 1787, Matra.

47 aṣ-Ṣiddīqī, *Īqāẓ*, pp. 34–7; ar-Ragrāgī, *ash-Shamūs*, p. 33.

48 Ibn al-Ḥājj, *ad-Durr*, fol. 140.

49 Abū al-Qāsim b. Aḥmad az-Zayānī, *al-Bustan az-ẓarīf fī dawlat awlād Mawlāy ʿAlī ash-Sharīf* (1283/1817–18), A.N., Aix-en-Provence, 20 mi 1 (a), fol. 105.

50 ad-Duʿayyif, *Tārīkh*, fol. 170.

51 The description of S. D. Goitein on the Middle Ages is in many respects comparable: *A Mediterranean Society*, vol. I: *Economic Foundations* (Berkeley and Los Angeles, 1967), p. 70, and pp. 148f.

52 Corcos, *Studies*, pp. 109–13. Some of the merchants' families, e.g., Corcos and Levy-Ben Sussan, left Essaouira when trade at the port languished in the first decades of the nineteenth century, but members of their family returned several decades later. A letter sent by French consul Chénier in 1768 seems to corroborate the Corcos document. Chénier refers to Sumbal gathering together merchants from Agadir and Essaouira, and suggests that

the purpose might be to farm out the ports. Chénier, *Correspondance*, p. 101 (letter sent from Marrakesh: 6 May 1768).

53 Corcos, *Studies*, p. 114. Various letters from this period show that in the first two decades of the nineteenth century the most important merchant house was Macnin. Macnin advanced credit to numerous local notables; for example, S.L., 13 Jumādā I 1226 /5 June 1881 (loan of 384 riyāl to Sīdī ʿAbd al-Qādir).

54 Jonathan I. Israel, *European Jewry in the Age of Mercantilism: 1550–1750* (Oxford, 1985), pp. 49, 113.

55 Corcos, *Studies*, p. 114; Rōmānellī, *Massāʾ*, p. 119.

56 The Boujnah house was later represented by Aaron Amar, who was known as 'Boujnah' owing to his association; oral communication of Samuel Levy. Many documents relating to the business of Boujnah are found in the S.L. papers.

57 Corcos, *Studies*, pp. 79, 112 n111, 114. A letter in the C.A., (13 March 1774) is addressed to Moses Guedalla in Amsterdam.

58 Chénier, *Correspondance*, pp. 69 (16 January 1767), 130–1 (30 May 1769), 197 (30 May 1771), 297 (8 April 1773), 715 (9 January 1779); F.O. 52/1, Tetuan: 23 December 1765, Popham.

59 R.G.S., MS 1828, folios 48–9, 67–8.

60 Fr. A. Luengo, 'Mogador – fondación de la mission católica', *Mauritania* (1 August 1940), 152–4.

61 Lourido-Díaz, *Marruecos*, pp. 208–9; Lourido-Díaz, 'Le commerce entre le Portugal et le Maroc pendant la deuxième moitié du XVIIIe siècle', *Revue d'Histoire Maghrebine*, 5 (1976), 43–6.

62 A number of Judeo-Arabic letters pertaining to Dutch activities in Agadir and Essaouira have been discovered in the archives of Schoonhoven. One is dated Agadir: 28 Elul 5531 /7 September 1771, Yaḥyā b. Aharōn Wīzgān to Hendrik Willem Uhlman (the latter was formerly the vice-consul of Agadir). I am indebted to Paulo De Mas for sending me several copies of letters from these archives. A British merchant who resided in Essaouira and Agadir wrote one of the most detailed accounts of Morocco and its trade during the latter part of the eighteenth and early nineteenth century: James Grey Jackson, *An Account of the Empire of Morocco and the Districts of Sus and Tafilelt* (London, 1814). On the French merchants of Essaouira, see M. Hosotte-Reynaud, 'Un négociant à Mogador à la fin du XVIIIe siècle et sa correspondance avec le consul de France à Salé', *Hespéris*, 44 (1957), 335–45.

63 Foreign maritime trade decreased in this period due to both internal and external factors: the Moroccan plague epidemic of 1799–1800, and the Napoleonic wars. El Mansour, 'Political and Social Developments', pp. 152–4. Foreign contemporary sources give the impression that Sultan Sulaymān had an aversion to commerce. In fact, although the number of foreign merchants was limited, the extent of foreign trade conducted by Jewish merchants in Essaouira in the second decade of the nineteenth century was quite substantial. B.L., Add. MS 41512, 21 July 1813, Joseph

Dupuis (statistics for British trade with Essaouira in 1812).

64 *Mellahs* had already existed in Fez, Meknes and Marrakesh for several hundred years. The reasons for the construction of the *mellahs* were due to a combination of factors. First of all, the authorities wished to protect the Jews from potential outbreaks of violence either by the rural or urban Muslim population, and thus secure greater stability in the cities. Secondly, the authorities wanted to confine Jewish activities and rites to an exclusively Jewish neighbourhood which would not be offensive to Muslim sensibilities. It could be conjectured that this became an important issue in the early nineteenth century, as the Jewish population increased in proportion to the Muslims at the coastal ports. On the origins of the *mellahs* in Morocco generally, see Corcos, *Studies*, pp. 75–89; Norman A. Stillman, *The Jews of Arab Lands: A History and Source Book* (Philadelphia, 1979), pp. 80–1.

65 On the creation of the *mellah* in Essaouira, see Corcos, *Studies*, pp. 120–3. An original letter dated 1807 concerning Sulaymān's order to create *mellahs* is edited in Dawid ʿŌbadiya, *Qehīllat Ṣefrū* (3 vols., Jerusalem, 1975–6) vol. 1, p. 35. On the creation of the *mellahs* of Rabat and Salé, see K. L. Brown, 'An Urban View of Moroccan History: Salé, 1000 to 1800', *Hespéris-Tamuda*, 12 (1971), 73–5.

3 Merchants of the Sultan

1 Cf. Selma Stern, *The Court Jew* (Philadelphia, 1950), pp. 9–12.

2 J.-L. Miège, 'La bourgeoisie juive du Maroc au XIXe siècle: rupture ou continuité', in M. Abitbol (ed.), *Judaïsme d'Afrique du Nord aux XIXe–XXe siècles* (Jerusalem, 1980), pp. 30–6.

3 Cf. Laroui, *Les origines sociales et culturelles du nationalisme marocain (1830–1912)* (Paris, 1977), pp. 106–8.

4 In medieval times, *tājir* denoted a large-scale merchant. Cf. Goitein, *Mediterranean Society*, p. 149. The term is often discussed for Morocco: Tourneau, *Fès*, pp. 481–94; Charles René-Leclerc, 'Le commerce et l'industrie à Fez', *R.C.* (1905), 249.

5 A.E., Maroc, M.D. 4, December 1847, Solange-Bodin.

6 Cf. Michel Abitbol, 'Une élite économique juive au Maroc pré-colonial; les tujjar al-Sultan' (in Hebrew), in Abitbol, *Judaïsme*, pp. 26–33; Laroui, *Les origines*, pp. 105–6.

7 D.A.R., Essaouira 1, 24 Ramaḍān 1270/20 June 1854, Muḥammad Brīsha to Sultan.

8 In one instance, two Muslim and 11 Jewish *tujjār* received linens. The Muslim received completed garments while the Jews received pieces. K.H., 28 Muḥarram 1285/21 May 1868.

9 F.O., 174/4, 18 November 1839, Willshire; F.O., 174/20, Marrakesh: 4 March 1815, Willshire.

10 El Mansour, 'Political and Social Developments', p. 162; F.O., 52/28, 16 January 1827, Chaillet.

11 A.E., C.C.C. Mogador 1, 22 January 1838, Delaporte.

12 Willshire and Robertson absconded during the 1844 attack, never to return, and Bolelli was killed during the pillaging of the town that followed the bombardment. F.O., 174/49, 'Mr Willshire's Narrative of Eight Days Events at Mogadore'; 21 November 1844, Grace to Hay.

13 The protection extended to *tujjār* by the *makhzan* may have helped facilitate the spread of consular protection when the foreign powers began to intervene more vigorously and to demand that the Sultan extend both extraterritorial rights for their Moroccan protégés and dahirs of *tawqīr* and *iḥtirām*. Mohamed Kenbib, 'Structures traditionelles et protection diplomatique dans le Maroc précolonial', in René Gallisot (ed.), *Structures et cultures précapitalistes* (Paris, 1981), pp. 448–51.

14 A.E., C.C.C., Mogador 3, 15 November 1854, Tippel; 15 April 1868, Beaumier.

15 K.H., K^{46}, Rabīʿ II 1279 / September–October 1862 to Dhū al-Ḥijja 1279 / May–June 1863; K.H., *qawāʾim ḥisābiyya*, 22 Ramaḍān 1280 / 1 March 1864 to 22 Shawwāl 1280 / 31 March 1864.

16 K.H., K^{120}. The original old debt still appears in this register except in cases where it was completely settled.

17 K.H., K^{120}, Rabīʿ I 1301 / December 1883–January 1884 to Rajab 1301 / April–May 1884. The names are often abbreviated, making it difficult to give the exact numbers. Approximately 90 names are listed in five months.

18 It was reported in 1906 that only a small number of Muslims and Jews owned their own houses, and in the *mellah* about 20 per cent were privately owned. E. Pobeguin, 'Notes sur Mogador', *R.C.* (1906), 49–50. The Alliance director in 1907 reported that nine-tenths of the property in the *casbah* belonged to the *makhzan*. A.I.U., Maroc XXXVIII E 660 b, 12 February 1907, Taourel.

19 This excludes markets and industries leased to tax farmers. In Essaouira, almost 63,000 ūqiya were raised from *makhzan* houses. K.H., K^{80}, 1292 / 1875–6, and K^{93}, 1296 / 1878–9.

20 A long account on the history of *makhzan* and *ḥubus* property in Essaouira and other towns in Morocco is found in F.O., 835 / 164. This subject has also been studied by E. Michaux-Bellaire, 'Les biens habous et les biens du Makhzen du point de vue de leur location et de leur aliénation', *Revue du Monde Musulman*, 5 (1908), 436–57. The article is useful but his distinction between *habous* and *makhzan* properties is slightly misleading in the case of Essaouira where the sale of the 'keys' was prevalent for both types of property. The importance of *ḥazaqa* in Morocco has been analysed by Haim Zafrani, *Les Juifs du Maroc. Vie sociale, économique et religieuse* (Paris 1972), pp. 188–95. We were unable to locate any precolonial registers of *ḥubus* property. A register of *ḥubus* in French and Arabic for 1924 was located (referred to as B.G., Habous), probably a part of Michaux-Bellaire's collection at one time. It demonstrates that many descendants of Essaouira's principal merchants in an earlier period were still tenant-holders at that date. This register has been analysed by Thomas Park, 'Administration', pp. 487–94.

21 It was the person who had purchased the key rights, *miftāḥ*, whose name found its way on the revised registers. *Al-Moghreb Al-Aksa*, 16 March 1907.

22 His property was valued at 15,000 riyāl and his debt owed from the new loan was 7,000 riyāl. D.A.R., Essaouira 2, 21 Rabīʿ I 1285/12 July 1868, Bū ʿAshrīn to Bannīs.

23 For other towns, cf. Brown, *People*, pp. 66 ff; Norman Cigar, 'Société et la vie politique à Fès sous les premiers 'Alawites (*ca.* 1660/1830)', *Hespéris-Tamuda*, 18 (1978–9), 98–125.

24 See Corcos, *Studies*, p. 109, n. 106; Jackson, *An Account of the Empire*, p. 161.

25 S.L., Accounts, 1814–16; probably the Abraham Corcos appearing in the Macnin account books.

26 This is recorded in Meyer's family record book. C.A., Diary of Meyer Corcos (in Judeo-Arabic). The birth was on 15 Elūl 5604/30 August 1844.

27 The amount left by Willshire in Solomon Corcos' care is listed as follows:

specie	100,000 ūqiya
merchandise assessed	124,183
profit (*ribḥ*)	12,417 (i.e., 10% of merchandise)
debts	158,059
Total	394,659 ūqiya

C.A., 14 Ṣafar 1263/1 February 1847, *dahir* addressed o al-Ḥājj al-ʿArabī aṭ-Ṭarrīs, the governor of Essaouira; the *dahir* regarding Solomon Corcos: C.A., 28 Jumādā II 1263/23 June 1846. Cf. Michel Abitbol, *Témoins et acteurs: les Corcos et l'histoire du Maroc contemporain* (Jerusalem, 1980), p. 24. Willshire claimed that Corcos (Abraham) in Essaouira owed him a balance of 2,150,582 ūqiya (= 13,441 Spanish riyāl), and still had a large quantity of his unsold goods. F.O., 99/28, 26 March 1845, Willshire to Bidwell; F.O., 174/49, 11 July 1848, Grace to Hay.

28 C.A., Rabīʿ I 1270/4 December 1853, Bū ʿAshrīn to Jacob Corcos.

29 C.A., 7 Ramaḍān 1273/1 May 1857. This document is translated by Abitbol, *Témoins*, p. 38 (in French), p. 29 (in Hebrew).

30 C.A., 11 Rabīʿ II 1275/18 November 1858.

31 C.A., 12 Rabīʿ II 1276/12 November 1859.

32 C.A., 18 Jumādā I 1279/11 November 1862.

33 C.A., 1 Muḥarram 1301/2 November 1883. The death of Abraham Corcos is marked in the Jewish cemetery: 21 Elūl 5643/23 September 1883.

34 C.A., 11 Rajab 1280/23 December 1863; C.A. 18 Dhū al-Ḥijja 1274/30 July 1858; K.H., K[46], fabrics supplied by Corcos to the garrison are listed in Shaʿbān 1279/January–February 1863.

35 C.A., 3 Rabīʿ I 1270/4 December 1853.

36 Cf. Abitbol, *Témoins*, pp. 26–7. At one point, Bū ʿAshrīn appears to have

recognized that Abraham and Jacob in Essaouira had a disagreement with Haim in Marrakesh.

37 See above, pp. 137–8.

38 For example, Abraham Corcos reported on fighting among the Kunta, Awlād Bū Saba'a and Ragibāt in the Sahara: C.A., 11 Muḥarram 1282/6 June 1865, Bu 'Ashrin to Abraham Corcos. On another occasion, fighting between Ḥusayn Ū Hāshim and Daḥmān Bayrūk is reported: C.A., 5 Rabī' I 1288/24 June 1871, Musa b. Ahmad to Abraham Corcos.

39 In 1865, Abraham Corcos is listed as owing 735,818 ūqiya to the *makhzan* which made him the third highest debtor (see table 1). By 1886, he is listed as having paid back 120,000 ūqiya through the *amīn* Aḥmad Ibn Shaqrūn in Marrakesh: K.H., K^{295}.

40 C.A., 22 Muḥarram 1297/5 January 1880.

41 A document in the Corcos collection lists the debtors, drawn up for the U.S. consulate. Also in N.A., R.G. 84, 7 March 1888, Meyer Corcos to Lewis. On 4 June 1889, he was claiming $50,000.

42 Details are extrapolated from the customs duties they paid: K.H., K^{46}; *K. H., qawā'im ḥisābiyya.* On general traders, cf. Miège, II, p. 545.

43 Eugène Aubin, *Morocco of Today* (London, 1906), p. 297. On Ishu'a Corcos, see José Benech, *Essai d'explication d'un mellah* (Kaiserslauten, n.d.), pp. 41, 256–65.

44 F.O., 174/72, 1 September 1864, Elton to Hay.

45 F.O., 174/85, 1 May 1874, and F.O., 631/5, 21 May 1874, Beaumier to Hay (the French consul was acting temporarily as British consular agent); N.A., R.G. 84, 30 March 1874.

46 C.A., 7 Dhū al-Qa'da 1280/14 April 1864, Bū 'Ashrīn to Abraham Corcos.

47 C.A., 22 Shawwāl 1282/21 November 1875, 18 Muḥarram 1293/14 February 1876, Mūsā b. Aḥmad to Abraham Corcos.

48 For example, Mūsā b. Aḥmad wrote asking Abraham Corcos to take care of his nephew, the *faqīh* as-Sayyīd 'Aisā, and to instruct him on commercial matters. C.A., 13 Muḥarram 1288/4 April 1871.

49 K.H., K^{295}, Dhū al-Qa'da 1288/23 January 1872, al-'Arabī b. al-Qabbāj to Bannīs.

50 D.A.R., Essaouira 2, 12 Dhū al-Qa'da 1288/23 January 1872, al-'Arabī b. al-Qabbāj to Bannīs.

51 C.A., 24 Sha'bān 1291/6 October 1874, Mūsā b. Aḥmad to Abraham Corcos.

52 Halewī, (1891), 311. Cf. Miège, III, pp. 27–31, IV, p. 408.

53 Miège, III, p. 31.

54 Affidavits were taken in Judeo-Arabic for a consular law suit involving disputed property left by Solomon Corcos. The proceedings list the Corcos holdings. N.A., R.G. 84, Mogador, 3 August 1882.

55 There are two deeds in the Corcos collection, one for a house and another for a *funduq* during this period; C.A., 15 Dhū al-Qa'da 1285/27 February 1869; C.A., 13 Shawwāl 1282/1 March 1866. Ownership of the property was later

disputed by the descendants of the original owners who claimed that the property was mortgaged rather than purchased; N.A., R.G. 84, Mogador 29 August 1893 and 25 September 1893, Broome to Mathews.

56 C.A., 1 Shebet 5608/6 January 1848, notarized and signed by Rabbi Abraham b. Ya'qōb Ben 'Aṭṭār, Rabbi Yehūda [. . .], and Rabbi Shlōmō Abīqaṣiṣ. On the institution of *mashkanta*, see Zafrani, *Les Juifs*, pp. 179–80.

57 N.A., R.G. 84, Mogador, 1 March 1863, Abraham Corcos to McMath.

58 In 1864, Abraham Corcos granted protection to two of his agents in the Sous. The English merchant, David Perry, sought the same advantage for his agents but was turned down by the British vice-consul. F.O., 631/3, 9 March 1864, Elton to Hay.

59 The Corcos collection includes letters from Moses Montefiore to Abraham Corcos in Hebrew. Montefiore stayed with Corcos en route to Marrakesh. L. Loewe (ed.), *Diaries of Sir Moses and Lady Montefiore* (London, 1890), vol. II, p. 152.

60 A.I.U., Maroc XXXIV E 601, 15 November 1866, Hermann Cohen.

61 On rabbis and *dayyans* in Morocco, cf. Shlōmō Deshen, *Ṣībūr we-yeḥīdīm be-Marrōqō: sidrei ḥebra be-qehīllōt ha-yehūdīyyōt be-me'ōt ha-18 -19* (Tel Aviv, 1983), pp. 61–5. On the challenge to Elmaleh's authority, see my 'Anglo-Jewry and Essaouira (Mogador), 1860–1900: The Social Implications of Philanthropy', *Transactions of the Jewish Historical Society of England*, 28 (1984), 75–80.

62 There were also a number of other branches of the family who were distinguished in Essaouira's cultural life. See Abraham Laredo, *Les noms des Juifs du Maroc* (Madrid, 1978), pp. 289–92.

63 Joseph Elmaleh died in Gibraltar in 1823. There were two volumes published posthumously in Livorno in 1823 and 1855. See Zafrani, *Les Juifs*, pp. 33–5.

64 Corcos, *Studies*, p. 123.

65 The British merchant and vice-consul Willshire wrote about the increase of Jewish merchants and the departure of Christians. Elmaleh is one of the merchants mentioned at this time. F.O., 174/28, 9 December 1824, Willshire to Douglas.

66 Joseph Elmaleh is mentioned as the president of the committee of commerce. F.O., 631/1, 27 May 1831, Diary of the vice-consul Chaillet.

67 F.O., 174/49, 11 July 1848, Grace to Hay.

68 F.O., 830/2, 21 February 1861, Elton to Hay.

69 D.A.R., Essaouira 1, 29 Ṣafar 1281/3 August 1864 (properties are appraised and the documents notarized).

70 Of all the merchants, Elmaleh was the largest debtor to the *makhzan* at this time. See table 1.

71 K.H., 20 Jumādā I 1282/11 October 1865, 'Abd al-Wāḥid Aqaṣbī, 'Umar b. 'Amr al-Awsā to Bannīs. F.O., 631/3, 10 March 1866, Carstensen to Hay; C.A., 23 Sha'bān 1282/11 January 1866, Bū 'Ashrīn to Abraham Corcos.

72 F.O., 631/3, 13 March 1855, Carstensen to White.

73 Joseph Elmaleh was often referred to in foreign sources as head of the Jewish community or Chief Rabbi. His leadership of the community and functions

were informal for the most part until the 1880s when, in response to pressures from foreign Jewish organizations, a *maʿamad*, probably on an Anglo-Jewish model, was constituted. See my 'Anglo-Jewry', pp. 74–5. Though Elmaleh seems to have had the qualifications of *dayyan*, there is little evidence that he had any functions in the rabbinical court (*beit dīn*), which consisted of three *dayyan*s, of whom Abraham Ben ʿAṭṭār made the main decisions.

74 F.O., 830/2, 20 June 1860, Elton to Hay. He paid 702 ūqiya a month on his house, as opposed to Abraham Corcos who paid 494; K.H., K[93], 1296/1878–9.

75 The houses were contested by Guedalla's estate. F.O., 830/2, 8 September 1869, Elton to Hay; F.O., 631/4, 30 April 1869, Carstensen to Haim Guedalla.

76 F.O., 631/3, 24 June 1868, Carstensen to Hay; C.A., Diary of Meyer Corcos. At the time of my research in Essaouira, this house was still occupied by descendants of ʿAmram.

77 Listed in K.H., K[92], 1296/1878–9.

78 In the last decades of the nineteenth century, a tide of resentment arose in the *mellah* against the oligarchy's proprietorship. See my 'Anglo-Jewry', pp. 78–9.

79 An extension was granted on the payment of three months' customs duties. K.H., 8 Ramaḍān 1293/27 September 1876, Sultan to *umanāʾ* of Essaouira.

80 A.J., 95/add 5, 19 January 1886; D.A.R., Essaouira 4, 26 Rabīʿ III 1303/1 February 1886.

81 A.I.U., France VIII D 42, 24 December 1867, 20 October 1873. See Michael M. Laskier, *The Alliance Israélite Universelle and the Jewish Communities of Morocco, 1862–1962* (Albany, N.Y., 1983). pp. 62–3.

82 I wonder to what degree the 'hyperorganization' described by Geertz was a nineteenth-century development in Morocco caused by foreign influences. '*Suq:* the Bazaar Economy in Sefrou', in Clifford Geertz, Hildred Geertz, and Lawrence Rosen, *Meaning and Order in Moroccan Society* (Cambridge, 1979), pp. 165–8. That is, the *maʿamad* increased its power at the expense of the *shaykh al-yahūd* (the official intermediary between the Muslim authorities and the Jewish community), and sodalities proliferated due to foreign philanthropy and the transformation of the communal fiscal structure.

83 On Afriat origins, see Laredo, *Noms des Juifs*, pp. 359–60.

84 On the revolt, see Muḥammad al-Mukhtār as-Sūsī, *al-Maʿsūl*, 20 vols. (Casablanca, 1960–1), vol. v, pp. 142–4. For details on the Afriats and the martyrdom of Ifrane, see V. Monteil, 'Les Juifs d'Ifrane', *Hespéris*, 35 (1948), pp. 154–5; Flamand, *Quelques manifestations*, pp. 23–32. Victoria Ducheneaux of *National Geographic* has provided me with a typescript regarding this event; it is signed Ichia Ben Rabi Jacob Sabat of Mogador, translated 20 October 1953.

85 On the rise of Bayrūk, see Mustapha Naïmi, 'La politique des chefs de la confederation Tekna face à l'expansionnisme commercial européen', *Revue d'Histoire Maghrebine*, 11:35–6 (1984), 166–73.

86 The French refer to him as 'Nephtalie' or 'Joseph Ben Hazzan Nephtalie'.

Evidence demonstrates that this was Joseph Afriat. Subsequent Afriats in Essaouira were often called *awlād* Naftālī. A.N., S.O.M., Afrique IV, dos. 3, 17 April 1837, Delaporte; A.E., C.C.C., Mogador 1, 26 June 1839, Delaporte.

87 Miège, III, p. 23; A.E., C.C.C. Mogador 5, 26 April 1879, Beaumier.

88 K.H., K[46], Rajab 1279 /December 1862–January 1863.

89 D.A.R., Essaouira 2, Dhū al-Qaʿda 1283 / 18 April 1867, al-Hazan Bihi to Bannīs.

90 F.O., 830 /2, 21 February 1861, Elton to Hay; F.O., 631 /5, 2 October 1876, R. Hay to White; K.H., K[93].

91 K.H., K[93]; F.O., 174 /72, 1 September 1864, Elton to Hay.

92 Details on this property are somewhat sketchy since it was *makhzan* property 'granted' rent-free to Ḥusayn Ū Hāshim but explicitly built for French commerce. Although the *makhzan* collected the rent from the current tenant, the *qāʾid* of Iligh was actually 'subletting' the property, and the contracts were drawn up, first with a French merchant, Bonnet, who vacated the place before the lease terminated, and then with the Afriats who were in fact managing the property for the house of Iligh. It was also inhabited for a time by the Coriats, the family of Messod Afriat's widow. This complicated state of affairs led to a number of disputes over rent and possession between the Afriats, the U.S. consulate, the *makhzan*, and the house of Iligh, K.H., K[393]; A.E., C.C.C. Mogador 8, 24 November 1890, Hugonnet; N.A., R.G. 84, 27 June 1906, Broome to Hoffman Philip; A.I.U., Maroc XXXIII E 582, 15 December 1891, Benchimol; B.D., 1 Rabīʿ I 1310 /29 September 1892, Sultan to Muḥammad b. al-Ḥusayn Ū Hāshim.

93 Miège, III, pp. 32–3.

94 A.E., C.C.C. Mogador 5, 26 October 1873 and 26 April 1874, Beaumier; A.I.U., France VIII D 42, 27 August 1873, Beaumier to Crémieux, 26 October 1873, Beaumier to Albert Cohen.

95 Listed in K.H., K[386], containing monthly rent for Shawwāl 1306 /May–June 1889.

96 A British merchant, who became United States vice-consul, rented Abraham's house not long before the latter left Essaouira. N.A., R.G. 84, 27 June 1906, Broome to Hoffman Philip.

97 A.E., C.C.C. Mogador 7, 20 December 1886, Lacoste; A.E., C.P. Consuls 2, 5 February 1891, Hugonnet.

98 A.I.U., Maroc XXXVII bis E a, 19 July 1912, Loubaton.

99 F.O., 634 /4, 1 February 1870, 'Public Acts'.

100 F.O., 99 /338, Tangier: 4 August 1896, Nicolson. Jacob Afriat's investments are listed in his will, dated 18 August 1881. A copy of this will was generously provided to me by his descendants in Casablanca.

101 F.O., 631 /4, 25 August 1865. The scope and nature of his import trade can be inferred from the customs duties paid. K.H., K[46]; K.H., *qawāʾim ḥisābiyya*.

102 I am indebted to Victoria Ducheneaux for this information.

103 Laredo, *Noms des Juifs*, p. 360.

104 C.A., Diary of Meyer Corcos; J.-L. Miège, 'Les Juifs et le commerce transsaharien au dix-neuvième siècle', in M. Abitbol (ed.), *Communautés juives des marges sahariennes du Maghreb* (Jerusalem, 1982), p. 395.
105 Jacob Ohayon, '*Les origines des Juifs de Mogador*', MS at the Ben Zvi Institute (n.d.), pp. 5–6.
106 See Miège, II, pp. 40, III, pp. 32–6.
107 K.H., K[46]; K.H., *qawā'im ḥisābiyya.*
108 aṣ-Ṣiddīqī, *Īqāẓ*, p. 72.
109 *Ibid. Tawqīr* and *iḥtirām* was a privilege often granted to *shurafā'*.
110 aṣ-Ṣiddīqī, *Īqāẓ*, pp. 67, 72–3. The author claims that the *dahir* signified his appointment, but other documentation demonstrates that he was the *amīn* at least a year earlier – in 1841 he is referred to as an employee at the customs. F.O., 99/7, 25 January 1841, Willshire. One year later (and also before the *dahir*), he was summoned to the Sultan to liquidate the accounts of the former *qā'id*, az-Zamrānī. A.E., C.C.C., Mogador 2, 19 February 1842, Beuscher.
111 aṣ-Ṣiddīqī, *Īqāẓ*, p. 48.
112 F.O., 635/5, 'Marine Protests and Manifests', 24 June 1845. Until 1850 in this series, Tūfal'azz appears as one of the main shippers of Essaouira.
113 aṣ-Ṣiddīqī, *Īqāẓ*, pp. 73, 86.
114 It seems that Maḥjūb took over responsibility for paying off the interest-free loan (*salaf*) originally granted to Muḥammad (see table 1). Maḥjūb Tūfal-'azz paid a total of 16,735 ūqiya in customs duties in the extant records from 1862–4. K.H., K[46]; K.H., *qawā'im ḥisābiyya.*
115 K.H., K[295], Dhū al-Qa'da 1282/March–April 1866.
116 D.A.R., Essaouira, 2, 30 Muḥarram 1286/12 May 1869, Sultan to 'Amāra.
117 D.A.R., Essaouira 2, revenues for February 1873 (Gregorian date listed).
118 D.A.R., Essaouira 9, Shawwāl 1288/1872; K.H., K[93], 1296/1878.
119 D.A.R., Essaouira 2, 8 Rabī' II 1288/27 June 1871, al-'Arabī Faraj and 'Abd ar-Raḥmān Aqaṣbī to Bannīs.
120 F.O., 99/158, 1873.
121 K.H., K[295]; K.H., K[93].
122 See above, p. 48.
123 D.A.R., 'Amāra dos., 24 Rabī' II/15 March 1882, Sultan to 'Amāra.
124 In Jumādā I 1301/February–March 1884, 3,826.83 ūqiya were sent through Tūfal-'azz for the construction of Tiznit, while at the same time constructions on his house were under way. At the end of the register, he was still holding 8,460.66 ūqiya from expenses for Tiznit. K.H., K[120].
125 K.H., K[120].
126 Le Tourneau, *Fès*, pp. 451–2.
127 El Mansour, 'Political and Social Developments', pp. 112, 151. Sīdī al-Makkī Būhillāl lived in Timbuktu for some years, and his brother was head of the Eastern caravan. A.N., S.O.M., Afrique III, dos. 5 b, 'Nota interesante sobre el Niger, Tombukt, Housa y el mar mediterraneo de Africa', Badia.

128 F.O., 635/5, 'Marine Protests and Manifests', 14 June 1845, and subsequent references in the series.
129 Muḥammad Dā'ūd, *Tārīkh Tiṭwān*, 6 vols. (Tetuan, 1959–66), vol. III, p. 336.
130 N.A., R.G. 84, 20 December 1862, Corcos to McMath; A.E., C.C.C., Mogador 4, 27 December 1862, Destrees; F.O., 631/2, Public Acts, 18 June 1862 (involving Perry and Co.).
131 F.O., 631/3, 11 February 1869, Carstensen to Hay.
132 D.A.R., 'Amāra dos., 25 Ṣafar 1298/27 January 1881, aṭ-Ṭālib Būhillāl to 'Amāra.
133 K.H., K[46]; K.H., *qawā'im ḥisābiyya.*
134 D.A.R., Essaouira 2, 4 Rabī' I 1287/4 June 1870, notarized copy of sharifian letter.
135 D.A.R., Essaouira 2, 1 Jumādā I 1288/19 July 1871, Muslim petitioners: Aḥmad Būhillāl, Mukhtār al-Warzāzī, Jewish petitioners: Dinar [Ohana], Judah [Levy-Yuly], Yamin Acoca, Salam Amar [Ben Messas].
136 D.A.R., Essaouira 3, 10 Rabī' II 1290/7 June 1873 (notarized document); 28 Jumādā I 1290/25 June 1873, Muḥammad b. 'Abd ar-Raḥmān Brīsha and 'Abd ar-Raḥmān b. al-Ḥasan to Sultan.
137 K.H., 27 Rabī' I 1302/14 January 1885, Ibn Zākūr, Brīsha, and Ibn al-Ḥasan to Sultan.
138 K.H., 3 Dhū al-Ḥijja 1302/13 September 1885, Ibn Zākūr, Brīsha, and Ibn al-Ḥasan to Sultan.
139 K.H., K[120].
140 D.A.R., Essaouira 4, 25 Sha'bān 1306/26 April 1889, Aḥmad b. 'Abd al-Kabīr at-Tāzī, 'Abd as-Salām Gharsiya, 'Abd ar-Raḥmān b. al-Ḥasan to Sultan.
141 Laroui, *Les origines*, pp. 104–8; Brown, *People*, pp. 158–63.
142 Laroui, *Les origines*, p. 107.
143 It was largely the silk industry that Beirut traders developed in Lebanon and Syria. See Fawaz, *Merchants*, pp. 63 ff; Dominique Chevalier, *La société du Mont Liban à l'époque de la révolution industrielle en Europe* (Paris, 1971), pp. 294–5. The transition in Egyptian agriculture in the nineteenth century to cash crops, especially cotton, has been extensively studied. Roger Owen, *Cotton and the Egyptian Economy: 1820–1914* (Oxford, 1969).
144 Cf. Miège, III, p. 31–5.
145 F. Nataf, *Le crédit et la banque au Maroc* (Paris, 1929), p. 53.
146 Debts were owed in Dundee, Birmingham, Hamburg, and Marseille amounting to $15,000. Meyer and Aaron Corcos valuated their houses in the *mellah* at $17,000, although the creditors felt that this was much too high given the commercial slump in the town. When the two brothers were declared bankrupt in 1900, scores of creditors in town came forward with claims. N.A., R.G. 84, 4 September 1896, legal statement signed by M. and A. Corcos; 22 November 1896, Broome to Cobb; 10 December 1897, Broome to Burke; 31 May 1900, affidavit of creditors.
147 By 1912, Reuben Elmaleh was reduced to appealing to the Alliance for a

pension so that he could retire in Jerusalem, his business having been inactive for some time. A.I.U., Maroc III B 14, 18 December 1912.

148 The declining fortunes of the Jewish merchants can be followed in the Alliance correspondence. A.I.U., Maroc III B 14, 29 May 1899, petition signed: J. D. Ohana, S. J. Afriat, Jacob H. Corcos, S. Hadida, N. J. Afriat, Léon Corcos, D. Corcos, Meyer Corcos; A.I.U., France XV F 26, Annual Report 1910–11, Loubaton.

149 Miège, III, p. 33.

150 Bernard Lewis, *The Jews of Islam* (Princeton, 1984), pp. 163–9.

151 See Stillman, *The Jews*, pp. 100–2.

152 Goitein *Mediterranean Society*, (pp. 70–9) sees a large and powerful merchant 'class' in the eighth and ninth centuries, though lacking political power. On the importance of the merchants in Mamluk cities and their status in society, see Ira M. Lapidus, *Muslim Cities in the Later Middle Ages* (Cambridge, Mass. 1967), pp. 117–30.

153 Cf. Raymond, *Grandes villes*, pp. 89–92.

154 Cigar, 'Socio-economic', p. 60.

155 Domingo Badia Y Leyblich, *Travels of Ali Bey in Morocco, Tripoli, Cyprus, Egypt, Arabia, Syria, and Turkey between the years 1802 and 1807* (London, 1816), vol. I, p. 147.

156 James Richardson, *Travels in Morocco* (London, 1860), vol. II, p. 1.

157 F.O., 174/126, 15 September 1831, Hay; 10 October 1831, Sultan to Hay; 22 Jumādā I 1247/29 October 1831, Sultan to Hay; F.O., 99/1, 9 February 1838, Hay to Palmerston.

158 Riley, *Authentic Narrative*, pp. 411–12; Charles A. Payton, *Moss from a Rolling Stone, or Moorish Wanderings and Rambling Reminiscences* (London, 1879), p. 27.

159 Scattered information on amounts given in marriages are found in Jewish marriage contracts (*ketūba*s). Reuben b. Joseph Elmaleh paid $5,000 (about £1,053) in 1871, while his cousin Reuben b. Amram paid $18,000 (about £3,789) the same year. From the collection of the Abecassis family of Essaouira. The price of marriages in *ketūba*s in the S.L. collection between 1859 and 1887 range from $2,600 and $26,000.

160 Raymond Thomassy, *Le Maroc et ses caravanes ou relations de la France avec cet Empire* (Paris, 1845), pp. 326–7. On the growing taste for European products, see Miège, IV, pp. 388–96. Foreign material objects were also found in the homes of the Muslim *makhzan* class. J. Leclerq, 'Mogador', *Revue Britanique*, 6 (1880), 403; A.E., C.C.C. Mogador 4, 21 October 1865, Gay.

161 J.-L. Miège, 'Origine et développement de la consommation du thé au Maroc', *Bulletin Economique et Social du Maroc*, 20, 71 (1956), 377–98.

162 Payton, *Moss*, pp. 83–4.

163 See Raymond, *Grandes villes*, pp. 305–13.

164 The houses of the old *casbah* which belonged to the few remaining Jews of Essaouira were still decorated in this manner at the time of my research in 1981. For nineteenth-century descriptions, see Arthur Leared, *Marocco and*

the Moors (London, 1876), p. 67; J.-L. Miège, *Une Mission française à Marrakech en 1882* (Aix-en-Provence, 1968), p. 97 (from a MS of Brueille in 1882); *Times of Morocco*, 18 August 1888; A.I.U., Maroc XXXIII E 582, 15 December 1891, Benchimol; William B. Leech, 'Notes on a Visit to Mogador', *Journal of the Manchester Geographical Society*, 18 (1902), 61.

165 Riley, *Authentic Narrative*, p. 406.

166 J.-L. Miège, 'Le Maroc et les premières lignes de navigation à vapeur', *Bulletin de l'Enseignement Public au Maroc*, no. 236 (1956), 37–47.

167 Schroeter, 'Anglo-Jewry', pp. 62–6.

168 At one stage, the *makhzan* tried to halt the growing number of Jews leaving for Palestine from the northern ports. K.H., 23 Jumādā I 1261/19 May 1846, Sultan to Būsilhām b. ʿAlī.

169 A.I.U., France, XV F 26, 1891–2, Annual Report, Benchimol.

4 Port and bazaar

1 P.P., LXXX (1884), 95.

2 F.O., 174/72, 17 May 1863, Elton to Hay.

3 F.O., 830/1, 3 February 1856, Grace to Hay; Auguste Beaumier, 'Mogador et son commerce maritime', *Annales du Commerce Extérieur*, Etats-Barbaresques, Faits Commerciaux, no. 17 (1875), 116–17.

4 K.H., 16 Rajab 1302/1 May 1885, Sultan to Muḥammad Gannūn (cited by at-Tūzānī, p. 92). The old building was eventually converted into a prison. Budgett Meakin, *The Land of the Moors* (London, 1901), p. 208.

5 See chap. 3, n. 64.

6 Payton, *Moss*, pp. 170–1.

7 See Rosemary Arnold, 'Separation of Trade from Market: The Great Market of Whydah', in Polanyi, *et al.*, *Trade and Market*, pp. 177–87.

8 The question of currency in circulation is discussed in detail in chap. 7.

9 D.A.R., Essaouira 2, 6 Dhū al-Qaʿda 1289/5 January 1873, Muḥammad b. al-ʿArabī al-Qabbāj to Bannīs.

10 On the *diwāna*, see at-Tūzānī, *al-Umanā'*, p. 72.

11 Cf. Brown, *People*, pp. 129–35.

12 Cf. Le Tourneau, *Fès*, p. 306.

13 Marrakesh, for example, had a *sūq al-jadīd*. Paul Lambert, 'Notice sur la ville de Maroc', *B.S.G.*, 5e sér., 16 (1868), 439.

14 aṣ-Ṣiddīqī, *Īqāẓ*, p. 37. Some 55 shops are listed in a *ḥubus* register dating from the beginning of the protectorate. B.G., Habous, Essaouira. A register of 1296/1878–9 lists 36 shops paying rent to the *makhzan*, which was much more than any other market paid. K.H., K^{93}.

15 *Times of Morocco*, 11 August 1888. The drapers are still to be found there today, though the area is not shut off at night.

16 The goods sold there were broadly known as *ʿiṭr* or *ʿiṭriya*, derived from the root *ʿa-ṭ-r*, ato perfume. The original meaning of *al-ʿiṭāra* (the place) seems to have been indeed perfumeries, and related to this, apothecary. See the

definition of R. Dozy, *Supplément aux dictionnaires arabes*, II (Leiden, 1881), p. 137.

17 Diverse products are listed under *ʿiṭriya* in a table of import and export duties paid for a period of one year. D.A.R., Essaouira 1, Shaʿbān 1268–Rajab 1296/1852–3. For a list of products at the *ʿiṭāra* of Fez, see Charles René-Leclerc, 'Le commerce et l'industrie à Fez', *R.C.* (1905), 310–12, 315.

18 On the development of shopkeeping in Europe, see Fernand Braudel, *The Wheels of Commerce* (London, 1982), pp. 60–75.

19 'Travaux dans la rade et dans la ville de Mogador', *Nouvelles Annales de la Marine*, 30 (1863), 285; F.O., 174/72, 1 September 1864, Elton to Hay.

20 'Travaux dans la rade et dans la ville de Mogador', 285.

21 Starting in Rajab 1282/November–December 1865, constructions in the new *mellah* are listed as one of the major town expenditures. K.H., K^{295}.

22 K.H., 20 Rabīʿ I 1282/13 August 1865, ʿAbd al-Wāḥid Aqaṣbī and ʿUmar b. ʿAmr al-Awsā to Bannīs.

23 D.A.R., Essaouira 1, 26 Ramaḍān 1282/12 February 1866, Aqaṣbī and ʿUmar b. ʿAmr to Bannīs.

24 Halewī, (1891), p. 565.

25 F.O., 174/292, 9 February 1885, Payton to Hay.

26 Payton, *Moss*, p. 170.

27 See particularly René-Leclerc, 'Le Commerce', pp. 306–8; E. Michaux-Bellaire and G. Salmon, 'El-Qçar El-Kebir: une ville de province au Maroc septentrional'. *Archives Marocaines*, 2 (1904), p. 92; Geertz, '*Suq*', p. 131.

28 Other names besides *funduq* used for caravanserai are *qaysariyya*, *khān*, and *wakāla*. Raymond, *Grandes villes*, pp. 248–9.

29 Geertz makes no distinction between the different kinds of *funduq*s, which might suggest that they were fairly uniform in Sefrou. René-Leclerc distinguished between *funduq*s which were carvanserais and commerce *funduq*s. See above, note 28. This distinction also applied to Essaouira.

30 Michaux-Bellaire and Salmon, 'El Qçar El-Kebir', p. 32.

31 Geertz, '*Suq*', p. 131.

32 The comprehensive list of *hubus* property established by the French lists only a sugar *funduq* containing 72 stalls, and another two *funduq*s in Sūq Wāqa. B.G., Habous, Essaouira.

33 There are four full *funduq*s and five half *funduq*s listed in 1296/1878–9. Two are in the old *mellah*, and seven are in the *medina*. K.H., K^{93}.

34 See above, pp. 198–9.

35 The *qāʾid*'s description of the incident is summarized in the Sultan's reply to Qāʾid ʿAmāra. D.A.R., ʿAmara dos., 5 Muḥarram 1292/11 February 1875.

36 D.A.R., ʿAmāra dos., 10 Muḥarram 1287/12 April 1870.

37 D.A.R., ʿAmāra dos. 29 Rajab 1291/11 September 1874, Sultan to ʿAmāra.

38 Raymond, *Grandes villes*, pp. 179–80.

39 There are numerous listings of stables (*riwāʾ*, pl. *arwī*) belonging to the *makhzan* and the *ḥubus*. K.H., K^{93}; B.G., Habous, Essaouira.

40 A.I.U., Maroc XXXIV E 584, 12 October 1875, Benchimol.
41 Raymond, *Grandes villes*, p. 262.
42 A register of expenditures lists constructions on a textile workshop (*fabrīka al-khiyāṭa*). K.H., K[295]. The construction of a steam mill is reported in the 1870s. Leared, *Marocco*, p. 72. A consular report for 1883 refers to two steam mills. P.P., 1884, LXXX, p. 100.
43 A.E., Maroc, M.D. 4, December 1847.
44 F.O., 631/3, 28 January 1870, Carstensen to White.
45 J. D. Hooker and J. Ball, *Journal of a Tour in Morocco and the Great Atlas* (London, 1878), p. 335; account of Breiulle, in Miège, *Une mission*, p. 99. Today the main craft of note is woodmaking, but according to local tradition, this only started in the late 1880s. On the locales of artisans in Fez, see Le Tourneau, *Fès*, pp. 314–15.
46 J.-L. Miège, 'Note sur l'artisanat marocain en 1870', *Bulletin Economique et Social du Maroc*, 16 (1953), 91.
47 Descriptive accounts on ethnic specialization are confirmed by the names of the tenants listed in the *ḥubus* register. B.G., Habous, Essaouira.
48 Halewī, (1891), 581.
49 A.I.U., Maroc XXXIII E 582, 22 February 1894, Benchimol. L. de Campou, *Un empire qui croule: Le Maroc contemporain* (Paris, 1886), pp. 53–4.
50 A.E., C.C.C. Mogador 8, 31 March 1891, Hugonnet.
51 Cf. Geertz, '*Suq*', p. 171.
52 A.E., Maroc, M.D. 10, March 1867, Beaumier.
53 Payton, *Moss*, p. 285.
54 Riley, *Authentic Narrative*, p. 413.
55 See Geertz, '*Suq*', pp. 125–6.
56 The shops belonged to the *makhzan*. K.H., K[93], 1296/1878–9.
57 The *jūṭiya* made a big impression on foreigners. G. Beauclerk, *Journey to Morocco* (London, 1828), p. 237.
58 Riley, *Authentic Narrative*, p. 421.
59 Leclerq, 'Mogador', p. 421.
60 F.O., 174/292, 30 May 1883, Payton. In a *makhzan* register of 1300–1/1883–4, spanning 17 months (with one month missing), taxes were taken on the sale of slaves for only five months: Shaʿbān, Ramaḍān, Shawwāl, Dhū al-Qaʿda of 1300, and Ramaḍān of 1301. K.H., K[122]. An informant in Essaouira pointed out to me the place where the slave market was formerly held. It was in what is marked in nineteenth-century maps as the *jūṭiya*.
61 A.I.U., Maroc XXXIV E 588, 13 June 1902, Bensimhon.
62 Louis Massignon, 'Enquête sur les corporations musulmanes d'artisans et de commerçants au Maroc', *Revue du Monde Musulman*, 58 (1924), 49. The word is derived from the verb *ḥ-m-l*, to carry; thus *ḥammāla* is the place of the carriers.
63 Payton, *Moss*, p. 297.
64 Cf. Le Tourneau, *Fès*, pp. 309–14.
65 A certain Mawlāy ʿUmar b. Muḥammad al-ʿAlawī of Essaouira, in partnership with Muḥammad b. aṭ-Ṭayyib al-Maḥmūdi of Marrakesh, was

having trouble selling some goat skins so he entrusted them to a *dallāl*, Muḥammad Ū Bīhī al-Jadīrī. This led to a dispute. D.A.R., ʿAmara dos., 19 Muḥarram 1294/3 February 1877, Khalīfa ʿUthmān b. Muḥammad to ʿAmāra.

66 A.I.U., France XV F 26, Annual Report 1892–3, Benchimol.

67 In a census of the Jewish population, Jewish pedlars represented 13.75 per cent. A.I.U., Maroc XXXVII bis E b.

68 They earned only 50 centimes a day, according to Benchimol. A.I.U., Maroc XXXIII E 582, 22 February 1894.

69 About 10 francs a month, according to Hugonnet. A.E., C.C.C. Mogador 8, 31 March 1891.

70 A.I.U., France XV F 26, Annual Report 1900–1, Benchimol.

71 F.O., 631/3, 28 January 1870, Carstensen to White.

72 The governor is also sometimes called pasha (*basha*), though this term tended to relate more to the army. Cf. G. Salmon, 'L'administration marocaine à Tangier', *Archives Marocaines*, I (1904), 1.

73 *Ibid.*, pp. 3, 24.

74 These administrative changes are discussed in detail above, pp. 139–40, 158–9.

75 The domain of activities of the *amīn al-mustafād* can be seen in the *makhzan* register, K.H., K[122], 1300–1/1883–4. The functioning of this institution in Essaouira is studied in detail by Park, 'Administration', chap. 5.

76 See Ibn Khaldun, *The Muqaddimah*, trans. F. Rosenthal, (New York, 1958), vol. I, pp. 462–3; Raymond, *Grandes villes*, pp. 121–3; Geertz, '*Suq*', p. 196. Literally the *muḥtasib* was appointed to the *ḥisba*, as in the case of al-Ḥājj al-Hāshimī al-Gadīrī. aṣ-Ṣiddīqī, *Īqāẓ*, p. 125. For details on this institution in Morocco, see Brown, *People*, pp. 137–8; Massignon, 'Enquête', pp. 107–10; ʿAbd ar-Raḥmān Ibn Zaydān, *al-ʿIzz wa-ṣ-ṣawla maʿālim nuẓum ad-dawla*, 2 vols. (Rabat, 1961–2), vol. II, pp. 61–71.

77 Ibn Khaldun, *The Muqaddimah*, vol. I, pp. 461–2.

78 Godard, *Le Maroc*, p. 52.

79 *Ibid.*

80 For example, in the appointment of ʿAbd al-Qādir al-Fallāḥ. D.A.R., Essaouira 4, 22 Shawwāl 1310/9 May 1893, ʿUmar al-Lubarīs to Sultan.

81 The many monographs on the Moroccan administrative institutions by early French colonial writers – in particular, Michaux-Bellaire, Salmon, and Mercier – have been largely superseded by the studies of at-Tūzānī, *al-Umanāʾ*, and Park, 'Administration'. Still, for particular details it is worth mentioning the best monographs on Moroccan administrative institutions for other towns: L. Mercier, 'L'administration marocain à Rabat', *Archives Marocaines*, I (1904), pp. 59–96; Michaux-Bellaire and Salmon, 'El-Qçar El-Kebir'; Salmon, 'L'administration marocaine à Tanger,'. In general, see E. Michaux – Bellaire 'L'organisation de finances au Maroc', *Archives Marocaines*, 11 (1907), pp. 171–251; Aubin, *Morocco of Today*, pp. 158–205, 234–48. No study is as complete as Le Tourneau's book, *Fès*. On general patterns of administration of Arab cities during the Ottoman period, see Raymond, *Grandes villes*, pp. 121–9.

82 Zafrani, *Les Juifs*, pp. 106–9; Deshen, *Ṣībūr*, pp. 42 ff.

83 M. Obedia, *Les Juifs de Mogador*, typescript, n.d., pp. 15–16. A copy of this document was kindly given to me by Professor Miège. A case of a Jew imprisoned by the *shaykh* is reported to the Alliance. A.I.U., Maroc XXXIII E 582, 21 July 1896.
84 Zafrani, *Les Juifs*, pp. 170–1; cf. Deshen, *Ṣībūr*, pp. 56–7.
85 Halewī, (1891), p. 311. On this tax, see Zafrani, *Les Juifs*, p. 137.
86 Halewī, (1891), p. 565.
87 Halewī, (1891), p. 311. Zafrani states that it was the *shaykh al-yahūd* who was the highest dignitary in the Jewish community; *Les Juifs*, p. 106. This may traditionally have been the case, but it was never so in Essaouira.
88 Cf. Geertz, '*Suq*', pp. 164–8.
89 Cf. Brown, *People*, pp. 88–9.
90 Cf. Abraham L. Udovitch and Lucette Valensi, *The Last Arab Jews: The Communities of Jerba, Tunisia* (Chur, London, Paris, and New York, 1984), pp. 63–4.
91 A.E., Maroc M.D. 10, March 1867, Beaumier.
92 A.E., C.C.C. Mogador 8, 31 March 1891, Hugonnet; F.O., 631/1, 28 January 1870, Carstensen to White.
93 Cf. Le Tourneau, *Fès*, pp. 554–5.
94 Until the period when massive importation began, tea was mainly consumed by the wealthy. See W. Lempriere, *A Tour from Gibraltar to Tangier, Sallee, Mogadore, Santa Cruz, Tarudant and thence over Mount Atlas to Morocco*, 2nd edn (London, 1793), p. 308. Its consumption later became general. Paul-Eugène Bache, 'Souvenirs d'un voyage à Mogador', *Revue Maritime et Coloniale* (January–February, 1861), 87–8. See also chap. 3.
95 Bache, 'Souvenirs', p. 87; Miège, 'Origine', pp. 391–2.
96 Payton, *Moss*, pp. 28–9; cf. Le Tourneau, *Fès*, pp. 554–5.
97 aṣ-Ṣiddīqī, *Īqāẓ*, p. 76.
98 In 1887 the Sultan consulted the ulama of Fez and decided to prohibit tobacco and hashish. an-Nāṣirī, *Kitāb al-istiqṣā*, vol. IX, pp. 192–3; Miège, 'Origine', pp. 390–1.
99 *al-Wathā'iq*, 4, (1978), 357 ff.
100 Meakin, *The Land*, p. 212; C. Ollive, 'Géographie médicale: climat de Mogador et de son influence sur la phthisie', *B.S.G.*, 6e sér., 10 (1875), 372.
101 P.P., 1887, LXXXV, p. 135.
102 D.A.R., Essaouira 1, 3 Rabīʿ II 1282/26 August 1865, ʿUmar b. ʿAmr al-Awsā to Bannīs.
103 The division is comparable to the situation analysed in Jerba. Udovitch and Valensi, *The Last Arab Jews*, pp. 63–4.
104 Halewī, (1891), 311. On the special place of the *Zohar* in Moroccan Judaism, see Zafrani, *Les Juifs*, p. 62.
105 Joseph Thomson, *Travels in the Atlas and Southern Morocco* (London, 1889), pp. 73–9. Vestiges of this ritual were seen during my fieldwork in Essaouira.
106 Halewī, (1891), 581.
107 The British consul was appalled by the crowds of Jewish beggars in the *casbah* on Fridays. Payton, *Moss*, pp. 303–4. Cf. Halewī, (1891), 311.

108 *Jewish Missionary Intelligence*, 21 (August, 1905), 117.
109 Cf. Brown, *People*, p. 88.
110 Cf. Raymond, *Grandes villes*, p. 169.
111 This is mentioned in a *dahir* ordering special prayers to be performed every day of the week (called *ikhrāj al-lāṭif as-saghīr*). K.H., 2 Shawwāl 1270/28 June 1854, Muḥammad Brīsha to Sultan. The *lāṭif* was a prayer recited during crisis; the number of *lāṭif*s was sometimes determined by order of the Sultan. See K. Brown, 'The Impact of the *Dahir Berbère* in Salé', in E. Gellner and C. Micaud (eds.), *Arabs and Berbers* (London, 1972), p. 209n. Presumably the recitation on Fridays was longer than the other days (*awsaṭ*, denoting a *lāṭif* of medium, and *saghīr* of short, duration).
112 ar-Ragrāgī, *ash-Shamūs*, p. 33.
113 *Mu'na* and *ṣadaqa* were part of the expenditure of Essaouira. K.H., K[42], 1276–8/1860–2. Cf. at-Tūzānī, *al-Umanā'*, p. 97. In 1866, the *amīn* noted that the charity was insufficient. D.A.R., Essaouira 1, 13 Rabīʿ I 1283/5 August 1866, Muḥammad b. al-Mahjūb to Bannīs.
114 It is probable that the *makhzan* collected 10 per cent of the products sold in the *qāʿa*. Cf. Le Tourneau, *Fès*, p. 387.
115 For Marrakesh, for example, see Leared, *Marocco*, p. 169; for Salé, Brown, *People*, pp. 19–20; and for Fez, Le Tourneau, *Fès*, p. 392.
116 It has been pointed out that in Sefrou Jews were heavily concentrated in shoemaking and tailoring for a rural clientele. Geertz, '*Suq*', p. 170.

5 Beyond the walls

1 *Times of Morocco*, 11 August 1888.
2 Edmund Burke, 'Morocco and the Near East: Reflections on Some Basic Differences', *Archiv. Europ. Sociol.*, 10 (1969), 84.
3 Leared, *Marocco*, p. 71.
4 A.E., Maroc, M.D. 4, December 1847, Soulange-Bodin.
5 Distance is viewed as determining the difference between 'local' and 'long distance' trade in precolonial Western Africa. Local trade was within a radius of ten miles of the area of production. This distinction 'draws attention to the differences in degrees of specialisation, in types of commercial institutions, in the composition of the goods traded, and the nature of the consumer demands'. A. G. Hopkins, *An Economic History of West Africa* (London, 1973), p. 53.
6 G. Beauclerk, *Journey to Morocco*, p. 229.
7 For the sense of 'riding' and 'sitting' merchants, see Geertz, '*Suq*', p. 171.
8 Halewī, (1891), 581.
9 On the Jewish pedlar in Morocco, see Geertz, '*Suq*', pp. 170–2; Deshen, *Ṣībūr*, p. 35; Dale F. Eickelman, 'Religion and Trade in Western Morocco', *Research in Economic Anthropology*, 5 (1983), 338–41; K. L. Brown, 'Mellah and Madina: A Moroccan City and its Jewish Quarter (Salé, ca 1880–1930)', in S. Morag, I. Ben-Ami, and N. Stillman, *Studies in Judaism and Islam* (Jerusalem, 1981), pp. 266–70; Burke, 'Morocco and the Near East', pp. 86–7. The relationship between Muslim and Jew did not entail the social

competition which arose in relations between two Muslims. Lawrence Rosen, *Bargaining for Reality: the Construction of Social Relations in a Muslim Community* (Chicago and London, 1984) p. 152. For other parts of North Africa, see Udovitch and Valensi, *The Last Arab Jews*, p. 103; Harvey E. Goldberg, *The Book of Mordechai. A Study of the Jews of Libya* (Philadelphia, 1980), pp. 81–4.

10 Halewī, (1891), 581.

11 Jean-François Troin, *Les souks marocains* (Aix-en-Provence, 1975), pp. 82–3.

12 Edward Westermarck, *Ritual and Belief in Morocco* (London, 1926), vol. II, p. 45.

13 K.H., K^{122}.

14 Marrakesh was estimated to be at least a 32 hour journey from Essaouira. Auguste Beaumier, 'Itinéraire de Mogador au Maroc et du Maroc à Saffy', *B.S.G.*, 5e sér, 16 (1868), 326. Not the eight days suggested by Laroui, *Les Origines*, p. 54.

15 In one instance the term parasangs (*parsa'ōt*), an ancient Persian measure of length equivalent to about three and a quarter miles, is used for estimating the distance between Essaouira and Safi. Halewī, (1891), 565.

16 Halewī, (1891), 362.

17 Beaumier, 'Itinéraire', 327–8.

18 Halewī, (1891), 927, 941–2. The bodies of the victims were found at Ilasmin by the Jewish community of Kūzimt (the population of this community comprised about 40 Jewish men). The Jews of Kūzimt were accompanied by soldiers of the *qā'id* of the Ida Ū Būziya and Matūga. Jews were essential for the prosperity of these districts and therefore the *qā'id* guaranteed their safety. It seems as though the Jewish community of Kūzimt, whose origin is uncertain, was a sort of 'migrant' community, which probably returned to Essaouira for the Jewish festivals.

19 Edmond Doutté, 'Organisation sociale et domestique chez le H'ah'a', *R.C.* (1905), 13.

20 Montagne, *Les Berbères et le Makhzen*, p. 25. A. Marcet, *Le Maroc: voyage d'une mission française à la cour du Sultan* (Paris, 1885), p. 264.

21 B.D., 29 Ṣafar 1262 /26 February 1846, Muḥammad Bū Mah[dī] to Ḥusayn b. Hāshim (these letters are translated in French in a forthcoming posthumous publication of Paul Pascon).

22 Most authors of the colonial era depict a dichotomy between *Bled el-Makhzen* (lit. *bilād al-makhzan*), those areas which recognize the authority of the Sultan, and *Bled es-Siba* (lit. *bilād as-sība*), those areas of 'dissidence' – often mountainous and Berber regions – where the Sultan has no control and which he is unable to tax. This thesis is found particularly in Montagne, *Les Berbères et le Makhzen*. Reviewing most of the secondary literature, the subject is examined by Francisco Benet, 'Explosive Markets: the Berber Highlands', in Polanyi *et al.*, *Trade and Market*, pp. 188–217. The system is discussed in a paradigmatic manner by E. Gellner, *Saints of the Atlas* (Chicago and London, 1969), pp. 1–5. It should be noted here that the

Sultan maintains a symbolic legitimacy, and at times, is able to arbitrate in tribal 'dissident' regions. See the criticism of the *makhzan/sība* stereotype of Germain Ayache, *Etudes d'histoire marocain* (Rabat, 1979), pp. 159–176; Raymond Jamous, *Honneur et baraka: les structures sociales traditionnelles dans le Rif* (Cambridge and Paris, 1981), p. 241. For an important case study of the relationship between the *makhzan* and a tribal region, see the thesis of ʿAbd ar-Raḥmān al-Mūʾddin, '*al-ʿAlāqa bayn al-mujtamaʿ al-qarawīya wa-d-dawla fī Maghrib al-qarn at-tāsiʿ ʿashr: qabāʾil Ināwin wa-l-Makhzan, 1290/1873–1320/1902*', diblōm ad-dirāsāt al-ʿalyāʾ (Rabat, 1984). On the relationship of this stereotype to French policy during the protectorate, see Edmund Burke, 'The Image of the Moroccan State in French Ethnological Literature: a New Look at the Origin of Lyautey's Berber Policy', in Gellner and Micaud, *Arabs and Berbers*, pp. 175–99.

23 Ibn Manṣūr says that it is an old term, though he presents no evidence regarding its origin. *al-Wathāʾiq*, 4 (1978), 378.

24 For nineteenth century descriptions of *nazālas*, see Leared, *Marocco*, p. 103; Hooker and Ball, *Journal*, p. 110; Marcet, *Le Maroc*, p. 223; Halewī, (1891), 589; Hubert Gíraud, 'Itinéraire de Mogador à Marrakech (1890–92)', *C.R. de Séances du Congrès National de Géographie*, Marseille (1898), p. 4.

25 A case is reported in 1874 of a small party of Jews killed at a *nazāla* in the Shiadma. A.I.U., Maroc XXXIII E 571, 25 December 1874, Emile Altaras.

26 On the meaning and origin of the term, see E. Laoust, *Mots et choses berbères* (Paris, 1920). See D. M. Hart, *The Aith Waryaghar of the Moroccan Rif* (Tucson, 1976), pp. 303–5; Geertz, '*Suq*', pp. 137–8. '*Mezrag*' and '*zaṭṭāṭa*' appear to be referring to the same kind of situation (see below). Perhaps the terms differed from region to region.

27 D.A.R., Essaouira 3, Dhū al-Qaʿda 1292/19 December 1875, Sultan to ʿAmāra.

28 John Davidson, *Notes Taken during Travels in Africa* (London, 1836), p. 188.

29 This may be more specific to the Jew's relationship to a patron. It has been suggested that Jews and other low-status groups were exempt from *zaṭṭāt*. Hart, *Aith Waryaghar*, p. 304. Elsewhere, it has been mentioned that Jews paid a more exorbitant passage fee. Ross E. Dunn, *Resistance in the Desert: Moroccan Responses to French Imperialism, 1881–1912* (Madison, 1977), pp. 16–17.

30 Geertz, '*Suq*', pp. 137–8; Brown, 'Mellah and Medina', p. 269.

31 Westermarck, *Ritual*, vol. 1, p. 535. Westermarck mistakenly leads us to believe that *al-ʿār* implied 'curse' and 'sin'. It has been shown that its usage related to 'honour' and 'shame'. See K. L. Brown, 'The "Curse" of Westermarck', *Acta Philosophica Fennica*, 34 (1982), 219–59.

32 This system was noted by nineteenth-century observers: e.g., Foucauld, pp. 130–2; Walter B. Harris, *Tafilet: the Narrative of a Journey of Exploration in the Atlas Mountains and the Oases of the North-West Sahara* (London, 1895), pp. 98–9. It has been studied more recently by Jamous, *Honneur*, pp. 212–16. It has been observed that the killing of a Jew was regarded as a worse

offence than killing a Muslim, since Jews generally were not part of the political system, and the patron would retaliate with little mercy. Hart, *Aith Waryaghar*, p. 280; cf. Rosen, *Bargaining for Reality*, p. 153.

33 Georges Drague, *Esquisse d'histoire religieuse du Maroc. Confréries et zaouias* (Paris, 1951), pp. 197–8. On the *zawiya* and its geopolitical position, see Abdallah Hammoudi, 'Sainteté, pouvoir, et société: Tamgrout aux XVIIe et XVIIIe siècles', *Annales, E.S.C.*, 35 (1980), 626.

34 A.E., C.C.C., Mogador 6, 18 August 1879, Hélouis. Cf. Oscar Lenz, 'Voyage du Maroc au Sénégal', *B.S.G.*, 7e sér., 1 (1881), 206.

35 Laroui, *Les origines*, pp. 41–2.

36 Leared, *Marocco*, pp. 70–1.

37 C. Ollive, 'Commerce entre Timbouctou et Mogador', *Bulletin de la Société de Géographie de Marseille*, 4 (1880), 5.

38 Soulange-Bodin suggests 63–6 days. A.E., Maroc, M.D. 4, 11 February 1847. Another estimate is 68 days from Timbuktu to Essaouira. Ollive, 'Commerce', p. 6. Miège, in one place, concludes from the sources that the trip took between 65 and 80 days, and elsewhere he suggests from 70 to 75 days (II, p. 149; III, pp. 85–6).

39 Davidson, *Notes*, p. 87; V. Monteil, *Notes sur les Tekna* (Paris, 1948), p. 47; Felix A. Mathews, 'Northwest Africa and Timbuctoo', *Bulletin of the American Geographical Society*, 4 (1881), 211.

40 Auguste Beaumier, 'Premier établissement des Israélites à Tombouctou', *B.S.G.*, 5e sér., 19 (1870), 364.

41 Michel Abitbol, *Tombouctou et les Arma. De la conquête marocaine du Soudan nigérien en 1591 à l'hégemonie de l'Empire Peul de Macina en 1833.* (Paris, 1979), p. 187.

42 T. E. Zerbib, 'Slave Caravans in Morocco' *The Anti-Slavery Reporter*, ser. 4, 7:3 (1887), 98–9.

43 A.E., C.C.C. Mogador 7, 17 March 1887. Arthur Leared, 'The Trade and Resources of Morocco', *Journal of the Society of Arts*, 25 (1877), 536; Ollive, 'Commerce', p. 7. An earlier traveller estimated 500 pounds. René Caillié, *Travels through Central Africa to Timbuctoo and across the Great Desert to Morocco, Performed in the Years 1824–1828*, (London, 1830), vol. II, p. 94.

44 On this relay to trade, cf. Ross E. Dunn, 'The Trade of Tafilalt: Commercial Change in Southeast Morocco on the Eve of the Protectorate', *African Historical Studies*, 4 (1971), 277–9.

45 Leared suggests six to ten; 'Trade and Resources', p. 537. Records on caravans coming to and departing from Tazarwalt have been preserved in the register of Iligh. In 18 years, there were 3 to 4 caravans annually. Pascon, *La Maison*, p. 74.

46 Mathews, '*Northwest Africa*', p. 211.

47 D.A.R., Essaouira 2, 16 Rabīʿ I 1288 /5 June 1871, al-ʿArabī Faraj and ʿAbd ar-Raḥmān Aqaṣbī to Sultan.

48 K.H., 23 Shawwāl 1303 /25 July 1886, ar-Ragrāgī ad-Dawbilālī to Sultan.

49 K.H., K^{295}, 23 Jumādā I 1282 /14 October 1865.

50 K.H., K^{42}, 12 Ramaḍān 1276 /3 April 1860, 15 Ramaḍān 1276 /6 April 1860.

51 Various examples of these convoys for 1860–1 are enumerated in K.H., K[42]. As far as I have been able to determine, there were no reports of armed convoys being attacked between Marrakesh and Essaouira in the period under study.

52 Robert Brunschvig, 'Coup d'œil sur l'histoire des foires à travers l'Islam', in *Recueils de la Société Jean Bodin*, vol. V: *La Foire* (1953), 44, 52.

53 Doutté makes a distinction between the two: the *mawsim* is essentially religious and the market is subsidiary, while the *ammūgar* is mainly a fair for commercial transactions where religion is secondary; 'Organisation sociale', p. 13. In fact, no such distinction exists – though the latter literally means 'meeting'.

54 E. Westermarck, *Ceremonies and Beliefs Connected with Agriculture, Certain Dates of the Solar Year, and the Weather in Morocco* (Helsinki, 1913); Jacques Berque, *Structures sociales du Haut-Atlas*, (Paris, 1978), pp. 130–4, 276–9.

55 Jewish *ṣaddīq*s in Morocco have been studied by Issachar Ben Ami, *ha-ʿAraṣat ha-qidūshīm be-qereb yehūdei Marrōqō* (Jerusalem, 1984).

56 L. Voinot, *Pèlerinages judéo-musulmans au Maroc* (Paris, 1948).

57 On the Jewish veneration of saints at *hillūla*s, see Issachar Ben Ami, 'Folk Veneration of Saints among the Moroccan Jews' in Morag *et al.*, *Studies in Judaism and Islam* (Jerusalem 1984), pp. 283–344.

58 It was noted in the early twentieth century that the *mawsim* annually began on the first Thursday of March. Segonzac, *Au Cœur*, p. 416. In 1981, it officially began on the third Thursday of March. I have no direct evidence that trading was combined with pilgrimage in the Ragrāga *mawsim* of the nineteenth century. On the *mawsim* of the Ragrāga generally, see Doutté, *En Tribu*, pp. 360–2.

59 B.D., K[10], 28 Dhū al-Ḥijja 1291, and 7 Shawwāl 1293.

60 The commerce of Tazarwalt, organized and protected by the *shurafa'* of Iligh has been closely studied by Pascon, *La Maison*, pp. 43 ff. See also as-Sūsī, *Īllīgh*, pp. 252–3. Authors of the nineteenth century also discuss the *mawsim*. Lenz, 'Voyage', p. 206; Joachim Gatell, 'Description du Sous', *B.S.G.*, 6e sér., 1 (1871), 101.

61 Pascon, *La Maison*, p. 81, n. 37.

62 Some 29 *mawsim*s in Southwestern Morocco are listed in the thesis of ʿUmar Afā', '*Mas'alat an-nuqūd fi tārīkh al-Maghrib fī 'l-qarn at-tāsiʿ ʿashr (Sūs 1822–1906)*', diblōm ad-dirāsāt al-ʿalyā' (Rabat 1985), 86–7.

63 Segonzac, *Au Cœur*, pp. 526–8; Foucauld, *Reconnaissance au Maroc*, p. 169.

64 Davidson, *Notes*, pp. 87, 201–6, 112–14.

65 Segonzac, *Au Cœur*, pp. 526–8; Gatell, 'Description du Sous', p. 101; Foucauld, *Reconnaissance au Maroc*, pp. 169, 343.

66 On this routine among the Jews of Todgha, cf. Haïm Zafrani, *Pédagogie juive en terre d'Islam. L'enseignement traditionnel d l'hébreu et du Judaïsme au Maroc* (Paris, 1969), p. 35. Jewish pedlars throughout North Africa followed a similar cycle. Cf. Udovitch and Valensi, *The Last Arab Jews*, p. 104.

67 Troin, *Les souks*, vol. I, pp. 100–1.

68 The fluctuation in urban activity was perhaps indirectly influenced by the celebrations in the countryside at the end of Passover and the Ragrāga *mawsim*. See above, note 58.

69 Tawfīq, *al-Mujtama'*, vol. I, p. 223; José Alvarez-Pérez, 'Marruecos. Memoria geográfico-comercial de la demarción del consulado de Mogador', *Boletín de la Sociedad Geográfica de Madrid*, 2 (1877), 511.

70 Alvarez Pérez, 'Marruecos', pp. 502–3; P.P., 1878, LXXIV, 21–2.

71 There is much controversy over the origin of gums which came to Essaouira. Some authors claim that most of the gum arabic came from the region of Demnat, while others suggest that it came from the Sous, Shiadma, 'Abda, or Rahamna, etc. The other main gum exported from Essaouira, gum senegal, *'ilk awarwal* in Arabic, which is a variety of *acacia arabica*, mostly came from south of the Sahara, and perhaps also from the Saharan Sahel. In the customs duty register books, both 'arabic' and 'senegal' were known as "*ilk*'. Two other kinds of gums traded at Essaouira were gum ammoniac (*fas[h]ukh*), and a red gum called '*amarand*'. In Europe gums were used principally in paints and in the manufacture of textiles. In Morocco, they were used for various pharmaceutical purposes, as was formerly the case in Europe. Among the sources which discuss the gum trade, see James Curtis, *A Journal of Travels in Barbary in the Year 1801, with Observations on the Gum Trade of Senegal* (London, 1803), pp. 123–6, 139; Jackson, *Account of the Empire of Morocco*, pp. 134–6; Thomassy, *Le Maroc*, pp. 330–1; Hooker and Ball, *Journal*, pp. 337, 386–95; Leared, *Marocco*, p. 95; Alvarez Pérez, 'Marruecos', p. 513; F.O., 830/1, 3 February 1856, Grace; F.O., 631/6, 22 August 1878, R. Drummond Hay to Hooker. Miège also examined in detail gum imports from Essaouira from the 1850s. *Le Maroc et l'Europe*, vol. III, p. 87. On gum in Senegambia, see Philip D. Curtin, *Economic Change in Precolonial Africa: Senegambia in the Era of the Slave Trade* (Madison, 1975), vol. I, pp. 216–17, vol. II, pp. 64–5.

72 A.E., C.C.C. Mogador 2, 1 December 1843, Hélouis-Jorelle; Miège, *Doc.*, p. 174 (14 August 1884, Mahon).

73 K.H., 20 Ṣafar 1303/28 November 1885, Aḥmad b. al-Ḥasan ad-Darāwī to Sultan.

74 Alvarez Pérez, 'Marruecos', p. 511. The tithes (*a'shār*) on olives apparently were collected between November and December. K.H., K[122]. In Īnūltān, the region around Demnat, olives were pressed in January. Tawfīq, *al-Mujtama'* vol. I, p. 227.

75 Mahon reports that in December, one of the three annual caravans arrives (see note 72 above). Other sources report on caravans arriving between February and April. Zerbib, 'Slave Caravans', p. 98. A.E., C.C.C., Mogador 7, 17 March 1887, Lacoste. *Times of Morocco*, 11 August 1887.

76 Curtis, *Travels in Barbary*, p. 139.

77 Troin, *Les Souks*, vol. I, p. 197.

78 *Ibid.*

79 F.O., 631/5, 10 December 1872.

80 See table in Miège, *Doc.*, p. 240; Miège, II, p. 545; Miège, 'Origine', p. 392.
81 This was the case, for example, in 1847. F.O., 99/36, Trade Report for Mogador, 1847.
82 P.P., 1881, XC, 83–4. Fish were plentiful in the year 1887. P.P., 1888, CII, 105–8.
83 On the development of steam navigation, see Miège, 'Le Maroc et les premières lignes', pp. 37–47.
84 A.E., C.C.C., Mogador 4, 11 November 1864.
85 On this caravan, see Le Tourneau, *Fès*, pp. 429, 590–1.
86 Henri Pirenne, *Economic and Social History of Medieval Europe* (London and Henley, 1936), p. 103.
87 Braudel, *The Wheels*, pp. 93–7.
88 On the persistence of archaic modes of transport, cf. Fernand Braudel, *The Mediterranean and the Mediterranean World in the Age of Philip II*, (New York, 1973), vol. I, pp. 282 ff.
89 Thomassy, *Le Maroc*, p. 330 (citing a letter of the French consul in the 1780s).
90 C. W. Newbury, 'North African and Western Sudan Trade in the Nineteenth Century: a Re-evaluation', *Journal of African History*, 7 (1966), 223–46.
91 J.-L. Miège, 'Le commerce trans-saharien au XIXe siècle. Essai de quantification', *Revue de l'Occident Musulman et de la Méditerranée*, 32, 2 (1981), 93–119; Ahmed Said Fituri, 'Tripolitania, Cyrenaica, and Bilad as-Sudan: Trade Relations during the Second Half of the Nineteenth Century', Ph.D. thesis (Michigan, 1982). The extent of the trans-Saharan trade with Morocco in the nineteenth century cannot be assessed from exports at the Moroccan seaports alone. Historically, the most important items exported from Timbuktu, such as slaves, ivory, and gold, were destined for the Moroccan domestic market. Research on Fez suggests that the trans-Saharan trade was greater at the end of the eighteenth century than in the second half of the nineteenth century, though the trade was still considerable until the very end of the nineteenth century. Cigar, 'Socio-economic', p. 62. It has been suggested that Tafilalt, an intermediate stage in the route leading south from Fez, was weakened by Essaouira's prosperity and the reconstruction of Tindouf in 1852. Dunn, 'The Trade of Tafilalt', pp. 279–80.
92 Miège, II, p. 152.
93 *Ibid.*, pp. 87–9, 358–71; IV, pp. 381–5.
94 Cf. Stambouli and Zghal, 'Urban Life', p. 4.
95 Cf. Hopkins, *Economic History*, p. 53; Owen, *The Middle East*, pp. 42–3.
96 Claude Meillassoux (ed.), *The Development of Indigenous Trade and Markets in West Africa* (Oxford, 1971), p. 67.
97 Abner Cohen, 'Cultural Strategies in the Organization of Trading Diasporas', in Meillassoux (ed.), *Development of Indigenous Trade*, pp. 266–81. His argument has also been taken up for the trans-Saharan trade. B. M. Perinbaum, 'Social Relations in the Trans-Saharan and Western Sudanese Trade: an Overview', *Comparative Studies in Society and History*, 15 (1973),

416–36. This theory of 'trade diasporas' is the basis of analysis in Curtin, *Economic Change*, pp. 59 ff; Curtin, *Cross-Cultural*, pp. 2–3.

98 This could sometimes give rise to legal disputes, and is reflected in the responsa literature of Morocco. See, for example, Masʿūd Khnāfō, *She'eilōt u- teshūbōt*, Bar Ilan, MS 192, folios 14–18.

99 Cf. Miège, II, pp. 92–4.

100 C.A.H.J.P., MA/MG, 2272, 30 January 1839, [. . .] to James Renshaw.

101 A.E., C.C.C., Mogador 3, June 1849.

102 Beaumier, 'Mogador', p. 112.

103 Pobeguin, 'Notes', p. 53. There is a case of merchandise arriving in Marrakesh on commission, where the recipient was absent. Yōsef Elmālīḥ, *Tōqfō shel Yōsef* (Livorno, 1823), responsum no. 91.

104 D.A.R., ʿAmāra dos., 2 Jumādā I 1287/31 July 1870, ʿAlī b. aṭ-Ṭayyib to ʿAmāra.

105 This is not to say that the wholesaler would not enter into a partnership with the retailer. In one responsum, everything is partnership except the shop. The question involves how to divide up the profits since the shopkeeper had left town. Abraham Qōrīyāṭ, *Berīt abōt* (Livorno, 1862), folios 114^b–115^a

106 Pobeguin, 'Notes', p. 53.

107 Braudel, *The Wheels*, p. 73.

108 Such a case is reported on Mukhtār b. ʿAzūz and his two Jewish commission agents, Massān and Yūsuf, the children of Ibn Dallāka. K.H., 15 Rabīʿ II 1281/17 September 1864, al-Mahdī b. al-Mashāwrī to Ibrāhīm b. Saʿīd.

109 'Caravanes de Timbouctou', *Revue Française de l'Etranger et des Colonies*, 8, 2^e sem. of 1888 (1889), 552–3.

110 Halewī, (1892), 627.

111 P.P., 1881, XC, pp. 81–2.

112 Pascon, *La Maison*, pp. 53–5.

113 B.D., K^3, folios 161^1 and 163^2. Ten years later Masʿūd is still receiving loans from Ḥusayn. B.D., K^{10}/16–6, 7 and 8; on 20 Ṣafar 1290/9 April 1873, he is entrusted with 800 French riyāl to buy feathers; on 18 Dhū al-Ḥijja 1290/6 February 1874, 233 riyāl were paid back, and on 29 Rabī I 1291/16 May 1874, another 438 riyāl were repaid.

114 A number of studies have discussed, in general terms, how the system operated in North Africa, and in specific towns in Morocco. Geertz, '*Suq*', pp. 133–4; Le Tourneau, *Fès*, p. 402; René-Leclerc, 'Le Commerce', p. 301; P. Ernest-Picard, *La monnai et le crédit en Algérie depuis 1830* (Algiers and Paris, 1980), p. 27. On the question of partnerships generally, see Abraham L. Udovitch, *Partnership and Profit in Medieval Islam* (Princeton, 1970). Many nuances of the different kinds of associations have been studied by Pascon, *La Maison*, pp. 53 ff.

115 Economic collaboration was also widespread in medieval Islam, but there were some reservations about interdenominational *commenda*. Udovitch, *Partnership*, pp. 227–30.

116 Zafrani, *Les Juifs*, pp. 181–8. For the medieval period, cf. Goitein, *Mediterranean Society*, pp. 169–83.

117 C.A., 5 Nīssan 5623/25 March 1863. The commodities are listed in Arabic in the document.
118 Cf. Udovitch, *Partnership*, pp. 170 ff.
119 *Commenda* agreements appear to have been made in riyāl in this period. In the medieval, as well as the modern period, copper coins were often viewed more as a commodity than a currency. *Ibid.*, p. 177.
120 The equivalent idea in Arabic is *amīn*. Udovitch, *Partnership*, p. 203.
121 *Ibid.*, p. 232.
122 Udovitch, *Partnership*, p. 246. One year was the standard time for the medieval Jewish partnerships, though sometimes two years were stipulated. Goitein, *Mediterranean Society*, p. 178.
123 C.A., 2 Ṭebet 5630/6 December 1869, signed Mōshe Hakōhen and Abraham Ben ʿAṭṭār.
124 For instance, Reuben Elmaleh, who had close ties with Daḥmān Bayrūk, loaned the latter money and asked him to recover debts. B.A., Shawwāl 1311/2 May 1894, Elmaleh.
125 C.A., 24 Rajab 1290/17 September 1873.
126 C.A., 1 Dhū al-Ḥijja 1285/15 March 1869. al-Waltītī appears to have been an important family from the Sous residing in Essaouira. as-Sūsī, *al-Maʿsūl*, vol. VIII, p. 200.
127 D.A.R., ʿAmāra dos., 19 Muḥarram 1294/3 February 1877, Khalīfa ʿUthmān b. Muḥammad to ʿAmāra.
128 Zafrani, *Les Juifs*, pp. 187–8.
129 Abraham Qōrīyāṭ, *Zekhūt abōt* (Pisa, 1812), folio 1[a].
130 On the predominance of ethnic minorities in commerce, see Brian L. Foster, 'Ethnicity and Commerce', *American Ethnologist*, 1 (1974): 437–48. See also the remarks of Landes, *Bankers*, p. 19.
131 N.A., R.G. 84, 15 January 1888, Corcos to Reade.
132 A letter to Solomon Corcos from a rural *qāʾid* in 1850 alludes to some lost goods. It would be unacceptable, according to this letter, that goods which Corcos confided, '*fī amān Allāh*', should be lost. C.A., 25 Muḥarram 1267/30 November 1850.
133 B.A., 22 Jumādā I 1281/24 September 1864.
134 The relations between Swiri merchants, Bayrūk, and the Tajakant are reflected in a letter of 1846. B.A., 11 Ramaḍān 1262/2 September 1846, Zubayr b. ʿAbd ar-Raḥmān to Sheikh Mubārak Bayrūk.
135 Laroui, *Les origines*, pp. 53–4.
136 The expenses incurred in dispatching these couriers are listed in the *makhzan* registers. K.H., K[120].
137 Sheikh Bayrūk sent a *raqqāṣ* to Zubayr, in the letter cited in note 134.
138 C.A., 17 Rabīʿ I 1282/10 August 1865, Muḥammad b. al-Madanī Bannīs to Abraham Corcos. Perhaps the *ḥazān* Yaʿqūb was the rabbi Yaʿqōb Abīḥaṣīra. See Joseph Chetrit, 'Shlomo Gozlan: un poète bilingue de Tamgrūt dans le Drâa', in Michel Abitbol, (ed.), *Communautés juives des marges sahariennes du Maghreb* (Jerusalem, 1982), p. 432.
139 Goitein, *Mediterranean Society*, pp. 14–16.

140 A collection of account registers of the Macnin merchant house, dating from the first two decades of the nineteenth century, has been discovered recently, and will be the object of a future study.

141 After Agadir was closed to foreign commerce, Uhlmann's agents moved to Essaouira. Archives of the Uhlmann trading house, in Schoonhoven, Holland, 28 Elul 5531/7 September 1771. I am grateful to Paulo De Mas who sent me copies of a number of letters from these archives.

142 F.O., 174/28, 11 November 1829, Chaillet to E. W. A. Hay. The Judeo-Arabic letter is dated 7 Ḥishōn.

143 Several legal statements are found in Judeo-Arabic in B.D., K[2] and K[3] (the latter is the register used in the study by Pascon in *La Maison*), and K[10] in 1881.

6 The politics of trade

1 On the reactions and effects of the war, see Wilfrid J. Rollman, 'The "New Order"', pp. 464–8, 495–9. On the legends and poetry to which the war gave rise, see Mohamed Lakhdar, *La vie littéraire au Maroc sous la dynastie ʿAlawide (1075–1311=1664–1894)* (Rabat, 1971), p. 316; A.E., Maroc, M.D. 4, December 1847, Soulange-Bodin; Doutté, *En Tribu*, pp. 353–7.

2 an-Nāṣirī, *Kitāb al-istiqṣā*ʾ, vol. VIII, p. 155, vol. IX, p. 3. ʿAbd ar-Raḥmān was appointed to Essaouira in 1230/1814–15, according to ar-Ragrāgī, *ash-Shamūs*, p. 24.

3 Sulaymān favoured inland over Atlantic trade, which did not necessarily imply internal economic weakness. El Mansour, 'Political and Social Developments', pp. 114–18.

4 F.O., 174/4, 18 November 1839.

5 Miège, II, p. 146 (lists imports and exports for 1836–42, in French francs); for competition with other ports, see III, pp. 63–5. British consular reports of Essaouira's trade are found in F.O., 52/39 for 1834, 52/41 for 1835, 52/45 for 1836, 99/1 for 1837, 99/4 for 1838, 99/6 for 1839, and 99/19 for 1843.

6 ʿAbd al-Mālik Ū Bīhī of the Haha, for instance, was *qāʾid* during part of the reign of Sulaymān. as-Sūsī, *Illīgh*, p. 242. The consul Delaporte compiled a list in Arabic of all the *qāʾid*s of Essaouira from the foundation of the town up until 1834, unfortunately without dates. A.N., Aix-en-Provence, F[80] 1589–A.

7 A.N., Aix-en-Provence, F[80] 1589–A, Delaporte's list.

8 Beauclerk, *Journey*, pp. 228–9; aṣ-Ṣiddīqī, *Īqāẓ*, p. 64.

9 His brother, Muḥammad b. ʿAbd ar-Raḥmān, was a very noted *qāʾid* of Tetuan. See *al-Wathāʾiq*, I (1976), 454n.

10 D.A.R., Essaouira I, 12 Shaʿbān 1255/21 October 1839.

11 The British vice-consul, Chaillet, lists a governor with two secretaries, a head of customs, and four clerks. F.O., 174/28, 29 December 1829.

12 A.E., C.C.C., Mogador I, 24 January 1840, 20 April 1840, 8 July 1870, Delaporte.

13 On this dispute, see Jean Serres, 'Comment Pellissier de Reynaud ne fut pas

consul de France à Mogador (1843)', in *Memorial Henri Basset* (Paris, 1928), vol. II, pp. 243–7.

14 A.E., C.C.C., Mogador 2, 16 November 1842, Beauscher.

15 aṣ-Ṣiddīqī, *Īqāẓ*, p. 68.

16 A.N., Aix-en-Provence, 2 EE 19 (18 mi 9), 3 July 1844, Bugeaud to Joinville.

17 There are a number of descriptive accounts of the bombardment of Essaouira: J. Rousseau des Roches, *Trois souvenirs: Tanger, Isly, Mogador* (Paris, 1846); H. de Ideville, *Le Maréchal Bugeaud, d'après sa correspondance intime et des documents inédits: 1784–1849* (Paris, 1882), pp. 297–545; Auguste Hubert Warnier, *Campagne du Maroc, 1844* (Paris, 1944); Phillipe Cossé-Brissac, 'Les rapports de la France et du Maroc pendant la conquête de l'Algérie (1830–1847)', *Hespéris*, 13 (1931), 143–6; Jacques Caillé, *Les français à Mogador en 1844* (Essaouira, 1952).

18 A.N., Aix-en-Provence, 2 EE 10 (18 mi 9), 17 August 1844, Joinville to Bugeaud.

19 F.O., 99/23, Gibraltar, 2 October 1844, Military Secretary's Office, Military Report. The prisoners were released by the French a year later. *al-Wathā'iq*, 2 (1976), 45–6 (8 Rajab 1261/13 July 1845, Būsilhām b.ʿAlī).

20 D.A.R., Essaouira 1, 21 Shaʿbān 1260/5 September 1844, Sultan to Muḥammad al-Mazmīzī. Allegedly 150,000 Spanish dollars were stolen in money and goods from the customs house. F.O., 99/23 Gibraltar: 2 October 1844, Military Secretary's Office.

21 F.O., 174/49, 1844 ('Mr. Willshire's Narrative of Eight Days' Events at Mogador').

22 As in the case of Abraham Corcos, recorded in the diary of his son Meyer, who was born on 30 August in the village of Kūzimt. See above, p. 35.

23 *Jewish Chronicle* (15 November 1844); *Voice of Jacob*, vol. IV, 89 (15 November 1844); F.O., 174/49, 1844, ('Willshire's narrative').

24 an-Nāṣirī, *Kitāb al-istiqṣā'*, vol. IX, p. 53.

25 F.O., 830/1, 21 November 1844, Grace to E. W. A. Hay; F.O., 99/18, 1 October 1844, E. W. A. Hay. In a letter to Bugeaud, the French foreign ministry reported that some of the Jewish refugees in Gibraltar had requested permission to go to Algiers. The Moroccan consulate would not grant them passports required for travel, in order to oblige them to return to Morocco. The French then decided to admit them. A.N., Aix-en-Provence, 30 H 26, Paris: 14 September 1844. The Corcos family returned in July, 1845.

26 F.O., 99/18, 1 October 1844, E. W. A. Hay.

27 D.A.R., Essaouira 1, 18 Ramaḍān 1260/1 October 1844, Sultan to aṭ-Ṭālib Sulaymān ash-Shiyāẓmī.

28 See above, note 20.

29 F.O., 830/1 and F.O., 174/49, 21 November 1844, William Grace to E. W. A. Hay.

30 F.O., 830/1, 3 February 1845, Grace to E. W. A. Hay.

31 F.O., 830/1, 18 April 1845, Grace to Postle.

32 D.A.R., Essaouira 1, 21 Dhū al-Qaʿda 1261/21 November 1845.

33 Thomassy, *Le Maroc*, p. 71.
34 On the 'new order' troops created after 1845, see Rollman, 'The "New Order"', pp. 547 ff.
35 Miège, *Doc.*, pp. 17–26 (letter dated 8 March 1845, D. de Nion and Hélouis-Jorelle).
36 S.L., 'Note explicative présentée à M[r] le Consul Général de France à Tanger par le Sr Joseph Cadouch, originaire du Maroc [Marrakesh] aujourd'hui naturalisé Français'.
37 an-Nāṣirī, *Kitāb al-istiqṣā'*, vol. IX, p. 54. On the ending of tribute paid to Sweden and Denmark after 1844, see Jacques Caillé, 'L'abolition des tributs versés au Maroc par la Suede et le Danemark', *Hespéris*, 45 (1958), 203–38.
38 Miège, II, pp. 228 ff.
39 F.O., 830/1, 2 December 1844, Grace to E. W. A. Hay.
40 A.E., Maroc, M.D. 4, December 1847, Soulange-Bodin.
41 F.O., 174/49, 21 August 1847, Grace to Hay.
42 A.E., C.C.C., Mogador 3, 27 February 1854, Senenza; F.O., 830/1, 7 February 1854, Grace to Hay. In contrast, aṣ-Ṣiddīqī tells us how Brīsha was cruel and a hinderance to the merchants (*Īqāẓ*, p. 76). Neither foreign nor Moroccan archives make any allusion to the *qā'id*'s arbitrariness.
43 A.E., C.C.C., Mogador 3, 5 December 1854, Tippel.
44 K.H., 18 Ramaḍān 1270/14 June 1854, Muḥammad Brīsha to Sultan.
45 One source refers to 100,000 piastres (i.e., riyāl). A.E., Maroc, M.D. 4, August 1846, Soulange-Bodin. Beaumier refers to 4,000 piastres each. A.E., C.C.C., Mogador 2, 11 December 1848.
46 A.E., C.C.C., Mogador 2, 11 September 1846, Soulange-Bodin.
47 F.O., 830/1, 18 April 1845, Grace to Postle.
48 A.E., C.C.C., Mogador 2, 11 December 1848, Beaumier.
49 F.O., 174/49 and F.O. 830/1, 21 August 1848, Grace to Hay.
50 A.E., C.C.C., Mogador 3, 11 December 1848, Beaumier.
51 Miège enumerates Moroccan customs legislation in a chart for 1817–1903 in *Doc.*, pp. 155–66. This chart should be used cautiously since, firstly, regulations were not always uniform in all the Morocco ports, and secondly, they were not always enforced.
52 M.C.C., M8/2/4, 18 June 1845, 9 February 1846.
53 M.C.C., M8/2/5, 18 July 1855.
54 F.O., 830/1, 21 November 1844, Grace to Hay.
55 F.O., 830/1, 1 August 1850, Grace to Hay.
56 El Mansour, 'Political and Social Developments', pp. 122–3.
57 an-Nāṣirī, *Kitāb al-istiqṣā'*, vol. IX, p. 61.
58 Michaux-Bellaire, 'L'organisation des finances', p. 214.
59 Each year customs on certain commodities from a number of ports were auctioned, and Muṣṭafā ad-Dukkālī and al-Qabbāj were among the principal purchasers, as can be seen from a letter. K.H., Mid-Ṣafar 1264/January 1848, Sultan to Būsilhām b. 'Alī.
60 Laroui, *Les origines*, pp. 292–4.
61 F.O., 830/1, 21 September 1850, Grace to Hay.

62 Miège, *Doc.*, pp. 33–9 (letter of 20 November 1850).
63 D.A.R., Essaouira 1, 1266/1850 (no day and month), ad-Dukkālī, al-Qabbāj to al-ʿArabī b. al-Mukhtār.
64 K.H., 1 Muḥarram 1267/6 November 1850.
65 In the letter cited in note 64, the Sultan mentioned a correspondence with aṭ-Ṭarrīs.
66 F.O., 830, 10 December 1850, Grace to Hay.
67 K.H., 16 Muḥarram 1267/21 November 1850, Sultan to Būsilhām b. ʿAlī. The text refers to a 3 riyāl duty imposed on goat skins.
68 F.O., 830/1, 27 February 1852, Grace to Hay.
69 F.O., 830/1, 7 December 1854, Grace to Hay.
70 Most of these are found in Miège. See above, note 51. Much information on the monopolies is found in F.O., 830/1.
71 F.O., 830/1, 17 February 1854, Grace to Hay.
72 K.H., 25 Rabīʿ II 1270/26 December 1853, Muḥammad Brīsha; 29 Rabīʿ II 1270/30 December 1853, and 9 Jumādā II 1270/9 March 1854, al-Khaṭīb to Muḥammad aṣ-Ṣafar.
73 F. R. Flournoy, *British Policy towards Morocco in the Age of Palmerston: 1830–1865* (Baltimore, 1935), pp. 165–81.
74 Texts of the treaty are found in P.P., 1857, XVIII, pp. 43–64; both English and Arabic versions are found in *al-Wathāʾiq*, 2 (1976), 157–92, 200–26.
75 F.O., 830/1, 1 September 1848, 21 September 1848, and 30 September 1848, Grace to Hay.
76 K.H., K[295]. Register of the port of Essaouira, dated 1282/1865–6 (tariff enumerated).
77 F.O., 830/1, 3 July 1855, Grace.
78 *al-Wathāʾiq*, 2 (1976), 203.
79 In theory it should be collected at harvest time. Since much of the production was outside the direct control of the *makhzan* and not usually taxed (e.g., in the Sous, Ida Ū Tanān, etc.), this might have lended itself to legal justification of levying a market and gate tax on olive oil in Essaouira. In a similar vein, the skin tax could be viewed as related to the *zakāh* (see app. C). In a register of 1 Ramaḍān 1276/23 March 1860 to 17 Shawwāl 1278/17 April 1862, 'gate entries, including the tax on what the sale of oil in the *qāʿa* brings' is listed under one heading. K.H., K[42].
80 In one instance, the British vice-consul refers to gate fees on 'all produce'. F.O., 830/2, 26 April 1857. This seems to be an exaggeration, and there is no evidence of any gate fee at this time, other than on olive oil (see app. C). On British protests to the authorities: F.O., 830/2, 11 May 1857, 6 August 1857, and 20 June 1857, Elton to Hay. Hay, however, in a letter to the *qāʾid* of Essaouira refers to the gate tax on oil. F.O., 99/84, 6 October 1857.
81 F.O., 830/2, 10 May 1859, Elton to Hay; 15 June 1859, Elton to Hay and Elton to Reade; 22 June 1859, Elton to Reade.
82 F.O., 99/84, Tangier: 7 September 1858, Hay. On British relations with Morocco, see Rollman, 'The "New Order"', pp. 474–80.
83 F.O., 830/1, 20 March 1856, Grace.

84 The growth in the import of these commodities has been enumerated by Miège, II, pp. 534–46, and Miège, *Doc.*, pp. 231–7.
85 A.E., C.C.C., Mogador 4, 15 April 1866, Beaumier.
86 *al-Wathā'iq*, 4 (1978), 254–5 (21 Dhū al-Qaʿda 1279 / 13 December 1862).
87 F.O., 830 / 2, 21 February 1861, Elton to Hay; F.O., 99 / 117, 24 July 1862, Elton to Hay.
88 F.O., 99 / 117, Tangier: 25 April 1863.
89 F.O., 99 / 121, Tangier: 4 October 1864, Hay. The supervisor of the constructions was al-Ḥājj aṭ-Ṭayyib Būjayda ar-Ribāṭī. He was appointed on 28 Jumādā I 1281 / 29 October 1864. D.A.R., Essaouira 2, copy of a sharifian letter (copied on 10 Dhū al-Qaʿda 1288 / 23 January 1872).
90 K.H., K295 (listed in the monthly expenditures).
91 F.O., 174 / 83, 22 Shaʿbān 1280 / 1 February 1864, Bū ʿAshrīn to Reade.
92 F.O., 174 / 72, 1 September 1864, Elton to Hay.
93 F.O., 174 / 72, 23 October 1865, Carstensen to Hay.
94 D.A.R., Essaouira 1, 6 Jumādā I 1282 / 27 September 1865, Sultan to al-Ḥasan; A.E., C.C.C., Mogador 4, 14 November 1865, Ferdinand Gay. A new *amīn* replaced Būjayda in 1872 to complete the constructions. D.A.R., Essaouira 2, 12 Dhū al-Qaʿda 1288 / 25 January 1872, al-ʿArabī Faraj to Bannīs.
95 F.O., 631 / 3, 19 January 1866, Carstensen to Hay.
96 F.O., 631 / 3, August 1870, report for 1869, Carstensen.
97 D.A.R., Essaouira 2, 4 Muḥarram 1287 / 6 April 1870, al-ʿAyāshī Bannīs to Bannīs.
98 D.A.R., Essaouira 2, 8 Rabīʿ II 1288 / 31 May 1871, 4 Jumādā II 1288 / 21 August 1871, 23 Ramaḍān 1288 / 6 Deocember 1871, 12 Dhū al-Qaʿda 128 / 23 January 1872, ʿAbd ar-Raḥmān Aqaṣbī and al-ʿArabī Faraj to Bannīs; 18 Ramaḍān 1289 / 19 November 1872, Muḥammad b. al-ʿArabī al-Qabbāj to Bannīs.
99 An account of these negotiations is found in F.O., 835, 164, pp. 26–7; copies of the original documents are also included in pp. 74–83.
100 Except for the Spanish consul, who still owed rent for his house in the new *casbah*. D.A.R., Essaouira 3, 3 Rabīʿ II 1290 / 3 May 1873, al-Qabbāj and Muṣṭafā Gassūs to Bannīs.
101 Such was the case of Ratto in 1873, who sought repairs on his warehouse. D.A.R., Essaouira 3, 10 Rajab 1290 / 3 September 1873, ʿAbd al-Karīm b. Zākūr and Muḥammad b. al-Ḥassānī to Mūsā b. Aḥmad; F.O., 631 / 4, 26 November 1873, Beaumier (as acting British vice-consul) to John Damonte. Beaumier suggested to him that he should pay.
102 Serafin E. Calderón, *Manuel del oficial en Marruecos* (Madrid, 1844), p. 69. The author claims that his information was based on a royal register that Sulaymān had in Tangier in 1821.
103 A.E., C.C.C., Mogador 3, 11 December 1848.
104 At the beginning of the century, the piastre, or Spanish dollar, was worth 12 ūqiya; from 1820 to 1830, it went up to about 13.5 ūqiya; by 1848, it had risen to 18 (see fig. 17).

105 The ūqiya was fluctuating during this period. In Essaouira, its average exchange in 1857 for purchasing imports was 24 ūqiya, for exports between 21 and 23.5 ūqiya. Between 1857 and 1859 in Iligh, for instance, the riyāl was worth 25 ūqiya. F.O., 830/2, 29 October 1857. Pascon, *La Maison*, p. 67.

106 Dividing value by quantity for cotton goods shows a general downward trend. Such a calculation is inconclusive since quantity is indicated by 'pieces' which varied greatly in size, type, and value at any given period. Import and export tables for specific items at Essaouira are found in Miège, *Doc.*, pp. 229–33, 241–2.

107 Although not identical, the figures in this source are too close to Calderón's (above, note 102) for comfort. Alermón y Dorreguiz, *Descripción del Imperio de Marruecos* (Madrid, 1859), p. 33.

108 It has been suggested that customs revenues constituted the principal source of state revenues, once Morocco had expanded foreign trade. Laroui, *The History of the Maghrib*, p. 54; Ayache, *Etudes*, p. 105. A study of *makhzan* revenues, however, shows that most revenues were still derived from rural taxes, even in Mawlāy al-Ḥasan's time. at-Tūzānī, *al-Umanā'*, p. 191.

7 Foreign intervention and domestic reforms

1 F.O., 830/2, 30 September 1859. A letter of allegiance (*bayʿa*) from the authorities is dated Ṣafar 1276/13 September 1859. *al-Wathā'iq*, 2 (1976), 370–1.

2 M. H. Picciotto, *Jews of Morocco, Report* (London, 1861), p. 60.

3 A collective letter from London from these Swiri Jews is addressed to the recently established 'Morocco Relief Fund', set up to help the refugees and victims. *Jewish Chronicle*, 2 March 1860 (letter dated 20 February 1860).

4 *Jewish Chronicle*, 31 January 1860, Moses Abitbol to the Editor.

5 aṣ-Ṣiddīqī, *Īqāẓ*, p. 85.

6 *Jewish Chronicle*, 31 January 1860, Moses Abitbol to the Editor.

7 Picciotto, *Jews*, p. 60.

8 On the Spanish–Moroccan war and its consequences, see Edward Szymański, 'La guerre hispano-marocain 1859–1860: début de l'histoire du Maroc contemporain (essai de périodisation)', *Rocnik Orientalistyczny*, 29:2 (1965), 53–65; Ayache, *Etudes*, pp. 97–109; Laroui, *Les Origines*, pp. 278–82; Rollman, 'The "New Order"', pp. 598–617.

9 These events are recorded in a number of sources: Dā'ūd, *Tārīkh*, vol. v, pp. 21–2, 35–6, 43; ʿAbd ar-Raḥmān Ibn Zaydān, *Itḥāf aʿlām an-nās bi jamāl akhbār ḥāḍirat Miknās* (5 vols. Rabat, 1929–33), vol. III, p. 447 (11 Rajab 1277/23 January 1861, Sultan to Bargāsh); aṣ-Ṣiddīqī, *Īqāẓ*, p. 85; F.O., 830/2, 16 September 1860, Elton to Hay; F.O., 830/2, 15 January 1861, Elton to Hay.

10 F.O., 99/109, Lambeth: 14 June 1861, M. Abitbol to John Russel.

11 The first 10 million came from the following sources: 5 from Fez, 2 from Essaouira, 1 from Muḥammad Bannīs who was in charge of finances, and 2 million from the English loan. Ibn Zaydān, *Itḥāf*, vol. III, p. 468.

12 *al-Wathā'iq*, 4 (1978), 223 (13 Ramaḍān 1278/14 March 1862, Sultan to Bargāsh). The Sultan authorized the Spanish to take half the duties in this letter.
13 On these events, see Miège, II, pp. 158, 373; Flournoy, *British Policy*, pp. 201–15; Szymański, 'La guerre', pp. 62–5; Ayache, *Etudes*, pp. 104–5. Texts of the loan are found in P.P., 1862, LXIV, pp. 453–73. The payment to the British was made via Tangier. Ibn Zaydān, *Itḥāf*, vol. III, p. 468.
14 B.L., Add. 39004, 13 November 1873, Hay to Layard.
15 A.E., C.C.C., Mogador 4, 8 April 1862, Ch. Destrées.
16 A.E., C.C.C., Mogador 4, 12 July 1862, Ch. Destrées.
17 See table 3.
18 Miège, II, pp. 560–1.
19 On the question of military, technical, and administrative reforms in Morocco, see Muḥammad al-Manūnī, *Maẓāhir yaqẓat al-Maghrib al-ḥadīth* (Rabat, 1973). On the reform of the military for this period, see Rollman, 'The "New Order"', pp. 620–9. For a comparative approach, see M. Brett, 'Modernisation in 19th Century North Africa', *The Maghreb Review*, 7:1–2 (1982), 16–22. On the Middle East, see Owen, *The Middle East*, pp. 57ff.
20 Amounting to a sum of 11,150,013.5 ūqiya (as opposed to 5.5 million in 1858–9). K.H., K^{295}, Dhū al-Ḥijja 1281/May 1865 to Dhū al-Ḥijja 1282/April 1866.
21 K.H., K^{33} and K^{43} (treasury registers from Marrakesh, listing some of these exchanges to pay the English).
22 K.H., K^{120}; D.A.R., Essaouira 4, 4 Rajab 1302/19 April 1885, Aḥmad al-Bannānī to Sultan; P.P., 1884–5, LXXVII, p. 662.
23 The first figure is from K.H., K^{120}, as calculated by at-Tūzānī, *al-Umanā'*, p. 107. The British consul also quotes a figure, but in pounds. P.P., 1884, LXXX, p. 101. This comes out at an exchange of 165.32 ūqiya to the pound. The subsequent figures are converted at this rate. P.P., 1884–5, LXXVII, p. 662; and 1886, LXVI, p. 289.
24 M. Nehlil, *Lettres chérifiennes* (Paris, 1915), doc. IX (30 Ramaḍān 1278/31 March 1862, Sultan to Muḥammad Idrīs al-Jarrārī); Ibn Zaydān, *Itḥāf*, vol. III, pp. 379–80 (Sultan to Bargāsh, same date). This measure is discussed in at-Tūzānī, *al-Umanā'*, pp. 36, 76, 261; and al-Manūnī, *Maẓāhir*, pp. 87–8. It has mistakenly been suggested that the development of the *amīn al-umanā'* and the port reforms took place during the reign of Maylāy al-Ḥasan. Mohamed Lahbabi, *Le gouvernement marocain à l'aube de XXe siècle* (Rabat, 1958), p. 157.
25 aṣ-Ṣiddīqī, *Īqāẓ*, pp. 79–81; F.O., 830/2, 23 June 1859 and 7 July 1859, Elton to Reade.
26 aṣ-Ṣiddīqī, *Īqāẓ*, p. 83.
27 A.E., C.C.C., Mogador 4, 27 December 1862, Destrées. He was perhaps a *bāshā* in the garrison of Essaouira, as a *dahir* to Essaouira's army announcing his appointment seems to suggest. aṣ-Ṣiddīqī, *Īqāẓ*, pp. 86–7.
28 K.H., K^{295}, Dhū al-Ḥijja 1281/April–May 1865.

29 F.O., 631/5, 5 August 1873, Beaumier (as acting British consular agent) to Hay. al-ʿAṭṭār is referred to as a Spanish protégé in this dispatch.

30 D.A.R., Essaouira 1, 28 Ṣafar 1282/23 July 1865, Aqaṣbī to Bannīs.

31 D.A.R., Essaouira 1, 6 Ramaḍān 1282/23 January 1866, Aqāsbī, ʿUmar b. ʿAmr al-Awsā, ʿAbd ar-Raḥmān b. al-Ḥasan, Muḥammad Amillāḥ (the four *umanāʾ*) to Bannīs.

32 K.H., K[295]. Expenditures are recorded each month in this register kept by Aqaṣbī. The responsibilities of the *umanāʾ* were precisely detailed by the Sultan, as an instruction book from that period shows. al-Manūnī, pp. 306–16.

33 C.A., 16 Ṣafar 1282/10 July 1865.

34 C.A., 4 Dhū al-Ḥijja 1282/20 April 1866. He was buried in the Darqāwa *zāwiya* in town. D.A.R., Essaouira 1, 18 Rabīʿ I 1283/31 July 1866, ʿAbd ar-Raḥmān b. al-Ḥasan, Muḥammad b. ʿAbdallāh, and Amillāḥ to Bannīs.

35 D.A.R., Essaouira 1, 18 Ṣafar 1284/21 June 1867, Beaumier to Bannīs.

36 C.A., 13 Jumādā II 1286/25 September 1869.

37 D.A.R., Essaouira 1, 20 Rabīʿ I 1282/13 August 1865. Some of the manifests are preserved in the archives for 1865–6. K.H., *qawāʾim ḥisābiyya*.

38 D.A.R., Essaouira 1, 6 Rabīʿ III 1282/29 August 1865, Sultan to Bargāsh.

39 D.A.R., Essaouira 1, 10 Shawwāl 1282/26 February 1866, Aqaṣbī, ʿUmar b. ʿAmr to Bannīs.

40 Corcos imported *kanānīsh* for the *makhzan*. C.A., 16 Shawwāl 1285/30 January 1869, Mūsā b. Aḥmad to Abraham and Jacob Corcos, and 23 Shaʿbān 1286/28 November 1869, Mūsā b. Aḥmad to Abraham Corcos. After the port reforms, account books became more detailed, listing duties with the names of shippers, revenues, expenditures, etc. K.H., K[46], and K[295].

41 D.A.R., Essaouira 2, 28 Dhū al-Ḥijja 1287/21 March 1871, Faraj and Aqaṣbī to Bannīs.

42 D.A.R., Essaouira 2, 3 Rabīʿ I 1288/23 May 1871, Faraj and Aqaṣbī to Bannīs.

43 D.A.R., Essaouira 3, 26 Ṣafar 1290/25 April 1873, ʿAbd al-Karīm Ibn Zākūr and Muḥammad al-Ḥisānī to Bannīs.

44 In 1879, a meat tax was established to pay for sanitary measures. The letter refers to the *umanāʾ al-mustafād* who were responsible for the collection of the tax. These *umanāʾ* were under the control of the *muḥtasib*. D.A.R., ʿAmāra dos., 2 Jumādā I 1296/24 April 1879.

45 at-Tūzānī makes no mention of this development, but only indicates that in most towns there was one *amin al-mustafādāt*, sometimes two (*al-Umanāʾ*, p. 114). I found no reference to the actual appointment of the *amīn al-mustafādāt* of Essaouira, who was al-Ḥājj Muḥammad b. Aḥmad Zunaybīr. But the official uses this title in a letter to Abraham Corcos. N.A., R.G. 84, 8 Shawwāl 1298/2 October 1881. The fact that he defines himself with this title – unusual in these kinds of letters – suggests that he was newly appointed to the town. Reference to the house is made in a letter of the new *amīn*, Muḥammad al-Ḥasnāwī. He complains of the *qāʾid* delaying the

handing over of the house held by his predecessor, Zunaybīr. D.A.R., ʿAmāra dos., 26 Dhū al-Qaʿda 1299 / 9 October 1882, Sultan to ʿAmāra.

46 al-Manūnī, *Maẓāhir*, p. 306.

47 D.A.R., Essaouira 1, 26 Ramaḍān 1282 / 12 February 1866, Aqaṣbī and ʿUmar b. ʿAmr to Bannīs.

48 D.A.R., Essaouira 1, 18 Shawwāl 1287 / 5 March 1866, Aqaṣbī and ʿUmar b. ʿAmr to Bannīs; K.H., 16 Dhū al-Qaʿda 1282 / 2 April 1866, Sultan to Khalīfa al-Ḥasan.

49 A.E., C.C.C., Mogador 6, 20 April 1879, Hélouis. at-Tūzānī, quoting an-Nāsirī, cites Jumādā I 1296 / April 1879 as the date of his appointment (*al Umanā*ʾ, pp. 45–6).

50 K.H., 28 Ramaḍān 1301 / 22 July 1884, Muḥammad b. ʿAbd ar-Raḥmān Brīsha, Muḥammad b. Zākūr, ʿAbd ar-Raḥmān b. al-Ḥasan to Sultan.

51 Miège, IV, p. 133.

52 The salaries of the foreign *umanā*ʾ were 85.5 riyāl each, and the two locals' salaries were 46 each. By subtracting one local, I have calculated a monthly total salary of 217.5 riyāl. K.H., K[295]. The figure for 1884, 6,971.5 ūqiya divided by 32.5, equals approximately 214.5 riyāl. K.H., K[120].

53 Park, 'Administration', pp. 224–6, 264–6.

54 D.A.R., Essaouira 1, 3 Rabīʿ II 1282 / 26 August 1865, ʿAbd as-Salām as-Suwīsī to Bannīs.

55 D.A.R., Essaouira 1, 28 Rajab 1282 / 17 December 1865, Aqaṣbī and ʿUmar b. ʿAmr to Bannīs.

56 D.A.R., Essaouira 1, 6 Jumādā I 1282 / 27 September 1865, 'Alī b. Muḥammad at-Tanānī, 'Umar b. ʿAbd as-Salām aṣ-Ṣawīrī, Hammu b. Muḥammad aṣ-Ṣawīrī, al-Ḥasan b. [. . .], ʿAbd al Wāḥid Aqaṣbī, Ibn al-Ḥasan, Muḥammad Amillāḥ to Bannīs.

57 D.A.R., Essaouira 2, 15 Shawwāl 1287 / 2 March 1866, al-ʿAyāshī Bannīs, ʿAbd al-Khāliq Faraj to Bannīs; and 25 Shawwāl 1287 / 12 March 1866, ʿAbd ar-Raḥmān b. al-Ḥasan to Bannīs.

58 There are numerous sources on this affair. It is discussed by aṣ-Ṣiddīqī, *Īqāẓ*, p. 103. The British merchant Grace had some claims against Amillāḥ who was the guarantor for his brother; the latter had some dealings with Grace and went bankrupt. D.A.R., Essaouira 2, 3 Rabīʿ I 1288 / 12 February 1871, Faraj and Aqaṣbī to Bannīs; F.O., 631 / 5, 4 September 1872. On the selling of the estate of Amillāh: D.A.R. Essaouira 9 (several undated letters from the *umanā*ʾ); D.A.R., Essaouira 2, 23 Ramaḍān 1288 / 6 December 1871, Faraj and Aqaṣbī to Bannīs; and 11 Dhū al-Qaʾda / 22 January 1872. Property and expenses are listed in two notarized documents: 10 and 14 Dhū al-Hijja 1288 / 20 and 24 February 1872. Corcos reported on the matter: C.A., 17 Muḥarram 1289 / 27 March 1872, Mūsā b. Aḥmad to Abraham Corcos. On the sale of Amillāḥ's property to al-Ḥanshāwī and money collected generally from his property: D.A.R., Essaouira 2, 18 Ramaḍān 1289 / 19 November 1872, and 13 Shawwāl 1289 / 14 December 1872, Muḥammad b. al-ʿArabī al-Qabbāj to Bannīs.

59 D.A.R., ʿAmāra dos., 21 Jumādā II 1292 / 25 July 1875, Sultan to ʿAmāra.

The two foreign *amīns* appointed in 1875 were Aḥmad at-Tāzī and al-ʿArabī Faraj ar-Ribāṭī (the latter had already served a term in 1871–2).

60 D.A.R., ʿAmāra dos., 11 Jumādā II 1291 /26 July 1874, Sultan to ʿAmāra.

61 Mawlāy al-Ḥasan himself was more directly involved in administration than his predecessor. Most letters from the *umanāʾ* in the archives for this period are addressed directly to the Sultan, rather than to the *amīn al-umanāʾ* as in the preceding period.

62 D.A.R., ʿAmāra dos., 24 Jumādā I 1294 /6 June 1877, Sultan to ʿAmāra (regarding the confiscation of some frankincense).

63 Manuel Pablo Castellanos, *Descripción histórica de Marruecos y breve reseña de sus dinastías* (Santiago de Compostela, 1878), p. 118. The *umanāʾ* complained after three years that nothing had been accomplished. D.A.R., Essaouira 1, 20 Jumādā I 1282 /11 October 1865, Aqaṣbī, ʿUmar b. ʿAmr to Bannīs. Craig blamed the authorities. James Craig, 'Un aperçu de Maroc', *B.S.G.*, 5e sér., 19 (1870), 201. He received 9,750 ūqiya a month (equal to about £60), while his interpreter received 633.75 uqiya (about £4). K.H., K295.

64 Beaumier, 'Mogador', pp. 116–18.

65 Miège, IV, p. 132 and n; Lahbabi, *Le gouvernement*, pp. 189–90.

66 Cf. Burke, *Prelude to Protectorate in Morocco*, pp. 34–6, 39–40.

67 The Sous had abundant copper ore and historically was a source for copper coins. Afāʾ, '*Masʾalat*', pp. 346–51.

68 Thomas K. Park, 'Inflation and Economic Policy in 19th Century Morocco: The Compromise Solution', *The Maghreb Review*, 10:2–3 (1985), 52.

69 *Ibid.*, p. 51.

70 In the books of the Macnin house of commerce, the Spanish hard dollar (with the $ sign), is used for all accounts. S.L., Judeo-Arabic account books of the Macnin house of commerce, 1815–16.

71 El Mansour, 'Political and Social Developments', pp. 132–7.

72 Robert Jannasch, *Die deutsch Handelsexpedition 1886* (Berlin, 1887), p. 79.

73 Cf. Pascon, *La Maison*, p. 63.

74 The equivalences in European currency suggests that the former weighed 2.28 grams and the latter, 1.30. In reality, the intrinsic value varied considerably. *Ibid.*

75 Miège, II, pp. 220–2, III, pp. 99–106.

76 K.H., 8 Ṣafar 1262 /5 February 1845, Sultan to ʿAbd al-Qādir Ashʿāsh.

77 K.H., 1 Rabīʿ I 1264 /7 March 1848, Sultan to Ashʿāsh.

78 K.H., 9 Shaʿbān 1264 /11 July 1848 and 4 Dhū al-Ḥijja 1264 /1 November 1848, Sultan to Ashʿāsh.

79 aṣ-Ṣiddīqī, *Īqāẓ*, p. 71.

80 A.E., C.C.C., Mogador 3, 18 June 1849, 29 August 1849, De Vallet.

81 K.H., mid-Jumādā II 1266 /April 1850, Sultan to Būsilhām b. ʿAlī; A.E., C.C.C., Mogador 3, 22 May 1850, Flory.

82 F.O., 830 /1, 21 January 1852, Grace.

83 F.O., 830 /2, 20 October 1857.

84 F.O., 99 /139, Tangier: 27 September 1869 in Miège, *Doc.*, pp. 123–8.

85 *Ibid.*
86 These monetary issues have been clarified by Park, 'Administration', pp. 104ff.
87 Contrary to Ayache's suggestion that the 5f became the reference currency, Park has shown how the conversion to the *bilyūn* system underlines that the Spanish dollar was still the main reference currency. *Ibid.*, pp. 116–24.
88 For example, 80,000 riyāl were sent in three ships to al-Malīḥ in 1866. D.A.R., Essaouira 1, 11 Shaʿbān 1283/19 December 1866, Muḥammad b. ʿAbdallāh and al-ʿArabī ash-Sharrāṭ to Bannīs. Earlier that year, 590 French riyāl were sent to al-Malīḥ, care of Abraham Corcos. C.A., 20 Ramaḍān 1282/6 February 1866, ʿAbd an-Nabī Marrūr to Abraham Corcos. 10,000 riyāl were sent to Ibn ʿAzūz in 1871 after being exchanged in Marrakesh. D.A.R., Essaouira 2, 22 Rabīʿ I 1288/11 June 1872, Aqaṣbī and Faraj to Bannīs; another 5,000 were sent shortly thereafter: 13 Jumādā I 1288/31 July 1871.
89 Cf. Park, 'Administration', pp. 107–9.
90 Tazlaght refers to a place in the Sous about 40 miles from Tafraoute where the copper ore was mined. Afā', '*Mas'alat*' p. 348.
91 C.A., 22 Shaʿbān 1279/12 February 1863, *dahir* addressed to the *tujjār* of Essaouira.
92 Miège, III, p. 128.
93 C.A., 20 Dhū al-Qaʿda 1280/3 May 1864.
94 F.O., 631/3, 30 January 1864, Elton to Hay; 30 November 1864 and 3 January 1865, Carstensen to Hay.
95 C.A., 24 Rabīʿ I 1283/6 August 1866, Bū ʿAshrīn to Abraham Corcos; K.H., K[295], 24 Rabīʿ I 1283/6 August 1866, copy of a letter from the Sultan to Aqaṣbī and ʿUmar b. ʿAmr.
96 Cf. Miège, III, pp. 146–7.
97 A.N., F[12] 6564, Casablanca: December 1869.
98 F.O., 631/3, 3 February 1868, trade report for 1867, and 3 September 1867, Carstensen to Hay.
99 D.A.R., Essaouira 2, 17 Shaʿbān 1285, ʿAbd al-Ḥafīẓ Barrāda and Muḥammad b. ʿAbdallāh to Bannīs. E.g., 520 ūqiya were sent from the Marrakesh treasury to Essaouira on 29 Ramaḍān 1284/24 January 1868. K.H., K[48].
100 Hay in Miège, *Doc.*, p. 127.
101 D.A.R., Essaouira 2, 28 Shawwāl 1285/11 February 1869, Muḥammad Ibn Mūsā and ʿAbd al-Qādir Ghannām to Bannīs. See also Ayache, *Etudes*, p. 133.
102 Hay agreed with the Moroccan government on this measure. Hay in Miège, *Doc.*, pp. 126–8.
103 D.A.R., Essaouira 3 Dhū al-Qaʿda 1285/25 February 1869, Barrāda and Muḥammad b. ʿAbdallāh to Bannīs; Miège, III, pp. 139–43.
104 Ibn Zaydān, *Itḥāf*, vol. III, pp. 481–3; an-Nāṣirī, *Kitāb al-istiqṣā'*, vol. IX, pp. 120–1. It has been suggested that the measure implied the replacement as the base standard of the intrinsically larger dirham of 2.9 grams (as had existed

in the eighteenth century) for one of 0.7 grams. Ayache, *Etudes*, pp. 135–7. This was not the case. The essence of the reform was the establishment of a new accounting dirham at a 10 unit system, corresponding to the ūqiya. Furthermore, the dirham value would not be allowed to float. Without distinguishing that the dirham of account was established alongide the newly minted coints, the reform, as Ayache understands it, would have been totally irrational. On the dirham, cf. Park, 'Administration', pp. 152–4. This system is explained in a report: A.N., F[12] 6564, Casablanca.

105 D.A.R., Essaouira 2, 9 Ṣafar 1287/11 May 1870, al-Ayāshī Bannīs to Bannīs.

106 D.A.R., Essaouira 9, two undated letters (their contents place them about Jumādā I 1287/July–August 1870; they appear to be the notes of Bannīs sent to the Sultan).

107 D.A.R., Essaouira 2, 9 Ṣafar 1287/11 May 1870, al-Ayāshī Bannīs to Bannīs; see also 25 Ṣafar 1287/27 May 1870, Bannīs and Faraj to Bannīs.

108 Park, 'Inflation', pp. 52–3; and Park, 'Administration', pp. 128, 152–3.

109 D.A.R., Essaouira 2, 6 Dhū al-Qaʿda 1289/5 January 1873, Muṣṭafā Gassūs and Muḥammad b. al-ʿArabī al-Qabbāj to Bannīs. They claim that the *umanāʾ* before them had brought a new scale that was very accurate; an *ʿadl* from Marrakesh was appointed.

110 D.A.R., Essaouira 2, 25 Ṣafar 1287/27 May 1870, al-ʿAyāshī Bannīs and Faraj to Bannīs.

111 D.A.R., Essaouira 2, 26 Jumādā I 1287/24 August 1870; D.A.R., Essaouira 9, n.d. (circa Jumādā I 1287/August 1870).

112 al-Manūnī, *Maẓāhir*, pp. 311–12.

113 N.A., R.G. 84, 12 Ṣafar 1287/14 May 1870, *umanāʾ* of Essaouira to Abraham Corcos (to begin retroactively on 1 Muḥarram/3 April).

114 aṣ-Ṣiddīqī, *Īqāẓ*, p. 97 (Rabīʾ II 1291/May–June 1874, Sultan to ʿAmāra).

115 K.H., K[93].

116 The *muḥtasib* reported that protégés were refusing to pay rents. D.A.R., ʿAmāra dos., 25 Dhū al-Qaʾda 1297/29 October 1880, Sultan to ʿAmāra. On Corcos and Ohana: N.A., R.G. 84, 17 Shaʿbān 1302/1 June 1885, ad-Dawbilālī and Muḥammad b. ʿAbd ar-Raḥmān Brīsha to Meyer Corcos; and 1 Ramaḍān 1302/14 June 1885, Corcos to Dawbilālī and Brīsha.

117 D.A.R., ʿAmāra dos., 10 Ṣafar 1295/13 February 1878, Sultan to ʿAmāra.

118 K.H., K[122] (rents here are calculated in the dirham accounting system at 4 ūqiya the dirham; I have translated this into the ūqiya system used for the other accounts).

119 N.A., R.G. 84, 28 Rajab 1303/2 May 1886 and 26 Ramaḍān 1303/28 June 1886, ad-Dawbilālī to Meyer Corcos; 28 Rajab 1303/2 May 1886, 25 Ramaḍān 1303/27 June 1886, and 29 Ramaḍān 1393/1 July 1886, Corcos to ad-Dawbilālī.

120 D.A.R., Essaouira 2, 10 Jumādā I 1288/28 July 1871, petition of Būhillāl, al-Warzāzī, Dinar (Ohana), Judah (Levy-Yuly), Salām ʿAmar (Ben Messas), to Bannīs.

121 Leared, *Marocco*, p. 344.

122 D.A.R., Essaouira 2, 12 Dhū al-Qaʿda 1288 /23 January 1872, al-Qabbāj to Bannīs.
123 an-Nāṣirī, *Kitāb al-istiqṣā*ʾ, vol. IX, p. 173.
124 *Ibid.*
125 P.P., 1878, LXXIV, p. 21; D.A.R., ʿAmāra dos., 29 Ṣafar 1295 /4 March 1878, Mūsā b. Aḥmad to ʿAmāra.
126 F.O., 631 /6, 25 March 1878, R. Hay to British merchants of Mogador. Cf. Miège, III, p. 433. I have found no specific reference to the annulment of the regulation, but since complaints appear to have ceased after the summer of 1878, we can assume that the order was abandoned.
127 Miège, III, pp. 435–6. On the rise of prices and the famine, see as-Sūsī, *al-Maʿsūl*, vol. X, pp. 11–12; an-Nāṣirī, *Kitāb al-istiqṣā*ʾ, vol. IX, p. 164.
128 P.P., 1884, LXXX, p. 101.
129 K.H., Jumādā II 1301 /March–April 1884, Idrīs b. Muḥammad Bannīs, al-Arabī Faraj, and ʿAbd ar-Raḥmān b. al-Ḥasan to Sultan.
130 P.P., 1884–5, LXXVII, p. 663.
131 On the mint of the Ḥasanī riyāl in Europe, see Afāʾ, '*Masʾalat*', pp. 28–46.
132 al-Manūnī, *Maẓāhir*, pp. 85–6.
133 Ibn al-Ḥājj, *ad-Durar*, vol. II, (18 Ṣafar 1301 /19 December 1883, Sultan to ʿAbdallāh b. Aḥmad).
134 K.H., 21 Rabīʿ I 1301 /21 January 1884.
135 D.A.R., Essaouira 4, 12 Shaʿbān 1301 /7 June 1884, Ibn Zākūr, Ibn al-Ḥasan, and Brīsha to Muḥammad b. al-ʿArabī b. al-Mukhtār.
136 P.P., 1886, LXVI, p. 281; *dahir* dated 17 Rabīʿ II 1302 /6 December 1884, in Ibn al-Ḥājj, *ad-Durar*, vol. II. The *umanā*ʾ of grain in the Shiadma reported receiving the order. K.H., 8 Shaʿbān 1302 /23 May 1885.
137 The depreciation of the Spanish riyāl may have brought down the Ḥasanī. Park, 'Administration', p. 134. One view suggests that the demise of the Moroccan riyāl was caused by the French, who did not mint a coin of equal value to the 5**f**. al-Manūnī, *Maẓāhir*, pp. 86–7.
138 Park, 'Administration', p. 161.
139 Park, 'Inflation', p. 55.
140 See Laroui, *Les origines*, pp. 200–2; an-Nāṣirī, *Kitāb al-istiqṣā*ʾ, vol. IX, p. 101.
141 F.O., 830 /2, 10 December 1860, Elton to Hay.
142 The variation from month to month in the register for this period suggests a direct administration rather than a tax farm. K.H., K^{46}, Rabīʿ II 1279 /26 September 1862–19 May 1863.
143 F.O., 830 /2, 24 March 1861. There is only one revenue referred to as '*kunṭrada*' in K.H., K^{46}. This has to be the *ṭarqa* since the regular instalments for the eight months of the register come out to about 80,000 ūqiya by the end of the year, corresponding to the consular report.
144 D.A.R., Essaouira 1 (summary of a register book).
145 K.H., K^{46}.
146 See Miège, *Doc.*, pp. 234–7, 239.
147 Ayache, *Etudes*, p. 121.

148 K.H., 2 Sha'bān 1281 /31 December 1864, Sultan to Mawlāy al-Ḥasan.
149 C.A., 14 Jumādā I 1281 /15 October 1864.
150 K.H., 18 Rabī' II 1283 /30 August 1866.
151 K.H., 12 Shawwāl 1283 /17 February 1867.
152 C.A., 22 Rabī' I 1285 /13 August 1868. Bū 'Ashrīn to Abraham Corcos. I have not found a list of the 11 merchants. The contract began 1 Ṣafar 1285 /24 May. 1868. D.A.R., Essaouira 2, 1 Ṣafar 1285 /May 1868 to mid-Ramaḍān 1288 /November 1871 (accounts of the gate taxes).
153 C.A., 22 Ṣafar 1287 /24 May 1870, Mūsā b. Aḥmad to Abraham Corcos.
154 C.A., 25 Muḥarram 1285 /18 May 1868; and 1 Ṣafar 1285 /24 May 1868.
155 C.A., 22 Rabī' II 1285 /12 August 1868.
156 C.A., 23 Rabī' II 1285 /13 August 1868.
157 C.A., 6 Sha'bān 1285 /22 November 1868, Bū 'Ashrīn to Abraham Corcos.
158 D.A.R., Essaouira 2, 1 Ṣafar 1285 /May 1868 to mid-Ramaḍān 1288 /November 1871.
159 K.H., Shawwāl 1288 /10 January 1872, Sultan to Khalīfa al-Ḥasan.
160 D.A.R., Essaouira 2, 12 Dhū al-Qa'da 1288 /23 January 1872, Faraj and Aqaṣbī to Bannīs.
161 C.A., 7 Dhū al-Ḥijja 1288 /17 February 1872, Bū 'Ashrīn to the Jewish tax farmers of Essaouira (*jama'at ahl adh-dhimmat al-mushtariyyīn kunṭradāt abwāb aṣ-Ṣawīra*).
162 C.A., 11 Rabī' II 1289 /18 June 1872, Mūsā b. Aḥmad to tax-farmers.
163 Mohamed Kenbib, 'Les protections étrangères au Maroc aux XIXème siècle–début du XXème', thèse de 3ème cycle (Paris, 1980).
164 D.A.R., Essaouira 3, 11 Sha'bān 1290 /4 October 1873, Sultan to 'Amāra.
165 F.O., 631 /5, 27 February 1874, Beaumier (as acting British consular agent) to Hay.
166 D.A.R., 'Amāra dos., 7 Dhū al-Ḥijja 1290 /26 January 1874, Sultan to 'Amāra.
167 C.A., 24 Dhū al-Ḥijja 1290 /12 February 1874.
168 F.O., 631 /5, 1 April 1874, Beaumier to Hay.
169 K.H., 16 Jumādā I 1291 /1 July 1874, Sultan to 'Uthmān.
170 K.H., 10 Rajab 1291 /23 August 1874, Muḥammad Gannūn and aṭ-Ṭayyib al-Gharbī to Sultan.
171 In both cases, there was a period of a month and a half between the time when the Sultan agreed on the new contract and the actual transfer of administration to the new company.
172 Were the tax farmers able to recuperate the 113,333 mithqāl a year (i.e., one-third of 340,000) contract? We do not have data for the years that the gates were farmed out in the 1870s. Some comparisons might be made with a period when the gates were administered directly by the *makhzan*. In 1301 /1883–4, a year for which we have records, the revenue from the gates amounted to 70,145 mithqāl, a much lower amount than that paid by the tax-farmers. It should be noted that foreign trade in 1884 was significantly lower than the average for 1874–7. Presumably, therefore, gate taxes would have been much lower in 1884. In 1302 /1884–5, the gates amounted to about

87,890 mithqāl – a marginal increase in light of the increase in trade. K.H., K[122] and K[131]; P.P., 1878, LXXIV, p. 18 (for the trade of 1874–7); and P.P., 1884–5, LXVII, p. 656.

173 N.A., R.G. 84, 30 March 1874, A. Corcos to Mathews.

174 F.O., 631/5, 1 April 1874, Beaumier to Hay.

175 F.O., 631/5, 21 May 1874, 25 July 1874, and 8 August 1874, Beaumier to Hay. Statistics on goat skin exports are found in Miège, *Doc.*, pp. 232–3.

176 D.A.R., ʿAmāra dos., 1 Jumādā II 1292/5 July 1875.

177 D.A.R., Essaouira 3, 28 Rajab 1292/30 August 1875, and 20 Dhū al-Qaʿda 1292/18 December 1875, Sultan to ʿAmāra (and reply appended at bottom).

178 Kenbib, 'Les protections', pp. 185–6.

179 The concession had formerly been held by ʿAbd al-Majīd al-Ḥarīshī, with a partner, ʿAbd al-Majīd as-Saqqāt. The transfer to ʿAkkan Corcos was further complicated by the disclosure that al-Ḥarīshī in fact no longer held the concession; rather, it was in the hands of a certain ʿAmūr who was already paying the one-third supplement. D.A.R., Essaouira 2, 18 Shawwāl 1285/11 February 1869, and 14 Dhū al-Ḥijja 1285/28 March 1869, ʿAbd al-Ḥafiẓ Barrāda, Muḥammad b. ʿAbdallāh to Bannīs. al-Ḥarīshī was one of the *tujjār* in Essaouira, and was involved in the construction of the new houses and shops at Bāb al-Mellah in 1865. D.A.R., Essaouira 1, 20 Rabī I 1282/13 August 1865, ʿAbd al-Wāḥid Aqaṣbī.

180 The documentation is too scanty to trace the exact history of the tax-farmers. A 1301/1883–4 register lists some debts owed by the two companies of tax-farmers for their monopolies, but does not specify the dates nor precisely how much was paid off. K.H., K[120].

181 In this part of the register, the date is not clearly marked. In other parts in the register, 1292/1875–6 is given for some of the cities listed. However, the listing of properties in Essaouira are almost identical to K[93], which dates from 1296–7/1878–80. Another indicator is that the exchange rate of the riyāl is 62 ūqiya in the register, which corresponds to the exchange in 1878.

182 K.H., K[295], May 1865–April 1866. A total of 5,575,066.75 ūqiya profit came from customs, and 1,123,036.7 from other sources. A sizeable part of the other revenues was the merchants reimbursing the *makhzan* on their loans.

183 Miège, III, pp. 288–90; Leland L. Bowie, 'The Protégé System in Morocco, 1880–1904', Ph.D. thesis (Michigan, 1970), pp. 63–7; Kenbib, 'Les protections', pp. 189–93; at-Tūzānī, *al-Umanā'*, pp. 127–8.

184 P.P., 1882, LXXXI, 30 March 1881, p. 45.

185 Ayache, *Etudes*, pp. 118–21.

186 an-Nāṣirī, *Kitāb al- istiqṣā'*, vol. IX, p. 179.

187 at-Tūzānī, *al-Umanā'*, pp. 128–9. The *dahir* was sent to the *amīn al-mustafādāt* of Essaouira. aṣ-Ṣiddīqī, *Īqāẓ*, pp. 123–4. It arrived on 7 Rabīʿ I 1303/14 December 1885. This is recorded in the daily tax ledger of Essaouira. K[131].

8 The struggle for the southwest

1 A.E., C.C.C., Mogador 1, 17 May 1841, Beuscher. Bayrūk visited Essaouira in 1828. F.O., 52/3, 30 June 1829, Chaillet.

2 He was subsequently killed in the Hamad Draʿ, but his somewhat cryptic journal was published posthumously. Davidson, *Notes*. Numerous letters on his mission are found in F.O., 52/41–5. An interesting French account of his death by Delaporte is found in A.N., Aix-en-Provence, F[80] 1589–A.

3 Paul Marty, 'Une tentative de pénétration pacifique dans le sud marocain en 1839', *Revue de l'Histoire des Colonies Françaises*, 9:2 (1921), 101–16. Details are found in the dispatches of Delaporte to the ministry, in A.E., C.C.C., Mogador 1.

4 This event is reported in a number of sources: F.O., 99/25, Gibraltar: 9 April 1845, General R. W. Wilson to Hay; F.O., 99/29, Gibraltar: 25 April 1845, Wilson to Lord Stanley; F.O., 99/26, 30 April 1845 (extract); *al-Wathāʾiq*, 2 (1976), 11 (10 Jumādā II 1261/16 June 1845, Muḥammad b. Idrīs to Būsilhām b. ʿAlī); B.D., 29 Dhū al-Qaʿda 1261/21 November 1845, Muḥammad b. ʿAbd ar-Raḥmān to Ḥusayn Ū Hāshim.

5 N.A., T61/6, 29 August 1848, Thomas N. Carr to the president.

6 M.C.C., M8/2/5, 20 November 1856.

7 Beaumier later writes that Bayrūk was given three quarters duties on ostrich feather exports in 1856. Bayrūk went to Marrakesh to conclude this agreement, and passed through Essaouira to establish a commercial house at the port. He died in 1859. A.E., C.C.C., Mogador 4, 20 May 1866, Beaumier.

8 F.O., 830/1, 21 August 1848, Grace to Hay; A.E., C.C.C., Mogador 3, 11 December 1848.

9 B.D., 8 Rabīʿ II 1270/8 January 1852.

10 A.N., BB[4] 675 (Marine), 31 July 1853, Capt. of vessel 'Maisonneuve' at Cadix; A.E., C.C.C., Mogador 3, 28 May 1853, Senenza. No trace of negotiations between Altaras and Ḥusayn are found in the archives of Iligh, which Pascon believed cast doubt on the whole episode (personal communication).

11 Sulphur sold to Ḥusayn is listed in K.H., K[42], totalled up in 1279/1862–3. On Ḥusayn's house, see chap. 3, note 92.

12 Ross E. Dunn, *Resistance*, pp. 110–11.

13 The houses are listed in K.H., K[93].

14 According to the French consul, the residents of Essaouira preferred the powerful *qāʾid* of Haha, ʿAbdallāh Ū Bīhī, as governor, rather than aṭ-Ṭarrīs of Tetuan. A.E., C.C.C., Mogador 2, 31 May 1842, Beuscher.

15 L. Justinard, 'Notes d'histoire et de littérature berbères: les Haha et les gens du Sous', *Hespéris*, 8 (1928), 333–56.

16 Montagne, *Les Berbères et le Makhzen*, pp. 108–9.

17 A.E., C.C.C., Mogador 2, 31 May 1842, Beuscher; and 1 December 1843,

Hélouis-Jorelle. According to aṣ-Ṣiddīqī (*Īqāẓ*, p. 90), he was appointed on the death of his father.

18 Some reports accused Ū Bīhī of letting in the marauders. F.O., 99/29, 15 October 1845, Dupuis.

19 A.E., Maroc, M.D. 4, 11 February 1847, Soulange-Bodin.

20 A.E., C.C.C., Mogador 3, 12 November 1848, Beaumier.

21 A.E., C.C.C., Mogador 3, 1 May 1850, Flory.

22 In 1854, for example. K.H., 24 Jumādā I 1270/22 February 1854, ʿAbdallāh Ū Bīhī to Sultan.

23 A.E., C.C.C., Mogador 3, 10 December 1855, Tippel; aṣ-Ṣiddīqī, *Īqāẓ*, p. 90. These events are recounted in Justinard, 'Notes', p. 341.

24 Montagne, *Les Berbères et le Makhzen*, p. 380; J. Fuchs, *Evolution d'un grand commandement marocain: le caid Mtougi et le protectorat*, C.H.E.A.M., MS 2137, p. 5.

25 as-Sūsī, *al-Maʿsūl*, vol. XV, pp. 12–13 (Muḥarram 1285/April–May 1868, Muḥammad b. Aḥmad adh-Dhayb al-Wāzghī).

26 There is a tradition that the Sultan had ʿAbdallāh Ū Bīhī poisoned because of secret dealings with Ḥusayn Ū Hāshim of Tazarwalt. Montagne, *Les Berbères et la Makhzen*, pp. 110, 282–3; Justinard, 'Notes', pp. 344–5. The *qāʾid* owned much property in Essaouira when he died. aṣ-Ṣiddīqī, *Īqāẓ*, pp. 90–1. He was alleged to have made 60 pieces of property into *ḥubus* in town, ar-Ragrāgī, *ash-Shamūs*, p. 86n. His rural holdings were seized by the state after his death. In Jumādā II 1292/July–August 1875, his 11 orchards were collecting 3,093 ūqiya a month. K.H., K^{80}.

27 F.O., 174/72, 26 June 1863, Elton to Hay. The treaty with Spain in 1861 essentially recognized and reaffirmed the stipulations of the 1856 treaty with Britain. See ʿAbd al-Wahhāb Ibn Manṣūr, *Mushkilat al-ḥimāyāt al-qunṣilīya bi-l-Maghrib min nashʾatihā ilā muʾtamar Madrid Sanat 1880* (Rabat, 1977), p. 77.

28 For Egypt, cf. Landes, *Bankers*, p. 91. For Morocco, the question of 'protection' has received considerable scholarly attention, and several theses have dealt specifically with the subject. E. F. Cruickshank, *Morocco at the Parting of the Ways* (Philadelphia, 1935). This is largely superseded by Bowie, 'Protége System'; see also Bowie, 'An Aspect of Muslim–Jewish Relations in Late Nineteenth-Century Morocco: A European Diplomatic View', *International Journal of Middle Eastern Studies*, 7 (1976), 3–19. A good source book for documents has more recently been published by Ibn Manṣūr, *Mushkilat al-ḥimāyāt*. For a study of the effects on Moroccan society based on Moroccan sources, see Kenbib, 'les protections'.

29 B.G., Bargāsh, 27 Shawwāl 1279/17 April 1863, Sultan to Bargāsh. See also, B.G., Bargāsh, 25 Rabī I 1280/9 September 1863, Sultan to Bargāsh.

30 On this agreement and the consequences, see Miège, II, pp. 403–7; Bowie, 'Protégé System', pp. 12–13; Ibn Manṣur, *Mushkilat al-ḥimāyāt*, pp. 20–1; and Kenbib, 'Les protections', pp. 29–31.

31 Bargāsh wrote to the governors after the agreement outlining the categories

of protections and indicating that the protégés should be registered. K.H., n.d. (see note 32).

32 Lists of protégés sent to the *makhzan* are found in K.H., 17 Sha'bān 1282/5 January 1866; D.A.R., Essaouira Misc., 11 Ṣafar 1285/3 June 1868 (for Bolelli and Elmaleh, with the seal of their consulates); on Corcos in N.A., R.G. 84, 10 August 1863, and 18 January 1864, Corcos to McMath.

33 F.O., 631/3, 3 June 1868, Carstensen to Hay. There was a brief reaction to the proliferation of protégés between 1864 and 1868. Miège, III, p. 253.

34 Kenbib, 'Les protections', p. 20.

35 F.O., 99/150 (this document is found in Miège, *Doc.*, pp. 159–63; his reference mistakenly reads F.O., 99/250).

36 Kenbib, 'Les protections', p. 20.

37 C.A., 22 Jumādā I 1280/4 November 1863, copy of a sharifian letter, (copied on 10 Jumādā II 1280/22 November 1863).

38 Leared, *Marocco*, pp. 125, 132–3.

39 F.O., 631/3, 4 February 1867, 10 September 1868, and 6 September 1870, Carstensen to Hay; F.O., 631/5, 6 March 1871, Carstensen to Hay.

40 *al-Wathā'iq*, 4 (1978), 254–5 (21 Dhū al-Qa'da 1279/10 May 1863).

41 A.E., Maroc, M.D. 4, March 1867. Cf. Kenbib, 'Les protections', p. 183.

42 *al-Wathā'iq*, 4 (1978), 352–3 (22 Ramaḍān 1283/28 January 1867).

43 Miège, II, p. 493.

44 F.O., 99/117, Tangier: 13 December 1869.

45 Maxime Rodinson, *Islam and Capitalism* (London, 1974), pp. 35–45.

46 F.O., 99/130, Tangier: 13 December 1869, Hay; and F.O., 99/142, Tangier: 15 February 1870, Hay. On the many problems related to applying Muslim law to protégés during this period, see the *dahir*s in Ibn Zaydān, *al-'Izz*, vol. II, pp. 40–54. The dispute between al-Ḥājj Aḥmad b. Ibrāhīm al-Yaḥyāwī and Perry stands out in this period. aṣ-Ṣiddīqī, *Īqāẓ*, pp. 98–100; F.O., 631/3, 3 June 1868, and 10 March 1869, Carstensen to Hay.

47 N.A., R.G. 84, 9 May 1869, Corcos to McMath.

48 F.O., 99/117, Tangier: 13 December 1869, and F.O., 99/142, Tangier: 15 February 1870.

49 D.A.R., Essaouira I, 14 Ṣafar 1281/19 July 1864 (the reply is written on the same letter).

50 Kenbib, 'Les protections', pp. 239–40.

51 C.A., 10 Dhū al-Qa'da 1283/16 March 1867.

52 F.O., 631/3, 20 July 1865, Carstensen to Hay.

53 K.H., 26 Muḥarram 1283/10 June 1866, Sultan to Khalīfa al-Ḥasan.

54 F.O., 631/3, 23 March 1866.

55 Ibn Zaydān, *Itḥāf*, vol. III, pp. 388–90 (22 Ramaḍān 1284/17 January 1868, Sultan to Bargāsh).

56 Many cases could be cited: e.g., a man employed by Daniel Cohen took sanctuary at a shrine in Safi. F.O., 631/4, 14 July 1866, Carstensen to Elton.

57 In 1873, for example, the British consulate intervened on behalf of Grace who complained of the release of a certain al-Ḥusayn, who owed 570 riyāl.

D.A.R., ʿAmāra dos., 29 Ṣafar 1290/28 April 1873, Sultan to ʿAmāra.

58 The foreign merchants and protégés often petitioned their consulates on these matters. D.A.R., Essaouira Misc., 6 March 1871, Moses Corcos to Beaumier, 27 May 1871, Bonnet and Cie, Crespo to French Consulate. The *makhzan*'s help was also solicited by foreign merchants for the settlement of claims. In 1871, Curtis claimed that a Jewish agent of his in Marrakesh was robbed in the *mellah* there. K.H., 8 Rajab 1288/23 September 1871, Sultan to Ibrāhīm al-Agrāmī.

59 F.O., 99/139, Tangier: 13 December 1869.

60 aṣ-Ṣiddīqī, *Īqāẓ*, p. 104 (5 Dhū al-Qaʿda 1289/4 January 1873).

61 D.A.R., ʿAmāra dos., 1 Rabīʿ II 1290/29 May 1873, Sultan to Khalīfa al-Ḥasan. The governor reported the new practice to Abraham Corcos in the latter's capacity as American vice-consul. N.A., R.G. 84, 18 Rabīʿ I 1290/16 May 1873.

62 Referred to in Miège, II, p. 551.

63 Several cases unfold in the archives: the murder in the Shiadma of a Jewish traveller, daughter and son; the murder of a merchant from Iligh and two more from Tamillāḥt in Ida Ū Issarān en route to Essaouira. A.I.U., Maroc XXXIII E 571, 25 December 1874, Emile Altaras; F.O. 174/91, 1 March 1875, enclosing a memo. from the A.J.A. Compensation was still being sought in 1878. *A.J.A. Annual Report*, 7 (1878), pp. 85–7 (8 March 1878, Hay to Earl of Derby, 3 April 1878, Hay to Marquis of Salisbury, 29 March 1878, R. Hay to Hay). Anflūs described the general disturbances to the Sultan. K.H., 21 Ramaḍān 1291/1 November 1874.

64 A.I.U., France VIII D 42, 31 January 1875, Beaumier to Crémieux.

65 F.O., 631/5 31 August 1875, R. Hay to Hay. Considering the amount of traffic, the number of murders in these years was actually quite limited. Between 1865 and 1880 – and this includes the famine year of 1878–9 – the number of Jewish victims was reported at 41 in the area of Essaouira. *B.A.I.U.*m 1e sem. (1880), 32.

66 C.A., 26 Muḥarram 1295/30 January 1878, 12 Ṣafar 1295/15 February 1878, 29 Jumādā I 1295/31 May 1878, and 20 Jumādā II 1295/21 June 1878, Anflūs to Corcos; 5 Rabīʿ I 1295/10 March 1878, and 8 Jumādā II 1295/9 June 1878, Mūsā b. Aḥmad to Corcos; s.d., Mūsā b. Aḥmad to Corcos and Afriat.

67 C.A., 3 Ramaḍān 1295/31 August 1878.

68 Ibn Zaydān, *Itḥāf*, vol. II, pp. 380–1 (5 Dhū al-Qaʿda 1299/18 September 1882, Sultan to Bargāsh).

69 aṭ-Ṭālib ʿAbd al-Waḥid b. al-Mawwāz was sent to Agadir. D.A.R., ʿAmāra dos., 18 Jumādā II 1297/28 May 1880, Sultan to ʿAmāra; A.E., C.C.C., Mogador 6, 6 December 1880 and 17 January 1881, Mahon.

70 C.A., 13 Ramaḍān 1297/19 August 1880, Muḥammad b. al-ʿArabī to Corcos.

71 D.A.R., ʿAmāra dos., 1 Shawwāl 1297/6 September 1880, Anflūs to ʿAmāra.

72 Bowie, 'The Protégé System', pp. 161–5.

73 K.H., 23 Dhū al-Qaʿda 1301 / 14 September 1884, al-Ḥasan Būkhlāf al-Būzyād to Sultan, 4 Shawwāl 1302 / 18 July 1885, ʿAdī b. ʿAlī to Sultan.
74 D.A.R., Yahūd, 25 Ṣafar 1303 / 3 December 1885. Various other responses to the *dahir* are found in this series. The *dahir* sent to Qadi Ḥamīd Banānī is found in Aḥmad Ibn al-Ḥājj, *Durar al-jawhariyya fī madḥ al-khilāfat al-Ḥasaniyya*, vol. II, K.H., MS 512 (folio not enumerated).
75 Kenbib, 'Les protections', pp. 39–41.
76 Ibn Zaydān, *Itḥāf*, vol. II, p. 389 (25 Shawwāl 1298 / 20 September 1881, Sultan to Bargāsh).
77 The tax on foreigners and protégés was in fact never levied. In 1884, it was renounced definitely by the Sultan. at-Tūzānī, *al-Umanāʾ*, pp. 151–2; Miège, III, pp. 289–90.
78 aṣ-Ṣiddīqī, *Īqāẓ*, pp. 115–17 (6 Jumādā I 1300 / 15 March 1883, Sultan to Qāʾid al-ʿAyāshī ash-Shiyāẓmī).
79 For example, 'aṭ-Ṭālib Aḥmad b. ʿAbdallāh ad-Dimānī, residing in Shiadma, mentioned that he has property in Essaouira and Ḥarārtha in the Haha in partnership with someone who cultivates with him . . . he claims that what he owns [there] was sold [without his permission]'. D.A.R., ʿAmāra dos., 12 Jumādā I 1298 / 12 April 1881, ʿUthmān to ʿAmāra.
80 F.O., 174 / 105, 29 April 1881, Payton to Hay.
81 F.O., 99 / 208, 1 May 1883, Payton to Hay; 19 July 1883, memo. of Hay; A.E., C.P., Consuls 2, 22 May 1883, and 14 October 1884, Bertrand; 2 September 1884, Monteil. Controversy over Ratto's holdings continued for some years. Numerous Arabic documents, including title deeds, contracts of debts, and various other notarized documents, have been preserved. F.O., 631 / 11.
82 K.H., 4 Shawwāl 1302 / 17 July 1885, ʿAdī b. ʿAlī an-Naknāfī to Sultan.
83 F.O., 174 / 275, 14 January 1902, Broome to Madden.
84 K.H., 16 Jumādā I 1303 / 20 February 1886, Sheikh al-Makkī b. Ḥamīd ad-Dukkālī al-Hashtūkī, al-Ḥājj Aḥmad al-Būzdī, and Muḥammad b. ʿAbd al-ʿAzīz ash-Shiyāẓmī to Sultan.
85 K.H., 22 Jumādā I 1303 / 26 February 1886, Aḥmad b. Saʿīd al-ʿAisa.
86 N.A., R.G. 84, 16 June 1867 and 21 July 1867, Corcos to McMath. F.O., 174 / 290, 14 June 1867, Corcos to Carstensen; 25 June 1867, Mathews to White. F.O., 631 / 4, 14 June 1867, Carstensen to Corcos. F.O., 631 / 3, 23 August 1867, Carstensen to White.
87 A.E., C.C.C., Mogador 4, 12 June 1866. N.A., R.G. 84, 27 November 1867, 8 December 1867, 10 December 1867, 27 December 1867, 13 January 1868, 17 January 1868, and 16 February 1868, Corcos to McMath; and 9 March 1868, McMath to Corcos. A later source goes so far as to say that through Masʿūd's 'ill-gotten money', a war was started between the Haha and the Shiadma, and the Shiadma revolt was instigated. F.O., 99 / 158, R. Morris and Company (in a petition regarding the late Carstensen), 1873. F.O., 174 / 72, 13 April 1868, Carstensen to Hay. The *makhzan* also accused him of arming the rebels. Ibn Zaydān, *Itḥāf*, vol. III, pp. 386–8 (18 Rabīʿ II 1284 / 19 February 1869, Bū ʿAshrīn to Abraham Corcos).

88 Mas'ūd owed money to a number of merchants which was still being claimed in 1869. C.A., 26 Shawwāl 1285/9 February 1869, Bū 'Ashrīn to Abraham Corcos.
89 F.O., 631/3, 13 April 1868, Bū 'Ashrīn to Abraham Corcos.
90 C.A., 26 Ramaḍān 1284/21 January 1868, Bū 'Ashrīn to Abraham Corcos.
91 K.H., 18 Jumādā I 1284/9 September 1867, Sultan to al-Ḥasan.
92 F.O., 174/72, 18 September 1867, Carstensen to Hay.
93 N.A., R.G. 84, 3 June 1868, Corcos to McMath.
94 F.O., 631/3, 27 April 1868, Carstensen to Hay.
95 N.A., R.G. 84, 4 June 1868, Corcos to McMath.
96 The two head *amīn*s write about these dismissals. D.A.R., Essaouira 2, 10 Ṣafar 1285/2 June 1868, Muḥammad at-Tāzī, 'Abd al-Karīm at-Tāzī to Bannīs.
97 The new qadi, 'Allāl b. 'Abd aṣ-Ṣadiq, had been an '*adl* at customs. F.O., 830/2, 6 June 1860, Elton to Hay. He later becmae qadi of the Shiadma before his appointment to Essaouira. Aṣ-Ṣiddīqī, *Īqāẓ*, pp. 83–5; on 'Ali at-Tanānī, see pp. 88–9.
98 D.A.R., Essaouira 2, 13 Rajab 1285/31 October 1868, 'Umar b. 'Abd as-Salām aṣ-Ṣawīrī to Bannīs; 14 Rajab 1285/1 November 1868, 'Abd al-Karīm at-Tāzī to Bannīs.
99 F.O., 174/72, 1 September 1864, Elton to Hay.
100 The qadi initially had someone else appointed. The Sultan wrote back that at-Tanānī could be reinstated if there was no one else. The new '*adl* was causing problems with the merchants, allegedly devoting as much time for his own profits in the shops of the '*udūl* as at customs. D.A.R., Essaouira 3, 27 Ṣafar 1290/26 April 1873, 'Abd al-Karīm Ibn Zākūr, Muḥammad al-Ḥisānī to Bannīs.
101 aṣ-Ṣiddīqī, *Īqāẓ*, p. 107; D.A.R., Essaouira 3, 22 Rabī' II 1290/19 June 1873, 'Abd al-Karīm Ibn Zākūr and Muḥammad al-Ḥisānī to Bannīs.
102 aṣ-Ṣiddīqī, *Īqāẓ*, p. 87. Rather ironically, only a few months after his removal, Abraham Corcos petitioned the Palace to help the children of al-Mashāwrī, who had fallen into poverty. C.A., 23 Rajab 1285/19 November 1868, Bū 'Ashrīn to Corcos. A few months later, Corcos bought a piece of property from one of the sons of the *qā'id* (see chap. 3, note 55).
103 In 1874, for example, reports reached Essaouira that the *shaykh al-yahūd* of Iligh was oppressing the Jews there. Joseph Elmaleh asked the French consul to intervene 'due to the great affinity with the ruler (of Iligh)'. A.I.U., Maroc I C 3, 20 February 1874, Almaleh to Crémieux (in Hebrew).
104 B.D., 14 Dhū al-Ḥijja 1277/26 June 1861, 11 Rabī' I 1278/16 September 1861, Sultan to Ḥusayn Ū Hāshim. Some 199 loads were sent from Essaouira which he bought for 3,720 ūqiya. D.A.R., Essaouira 1, (summary of a register book).
105 F.O., 174/72, 14 May 1862, Elton to Hay; B.D., 13 Muḥarram 1279/11 July 1862, Sultan to Ḥusayn Ū Hāshim, and 2 Rabī' I 1279/28 August 1862, Sultan to tribe of Gazūla and Takna.
106 B.D., 2 Jumādā II 1284/12 November 1864. At this time Daḥmān Bayrūk

appears anxious to extend his business with Essaouira. B.A., 22 Jumādā I 1281, William Grace to Daḥmān.

107 A.E., C.C.C., Mogador 4, 20 May 1866 and 26 May 1866, Beaumier; Miège, *Doc.*, p. 117 (4 May 1869, Beaumier).

108 K.H., 13 Muḥarram 1283 /28 May 1866. Also reporting on a letter sent back by Ḥusayn Ū Hāshim through ʿAbdallāh Ū Bīhī. K.H., 25 Muḥarram 1283 /9 June 1866.

109 A.E., C.C.C., Mogador 4, 27 July 1886; B.D., 19 Rabīʿ I 1283 /1 August 1866.

110 B.D., 2 Jumādā II 1284 / 1 October 1867.

111 The following estimates have been made for the trans-Saharan trade through Essaouira: for 1851–5, f500,000; 1856–60, f650,000; 1861–5, f1,500,000 (or 20 per cent of Essaouira's exports); and 1865–74, f8–900,000. Miège, III, p. 97.

112 On rural taxes after the Spanish–Moroccan war, see Ayache, *Etudes*, pp. 112–18. This may have been the cause of the revolt in Raḥāmna soon after the new taxes were imposed. On the revolt, see an-Nāṣirī, *Kitāb al-isitqṣāʾ*, vol. IX, pp. 110–11; cf. Pascon, *Le Haouz*, vol. I, pp. 198–200.

113 F.O., 631 /3, 3 February 1868 (trade report for 1867) Carstensen to Hay; A.E., C.C.C., Mogador 4, 12 July 1868 and 9 August 1868, Hecquart; F.O., 174 /72, 3 February 1869, Carstensen to Hay.

114 C.A., 29 Rabīʿ II 1286 /7 August 1869. Here I have translated *fasād* as 'anarchy'. It is the most common word in the documents for dissidence, sedition, rebellion, corruption, etc. It denotes 'moral depravity', the authorities' view of any kind of activity countering government control. The word *fitna* is also sometimes used. I have not encountered the word *sība* in any documents.

115 K.H., 18 Muḥarram 1288 /9 April 1871, Sultan to al-Ḥasan, 19 Rabīʿ I 1288 /8 June 1871, al-Ḥasan to Muḥammad al-Jillānī, 2 Rabīʿ II 1288 /21 June 1871, Sultan to Muḥammad b. ʿAbdallāh Ū Bīhī; D.A.R., ʿAmāra dos., 26 Rabīʿ I 1288 /15 June 1871, ʿAmāra to Mūsā b. Aḥmad, 29 Rabīʿ I 1288 /18 June 1871, ʿUmar b. Aḥmád to ʿAmāra; cf. Hooker and Ball, *Journal*, pp. 294, 298, 304, 330–2; aṣ-Ṣiddīqī, *Īqāẓ*, pp. 100–1. aṣ-Ṣiddīqī relates that Azghār was sacked on 15 Rabīʿ II, and that the *khalīfa* of Ū Bīhī was killed there, but the date given does not correspond to the other sources I have cited.

116 F.O., 631 /5, 10 June 1871, Carstensen to Hay; N.A., R.G. 84, 12 June 1871, Corcos to Mathews.

117 F.O., 631 /5, 12 June 1871 and 20 June 1871, Carstensen to Hay.

118 K.H., 22 Rabīʿ II 1288 /11 July 1871, ʿUmar b. Saʿīd al-Matūgī to Sultan. Perhaps he was colluding with Ḥusayn of Iligh; in the above letter, the Sultan 'learned of the aid of Wild Hāshim (i.e., of Iligh) in the sedition (*fasād*) of the Hawwāra and Shtūka and other [tribes] with al-Ḥaḥī, and his diverting *makhzan* money to them'.

119 K.H., 8 Dhū al-Ḥijja 1288 /18 February 1872, Sultan to al-Ḥasan.

120 F.O., 631 /5, 25 March 1872, Carstensen to Hay.

121 F.O., 631/5, 1 October 1872, Carstensen to White.

122 K.H., 8 Rabīʿ I 1290/5 June 1873, ʿAbdallāh b. ʿUmar al-Baṭmī.

123 D.A.R., Essaouira 3, 20 Rabīʿ II 1290/17 June 1873, ʿAbd al-Karīm at-Tāzī to Bannīs.

124 Montagne, *Les Berbères et le Makhzen*, p. 386.

125 A.E., C.C.C., Mogador 5, 20 November 1873, Beaumier.

126 Accounts of the uprising are found in A.E., C.C.C., Mogador 5, 7 November 1873, Beaumier; N.A., R.G. 84, 7 November 1873. I did not uncover ʿAmāra's reports on the event, but a few details are found in responses to his letters. D.A.R., ʿAmāra dos., 30 Ramaḍān 1290/21 November 1873, Sultan to ʿAmāra, 3 Shawwāl 1290/24 November 1873, Mūsā b. Aḥmad to ʿAmāra.

127 K.H., 7 Shaʿbān 1291/19 September 1874, Sultan to Khalīfa ʿUthmān.

128 F.O., 631/5, 21 May 1875, and 28 May 1875, R. Hay to Hay. On the rise of Anflūs, see E. Doutté, 'Dans le sud marocain, au pays des Anfloûs', *Revue de Paris* (15 March 1913), 435–6.

129 D.A.R., ʿAmāra dos., 2 Ṣafar 1293/28 February 1876.

130 D.A.R., ʿAmāra dos., 11 Shaʿbān 1291/24 September 1875, Sultan to ʿAmāra; K.H., 19 Shaʿbān 1291/1 October 1875, Sultan to Khalīfa ʿUthmān.

131 E.g., concerning the arrest of aṭ-Ṭālib Mubārak b. ʿAlī Tughman. D.A.R., ʿAmāra dos., 11 Ṣafar 1291/30 March 1874, Sultan to ʿAmāra.

132 E.g., the case of ʿUmar al-Gurḍī (of Ida Ū Gurḍ) in 1874. D.A.R., ʿAmāra dos., 30 Rajab 1291/12 September 1874, Sultan to ʿAmāra. According to Montagne (*Les Berbères et le Makhzen*, p. 381), the Ida Ū Gurḍ were noted soldiers.

133 K.H., 21 Ramaḍān 1291/1 November 1874, Anflūs to Sultan.

134 D.A.R., Essaouira 3, 20 Rabīʿ II 1290/17 June 1873, ʿUthmān to ʿAmāra.

135 On banditry as a reaction to poverty and oppression, see Fernand Braudel, *The Mediterranean*, vol. II, p. 734 ff.

136 The events in Marrakesh are described in a letter to the *qāʾid* of Essaouira. D.A.R., ʿAmāra dos., 29 Jumādā II 1289/3 September 1872, al-Hāshim b. Aḥmad to ʿAmāra. Despite the gravity of the incident described, the Marrakesh uprising has received no attention from historians.

137 an-Nāṣirī, *Kitāb al-istiqṣāʾ*, vol. IX, p. 129; Ibn Manṣūr in *al-Wathāʾiq*, 3 (1977), pp. 278–86; Jacques Berque, *L'intérieur du Maghreb: XVe–XIXe siècle* (Paris, 1978), pp. 489–92; Laroui, *Les origines*, pp. 129–31; al-Manūnī, *Maẓāhir*, p. 300.

138 Cf. Pascon, *Le Haouz*, pp. 198–9.

139 These reforms are discussed at length by at-Tūzānī, *al-Umanāʾ*, pp. 40–3, 149 ff. For a regional view of these reforms, see al-Mūʾddin, '*al-ʿAlaqa*', pp. 313–26.

140 at-Tūzānī, *al-Umanāʾ*, pp. 46, 149.

141 The domains of these *qāʾids* are recorded in K.H., K^{80}, Jumādā II 1299/April–May, 1882.

142 K.H., 10 Rabīʿ II 1297/22 March 1880, *umanāʾ* of Shiadma to Sultan;

D.A.R., ʿAmāra dos. 10 Dhū al-Qaʿda 1296/24 October 1879, Sultan to ʿAmāra; D.A.R., Essaouira 4, 27 Ṣafar 1302/18 December 1884, Aḥmad Banānī (qadi) to Muḥammad b. al-ʿArabī b. al-Mukhtār. This is discussed in at-Tūzānī, *al-Umanāʾ*, pp. 184–5.

143 at-Tūzānī, *al-Umanāʾ*, pp. 150–2; Burke, *Prelude*, pp. 35–6; Kenbib, 'Les protections', pp. 158–65. The text of the 1881 agreement is found in P.P., 1882, LXXXI (30 March 1881), pp. 45–6.

144 From 1297/1879–80 onward, many *kanānīsh* of the *khirṣ* for the Shiadma and Hashtūka are found in the archives (see bibliography, p. 295).

145 K.H., Shawwāl 1301/1 August 1884, ad-Dawbilālī to Sultan.

146 K.H., 16 Shaʿbān 1302/31 May 1885, al-Bashīr and al-Hāshimī (*amīn*s of Ragrāga) to Sultan. Already in 1880, the *umanāʾ* of the Shiadma attempted to tax the Ragrāga *zāwiyas*. The Sultan warned them to respect the right of the *zāwiya*. *Dahir* dated 14 Rabīʿ II 1297/26 March 1880. I am grateful to Taïeb Amara for providing a copy of this document and other documents relating to the Ragrāga.

147 K.H., 10 Dhū al-Ḥijja 1302/20 September 1885, *khalīfa* of Saʿīd b. ʿUmar ash-Shiyāẓmī to Sultan. I have translated *nuzūl* – the force sent – as dragoon. See the definition of Abderrahman El-Mouden, 'Etat et société rurale à travers la *ḥarka* au Maroc du XIXème siècle', *The Maghreb Review*, 8:5–6 (1983), 142.

148 Cf. Berque, *L'intérieur*, pp. 482–3.

149 A.E., C.C.C., Mogador 4, 29 March 1864, Huet. A little over five years later, another *ḥarka* was sent to the Sous. F.O., 174/72, 30 November 1869, Carstensen to Hay. On the terminology used in the documents, see El Mouden, 'Etat et société', pp. 141–2.

150 K.H., 1280/1863–4, list of taxes from the tribes of the Sous.

151 The *khalīfa* reported on the *maḥalla* to Ḥusayn Ū Hāshim. B.D., 30 Rabīʿ I 1280/14 September 1863.

152 See above, pp. 180–1.

153 Miège, III, p. 323–6; Miège, *Doc.*, pp. 117–22 (May 1869, Beaumier); Leared, *Marocco*, pp. 362–5; A. Le Chatelier, *Tribus du sud-ouest marocain* (Paris, 1891), p. 80; Oskar Lenz, *Timbouctou: voyage au Maroc, au Sahara et au Soudan* (Paris, 1886), p. 360; B.L., Add 39000, 1 December 1871, Hay to Layard; A.E., C.C.C., Mogador 5, 1 October 1874, Beaumier. Abraham Corcos kept the *makhzan* informed on the last stages of the settlement. C.A., 13 Rajab 1291/26 August 1874, 26 Ramaḍān 1291/6 November 1874, and 21 Shawwāl 1291/1 December 1874, Mūsā b. Aḥmad to Corcos.

154 N.A., R.G. 84, 24 January 1878, and 6 February 1878, Corcos to Mathews; F.O. 174/85, 4 January 1878, and 4 February 1878, R. Hay to Hay.

155 F.O., 174/85, 14 February 1878, R. Hay to Hay.

156 *al-Wathāʾiq*, 3 (1977), 465–8 (3 Muḥarram 1294/18 January 1877, Sultan to Ḥabīb Bayrūk).

157 A.E., C.C.C., Mogador 6, 18 August 1879, Hélouis.

158 K.H., 19 Jumādā II 1297/29 May 1880, Sultan to ʿAllāl Ū Bīhī; D.A.R., ʿAmāra dos., 18 Jumādā II 1297/28 May 1880, Sultan to ʿAmāra.

159 B.D., 21 Rajab 1297/29 June 1880, Sultan to Ḥusayn; A.N., S.O.M., Afrique IV, dos., 4, 12 June 1880, Mahon; N.A. T61/13, Tangier: 14 June 1881, Mathews.

160 On this episode, see Miège, III, pp. 308–16; F.V. Parsons, *The Origins of the Morocco Question 1880–1900* (London, 1976), p. 106; A.N., S.O.M., Afrique IV, dos., 4, 12 June 1880, 23 June 1880, and 24 June 1880, Mahon, 10 Rajab 1297/18 June 1889, Ḥusayn to Mahon (the latter document is found in Miège, *Doc.*, p. 171); A.E., C.C.C., Mogador 6, 25 June 1880, Mahon, Marseille: 27 August 1880, Cohen, Julien & Cie to Ministère des Affaires Etrangères; N.A. T61/13, Tangier: 14 June 1881, Mathews; F.O., 174/105, 26 October 1881, Payton to Hay.

161 Donald Mackenzie, *The Flooding of the Sahara* (London, 1877), pp. xi, 197.

162 On the history of this company, see F. V. Parsons, 'The Northwest African Company and the British Government, 1875–1895', *Historical Journal*, 1 (1958), 136–53; Miège, III, pp. 299–309. According to Mukhtār as-Sūsī, Muḥammad Bayrūk settled at Tarfāya in 1290/1873–4. *al-Maʿsūl*, vol. XIX, p. 278.

163 Ibn Zaydān, *Itḥāf*, vol. III, pp. 333–5 (22 Ramaḍān 1297/28 August 1880, Sultan to Bargāsh); a copy of the original document is found in Nehlil, *Lettres cherifiennes*, doc. XLVIII. On the British position, see Miège, III, pp. 345–6.

164 Donald Mackenzie, *The Khalifate of the West* (London, 1911), pp. 168–9; Joseph C. Lee, 'The North-West Coast of Africa', *Journal of the Manchester Geographical Society*, 2 (1886), 146–7.

165 Miège, III, pp. 314–15.

166 *Ibid.*, pp. 316–18; F.O., 174/105, 9 November 1881, 'Extracts from the prospectus of the Sus and North African Trading Company (Ltd.)'; W. H. C. Andrews, *A Pamphlet and Map of Southern Morocco or 'Sûs' and 'Ait Bou Amaran'* (London, 1884), pp. 7–11. Ḥusayn allegedly signed an agreement between the four merchants and the Aït Bāʿamrān. The document is translated in E. Gérenton, 'Les expéditions de Moulay el Hasan dans le Sous: 1882–1886', *R.C.*, (1924), p. 268.

167 Miège, III, pp. 316, 318, Parsons, *Origins*, pp. 106, 174.

168 A copy of the *dahir* of Mawlāy al-Ḥasan on his arrival to the Sous sets out the aims of the *ḥarka*. Ibn al-Ḥājj, *Durar*, vol. I (29 Shaʿbān 1299/16 July 1882). an-Nāsirī (*Kitāb al-istiqṣā*ʾ vol. IX, pp. 174–5) says the prime purpose of the mission was to prevent the Spanish from taking possession of the port ceded to them in the war, and to prevent further illicit trade. This view is supported by oral sources recorded in Louis Arnaud, *Au temps des "Mehallas" ou le Maroc de 1860 à 1912* (Casablanca, 1952), p. 61. Mackenzie claims that the *ḥarka* was organized to wipe out Cape Juby. *Khalifate*, pp. 170–2. It was also claimed that the expedition was organized to subjugate the tribes who signed the treaty with Curtis, *et al.* Andrews, *Pamphet*, p. 11. All of these factors were probably important. Cf. Montagne, *Les Berbères et le Makhzen*, pp. 111–12; Gérenton, 'Les expéditions', pp. 267–9.

169 Cf. Berque, *L'intérieur*, pp. 482–3. The *ḥarka*s of Mawlāy al-Ḥasan have

been studied in detail. See Daniel Nordman, 'Les expéditions de Moulay Hassan', *Hespéris-Tamuda*, 19 (1980–81), 123–52; Mohamed Aafif, 'Les harkas hassaniennes d'après l'œuvre d'A. Ibn Zidane', *Hespéris-Tamuda*, 19 (1980–81), pp. 153–68.

170 For details on the expedition, see Gérenton, 'Les expéditions', pp. 269–75; Arnaud, *Au temps*, pp. 61–3, Foucauld, *Reconnaissance au Maroc*, pp. 343–6; an-Nāsirī, *Kitāb al-istiqṣā'*, vol. IX, pp. 174–7; F.O., 174/291, 2 June 1882, Payton. There were negotiations with Ḥusayn Ū Hāshim, who was kept informed of the *ḥarka*s advance. B.D., 9 Ramaḍān 1299/25 July 1882, Sultan to Ḥusayn. A day-to-day itinerary is found in Ibn al-Ḥājj, *ad-Durar*, vol. I.

171 Negotiations continued with the Spanish for agreeing on a site. The British were holding the *makhzan* responsible for the protection of property at Cape Juby, while the Sultan insisted on the illegality of the settlement. Nehlil, *Lettres cherifiennes*, doc. LXII (25 Dhū al-Ḥijja 1299/8 November 1882, Sultan to Bargāsh), doc. LXI (16 Dhū al-Qaʿda 1299/29 September 1882, Sultan to Bargāsh).

172 According to a French military report on the expedition, some 41 *qā'id*s were appointed. M.G., Maroc 3H21, 1883, Erckmann. On the appointment of Daḥmān Bayrūk, see as-Sūsī, *al-Maʿsūl*, vol. XIX, p. 279.

173 Segonzac, *Au Cœur*, p. 273.

174 Lee ('North-West Coast', p. 148) recounts that the tribes resumed trade in the autumn of 1882.

175 Ibn Zaydān, *Itḥāf*, vol. II, pp. 381–2 (29 Jumādā II 1300/7 May 1883, Sultan to Bargāsh). See Andrews, *Pamphlet*, pp. 12–16; and reports of the British consulate of Mogador. F.O., 635/3, 16 March 1883, Diary of the consulate; F.O., 99/215, April 1883.

176 N.A., R.G. 84, 23 May 1883, Corcos to Mathew.

177 Ibn Zaydān, *Itḥāf*, vol. II, p. 395 (30 Jumādā I 1300/8 April 1883, Sultan to Bargāsh); aṣ-Ṣiddīqī, *Īqāẓ*, p. 119; K.H., 12 Dhū al-Ḥijja 1300/14 October 1883, Aḥmad al-ʿAbūbī to Sultan.

178 Ibn Zaydān, *Itḥāf*, vol. II, pp. 383–6; F.O., 99/216, *passim*; Andrews, *Pamphlet*, p. 31.

179 Mackenzie, *Khalifate*, p. 189.

180 K.H., K^{120}; calculated by at-Tūzānī, *al-Umanā'*, p. 107.

181 K.H., K^{120}, Jumādā I 1301/February–March 1884. In the following months the costs of supporting the army in Tiznit and the Sous grew.

182 K.H., 16 Dhū al-Ḥijja 1300/18 October 1883, Idrīs b. Muḥammad Bannīs, Ibn al-Ḥasan, and Faraj to Sultan, 1 Rabīʿ I 1301/31 December 1883, [. . .] to Sultan, 7 Jumādā II 1301/5 March 1884, Bannis, Ibn al-Ḥasan, and Faraj to Sultan, 12 Dhū al-Ḥijja 1300/4 October 1883, Aḥmad al-ʿAbūbī to Sultan.

183 K.H., 15 Dhū al-Ḥijja 1301/6 October 1884, 19 Rajab 1302/4 May 1885, 23 Rajab 1302/8 May 1885, 8 Ramaḍān 1302/21 June 1885, Muḥammad b. ʿAbd ar-Raḥmān Brīsha, Muḥammad b. Zākūr, ʿAbd ar-Raḥmān b. al-Ḥasan.

184 K.H., 13 Shawwāl 1302 /26 July 1885, ʿAbd ar-Raḥmān b. al-Ḥasan.
185 See Arnaud, *Au temps*, p. 65; Gérenton, 'Les expéditions', pp. 275, 278.
186 K.H., 30 Rajab 1301 /26 May 1884, *umanāʾ* of Banī Issāran to Sultan. The tribes had an important role in purveying the *ḥarka*s. Often the *qāʾid*s and the *umanāʾ* preceded the Sultan to stock up on provisions. See Mohamed Aafif, 'Les harkas hassaniennes d'après l'œuvre d'A. Ibn Zidane', *Hesperis-Tamuda*, 19 (1980–1), 165. Concerning preparations for the *ḥarka*, see Ibn Zaydān, *al-ʿIzz*, vol. I, pp. 189–208.
187 K.H., 2 Jumādā I 1302 /17 February 1885, az-Ziltanī to Sultan. The texts refer to *ḥarka* and the *maḥalla* in the Sous already in 1884. Technically speaking, therefore, the *ḥarka* could exist without the presence of the Sultan. See El Mouden, 'Etat et société', pp. 141–2.
188 K.H., 30 Jumādā I 1302 /17 March 1885, 6 Rajab 1302 /21 April 1885, ʿAdī b. ʿAlī an-Naknāfī to Sultan, 8 Jumādā II 1302 /25 March 1885, *khalīfa* of az-Ziltanī to Sultan, 2 Jumādā II 1302 / 19 March 1885, *umanāʾ* of province of Qāʾid az-Ziltanī to Sultan (2 letters), 6 Jumādā II 1302 /23 March 1885, al-Maḥjūb b. Aḥmad al-Gallūlī to Sultan.
189 K.H., 8 Rajab 1302 /23 April 1885, ʿAdī b. ʿAlī an-Naknāfī to Sultan.
190 K.H., 18 Rajab 1302 /3 May 1885, az-Ziltanī to Sultan.
191 K.H., 22 Rajab 1302 /7 May 1865, Muḥammad ash-[. . .] at Taknī to Sultan.
192 as-Sūsī, *Khilāl*, vol. IV, p. 100. The author lists 10 *qāʾid*s appointed to the Hawwāra. See also F.O., 174 /292, 15 September 1884, Johnston to White.
193 K.H., 20 Ṣafar 1301 /21 December 1883, Ḥusayn Ū Hāshim to Sultan.
194 K.H., 20 Shaʿbān 1301 /15 June 1884, 26 Shaʿbān 1301 /21 June 1884, al-Maḥjūb b. Aḥmad al-Gallūlī to Sultan, 29 Rabīʿ II 1302 /15 February 1885, Muḥammad al-Yazīd al-Masgīnī to Sultan.
195 F.O., 174 /292, 15 September 1884.
196 K.H., 10 Ramaḍān 1301 /14 July 1884, ʿAlī b. ʿAbdallāh al-Fillāwī to Sultan, 6 Shawwāl 1301 /30 July 1884, [. . .] to Sultan.
197 K.H., 15 Shaʿbān 1302 /30 May 1885, al-ʿAbūbī to Sultan; F.O., 174 /292, 9 June 1885, Payton to Hay.
198 B.D., 10 Rabīʿ II 1303 /16 January 1886.
199 This process can be seen in 18 letters sent by the Sultan to Ḥusayn between 1882 and 1886, translated in Gérenton, 'Les expéditions', pp. 281–6.
200 K.H., 30 Jumādā I 1303 /6 March 1886, Muḥammad b. Zākūr, Muḥammad b. ʿAbd ar-Raḥmān Brīsha, ʿAbd ar-Raḥmān b. al-Ḥasan to Sultan.
201 F.O., 174 /292, 8 April 1886, Payton to Hay; N.A., R.G. 84, 3 April 1886, Meyer Corcos to Mathews; aṣ-Ṣiddīqī, *Īqāẓ*, pp. 124–5.
202 K.H., 7 Rajab 1303 /11 April 1886, and 25 Rajab 1303 /29 April 1886, az-Ziltanī to Sultan.
203 Ibn al-Ḥājj, *ad-Durar*, *dahir* of Sultan dated 27 Shaʿbān 1303 /31 May, 1866; Miège, (*Doc.*, Goulimime: 26 May 1886, De Breuille); an-Nāṣirī, *Kitāb al-istiqṣā*, vol. IX, pp. 180–2.
204 K.H., 17 Shawwāl 1303 /19 July 1886, Aḥmad b. al-ʿArabī al-Manbīhī, Masʿūd b. Aḥmad al-Matūgī, and Aḥmad b. ʿAbdallāh aṣ-Ṣawīrī to Sultan,

17 Shawwāl 1303/19 July 1886, and 19 Shawwāl 1303/21 July 1886, al-Gallūlī to Sultan; as-Sūsī, *Khilāl*, vol. IV, pp. 88–9.

205 K.H., 18 Shawwāl 1303/20 July 1886.

206 K.H., 18 Dhū al-Qaʿda 1303/18 August 1886, ar-Ragrāgī ad-Dawbilālī to Sultan.

207 On the appointment of the *qāʾids* to the Sous, see Le Chatelier, *Tribus*, pp. 39, 43, 79; Montagne, *Les Berbères et le Makhzen*, p. 113. The names of 40 *qāʾids* appointed are listed in Gérenton, 'Les expéditions', p. 280. A letter from Mawlāy al-Ḥasan to Daḥmān Bayrūk, refers to a warehouse in Essaouira. B.A., 1304/1886–7. Reference is also made to the house of Qāʾid ʿAlī b. Masʿūd al-Akhṣāṣ. K.H., 17 Rajab 1303/21 April 1886, al-Akhṣāṣ to Sultan. In 1889 it was reported that a house in the new *casbah* was granted to a sheikh of Wad Noun. 'This is the seventh sheikh from that district who has been provided with quarters in Mogador in this way for the purpose of bringing them under the jurisdiction of the Moorish government, with a view to securing their submission and preventing them from treating with Christians down there on their account'. *Times of Morocco*, 4 May 1889.

208 An agreement was reached between the British and the Moroccans in 1895, to pay compensation for the withdrawal of the company. The agreement implied that the British government recognized Moroccan sovereignty over the area. Parsons, 'North West African Company', p. 152.

209 Montagne, *Les Berbères et le Makhzen*, p. 113.

9 The people of Essaouira in precolonial times

1 Miège, III, p. 26, IV, p. 404; see André Adam, *Histoire de Casablanca (des origines à 1914)* (Aix-en-Provence, 1968), p. 98.

2 Many contradictory figures in app. B have been dismissed in my estimates.

3 Montagne, *Les Berbères et le Makhzen*, pp. 103–4.

4 Estimates on the population of Goulimime include in 1819, about 800 by Charles Cochelet, *Narrative of the Shipwreck Sophia on the 30th of May 1819, on the Western Coast of Africa and the Captivity of a Part of the Crew in the Desert of Sahara* (London, 1822), p. 61; in 1842, 1,800–2,000 by Bouet, A.N., S.O.M., Afrique IV, dos. 3, 15 March 1842; in 1844, 2,000 by Calderón, M.G., Maroc DHI, dos. VIII, May 1844; in 1848, 4,000 by Carr, N.A. T61/6, Tangier: 29 August 1848; in 1869, 3,000 by Joachim Gatell, 'Description du Sous', p. 265; and in 1886, 4,000 by Jannasch, *Handels expedition*, p. 37.

5 Paul Pascon and Daniel Schroeter, 'Le cimetière juif d'Iligh (1751–1956): Etude des épitaphes comme documents d'histoire démographique', in Pascon, *La Maison*, p. 138. A version of this article also appears in: *Revue de l'Occident Musulman et de la Méditerranée*, 34:2 (1982).

6 Noin, *La population*, vol. I, pp. 270–1.

7 See Schroeter, 'Merchants and Pedlars', pp. 50 ff.

8 Fernand Braudel, *The Structures of Everyday Life* (London, 1981), p. 78.

9 On cycles of famines and epidemics in Morocco, see B. Rosenberger and H.

Triki, 'Famines et épidemies au Maroc aux XVIe et XVIIe siècles', *Hespéris-Tamuda*, 14 (1973), 109–75; Charles Bois, 'Années de disette, années d'abondance, sécheresse et pluies au Maroc', *Revue pour l'Etude des Calamités*, nos. 26–7 (1949), 1–31. On demographic calamities in Tunisia and the Mediterranean, see Lucette Valensi, *Fellahs tunisiens: l'économie rurale et la vie des campagnes au 18e et 19e siècles* (Paris and The Hague, 1977), pp. 266 ff.

10 See Miège, II, p. 461; F.O., 830/1, 11 November 1848, Grace to Hay.

11 *al-Wathā'iq*, 4 (1978), 331 (18 Rabīʿ II 1281/10 September 1865, Sultan to Bargāsh); this was protested by the merchants of Fez.

12 F.O., 174/72, 2 October 1865, Carstensen to Hay. Bū ʿAshrīn's son, returning from the hajj, was quarantined on the island and Corcos took care of him when he landed in town. C.A., 7 Rabīʿ II 1282/30 August 1865, 20 Jumādā I 1282/11 October 1865, 6 Jumādā II 1282/27 October 1865, Bū ʿAshrīn to Abraham and Jacob Corcos.

13 D.A.R., Essaouira 2, 10 Jumādā I 1285/29 August 1868, Bargāsh to ʿAmāra; F.O., 631/3, 17 August 1868, Carstensen to Hay; A.I.U., France VIII D 42, 10 August 1868, Hecquart to Crémieux.

14 This is equally true of Europe and America until the end of the nineteenth century. William McNeill, *Plagues and People* (New York, 1976), pp. 229–30.

15 The British vice-consul claimed that 30 died and that another 10 to 20 were on the verge of death. F.O., 174/72, 23 October 1865, Carstensen to Hay.

16 Thomson, *Travels in the Atlas*, p. 67.

17 F.O., 52/39 Tangier: 29 June 1835, E. W. A. Hay (based on the vice-consul Willshire's reports); Auguste Beaumier, 'Le choléra au Maroc, sa marche du Sahara jusquʿau Sénégal en 1868', *B.S.G.*, 6e sér., 3 (1872), 301; Beaumier, 'Le Maroc', *B.S.G.*, 5e sér., 14 (1867), 11–12.

18 Beaumier, 'Le choléra', p. 299.

19 aṣ-Ṣiddīqī, *Īqāẓ*, p. 76. In the earlier part of the epidemic, a higher number of Muslim deaths were reported. A.E., C.C.C., Mogador 3, 26 July 1855, Grace to Hay. Evidence from the Jewish cemetery suggests that Jewish deaths accelerated in August of 1855.

20 A.E., C.C.C., Mogador 4, 11 September 1868, Hecquart.

21 Beaumier, 'Le choléra', p. 229.

22 A.E., C.C.C., Mogador 4, 11 September 1868, Hecquart.

23 In 1873, Beaumier reports to the Alliance Israélite Universelle of the daily growth of the Jewish population. A.I.U., France VIII D 42, 22 February 1873. The British consul reports of the 'continued influx of Jews from all parts of the interior'. F.O., 631/5, 4 May 1875, R. Hay to J. Hay.

24 A.I.U., Maroc XXXIV E 584, 25 September 1878, Benchimol.

25 Miège, III, pp. 443–4.

26 Foucauld, *Reconnaissance au Maroc*, pp. 108, 127, 143, 151.

27 These events are recounted in Miège, III, pp. 390–4. They are reported extensively in F.O., 631/6, 174/85, and 99/182. See especially R. Drummond Hay's consular report in P.P., 1878–9, LXXI. Besides the charities established by the consular corps and the Jewish elite, a Protestant mission

run by a Jewish convert began to distribute food to the Jewish poor, and hoped to find prospective converts. See J. B. Ginsburg, *An Account of the Persecution of the Protestant Mission among the Jews at Mogador, Morocco* (London, 1880).

28 These figures are entirely conjecture. I have attempted to compare various estimates of the population (see app. B) with reports of mortality of residents and refugees. Schroeter, 'Merchants and Pedlars', pp. 66–7.

29 *Ibid.*, pp. 67–9.

30 In a case before the rabbinical court (5657/1896–7), a certain Yiṣḥaq Būganīm from a village in the Sous seeks to divorce his wife. During the famine of 5643/1882–3, everyone in the *mellah* of the village migrated for survival, except Būganīm and another man, who later went to Essaouira. The reason he wishes divorce is because his wife has given birth only to daughters and he desires sons. Masʿūd Khnāffō, *Sheʾeilōt ū-teshūbōt*.

31 On the vaccinations, see *A.J.A. Annual Report*, 5 (1876), 60. In the 1880s and 1890s, Essaouira was struck by smallpox epidemics of major proportions on several occasions. F.O., 174/292, 21 January 1883; A.E., C.C.C., Mogador 7, 10 August 1888; *Times of Morocco*, 30 January 1892, 6 February 1892, 13 February 1892, and 5 March 1892; A.I.U., Maroc XXXIII E 582, January–February 1892, Benchimol; Halewī, (1892), 289.

32 Mocatta Library Archive, 'Committee for the Relief of the Sufferers at Mogadore', De Sola Pamphlets 6.

33 *Jewish Chronicle*, 17 August 1860.

34 Picciotto, *Jews*, pp. 24–5.

35 *Jewish Chronicle*, 7 November 1862.

36 L. Loewe (ed.), *Diaries*, vol. II, pp. 145–61; H. Guedalla, *Refutation of an Anonymous Article in the 'Jewish World', Secret History of Sir Moses Montefiore's Mission in 1863–4* (London, 1880). He was accompanied by a doctor, who left an account of the journey: Thomas Hodgkin, *Narrative of a Journey to Morocco in 1863 and 1864* (London, 1866). Moroccan documents on the events connected to the Montefiore visit are found in *al-Wathāʾiq*, 4 (1978), 266–95.

37 See Schroeter, 'Anglo-Jewry', pp. 65, 67–8.

38 F.O., 174/83, 28 Shaʿbān 1280/7 February 1864, 1 Ramaḍān 1280/9 February 1864, Reade to Bū ʿAshrīn and reply.

39 C.A., 14 Ramaḍān 1280/22 February 1864, Bū ʿAshrīn to Abraham and Jacob Corcos.

40 F.O., 631/5, 4 May 1875, R. Hay to Hay.

41 Laskier, *The Alliance Israélite Universelle and the Jewish Communities of Morocco, 1862–1962* (Albany, N.Y., 1983), pp. 32–4.

42 The utilization of social reform for spreading French influence was a clear policy pursued by the consulate in Essaouira. A.E., C.C.C., Mogador 4, 21 October 1865, Gay. Details of the improvements and the foundation of the school and hospital are found in numerous sources: A.E., C.C.C., Mogador 4, 10 June, 12 October, 21 October, and 4 November 1865, Gay; Miège, *Doc.*, pp. 75–6 (8 January 1866, Beaumier to Crémieux); *ha-Magīd*, 10 (3

January 1866); *Archives Israélites*, 27 (1866), 168–70; Adolphe Crémieux, 'Les Israélites de Mogador', *Univers Israélite* (1866); A.I.U., France VIII D 42, 8 January 1866, Gay to Crémieux, 24 December 1867, 30 June 1869, Beaumier to Crémieux; A.E., C.C.C., Mogador 4, 12 March 1868, Beaumier; A.I.U., Maroc XXXIV E 601, 7 May 1869, Cohen.

43 Laroui, *Les origines*, p. 310.

44 On this problem in Demnat and Morocco generally, see Ahmed Toufiq (Tawfīq), 'Les Juifs dan la société marocaine du 19e siècle: l'exemple des juifs de Demnate', in *Juifs du Maroc, identité et dialogue* (Grenoble, 1980).

45 A.E., Maroc, M.D. 10, March 1867, Beaumier.

46 At the end of 1893, the Jews were ordered to pay arrears for 18 years of *jizya*. A.I.U., Maroc XXXIII E 582, December 1893, Benchimol. Protégés in Marrakesh also began to refuse to pay the *jizya*. K.H., 13 Ramaḍān 1283 / 19 January 1867, Sultan to Khalīfa al-Ḥasan. However, the community as a whole continued to pay the tax until the twentieth century. al-Manūnī, *Maẓāhir*, p. 44.

47 A.I.U., France VIII D 42, 30 June 1869, Beaumier to Crémieux.

48 Laskier, *Alliance Israélite*, pp. 62–3.

49 A.J., 95 /add 4, A.J.A. Executive Committee Minutes, see, for example, 20 December 1874, 21 February 1875, 28 March 1875, 14 November 1875, 24 February 1876, 8 March 1877, 19 September 1877; *A.J.A. Annual Report*, 5 (1876), pp. 31–3.

50 Hirsch in *B.A.I.U.*, 1e sem., 4 (1877), 45–6.

51 See above, note 34.

52 A.I.U., France VIII D 42, 2 January 1874, Beaumier to Crémieux.

53 It was estimated in 1875 that the *mellah* comprised 248,000 square metres out of a total of 280,000. Beaumier, 'Mogador', p. 118. Beaumier's figure of 10,000 Jews may be exaggerated, although the *mellah* was certainly inflated by rural migrants at this time.

54 A.I.U., Maroc XXXIV E 584, 21 January 1875, Benchimol; Halévy in *B.A.I.U.*, 1e sem., 4 (1877), pp. 46–7; A.I.U., Maroc III B 14, 21 January 1875, Daniel d'Abraham Cohen; A.I.U., France IX A 73, 13 August 1876; *A.J.A. Annual Report*, 5 (1886), 60. The A.J.A. decided that it could carry out its vaccination programme under the *Ḥebrat Meshībat Nefesh*.

55 Though later the tax was not always used for that purpose. N.A., R.G. 84, 20 September 1895, Broome to L. de Marinas.

56 A.I.U., Maroc III B 14, 28 April 1882 (in Hebrew). The elected officers were: Joseph Elmaleh as honorary president, Jacob Afriat as president, Amram Elmaleh as vice-president, Aaron Elmaleh as secretary, and Joshua Belisha as treasurer. A.I.U., Maroc III C 10, 31 April 1882, signed Joseph Elmaleh, Aaron Elmaleh, sent by Jacob Afriat.

57 A.I.U., Maroc III B 14, 14 May 1882 and 11 August 1882.

58 Halewī, (1891), 311.

59 *Times of Morocco*, 30 November 1889, 18 January 1890, 28 March 1891, and 1 August 1891. For details on these charges, see Schroeter, 'Anglo-Jewry', pp. 76–80.

60 A.I.U., Maroc I C 9, 20 Sīwan 5642/7 June 1882.
61 I have studied this question in detail elsewhere. 'The Politics of Reform in Morocco: The Writings of Yiṣḥaq Ben Yaʿīs(h) Halewī in *Haṣfīrah* (1891)', paper presented to The Second International Congress for the Study of Sephardi and Oriental Jewry, Jerusalem, December 23–8, 1984 [publication of the acts forthcoming]. The literary movement in Essaouira has been studied in depth by Yōsef Shīṭrīt, 'Mūdaʿūt ḥadasha le-anōmaliyūt ū-le-lashōn – nīṣaneyah shel tenūʿat haskalah ʿivrīt be-Marrōkō be-sōf ha-meʾah ha-19', *mi-Qedem ū-mi-Yam*, 2 (1986), 129–68.
62 Miège, II, p. 573, III, p. 456, IV, p. 408.
63 as-Sūsī, *al-Maʿsūl*, vol. XV, pp. 11–14.
64 F.O., 631/3, August 1870 (trade report for 1869), Carstensen; A.E., C.C.C., Mogador 5, 19 November 1869, Beaumier. Export of goats skins from Essaouira jumped from a total of 69,497 dozen in 1868 to 119,375 in 1869; value of exports increased from f1,506,825 to f2,987,660; while this was a 58 per cent increase in quantity, it was only a 51 per cent increase in value. Calculated from Miège, *Doc.*, p. 233.
65 N.A., R.G. 84, 13 Rabīʿ I 1287/13 June 1870, *umanāʾ* of Essaouira to Abraham Corcos.
66 F.O., 174/293, 7 June 1887, Payton to Green. From the 1890s on, German credit to individuals at all levels became prevalent. Park 'Administration', pp. 423–4. Kenneth Brown relates that the people of Salé still talk of German open-handedness at the turn of the century – of the way Morocco had become the dumping ground for European imports (oral communication).
67 As was done for Īnūltān: Tawfīq, *al-Mujtamaʿ*, vol. I, pp. 233–46.
68 E.g., as compared with Īnūltān. *Ibid.*, pp. 341–2.
69 Cf. Laroui, *Les origines*, pp. 49–51.
70 ar-Ragrāgī, *ash-Shamūs*, p. 36.
71 Soulange-Bodin reported that the militiaman received 2 ducats (i.e., 20 ūqiya) a month. A.E., Maroc, M.D. 4, December 1847. The same salary was still maintained in the 1890s. Park, 'Administration', pp. 276, 280.
72 D.A.R., Essaouira I, 18 Rabīʿ I 1288/31 July 1866, Muḥammad b. al-Maḥjūb to Bannīs.
73 Average prices of barley sold in the *raḥba* were estimated at 35 ūqiya in 1864, 38 in 1865, 34 in 1866, and 26 ūqiya in 1867 (up to February 11). F.O., 631/3, 11 February 1867, Carstensen to Hay. For 1884–6 (prices were particularly high in 1883 because of the monetary crisis), high and low figures are cited in sterling by the British consul. I have converted this to ūqiya at a rate of 125 to the riyāl (£1 = f25 of 5f pieces). P.P., 1897, XCII, p. 133. In 1875, Beaumier claimed that the kharūba of barley was equal to 71 kg. (= 156 lb.). 'Mogador', p. 113. In 1883, it was estimated by the British consul at 320 lb. P.P., 1884, LXXX, p. 99. Kharūbas for other grains also had various weights.
74 Rollman, 'The "New Order"', p. 694.
75 K.H., 6 Rabīʿ III 1301/4 February 1884, Idrīs b. Muḥammad Bannīs,

Faraj, and Ibn al-Ḥasan to Sultan, 11 Jumādā I 1301 /10 March 1884, al-Maḥjūb b. Muḥammad Tūfal-ʿazz to Sultan.

76 N.A., R.G. 84, 7 Dhū al-Ḥijja 1289 /5 February 1873.

77 N.A., R.G. 84, 6 Rajab 1290 /30 August 1873.

78 Cf. Rollman, 'The "New Order"', pp. 694–5.

79 K.H., 3 Rabīʿ I 1302 /21 December 1884, ad-Dawbilālī to Sultan. As we have seen on one occasion, when the uniforms were not distributed the militamen rebelled. aṣ-Ṣiddīqī, *Īqāẓ*, pp. 79–81.

80 A.E., Maroc, M.D. 10, March 1867 (translated at an exchange rate of 37.8 ūqiya to the French riyāl).

81 F.O., 631 /3, 28 January 1870, Carstensen to White. The figure cited is 9 pence which equals 45 French riyāl × 38 ūdiya = 17.1 ūqiya. Other towns and regions examined in the survey found that wages ranged from 4 to 6 pence or 7.6 to 11.4 ūqiya; a worker subsisted on 2 pence or 3.8 ūqiya a day. Miège's conversion table (4–6 pence = 3–5 ūqiya) is in error. 'Note sur l'artisanat', p. 93.

82 These figures are cited in English pence, which I have converted into ūqiya. P.P., 1890, LXXVI, pp. 170–1.

83 Available data does not cover the whole period from 1867 onward, but we know that in 1296 /1878–9, rents on *makhzan* properties for the *medina* totalled 9,298 ūqiya. K.H., K[93]. In Shawwāl 1306 /May–June 1889, 12,263 ūqiya were collected. K.H., K[386]. A rise of just over 25 per cent, while the ūqiya rose by over 100 per cent.

10 The end of an era

1 Miège, III, p. 432.

2 Trade with Marseille slowed down in 1870 because of apprehension about the Franco-Prussian war. This caused the export of goat skins and the import of sugar to decrease. F.O., 631 /5, 1 March 1871 (trade report for 1870).

3 Miège, III, p. 432.

4 D.A.R., Essaouira 2, 12 Dhū al-Qaʿda 1288 /23 January 1872, Faraj and Aqaṣbī to Bannīs. In the 1820s, one of Boujnah's ancestors was described as 'the most opulent man in Mogador'. Beauclerk, *Journey*, p. 251. Boujnah figures very prominently in the 1820s in the commercial correspondence of S.L. He may in fact have been the merchant Aaron Amar, who was called Boujnah because he represented the Boujnah firm of Algiers (oral communication from M. Samuel Levy).

5 The difficulties of these merchants can be traced in several letters. D.A.R., Essaouira 2, 24 Rabīʿ I 1287 /24 June 1870, Mūsā b. Aḥmad to ʿAmāra, 3 Rabīʿ I 1288 /23 May 1871, 16 Ramaḍān 1288 /29 November 1871, and 2 Dhū al-Qaʿda 1288 /13 January 1872, Faraj and Aqaṣbī to Bannīs; 18 Ramaḍān 1289 /19 November 1872, Muḥammad al-Qabbāj to Bannīs.

6 P.P., 1874, LXVII (Report of Beaumier, as acting vice-consul, for 1873, dated 31 March 1874), p. 729.

7 Miège, III, pp. 449–58.

8 C.A., 1 Ṣafar 1292/9 March 1875, Mūsā b. Aḥmad to Abraham and Jacob Corcos.

9 The *makhzan* was unwilling to make the loan at this point. C.A., 22 Muḥarram 1297/5 January 1880, Aḥmad b., Mūsā to Abraham and Jacob Corcos, and 13 Ramaḍān 1297/19 August 1880, Muḥammad b. al-ʿArabī b. al-Mukhtār to Abrahm Corcos.

10 N.A., R.G. 84, 11 Ramaḍān 1301 /5 July 1884, Faraj, ad-Dawbilālī to Meyer Corcos.

11 N.A., R.G. 84, 7 March 1888, Meyer Corcos to Lewis.

12 Ibn Zaydān *Itḥāf*, vol. II, pp. 379–80; F.O., 99/200, London: 27 January 1881, 21 April 1881, J. & E. Carter to Earl Granville; F.O., 99/214, Manchester: March 1885, and 23 January 1885, S. A. Meyer and Co. to Earl Granville; 13 February 1884, Broome to Payton. The case is also discussed in Kenbib, 'Les protections', pp. 225–6.

13 K.H., 3 Dhū al-Ḥijja 1302/23 September 1885, Muḥammad b. Zākūr, Muḥammad b. ʿAbd ar-Raḥmān Brīsha, and ʿAbd ar-Raḥmān b. al-Ḥasan.

14 Miège, III, pp. 446–9; F.O., 631/7, 25 March 1880. The German merchant, Theodor Brauer, was on the verge of bankruptcy, but was saved by his correspondents in Europe. Pierre Guillen, *L'Allemagne et le Maroc de 1870 à 1905* (Paris, 1967), pp. 57–8.

15 See above, pp. 44–5.

16 Their private holdings in Essaouira amounted to 11 houses, 5 shops, and 1 store. F.O., 631/8, 'Mogador Free-Hold list', 1844–1914.

17 D.A.R., ʿAmāra dos., 4 Shaʿbān 1292/5 September 1875, Sultan to ʿAmāra; C.A., 22 Shawwāl 1292/21 November 1875, 18 Muḥarram 1293/14 February 1876, Mūsā b. Aḥmad to Abraham Corcos. In 1881, the *umanāʾ* were ordered to hand over the properties to Musa and to release him from the 933,923 ūqiya debt owed the *makhzan*. K.H., K120, 9 Rajab 1298/7 June 1881, copy of sharifian letter to *umanāʾ* (al-ʿArabī Faraj, and Idrīs Bannīs), and their reply, 20 Rajab 1298/18 June 1881.

18 From the 1890s, however, German penetration in the countryside grew more significantly. See Park, 'Administration', pp. 417–29.

19 Leared, 'The Trade and Resources', p. 535.

20 Miège, III, p. 31.

21 Kenbib, 'Les protections', pp. 101–3, 169; on later years, pp. 212–17.

22 Exports from the region did grow considerably from about 1900. See Park, 'Administration', pp. 60–2.

23 All these forms of wealth were noted several hundred years earlier by Ibn Khaldun, *The Muqqadimah*, vol. II, pp. 283–5, 336–9.

24 This was even more the case with German penetration. Cf. Park, 'Administration', pp. 420–4.

25 See Miège, IV, pp. 369, 395 ff.

26 Ayache, *Etudes*, pp. 137–8; at-Tūzānī, *al-Umanāʾ*, pp. 33–5; Tawfīq, *al-Mujtamaʿ*, vol. I, pp. 275 ff.

27 Brown, *People*, pp. 129–31.

28 Cigar, 'Socio-economic', pp. 63–4.

29 Aḥmad b. Masʿūd al-Hadrī, *Sināʿat al-ʿarʿār min al-Ḥasan al-awwal ilā al-Ḥasan ath-thānī*, MS of author in Essaouira. The first half was mimeographed in the first number of a review of the *Association Culturelle d'Essaouira.*

30 Cf. Park, 'Administration', pp. 59–65. In fact, as is shown here, exports were growing in the decade or so before 1912. Park estimates that the export of specie averaged about 2.5 per cent of Essaouira's international commerce from 1876–1912.

31 Park estimates that prices for commodities rose between 1862 and 1887 at a rate of 4.9 per cent a year in terms of flūs. 'Administration', pp. 161–2.

32 *Times of Morocco*, 7 November 1891, 12 December 1891 and 2 January 1892.

33 See Park, 'Administration', pp. 372–3.

34 On the development of Casablanca in the decade leading up to the protectorate, see Adam, *Histoire*, pp. 137ff. By 1890, Essaouira was competing for third place with El Jadida among Moroccan seaports in terms of the value of trade with Europe. Miège, IV, p. 376.

35 A. Redford, *Manchester Merchants and Foreign Trade* (2 vols. Manchester, 1934–56).

Bibliography

Archival sources

Morocco

al-Khizānat al-Ḥasaniyya, Rabat

The official correspondence was still not catalogued at the time of my research. Therefore, no reference numbers are given for administrative letters. There were also unbound dossiers of accounts (*qawā'im ḥisābiyya*) which were still not catalogued. The register books have been catalogued. The following were consulted for this study:

K^{33} Treasury of Marrakesh, 1274–8 / 1857–62

K^{42} Customs, town revenue, and expenditue of Essaouira, 1276–8 / 1859–62

K^{43} Treasury of Marrakesh, 1276–1302 / 1859–85

K^{46} Customs, town revenue, and expenditure of Essaouira, 1279 / 1862–3

K^{48} Old Treasury of Marrakesh, 1276–90 / 1859–74

K^{56} Military accounts and roll of Essaouira, 1281 / 1864–5

K^{80} Revenue from *makhzan* property in various cities, 1292–1302 / 1875–85

K^{93} Lists of *makhzan* property in various cities, 1296–7 / 1878–80

K^{109} Tax assessment (*khirṣ*) in the Hashtūka and Shiadma, 1298 / 1880–1

K^{120} Revenue and expenditure, port of Essaouira, 1301 / 1883–4

K^{122} Town revenue of Essaouira, 1300–2 / 1883–4

K^{131} Town revenue of Essaouira, 1302–4 / 1884–7

K^{295} Customs, town revenue, and expenditure of Essaouira, 1282 / 1865–6

K^{334} *Khirṣ* for some of the tribes of the Shiadma, 1297 / 1879–80

K^{335} *Khirṣ* for some of the tribes of the Shiadma, 1297 / 1879–80

K^{340} *Khirṣ* of the Hashtūka and Shiadma, 1298 / 1880–1

K^{350} *Khirṣ* of the Hashtūka and Shiadma, 1300 / 1882–3

K^{354} Revenue of the Haha, 1300–4 / 1882–7

K^{355} *Khirṣ* of the Shiadma, 1299 / 1881–2

K^{367} *Khirṣ* of the Shiadma, 1302 / 1884–5

K^{374} *Khirṣ* of the Shiadma, 1303 / 1885–6

K^{386} *Makhzan* property in Essaouira, 1306–8 / 1888–91

K^{393} Town revenue of Essaouira, 1307–8 / 1889–91

Direction del Archives Royales (Mudīriyya al-Wathā'iq al-Malakiyya), Rabat
The following collection was not yet catalogued. The Essaouira files are cited according to the order in which they are stored in the archives:
Essaouira. Correspondence with officials of Essaouira
ʿAmāra. Correspondence of Qā'id ʿAmāra b. ʿAbd aṣ-Ṣādiq
al-Yahūd. Correspondence relating to Jewish affairs

Bibliothèque Générale (al-Khizānat al-ʿĀmma), Rabat
Habous. List of *ḥubus* properties in Essaouira, 1924, and correspondence and documents relating to this property
Bargāsh. Correspondence of Muḥammad Bargāsh

France

Archives du Ministère des Affaires Etrangères, Paris
Correspondance Consulaire et Commercial, Mogador
Correspondance Politique, Maroc
Correspondance Politique de Consuls, Maroc 1, 1868–1881
Memoires et Document, Maroc

Archives Nationales, Paris
BB^4 Marine
F^{12} Commerce et Industrie

Archives Nationales, Section Outre-Mer, Paris
Afrique I through IV.

Archives Nationales, Section Outre-Mer, Aix-en-Provence
F^{80} Algérie

Archives du Ministère de la Guerre à Vincennes, Paris
Maroc 3H (formerly series C and D)

Archives de l'Alliance Israélite Universelle, Paris
Maroc, I through VII. Communities (political series)
Maroc, Ecoles. Reports and Correspondence of local School directors and leading personalities
France. General reports on Morocco and correspondence with the French government

Great Britain

Records of the Foreign Office, Public Record Office, London
52 Morocco, General Correspondence, Series I, 1761–1837
99 Morocco, General Correspondence, Series II, 1836–1905
174 Embassy and Consular Archives, Morocco Correspondence

631 Embassy and Consular Archives, Mogador Correspondence
830 Embassy and Consular Archives, Mogador, Registers of Correspondence
835 Embassy and Consular Archives, Casablanca Correspondences

British Library, London

Additional MSS. 38931–39164. The Layard Papers
Additional MSS. 41512, British Trade with Mogador

Anglo-Jewish Archives, London

A.J. 95. Minutes of the Anglo-Jewish Association
Gaster Papers

Archives of the Manchester Chamber of Commerce, Manchester

M8. Proceedings

United States

National Archives, Diplomatic Branch, Washington, D.C.

Record Group 84. American Consular Agency at Mogador. The volumes in this series have not yet been classified
T61. Despatches from the United States Consuls in Tangier

Israel

The Central Archives for the History of the Jewish People

MA/MG. Miscellaneous letters and rabbinical documents from Essaouira

Family collections

Corcos, Jerusalem. Documents include Arabic correspondence with the Palace, legal documents in Arabic, Hebrew, and Judeo-Arabic, and various other letters in European languages
Bū Damīʿa archives, Iligh, Tazarwalt. Arabic correspondence and commercial registers belonging to the *shurafāʾ* of Iligh
Bayrūk archives, Goulimime. Arabic correspondence and commercial registers of the Bayrūk family
Samuel Levy, Paris. These archives include Judeo-Arabic account books, legal documents in Arabic, Hebrew, and Judeo-Arabic, and miscellaneous letters in European languages

Books and studies in manuscript

Arabic and Hebrew

Akansūs, Muḥammad b. Aḥmad, *al-Jaysh al-ʿaramram al-khumāsī*, B.G., MS D 339

ad-Ḍuʿayyif, Muḥammad b. ʿAbd as-Salām, *Tārīkh*, B.G., MS D 660
ad-Dukkālī, Muḥammad b. Muḥammad al-Khayyāṭ . . . Ibn Ibrāhīm, *Taqāyīd tārīkhiyya*, Bodleian Library, Oxford, MS collection, Arab. C. 79
al-Ghazzāl, Aḥmad b. al-Mahdī, *Kitāb natījat al-ijtihād fī 'l-muhādana wa-l-jihād*, B.N., MS Fond Arabe, 2297
al-Hadrī, Aḥmad b. Masʿūd, *Sināʿat al-ʿArʿār min al-Ḥasan al-awwal ilā al-Ḥasan ath-thānī*, MS of author in Essaouira.
Ibn al-Ḥājj, Abū al-ʿAbbās Aḥmad, *ad-Durr al-muntakhab al-mustaḥsan fī baʿḍ maʾāthir amīr al-muʾminīn Mawlānā al-Ḥasan*, K.H., MS 1920
Durar al-jawhariyya fī madḥ al-khilāfat al-Ḥasaniyya, K.H., MS 512
Khnāffō, Masʿūd, *She'eilōt u-teshūbōt*, Bar Ilan, MS 192. Copy at Jewish National and University Library, Jerusalem, Micro. 36841
az-Zayānī, Abū al-Qāsim b. Aḥmad, *al-Bustān aẓ-Ẓarīf fī dawlat awlād Mawlāy ash-Sharīf*, A.N., Aix-en-Provence, 20 mi 1 (a)

European languages

Committee for the Relief of the Sufferers of Mogadore. Mocatta Library Archives, De Sola Pamphlets 6.
Fuchs, J., *Evolution d'un grand commandement marocain, le caid Mtougi et le Protectorat*, C.H.E.A.M., MS 2137
Obedia, M., *Les Juifs de Mogador*. Copy in the collection of Jean-Louis Miège
Observations on the Western Coast of the Morocco State during my Journey from Mogador to Tangier in July and August 1830; Memorandum Respecting the Foundation of Mogador, its Trade, etc., R.G.S., MS 1828
Ohayon, Jacob, *Les origines des Juifs de Mogador*, Ben Zvi Institute, Jerusalem

Unpublished theses

Afāʾ, ʿUmar, '*Masʾalat an-nuqūd fī tārīkh al-Maghrib fī' l-qarn at-tāsiʿ ʿashr (Sūs 1822–1906)*', Diblōm ad-dirāsāt al-ʿalyāʾ, Université Mohammed V. Rabat, 1985
Bowie, Leland L. 'The Protége System in Morocco 1880–1904', Ph.D. thesis, Michigan, 1970
Cigar, Norman, 'An Edition and Translation of the Chronicles from Muhammad al-Qadiri's Nashr Al-Mathani', D.Phil. thesis, Oxford, 1976.
El-Mansour, M. 'Political and Social Developments in Morocco during the Reign of Mawlay Sulayman, 1792–1822', Ph.D. thesis, S.O.A.S., London, 1981
Fituri, Aḥmad Said, 'Tripolitania, Cyrenaica, and Bilad as-Sudan: Trade Relations during the Second Half of the Nineteenth Century', Ph.D. thesis, Michigan, 1982.
Kenbib, Mohammed, 'Les protections étrangères au Maroc aux XIXème siècle–début du XXème', thèse de 3ème cycle, Paris VII, 1980
al-Mūʾddin, ʿAbd ar-Raḥmān, '*al-ʿAlaqa bayn al-mujtamaʿ al-qarawīya wa-d-dawla fī Maghrib al-qarn at-tāsiʿ ʿashr: qabāʾil Ināwin wa-l-makhzan, 1290/1873–1320/1902*', Diblōm ad-dirāsāt al-ʿalyāʾ, Université Moham-

med V. Rabat, 1984 [see also El Mouden, in published works, other languages].

Naïmi, Mustapha. 'L'infiltration des rapports marchands dans une formation économique traditionelle (essai de chronologie)', thèse de 3ème cycle, Paris X, 1981

Park, Thomas K., 'Administration and the Economy: Morocco 1880 to 1980. The Case of Essaouira', Ph.D. thesis, Wisconsin, 1983

Rollman, Wilfrid J., 'The "New Order" in a Pre-colonial Muslim Society: Military Reform in Morocco, 1844–1904', Ph.D. thesis, Michigan, 1983

Schroeter, Daniel J., 'Merchants and Pedlars of Essaouira: A Social History of a Moroccan Trading Town (1844–1886)', Ph.D. thesis, Manchester, 1984

Official publications

Great Britain

Accounts and papers. Parliamentary Papers. House of Commons. Consular Reports on Trade and Commerce

France

Annales du Commerce Extérieur. Faits Commerciaux

Spain

Anuario de la Dirección de Hidrografía

Morocco

al-Wathā'iq. Publication of the Direction des Archives Royales

Newspapers

ha-Maggīd, Lyck
ha-Ṣefīrah, Warsaw
Jewish Chronicle, London
Jewish Missionary Intelligence, London
Al-Moghreb Al-Aksa, Tangier
Times of Morocco, Tangier
Voice of Jacob, London

Published works

Arabic and Hebrew

Abīṭbūl, Micha'el 'Elīṭa Kalkalīt yehūdīt be-Marrōqō ha-pre-qōlōnīyālīt: tujjār as-Sulṭan [Une élite économique juive au Maroc pré-colonial; les tujjar al-Sultan'] in Michel Abitbol, (ed.), *Judaïsme d'Afrique du nord aux XIXe aux*

XXe siècles, Jerusalem, 1980, pp. 26–34 (in Hebrew section) [see also Abitbol, published works, other languages]
Ben-ʿAmī, Yissachar, *ha-Araṣat ha-qidūshīm be-qereb yehūdei Marrōqō*, Jerusalem, 1984 [see also Ben-Ami, published works, other languages]
Ben ʿAṭṭār, Abraham, *Shanōt Ḥayyīm*, Casablanca, 1958
Ben Nāʾīm, Yōsef, *Malkei Rabbanan*, Jerusalem, 1931
Dāʾūd, Muḥammad, *Tārīkh Tiṭwān*, 6 vols., Tetuan, 1959–1966
Deshen, Shlōmō, *Ṣībūr we-yeḥīdīm be-Marrōqō: sidrei ḥebra be-qehīllōt ha-yehūdīyyōt be-meʾōt ha-18-19*, Tel Aviv, 1983
Edraʿī, Moshe b. Yiṣḥaq, *Yad Mōshe*, Amsterdam, 5569/1808–9
Elmālīḥ, Yōsef, *Tōqfō shel Yōsef*, 2 vols., Livorno, 1823–1853
Ibn al-ʿArabī, aṣ-Ṣiddīq, 'Ṣafaḥāt min tārīkh aṣ-Ṣawīra', *Majallat al-Manāhil*, 9 (1978), 303–24
Ibn Manṣūr, ʿAbd al-Wahhāb, *Mushkilat al-ḥimāyat al-qunṣulīya bi-l-Maghrib min nashʾatihā ilā muʾtamar Madrid sanat 1880*, Rabat, 1977
Ibn Sūda, ʿAbd as-Salām b. ʿAbd al-Qādir, *Dalīl muʾarrikh al-Maghrib al-Aqṣā*, 2nd edn, 2 vols., Casablanca, 1960–5
Ibn Zaydān, ʿAbd ar-Raḥmān, *Itḥāf aʿlām an-nās bi-jamāl akhbār ḥaḍirat Miknās*, 5 vols., Rabat, 1929–33
al-ʿIzz wa-s-ṣawla fī maʿālim nuẓum ad-dawla, 2 vols., Rabat, 1962–2
al-Manūnī, Muḥammad, *Maẓāhir Yaqẓat al-Maghrib al-ḥadīth*, Rabat, 1973
an-Nāṣirī, Aḥmad b. Khālid, *Kitāb al-istiqṣāʾ li-akhbār duwal al-Maghrib al-Aqṣā*, 2nd edn, 9 vols., Casablanca, 1954–6
Nehlil, Mohammed, *Lettres chérifiennes*, Paris, 1915
ʿŌbadiya, Dawid, *Qehīllat Ṣefrū*, 3 vols., Jerusalem, 1975–6
al-Qādirī, Muḥammad, *The Bodleian Version of Muḥammad al-Qādirī's Nashr al-Mathānī: The Chronicles*, ed. Norman Cigar, Rabat, 1978
Qōrīyāṭ, Abraham, *Berīt abōt*, Livorno, 1862
Qōrīyāṭ, Abraham, *Zekhūt abōt*. Pisa, 1812 [grandfather of above].
ar-Ragrāgī, Aḥmad b. al-Ḥājj, *ash-Shamūs al-munīra fī akhbār madīnat aṣ-Ṣawīra*, Rabat, 1935
Rōmānellī, Shmūʾel, *Massāʾ ba-ʿarab*, ed. Ḥayyīm Schirmann, in *Ketābīm Nibḥarīm*, Jerusalem, 1968
Shitrit, Yosef, 'Mūdaʿūt ḥadasha le-anōmaliyūt ū-le-lashōn – niṣaneyah shel tenūʿat haskalah ʿivrit be-Marrōkō be-sōf ha-meʾah ha-19, *mi-Qedem ū-mi-Yam* 2, 1986.
aṣ-Ṣiddīqī, Muḥammad b. Saʿīd, *Īqāẓ as-Sarīra li-tārīkh aṣ-Ṣawīra*, Casablanca, n.d. [1961]
as-Sūsī, Muḥammad al-Mukhtār, *Illīgh qadīman wa-ḥadīthan*, Rabat, 1966
Khilāl Jazūla, 4 vols., Tetuan, n.d. [1959]
al-Maʿsūl, 20 vols., Casablanca, 1960–1
Tawfīq, Aḥmad, *al-Mujtamaʿ al-maghribī fī ʿl-qarn at-tāsiʿ ʿashr. Īnūltān (1850–1912)*, 2 vols., Rabat, 1978 [see also Toufiq, published works, other languages]
at-Tūzānī, Naʿīma Harrāj, *al-Umanāʾ bi-l-Maghrib fī ʿahd as-Sulṭan Mawlāy* al-*Ḥasan (1290–1311/1873–1894)*, Rabat, 1979

az-Zayānī, Abū 'l-Qāsim b. Aḥmad, *at-Turjumān al-mu'rib 'an duwal al-Mashriq wa-l-Maghrib*, ed. and tr. Octave Houdas, *Le Maroc de 1631 à 1812*, Paris, 1886

European languages

Aafif, Mohamed, 'Les harkas hassaniennes d'après l'œuvre d'A. Ibn Zidane', *Hésperis-Tamuda*, 19 (1980–1), 153–68

Abitbol, Michel, *Témoins et acteurs: les Corcos et l'histoire du Maroc contemporain*, Jerusalem, 1977

Tombouctou et les Arma. De la Conquête marocaine du Soudan nigérien en 1591 à l'hégemonie de l'Empire Peul du Macina en 1833, Paris, 1979

Abu-Lughod, Janet, *Rabat: Urban Apartheid in Morocco*, Princeton, 1980

Abun Nasr, Jamil M., *A History of the Maghrib*, Cambridge, 1971, 2nd edn. 1975

Adam, André, *Histoire de Casablanca (des origines à 1914)*, Aix-en-Provence, 1968

Alermón Y Dorreguiz, *Descripción del Imperio de Marruecos*, Madrid, 1859

Alvarez Pérez, José, 'Marruecos. Memoria geográfica-comercial de la demarción del consulado de Mogador', *Boletin de la Sociedad geográfica de Madrid*, 2 (1877), 499–518

Andrews, W. H. C., *A Pamphlet and Map of Southern Morocco, or "Sûs" and the "Ait Bou Amaran"*, London, 1884

Arlett, W., 'Survey of Some of the Canary Islands and of Part of the Western Coast of Africa in 1835', *Journal of the Royal Geographical Society*, 6 (1836), 285–310

Arnaud, Louis, *Au temps des "Mehallas" ou le Maroc de 1860 à 1912*, Casablanca, 1952

Arnold, Rosemary, 'Separation of Trade and Market: The Great Market of Whydah' and 'A port of Trade: Whydah on the Guinea Coast', in Karl Polanyi, Conrad M. Arensberg, and Harry W. Pearson, *Trade and Market in the Early Empires. Economies in History and Theory*, Glencoe, Ill., 1957, pp. 154–187

Attal, Robert, *Les Juifs d'Afrique du Nord: Bibliographie*, Jerusalem, 1973

Aubin, Eugène, *Morocco of Today*, London, 1906

Ayache, Germain, *Etudes d'histoire marocain*, Rabat, 1979

Bache, Paul-Eugène, 'Souvenirs d'un voyage à Mogador', *Revue Maritime et Coloniale*, (January–February, 1861), 81–99

Badia Y Leyblich, Domingo, *Travels of Ali Bey in Morocco, Tripoli, Cyprus, Egypt, Arabia, Syria, and Turkey between the years 1803 and 1807*, 2 vols., London, 1816

Baer, Gabriel, *Studies in the Social History of Modern Egypt*, Chicago and London, 1969

Balansa, A., 'Voyage de Mogador à Maroc', *B.S.G.*, 5e sér., 15 (1868), 312–34

Basset, René, *Relation de Sidi Brahim de Massat*, Paris, 1883

Basu, Dilip K. (ed.), *The Rise and Growth of Colonial Port Cities in Asia*, Lanham, Md. and London, 1985

Beauclerk, G., *Journey to Morocco*, London, 1828

Beaumier, Auguste, 'Le choléra au Maroc, sa marche du Sahara jusqu'au Sénégal en 1868', *B.S.G.*, 6e sér., 3 (1872), 287–305

'Itinéraire de Mogador au Maroc et du Maroc à Saffy', *B.S.G.*, 5e sér., 16 (1868), 321–39

'Le Maroc', *B.S.G.*, 5e sér., 14 (1867), 5–51

'Mogador et son commerce maritime', *Annales du Commerce Extérieur*, Etats-Barbaresques, Faits Commerciaux, no. 17 (1875), 105–20

'Premier établissement des Israélites à Tombouctou', *B.S.G.*, 5e sér., 19 (1870), 345–70

Ben-Ami, Issachar, 'Folk Veneration of Saints among Moroccan Jews' in S. Morag, I. Ben-Ami, and N. Stillman (eds.), *Studies in Judaism and Islam*, Jerusalem, 1984

Benech, José, *Essai d'explication d'un mellah*, Kaiserslauten, n.d.

Benet, Francisco, 'Explosive Markets: the Berber Highlands', in K. Polanyi *et al.*, *Trade and Market in Early Empires*, Glencoe, Ill., 1957, pp. 188–217

Benoit, Fernand, *L'Afrique méditerranéene; Algérie–Tunisie–Maroc*, 1931

Berque, Jacques, *L'intérieur du Maghreb; XVe–XIXe siecle*, Paris, 1978

Structures sociales du Haut-Atlas, 2nd edn, Paris, 1978

Berthier, Paul, *Les anciennes sucreries du Maroc et leurs réseaux hydrauliques*, 2 vols., Rabat, 1966.

Bois, Charles, 'Années de disette, années d'abondance, sécheresse et pluies au Maroc', *Revue pour l'Etude des Calamités*, nos. 26–7 (1949), 1–31

Bonelli, Emilio, *El Imperio de Marruecos y su constitución*, Madrid, 1882

Bowie, Leland, 'An Aspect of Muslim–Jewish Relations in Late Nineteenth-Century Morocco: A European Diplomatic View', *International Journal of Middle East Studies*, 7 (1976), 3–19

Braudel, Fernand, *Civilization and Capitalism: 15th–18th Century*, Vol. I: *The Structures of Everyday Life. The Limits of the Possible*, London, 1981; Vol. II: *The Wheels of Commerce*, London, 1982; Vol. III: *The Perspective of the World*, London, 1984

The Mediterranean and the Mediterranean World in the Age of Philip II, 2 vols., New York, 1973

Brett, Michael, 'Modernisation in 19th Century North Africa', *The Maghreb Review*, 7, 1–2 (1982), 16–22

Brignon, Jean, *et al.*, *Histoire du Maroc*, Casablanca, 1967

Brown, Kenneth L. 'The "Curse" of Westermarck, *Acta Philosophica Fennica*, 34 (1982), 219–59

'The Impact of the *Dahir Berbère* in Salé', in E. Gellner and C. Micaud (eds.), *Arabs and Berbers*, London, 1972, 201–15

'Mellah and Madina: A Moroccan City and its Jewish Quarter (Salé, *ca.* 1880–1930)' in S. Morag *et al.*, *Studies in Judaism and Islam*, Jerusalem, 1981, pp. 253–81

People of Salé. Tradition and Change in a Moroccan City: 1830–1930, Manchester, 1976

'An Urban View of Moroccan History: Salé, 100–1800', *Hespéris-Tamuda*, 12 (1971), 5–106

Brunschvig, Robert, 'Coup d'œil sur l'histoire des foires à travers l'Islam', in *Recueils de la Société Jean Bodin*, Vol. V: *La Foire* (1953), 43–74
Burke III, Edmund, 'The image of the Moroccan State in French Ethnological Literature: A New Look at the Origins of Lyautey's Berber Policy', in Ernest Gellner and Charles Micaud (eds.). *Arabs and Berbers: From Tribe to Nation in North Africa*, London, 1972, pp. 177–99
'Morocco and the Near East: Reflections on some Basic Differences', *Archiv, Europ. Sociol.* 10 (1969), 70–94
Prelude to Protectorate in Morocco. Precolonial Protest and Resistance: 1860–1912, Chicago and London, 1976
Caillé, Jacques, 'L'abolition des tributs versés au Maroc par la Suède et le Danemark', *Hespéris*, 45 (1958), 203–38
Les français à Mogador en 1844, Essaouira, 1952
La ville de Rabat jusqu'au Protectorat français, 3 vols., Paris, 1949
Caillié, René, *Travels through Central Africa to Timbuctoo and across the Great Desert, to Morocco, Performed in the Years 1824–1828*, 2 vols., London, 1830
Calderón, Serafin E., *Manuel del Oficial en Marruecos*, Madrid, 1844.
Campou, L. de, *Un Empire qui croule: Le Maroc contemporain*, Paris, 1886
'Caravanes de Timbouctou', *Revue Française de l'Etranger et des Colonies*, 8, 2e sem. of 1888 (1889), 552–3
Castellanos, Manuel Pablo, *Descripción histórica de Marruecos y breve reseña de sus dinastías*, Santiago de Compostella, 1978
Castries, H. de, 'Le Danemark et le Maroc: 1750–1767', *Hespéris*, 6 (1926), 327–49
Chénier, Louis, *Un Chargé d'affaires au Maroc. Le correspondance du consul Louis Chénier: 1767–1782*. 2 vols., ed. Pierre Grillon, Paris, 1970
The Present State of the Empire of Morocco, 2 vols., London, 1788
Chetrit, Joseph, 'Shlomo Gozlan: un poète bilingue de Tamgrût dans le Drâa', in Michel Abitbol (ed.), *Communautés juives des marges sahariennes du Maghreb*, Jerusalem, 1982
Chevallier, Dominique, *La société du Mont Liban à l'époque de la revolution industrielle en Europe*, Paris, 1971
Cigar, Norman, 'Société et la vie politique à Fès sous les premiers 'Alawites (*ca.* 1660/1830)', *Hespéris-Tamuda*, 18 (1978–9), 98–125
'Socio-economic Structures and the Development of an Urban Bourgeoisie in Pre-colonial Morocco', *The Maghreb Review*, 6, 3–4 (1981), 55–76
Cochelet, Charles, *Narrative of the Shipwreck Sophia on the 30th of May 1819, on the Western Coast of Africa and the Captivity of a Part of the Crew in the Desert of the Sahara*, London, 1822
Cohen, Abner, 'Cultural Strategies in the Organization of Trading Diasporas', in Claude Meillassoux (ed.), *The Development of Indigenous Trade in West Africa*, Oxford, 1971, pp. 266–81
Cohn, Albert, 'Voyage de M. Albert Cohn', *Univers Israélite*, 15 (1860), 699–701
Corcos, David, *Studies in the History of the Jews of Morocco*, Jerusalem, 1976
Cossé-Brissac, Philippe, 'Les rapports de la France et du Maroc pendant la conquête de l'Algérie (1830–1847)', *Hespéris*, 13 (1931), 35–115, 133–225
Craig, James, 'Un aperçu de Maroc', *B.S.G.*, 5e sér., 19 (1870), 177–203

Crémieux, Adolphe, 'Les Israélites de Mogador', *Univers Israélite* (1866), 329–31
Cruickshank, Earl F., *Morocco at the Parting of the Ways*, Philadelphia, 1935
Curtin, Philip D., *Cross-Cultural Trade in World History*, Cambridge, 1984
Economic Change in Precolonial Africa: Senegambia in the Era of the Slave Trade, 2 vols., Madison, 1975
Curtis, James, *A Journal of Travels in Barbary, in the Year 1801, with Observations on the Gum Trade of Senegal*, London, 1803
Davidson, John, *Notes Taken during Travels in Africa*, London, 1839
Deverdun, G., *Marrakech, des origines à 1912*, 2 vols., Rabat, 1959–66
Doutté, Edmond, 'Dans le sud marocain, au pays des Anfloûs', *Revue de Paris* (15 March 1913), pp. 428–48
'Organisation sociale et domestique chez le H'ah'a', *R.C.* (1905), 1–16
En Tribu, Paris, 1914
Dozy, R., *Supplement aux dictionnaires arabes*, 2 vols., Leiden, 1881
Drague, Georges, *Esquisse d'histoire religieuse du Maroc. Confréries et zaouias*, Paris, 1951
Dunn, Ross E., *Resistance in the Desert: Moroccan Responses to French Imperialism, 1881–1912*, Madison, 177
'The Trade of Tafilalt: Commercial Change in Southeast Morocco on the Eve of the Protectorate', *African Historical Studies*, 4 (1971), 271–304
Eickelmann, Dale F., 'Religion and Trade in Western Morocco', *Research in Economic Anthropology*, 5 (1983), 335–48
El-Mouden, Abderrahman, 'Etat et société rural à travers la *ḥarka* au Maroc du XIXème siècle', *The Maghreb Review*, 8, 5–6 (1983)
Ernest-Picard, P., *La monnai et le crédit en Algérie depuis 1830*, Algiers and Paris, 1930
Fawaz, Leila Tarazi, *Merchants and Migrants in Nineteenth Century Beirut*, Cambridge, Mass., 1983
Fernandez, Cesáreo, 'Mogador', *Anuario de la Dirección de Hidrografía*, 3 (1865), 259–78
Flamand, Pierre, *Quelques manifestations de l'esprit populaire dans les juiveries du sud marocain*, Casablanca, n.d. [1959]
Flournoy, Francis R., *British Policy towards Morocco in the age of Palmerston: 1830–1865*, Baltimore, 1935
Foster, Brian L., 'Ethnicity and Commerce', *American Ethnologist*, 1 (1974), 437–48
Foucauld, Charles de, *Reconnaissance au Maroc: 1883–1884*, Paris, 1888
Froidevaux, Henri, 'Une description de Mogador en 1765', *Annales de Geographie*, 2 (1893), 394–8
Gatell, Joachim, 'Description du Sous', *B.S.G.*, 6e sér., 1 (1871), 81–106
Geertz, Clifford, 'Ports of Trade in Nineteenth Century Bali', *Research in Economic Anthropology*, 3 (1980), 109–22
'*Suq:* The Bazaar Economy in Sefrou', in Clifford Geertz, Hildred Geertz, and Lawrence Rosen, *Meaning and Order in Moroccan Society*, Cambridge, 1979, pp. 123–310

Gellner, Ernest. *Saints of the Atlas*, Chicago and London, 1969
Gellner, Ernest, and Micaud, C. (eds.), *Arabs and Berbers*, London, 1972
Gérenton, E. 'Les expéditions de Moulay el Hasan dans le Sous: 1882–1886', *R.C.* (1924), 265–86
Ginsburg, J. B., *An Account of the Persecution of the Protestant Mission among the Jews at Mogador, Morocco*, London, 1880
Gíraud, Hubert, 'Itinéraire de Mogador à Marrakech (1890–92)', *C.R. des Séances du Congrès National de Géographie*, Marseilles (1898)
Godard, Léon, *Description et histoire du Maroc*, Paris, 1860
Le Maroc, notes d'un voyageur, Algiers, 1859
Goitein, S. D., *A Mediterranean Society*, Vol. I: *Economic Foundations*, Berkeley and Los Angeles, 1967
Goldberg, Harvey E., *The Book of Mordechai. A Study of the Jews of Libya*, Philadelphia, 1980
González-Palencia, A., 'Un Italiano en Mogador en 1783', *Africa* (June–August, 1948), 273–6
Gråberg di Hemsö, Jacopo, *Specchio geografico e statistico dell'Imperio di Marocco*, Genoa, 1834
Guedalla, H., *Refutation of an Anonymous Article in 'The Jewish World'; Secret History of Sir Moses Montefiore's Mission to Morocco in 1863–4*, London, 1880
Guillen, Pierre, *L'Allemagne et le Maroc de 1870 à 1905*, Paris, 1967
Hammoudi, Abdallah, 'Sainteté, pouvoir, et société: Tamgrout aux XVIIe et XVIIIe siècles', *Annales, E.S.C.*, 35 (1980), pp. 615–41
Harris, Walter B., *Tafilet: The Narrative of a Journey of Exploration in the Atlas Mountains and the Oases of the North-West Sahara*, London, 1895
Hart, David, *The Aith Waryaghar of the Moroccan Rif*, Tucson, 1976
Hodgkin, Thomas, *Narrative of a Journey to Morocco in 1863 and 1864*, London, 1866
Hooker, J. D. and Ball, J., *Journal of a Tour in Morocco and the Great Atlas*, London, 1878
Hopkins, A. G., *An Economic History of West Africa*, London, 1973
Hosotte-Reynaud, M., 'Un négociant à Mogador à la fin du XVIIIe siècle et sa correspondance avec le consul de France à Salé', *Hespéris*, 44 (1957), 335–45
Ibn Khaldun, *The Muqaddimah*, tr. F. Rosenthal, 3 vols., New York, 1958
Ideville, H. de, *Le Maréchal Bugeaud d'après sa correspondance intime et des documents inédits: 1784–1849*, 2 vols., Paris, 1882
Israel, Jonathan I., *European Jewry in the Age of Mercantilism: 1550–1750*, Oxford, 1985
Jackson, James Grey, *An Account of the Empire of Morocco and the Districts of Sus and Tafilelt*, 3rd edn, London, 1814
An Account of Timbuctoo and Housa Territories in the Interior of Africa, London, 1820
Jacques-Muenié, D., *Le Maroc saharien, des origines à 1670*, 2 vols., Paris, 1982
Jamous, Raymond, *Honneur et baraka: les structures sociales traditionnelles dans le Rif*, Cambridge and Paris, 1981

Jannasch, Robert, *Die deutsche Handelsexpedition 1886*, Berlin, 1887
Jodin, André, *Les établissements du roi Juba II aux îles purpuraires (Mogador)*, Tangier, 1967
Justinard, L., 'Notes d'histoire et de littérature berbères: les Haha et les gens du Sous', *Hespéris*, 8 (1928), 333–56
Kenbib, Mohamed, 'Structures traditionnelles et protection diplomatique dans le Maroc précolonial', in René Gallissot (ed.), *Structures et cultures précapitalistes*, Paris, 1981
Lahbabi, Mohamed, *Le gouvernement marocain à l'aube du XXe siècle*, Rabat, 1958
Lakhdar, Mohamed, *La vie littéraire au Maroc sous la dynastie 'Alawide (1075–1311 = 1664–1894)*, Rabat, 1971
Lambert, Paul, 'Notice sur la ville de Maroc', *B.S.G.*, 5e sér., 16 (1868), 430–47
Landes, David S., *Bankers and Pashas: International Finance and Economic Imperialism in Egypt*, Cambridge, Mass., 1958
Laoust, E., *Mots et choses berbères*, Paris, 1920
Lapidus, Ira M., *Muslim Cities in the Later Middle Ages*, Cambridge, Mass., 1967
Laredo, Abraham, *Les noms des Juifs du Maroc*, Madrid, 1978
Laroui, Abdallah, *The History of the Maghrib: An Interpretative Essay*, Princeton, 1977
Les origines sociales et culturelles du nationalisme marocain (1830–1912), Paris, 1977
Larras, N., 'La population du Maroc', *La Géographie*, *B.S.G.*, 13, 2 (1906), 337–48
Laskier, Michael M., *The Alliance Israélite Universelle and the Jewish Communities of Morocco, 1862–1962*, Albany, N.Y., 1983
Leared, Arthur, *Marocco and the Moors*, London, 1876
'Mogador as a Winter Resort for Invalids', *The Lancet* (25 October 1873)
'The Trade and Resources of Morocco', *Journal of the Society of Arts*, 25 (1877), 531–41
Le Chatelier, A., *Tribus du sud-ouest marocain*, Paris, 1891
Leclerq, J., 'Mogador', *Revue Britanique*, 6 (1880), 397–418
'Sur les côtes du Maroc', *Revue Britanique*, 2 (1881), 319–52
Lee, Joseph C., 'The North West Coast of Africa', *Journal of the Manchester Geographical Society*, 2 (1886), 145–64
Leech, William B., 'Notes on a visit to Mogador', *Journal of the Manchester Geographical Society*, 18 (1902), 57–64
Lempriere, W., *A Tour from Gibraltar to Tangier, Sallee, Mogadore, Santa Cruz, Tarudant and thence over Mount Atlas to Morocco*, 2nd edn, London, 1793
Lenz, Oskar, *Timbouctou: voyage au Maroc, an Sahara et au Soudan*, Paris, 1886
'Voyage du Maroc au Sénégal', *B.S.G.*, 7e sér., 1 (1881), 199–226
Le Tourneau, Roger, *Fès avant le protectorat*, Casablanca, 1949
Fez in the age of the Marinides, Norman, Okla., 1961
Lewis, Bernard, *The Jews of Islam*, Princeton, 1984
Loewe, L. (ed.), *Diaries of Sir Moses and Lady Montefiore*, 2 vols., London, 1890

Lourido-Díaz, Ramon, 'Le commerce entre le Portugal et le Maroc pendant la deuxième moitié du XVIIIe siècle', *Revue d'Historie Maghrebine*, 5 (1976), 27–46

Marruecos en la segunda mitad del siglo XVIII. Vida interna: política, social y religiosa durante el Sultanato de Sīdī Muḥammad b. 'Abd Allāh (1757–1790), Madrid, 1978

Lovejoy, Paul E., 'Polanyi's "Ports of Trade": Salaga and Kano in the Nineteenth Century', *Canadian Journal of African Studies*, 16 (1982), 245–77

Luengo, Fr. A., 'Mogador – fondación de la mission católica', *Mauritania* (1 August 1940), 249–51

Mackenzie, Donald, *The Flooding of the Sahara*, London, 1877

The Khalifate of the West, London, 1911

McNeill, William, *Plagues and People*, New York, 1976

Marcet, A., *Le Maroc: voyage d'une mission française à la cour du Sultan*, Paris, 1885

Marty, Paul, 'Une tentative de pénétration pacifique dans le sud marocain en 1839', *Revue de l'Histoire des Colonies Françaises*, 9, 2 (1921), 101–16

Massignon, Louis, 'Enquête sur les corporations musulmanes d'artisans et de commerçants au Maroc', *Revue du Monde Musulman*, 58 (1924), 1–250

Mathews, Felix A., 'Northwest Africa and Timbuctoo', *Bulletin of the American Geographical Society*, 4 (1881), 196–219

Meakin, Budgett, *The Land of the Moors*, London, 1901

Meillassoux, Claude (ed.), *The Development of Indigenous Trade and Markets in West Africa*, Oxford, 1971

Mercier, L., 'L'administration marocaine à Rabat', *Archives Marocaines*, 1 (1904), 59–96

Michaux-Bellaire, E., 'Les biens habous et les biens du Makhzen au point de vue de leur location et de leur alienation', *Revue du Monde Musulman*, 5 (1908), pp. 436–57

'L'organisation des finances au Maroc', *Archives Marocaines*, 11 (1907), 171–251

Michaux-Bellaire, E. and Salmon, G., 'El-Qçar El-Kebir: une ville de province au Maroc septentrional', *Archives Marocaines*, 2 (1904), 1–228

Miège, Jean-Louis. 'La bourgeoisie juive du Maroc au XIXe siècle: rupture ou continuité', in M. Abitbol (ed.), *Judaîsme d'Afrique du Nord aux XIXe–XXe siècle*, Jerusalem, 1980, pp. 25–36

'Le commerce trans-Saharien au XIXe siècle. Essai de quantification', *Revue de l'Occident Musulman et de la Méditerranée*, 32, 2 (1981), 93–119

Documents d'histoire économique et sociale marocaine au XIXe siècle, Paris, 1969

'Les Juifs et le commerce transsaharien au dix-neuvième siècle', in M. Abitbol (ed.), *Communautés juives des marges sahariennes*, Jerusalem, 1982, pp. 391–404

'Le Maroc et les premières lignes de navigation à vapeur', *Bulletin de l'Enseignement Public au Maroc*, no. 236 (1956), 37–47

Le Maroc et l'Europe: 1830–1894, 4 vols., Paris, 1961–2

Une mission française à Marrakech en 1882, Aix-en-Provence, 1968

'Note sur l'artisanat marocain en 1870', *Bulletin Economique et Social du Maroc*, 16 (1953) 91–3

'Origine et développement de la consommation du thé au Maroc', *Bulletin Economique et Social du Maroc*, 20, 71 (1956), 377–98

Montagne, Robert, *Les Berbères et le Makhzen dans le sud du Maroc*, Paris, 1930

Monteil, Vincent, 'Les Juifs d'Ifrane', *Hespéris*, 35 (1948), 151–62

Notes sur les Tekna, Paris, 1948

Morsy, Magali, 'Moulay Isma'il et l'armée de métier', *Revue d'Histoire Moderne et Contemporaine* (April–June, 1967), 97–122

North Africa 1800–1900, London and New York, 1984

Mouliéras, Auguste, *Le Maroc inconnu*, 2 vols., Paris, 1895–9

Murphey, Rhoads, *The Outsiders: The Western Experience in India and China*, Ann Arbor, 1977

Naïmi, Mustapha, 'La politique des chefs de la confederation Tekna face à l'expansionnisme commercial européen', *Revue d'Histoire Maghrebine*, 11, 35–6 (1984), 153–73

Nataf, F., *Le crédit et la banque au Maroc*, Paris, 1929

Newbury, C. W., 'North African and Western Sudan Trade in the Nineteenth Century: A Re-evaluation', *Journal of African History*, 7 (1966), 223–46

Noin, Daniel, *La population rurale du Maroc*, 2 vols., Paris, 1970

Nordman, Daniel. 'Les expéditions de Moulay Hassan', *Hespéris-Tamuda*, 19 (1980–1), 123–52

Ollive, C. 'Commerce entre Timbouctou et Mogador', *Bulletin de la Société de Géographie de Marseille*, 4 (1880), 5–7

'Géographie médicale: climat de Mogador et de son influence sur la phthisie', *B.S.G.*, 6e sér., 10 (1875), 365–416

Owen, Roger, *Cotton and the Egyptian Economy 1820–1914*, Oxford, 1969

The Middle East in the World Economy, London and New York, 1981

Park, Thomas K., 'Inflation and Economic Policy in 19th Century Morocco: The Compromise Solution', *The Maghreb Review*, 10, 2–3 (1985), 51–6

Parsons, F. V., 'The North West African Company and the British Government, 1875–1895', *Historical Journal*, 1 (1958), 136–53

The Origins of the Morocco Question 1880–1900, London, 1976

Pascon, Paul, *Le Haouz de Marrakesh*, 2 vols., Rabat, 1977

La maison d'Iligh et l'histoire sociale du Tazerwalt, collaboration of A. Arrif, D. Schroeter, M. Tozy, and H. Van Der Wusten, Rabat, 1984

Pascon, Paul and Schroeter, Daniel, 'Le cimetière juif d'Iligh (1751–1955): Etude des épitaphes comme documents d'histoire sociale (Tazerwalt, sud-ouest marocain)', *Revue de l'Occident Musulman et de la Méditerranée*, 34, 2 (1982), 39–62

Payton, Charles A., *Moss from a Rolling Stone, or Moorish Wanderings and Rambling Reminiscences*, London, 1879

Perinbaum, B. M., 'Social Relations in the Trans-Saharan and Western

Sudanese Trade: An Overview', *Comparative Studies in Society and History*, 15 (1873), 416–36
Picciotto, Moses Haim, *Jews of Morocco, Report*, London, 1861
Pirenne, Henri, *Economic and Social History of Medieval Europe*, London and Henley, 1936
Pobeguin, E., 'Notes sur Mogador', *R.C.* (1906), 49–63
Polanyi, Karl, 'Ports of Trade in Early Societies', *Journal of Economic History*, 23 (1963), 30–45
Polanyi, Karl, Arensberg, Conrad M., and Pearson, Harry W. (eds.), *Trade and Market in Early Empires. Economies in History and Theory*, Glencoe, Ill., 1957
Ponasik, D. S., 'The System of Administered Trade as a Defense Mechanism in Preprotectorate Morocco', *International Journal of Middle East Studies*, 8 (1977), 195–207
Raymond, André, *Grandes villes arabes à l'époque ottomane*, Paris, 1985
The Great Arab Cities in the 16th–18th Centuries: An Introduction, New York and London, 1984
Redford, A., *Manchester Merchants and Foreign Trade*, 2 vols., Manchester, 1934–56
René-Leclerc, Charles, 'Le commerce et l'industrie à Fez', *R.C.* (1905), 229–53, 295–321, 336–50
Richardson, James, *Travels in Morocco*, 2 vols., London, 1860
Riley, James, *An Authentic Narrative of the Loss of the American Brig Commerce*, New York, 1817
Rodinson, Maxime, *Islam and Capitalism*, London, 1974
Rohifs, Gerhard, *Adventures in Morocco through the Oases of Draa and Tafilet*, London, 1874
Rosen, Lawrence, *Bargaining for Reality: the Construction of Social Relations in a Muslim Community*, Chicago and London, 1984
Rosenberger, Bernard, and Triki, Hamid, 'Famines et épidemies au Maroc aux XVIe et XVIIe siècles', *Hespéris-Tamuda*, 14 (1973), 109–75
Rousseau des Roches, J., *Trois souvenirs: Tanger, Isly, Mogador*, Paris, 1846
Salmon. G., 'L'administration marocaine à Tanger' and 'Le commerce indigène à Tanger', *Archives Marocaines*, 1 (1904), 1–55
Schroeter, Daniel J., 'Anglo-Jewry and Essaouira (Mogador): 1860–1900. The Social Implications of Philanthropy', *Transactions of the Jewish Historical Society of England*, 28 (1984), 60–88
'The Jews of Essaouira (Mogador) and the Trade of Southern Morocco', in M. Abitbol (ed.), *Communautés juives des marges sahariennes du Maghreb*, Jerusalem, 1982, pp. 365–90
'The Royal Palace Archives of Rabat and the Makhzen in the 19th Century', *The Maghreb Review*, 7, 1–2 (1981), 41–5
'The Town of Mogador (Essaouira) and Aspects of Change in Pre-colonial Morocco: A Bibliographical Essay', *Bulletin of the British Society for Middle Eastern Studies*, 6, 1 (1979), 24–38

Seddon, David, *Moroccan Peasants: A Century of Change in the Eastern Rif, 1870–1970*, Folkestone, 1981
Segonazac, René de, *Au Cœur de l'Atlas. Mission au Maroc, 1904–1905*, Paris, 1910
Serres, Jean, 'Comment Pellissier de Reynaud ne fut pas consul de France à Mogador (1843)', in *Memorial Henri Basset*, vol. 2, Paris, 1928, pp. 243–7
Stähelin, Alfred, 'Mogador', *Das Ausland*, 62 (1889), 611–14, 629–31
Stambouli, F. and Zghal, A., 'Urban Life in Pre-colonial North Africa', *British Journal of Sociology*, 27 (1976), 1–20
Stern, Selma, *The Court Jew*, Philadelphia, 1950
Stillman, Norman, *The Jews of Arab Lands: A History and Source Book*, Philadelphia, 1979
Stutfield, E. M., *El Maghreb, 1200 Miles' Ride through Morocco*, London, 1886
Szymański, Edward, 'La guerre hispano-marocaine (1859–60): début de l'histoire du Maroc contemporain (essai de périodisation)', *Rocnik Orientalistyczny*, 29, 2 (1965), 53–65
Terrasse, Henri, *Histoire du Maroc. Des origines à l'établissement du protectorat français*, 2 vols., Casablanca, 1950
Thomassy, Raymond, *Le Maroc et ses caravanes ou relations de la France avec cet Empire*, Paris, 1845
Thomson, Joseph, *Travels in the Atlas and Southern Morocco*, London, 1889
Toufiq, Ahmed, 'Les Juifs dans la société marocaine au 19e siècle: l'example des Juifs de Demnate', in *Juifs du Maroc, identité et dialogue*, Grenoble, 1980.
'Travaux dans la rade et dans la ville de Mogador', *Nouvelles Annales de la Marine*, 30 (1863), pp. 285–6
Troin, Jean-François, *Les souks marocains*, 2 vols., Aix-en-Provence, 1975
Udovitch, Abraham L., *Partnership and Profit in Medieval Islam*, Princeton, 1970
Udovitch, Abraham L. and Valensi, Lucette, *The Last Arab Jews: The Communities of Jerba, Tunisia*, Chur, London, Paris and New York, 1984
Valensi, Lucette, *Fellahs tunisiens: l'économie rurale et la vie des campagnes au 18e et 19e siècles*, Paris and The Hague, 1977
Le Maghreb avant la prise d'Alger, Paris, 1969
Voinot, L., *Pèlerinages judéo-musulmans au Maroc*, Paris, 1948
Wallerstein, Immanuel, *The Modern World System. Capitalist Agriculture and the Origins of the European World Economy in the Sixteenth Century*, New York, 1974
Warnier, Auguste Hubert, *Campagne du Maroc (1844)*, Paris, 1944
Westermarck, Edward, *Ceremonies and Beliefs Connected with Agriculture, Certain Dates of the Solar Year, and Weather in Morocco*, Helsinki, 1913
Ritual and Belief in Morocco, 2 vols., London, 1926
Wolf, Eric R., *Europe and the People without History*, Berkeley, Los Angeles, and London, 1982
Zafrani, Haïm, *Les Juifs du Maroc. Vie sociale, économique et religieuse*, Paris, 1972
Pédagogie juive en terre d'Islam. L'enseignement traditionnel de l'hébreu et du judaïsme au Maroc, Paris, 1969
Zerbib, T. E., 'Slave Caravans in Morocco', *The Anti-Slavery Reporter*, ser. 4, 7, 3 (1887), pp. 98–9

Index

Arabic language, 60, 78, 109, 114–15
argan tree and oil, 8, 101, 159, 206–7
Arksīs, port of, 190, 192
army, *al-ʿaskar al-jadīd*, 192, 207; garrison of Essaouira, 12–15, 70, 76, 83, 119–20, 122, 131, 135–6, 180, 183, 184, 206–7, 224; *qāʾid* of (also called *bāshā*), 94, 122, 135, 186, 192; reforms of the 121, 134, 135–6, 191, 217; *see also ḥarka*, *maḥalla*, *ʿabīd*, renegades
artisans, crafts, 15, 34, 69–75, 76, 79, 207–8, 213; decline of, 1, 64, 213; itinerant, 71; Jewish, 70–1, 203–4
Asbūya, tribe, 192
Ashʿāsh, ʿAbd al-Khāliq, 118–19; Muḥammad, 118, 123
aʿshār, 125, 127, 185–7, 174, 193; *see also* taxes
ʿĀshūrāʾ, 96, 183
al-ʿaskar al-jadīd, *see* army
Asrir, *mawsim* of, 98
Assāka, port of 162, 192, 194,
Assor, Moses, 132
Atlas Mountains, 14; Jews of, 91
al-ʿAṭṭār, ʿAbd al-Qādir, 133, 135, 166, 167, 224; al-ʿArabī, 135, 224
Attia, Messod, 211
Austro–Hungarian consulate, 44, 45, 166
al-Awsā, ʿUmar b. ʿAmr, 140
Ayache, Germaine, 213, 270 n. 87 n. 104
Azghār, 182

banditry, 90, 92, 128, 171–2, 182, 184–5, 189, 195, 209, 278 n. 65
Banī ʿAntar, settlers from, 13–14, 61
Banī Tāmar, 172, 182
banks, established in Tangier, 55–6; absence of, 55, 71, 109; investment in European, 5, 49–50, 51, 55–6
Bannīs, al-ʿAyashī, 137–8, 147, 148; Muḥammad b. al-Madanī, 48, 54, 63, 66, 135, 137–8, 140, 170, 185, 218
Bargāsh, Muḥammad, 128, 129, 157, 168, 170, 172, 174, 179
barley, 95, 106, 151, 193, 205, 206–8, 291 n. 73
barter, 63, 111
al-Bārūdī, al-Ḥājj Bujnān, 137
bāshā (as chief of militia), 122, 135; *see also* army, *qāʾid* of
Bawākhir mosque, 141
Bayrūk, family, 110, 189, 195; members, ʿAbdīn, 181, Daḥmān, 114, 180–1, 190, 191–2, 239 n. 38, Ḥabīb, 180–1, 187, 189, Muḥammad, 180, 190; Sheikh, 47–8, 115, 121, 161–2, 180–1, 275
Beaumier, consul, 26–7, 45, 79, 109, 123, 130, 137, 156, 157, 171–2, 180, 181, 198, 202, 207–8, 226
Béclard Agreement, 166–8
Beirut, 1, 55, 214
Belgian consulate, 166
Ben ʿAṭṭār, Abraham, 240 n. 73
Ben ʿAṭṭār, Yaʿqōb, 111
Bensaude, Abraham, 109–10, 154, 175, 211, 224; Mordecai, 189
Bensemana, Judah, 128, 154, 209
Bensusan, M.S. and Co., 44
Berbers, 11, 85; relations with Jews, 91, 115
Berque, Jacques, 95
Bīhī, al-Ḥājj ʿAbdallāh Ū, 52, 164–5, 182, 185, 276 n. 26; ʿAbd al-Mālik b. ʿAbdallāh, 112, 183–4, 260 n. 5; Muḥammad, 182–3
bills of exchange, 109
bilyūn, 145–6
Bitton, Abraham, 44, 211
Bled el-Makhzan/Bled es-Siba, 252, n. 22
boatmen, 14, 136, 139, 207
Bolelli, family, 24, 237 n. 12; Antonio, 166, 175
Bonnet, merchant, 211, 242 n. 92
Botbol, Messan, 211
Boujnah family, 18, 24, 209, 235 n. 56, 292 n. 4
bourgeoisie, 1, 34, 55–60; compared with European, 65
Braudel, Fernand, 110
Brauer, Theodor, 175, 190, 211
Brīsha, Muḥammad, 80, 118, 122–3, 133, 262 n. 42
brokers, 63, 64, 67, 73, 85, 111, 113, 114, 165, 205, *see also simsar*s
Broome, George, 166, 172, 175, 190, 211
Bū al-ʿAshrāt al-Gallūlī, 183–4, 185
Bū ʿAshrīn (aṭ Ṭayyib b. al-Yamānī), 36, 37, 145, 154–5, 173, 182, 200, 218
Bū Bakr, Sīdī (British protége), 167
Bū Iḥlās rebellion, 47–8
Bū Mahdī (*qāʾid* of Tarudant), 164
Bū Rīqī, 183
Buʿazza b. al-ʿAwwād aṣ-Ṣawīrī, 161–2
Bugeaud, Maréchal, 119
Būhillāl, family, 51, 53–4, 55, 56, 173, 209; members, Aḥmad, 53–4, 128, 210–11, aṭ-Ṭālib Ibn al-Ḥājj al-Makkī, 53–4
Būshtā, b. al-Baghdādī, 173

rural unrest and rebellion, 120–1, 156, 164–5, 168, 178–80, 182–5, 212, 281 n. 114; effect on trade, 37, 91–2, 120–1, 156, 172–3, 182, 189–90, 209; pillaging of Essaouira, 120, 164

Saʿīd ʿAbd an-Naʿīm, Sīdī (marabout), 90
ṣaddīqs, 82, 95, 97
Safi, 12, 18, 19, 91, 214
Sahara, 50, 110, 111, 163, 180
salaf, 23, 109, 112
Salé, 12, 54, 213; *mellah* of, 65; Muslim merchants from, 50
Samlāl, 193
as-Sarīfī, Buʿazza, 192
aṣ-Ṣawīra (name of Essaouira), 11–12
seasonal labour, 15, 75, 79, 105
Sebag family, 18
Shabānāt, 13, 14; quarter, 201
Shabbat, 81–4, 86–9, 100
Shaqrūn, Muḥammad b., 118
sharīʿa, 23, 54, 76–8, 111, 169, 178
ash-Sharrāṭ, al-ʿArabī, 137
Shavuoth, 95, 97
Shāwiya, 114, 120
shaykh al-yahūd (Heb. *nagīd*), 78–9, 241 n. 82
Shiadma, 3, 4, 8, 68, 73, 86–7, 90, 105, 144, 184, 187, 212, 230 n. 19; government of, 121, 163, 170, 173, 177, 185; murders in 171–2; rebellion in 120–1, 178, 180, 212; settlers from, 14–15
ash-Shiyāẓmī, Mubārak b. ʿAmr, 68
shops, shopkeepers, 34, 64–6, 71, 73, 80, 89, 109–10
Shriqi, *see* Delevante
Shtūka, 98, 164, 187, 193, 194
shurafāʾ (sing. *sharīf*), 5, 34, 97–8, 163, 195, 243 n. 109; tax-exempt status revoked, 186
Sī Ḥmād Ū Mūsā, *mawsim* of, 92, 97–8, 106, 110, 112
aṣ-Ṣiddīqī, Muḥammad, 80, 133, 135
Sīdī Yūsuf mosque, 15, 83
ṣilla, 224
silver coins, *see* riyāl
silversmiths, silver market, 74, 159, 224
simsārs, 165–6, 178
skin trade, goat and calves, 38, 50, 52, 63, 89, 106, 113, 124–5, 126–7, 157, 159, 170, 185, 205, 210, 214; hide market, 66–7, 74, 75, 77, 78, 80, 83–4, 89, 103, 106, 151–2; monopoly of, 124–5
slaves, slave trade, 13, 73, 74, 93, 94, 108, 159, 248 n. 60, 257 n. 91
smallpox, 198–200, 202
sōfers, 78
Soulange-Bodin, consul, 70, 85
Sous, 5, 38, 61, 89, 101, 105, 110, 115, 172, 180–5, 188, 198, 214, 223; army, 183, 192–3, 194–5; immigrants from, 12–15, 47–8, 196, 199, 202
Spain (Spanish), consulate, 165, 166, 187, 189; disputes with local authorities, 138; trade with Morocco, 19; war of 1859–60, 117, 131–4, 165, 185, 187, 200, 227; *see also recaudadores*
sqāla, 9–10
steamships, 22, 50, 56, 59, 65, 92, 106–7, 139, 216
Succouth, 95, 97, 98, 101, 102
sugar, 38, 52, 54, 58, 63, 64, 86, 106, 124, 128, 214
Sulaymān, Sultan, 13, 20, 24, 58, 117, 124, 126, 142
sulphur, 124–5, 159, 163, 180, 224
Sumbal, Samuel, 18, 234 n. 52
sūq (defined), 73, 216; *see also separate entries*, markets
sūq al-ʿaṭṭārīn, 64–5, 74, 224, 246 n. 16
sūq al-jadīd, 64, 72, 74, 109–10, 159
Sus and North African Trading Company, 190–2
Swedish consulate, 166
synagogues, 44–5, 79

Tafilalt, 114, 257 n. 91
Tagrazīn Laḥsan Ū, 182–4, 185
Tajakant, 114
tājir, *see tujjār as-Sulṭān*
Takna, 180, 191
ṭalaba, 83, 136–7, 138
Tamgrout, 92
Tamlalt, 154
at-Tanānī, ʿAlī, 179–80
Tangier, banks in, 55; bombardment of, 119; foreign representatives in, 40, 125–6, 129, 134, 162, 178, 197; Moroccan administration in, 118, 148
Tarfāya, 189
tariffs, 122, 123, 126–7, 142, 144, 146–7
ṭarqa, *see* tobacco and hashish monopoly
aṭ-Ṭarrīs, al-Ḥājj al-ʿArabī, 119, 120–1, 122, 125, 126
tartib, 186
Tarudant, 127, 164, 170, 181, 187, 193
Tashelḥit dialect, 11
Tatta, 93, 163
Tawdenni, 93
tawqīr and *iḥtirām*, 51, 186, 237 n. 13, 243 n. 109

Uhlmann, merchant, 115
ulama, 15, 34, 54, 124, 159, 179–80, 181
ʿ*ulūj*, *see* renegades
*umanā*ʾ (sing. *amīn*), of Essaouira, 32, 39–40, 44, 51–4, 63, 66, 68–9, 76–7, 118, 122–3, 126, 129, 135–42, 145–51, 154, 158, 167–8, 174, 180, 189–90, 205, 207, 209, 224; *amīn al-umanā*ʾ, 48, 76, 135, 139, 148, 269 n. 61; rural, 185–6, 193, 194; of treasury in Marrakesh, 133, 154; *see also* administration of Essaouira, customs duties
United States, consulate, 40–1, 69, 162, 166, 178–9, interests in Sous, 162
ūqiya /mithqāl system, 142–7, 149–50, 270 n. 104; *see also* money
urban topography, 2, 9, 11, 19, 63, 69, 70, 73, 79–80, 83, 89, 128–9
urban violence and protests, 8, 119–20, 132–3, 135–6, 169, 178–80, 182–5, 204, 207
urbanization, 40, 196, 216, 236 n. 64
usury, 168–9, 171, 177–8, 185, 212

Wad Māsa, 190
Wad Noun, 48, 98, 108, 157, 161, 179, 180, 187, 190, 195
Wad Qsab, 8, 13
Wad Ulghās, 181
wage-earners, 75, 79, 105, 206–8
wakīl, 53, 118, 172–3
Wallerstein, Immanuel, 6
warehouses, stores, 29, 30, 31, 48, 61, 65–7, 126, 128–9, 148
al-Warzāzī, Muḥammad, 51, 211
Wasmīn, Sīdī (marabout), 90
wax, 38, 70, 94, 111, 115
weights measures, 63, 76, 147, 205–6, 291 n. 73
West Africa, 71, 107, 108–9; *see also* trade, inland, trans-Saharan
wheels, absence of, 66, 92, 216
Willshire, merchant and vice-consul, 24, 35, 117, 237 n. 12, 238 n. 27
Wolf, Eric, 6
women, professions of, 70–1, 75, 79; bridal-price of, 58, 245 n. 159; dress of Jewish elite, 58, 71, 73; relations with Jewish pedlars, 86
wool, yarn sheep skins, 54, 71, 74, 75, 124–5, 127, 159, 209

al-Yamānī, al-Mahdī b. aṭ-Ṭayyīb, 173
Yom Kippur, 97, 98–101, 102
Yule, Thomas, 175, 190

Zagury, Abraham, 211
zakāh, 125, 185–6
az-Zamrānī, ʿAllāl, 118–19
zaṭṭāt, 91, 253 n. 29
*zāwiya*s, 15, 81, 90, 92, 162–3, 267 n. 34; as sanctuary, 54, 178, 186; taxation of, 185–6
Zerbib, Protestant missionary, 177
az-Ziltanī, Aḥmad, b. Mubārak, 193, 194